THE

LIFE AND TIMES

OF

JOHN HUSS;

OR, THE

Bohemian Reformation

OF

THE FIFTEENTH CENTURY.

BY

E. H. GILLETT.

IN TWO VOLUMES.
VOL. I.

BOSTON:
GOULD AND LINCOLN,
59 WASHINGTON STREET.
NEW YORK: SHELDON AND COMPANY.
CINCINNATI: GEORGE S. BLANCHARD.
1863.

Entered according to Act of Congress, in the year 1861,

By E. H. GILLETT,

In the Clerk's Office of the District Court of the United States, for the Southern District of New York.

EDWARD O. JENKINS,
Printer and Stereotyper,
20 North William Street, N. Y.

PREFACE.

The task of gathering up and combining in a connected narrative the memorials which yet remain of the life and labors of John Huss, together with the results, nearer or more remote, which followed his efforts, has long challenged the attention of the historical student. The movement which he originated in Bohemia, though engrossing for the time the observation of Europe, and fraught with far-reaching consequences, has been overshadowed by the more imposing Reformation of the succeeding century, and Huss, although in many respects the peer of Luther or Calvin, has, through neglect alone, been denied the place to which he is justly entitled by their side.

This neglect has been due, in part, to the fact that the period in which he lived has been less explored by historians; in part, to the premature and violent suppression of the Bohemian Reformation, so that its earliest records were mostly left to hostile pens; and in part, also, to the fact that the various materials necessary to elucidate the subject are so difficult of access.

The task, so long deferred, I have ventured to undertake. When I commenced it, I was not aware of a single work, in the English language, which could afford me any material aid. But, since that period, the last volume of "Neander's Church History" has been translated and published in this country, and the work of Bonnechose—"Reformers before the Reformation"—has been brought to my notice. But neither of these presents such a view of the subject as the great body of intelligent readers demand. The former is fragmentary and disconnected in its arrangement; while the American edition of the latter is impaired in value by chronological errors, and the whole account of the life of Huss previous to the Council of Constance is dispatched in a few pages. On some important points the work is quite meagre, while on others the author has fallen into errors, through a failure to consult some of the most important authorities.

I have felt that the Bohemian Reformation was justly entitled to a larger share of attention than it has yet received; and such leisure as professional duties would allow, during a course of several years, and rare opportunities of access to the necessary documents, have been employed in elucidating a period in modern history but little known, yet scarcely inferior, in interest and importance, to any that preceded or that have followed it, with the exception of the Great Reformation of the sixteenth century. The character, ability, and powerful influence of Huss,—his earnestness of purpose,—his lofty aims,—the vigor of his pen,—his heroic faith and martyr's death,—as well as the magnitude and significance of the conflict in which he was the acknowledged leader,—all combined to render him the central figure, around which the great events of his time may be appropriately grouped; while his tragic end, and the consequences which followed it in

Bohemia and elsewhere, open to our view those memorable scenes of conflict, where Hussite and Catholic, Bohemian and imperialist, Taborite and Calixtine, reformer and conservative, met in long, bitter, and deadly strife.

The incidents of the period thus presented to view, are many of them possessed of high dramatic interest. The conflicts of Huss at Prague, as the bold and fearless reprover of ecclesiastical corruption and papal indulgences, the champion of Wickliffe and the antagonist of the archbishop—his harsh treatment by the council, which first deposed the pope by whom he had been excommunicated—his heroic fidelity to his convictions—his manly defence, cruel imprisonment, and unjust execution,—all conspire to excite our interest in the issue of a struggle where the death of the leader is the signal for thousands to rise up to avenge his fall. As the drama proceeds, nearly all the leading minds and powers of Europe are brought forward upon the stage. The expiring brands of crusading zeal are kindled anew for the *auto de fé* of a kingdom, and invading armies, like waves dashed to foam upon the rocks, are shattered and dispersed by the fierce fanatic valor of those Taborites, who are the lineal predecessors of the peaceful Moravians.

In the progress of the drama, our attention is arrested by the bearing and efforts of individual actors. We have before us the abominable profligacy and sacrilegious impiety of John XXIII.—the impetuous spirit of the Cardinal of Cambray—the learning and ability of the great Chancellor of Paris University, John Gerson—the glowing invective and searching rebukes of Clemengis—the apostolic zeal of Vincent Ferrara—the iron will and pertinacity of

Benedict XIII.—the self-reliance of Zabarella—the almost fabulous eloquence of Jerome of Prague—the capricious humors of the drunken Wenzel—the unscrupulous or dissembling policy of Sigismund—the heroic fidelity of John de Chlum—the fearless investigation and utterance of Jacobel—the Cromwellian energy and strategic skill of the blind Zisca—and the prudent sagacity and unyielding firmness of the Great Procopius.

We see at last attained by arts and diplomacy, what the power of arms could not accomplish,—the Taborites weakened by dissension, and the Calixtines won back by compromise to the "Catholic" church. But the current which seemed lost over the broad marsh of a century, was to feed new fountains, the streams of which were at length to be gathered up to form the church of the United Brethren—an important tributary to that great tide of our common Protestantism, which rolls on to-day with the force and volume of an Amazon.

The sources from which the materials of the present work have been drawn are many and various. First in importance and value is the compilation of Van der Hardt, designed to illustrate the history of the Council of Constance, and which comprises three large folio volumes of from 1200 to 1600 pages each. Here are to be found, also, treatises of Gerson, D'Ailly, Clemengis, Ullerston, Jacobel, and others, the histories of Niem and De Vrie, various sermons and other documents of historical importance, beside a minute record of the proceedings of the council. Second only in importance to this, is the work, in two large folios, entitled "Johannis Hus, et Hieronomi Pragensis, Confessorum Christi, Historia et Monumenta."

In this we have the sermons, letters, commentaries, controversial and other treatises of Huss, beside narratives of his controversy at Prague and his trial at Constance. Quite full accounts of the arrest and trial of Jerome, and several works of Matthias of Janow, are also included in these volumes. The "History of the Hussites," by Cochleius, an inveterate and prejudiced opponent; the "History of Bohemia," by Æneas Sylvius, afterward raised to the popedom; and the "Diarium Belli Hussitici," by Laurence Bezezyna, a Calixtine, and Chancellor of New Prague, furnish some invaluable materials. Mansi's "History of the Councils" is a work of the highest authority, and has enabled me to verify many important points. Schmidt's "History of the Dutch," though by a Roman Catholic, is a work written in an impartial and liberal spirit, and its third and fourth volumes have been of material aid in throwing light on the condition and mutual relations of Bohemia and the German empire. The general church histories of Fleury, Godeau (Germ. Edit.), Schröckh, Gieseler, Neander, Natalis Alexander, and others, have been carefully consulted, and have been of service. Spittler's "History of the Cup," Monstrelet's "Chronicles," the works of Gerson in five folio volumes, the letters and treatises of Clemengis, Crevier's "History of the University of Paris," and L'Enfant's histories of the councils of Pisa, Constance, and Basle, have all yielded valuable materials in the composition of the work. Something has been gathered from the histories of the popes, by Cormenin and Bower, while Kohler's "Huss und Seine Zeit," Helfert's "Life of Huss," Becker's "Life of Huss," Richerius' "History of the Councils," Oudin's "Dictionary of English Writers," and Moreri's large work have been carefully consulted.

I have endeavored to write with historical impartiality, yet I have not wished to suppress my judgment of the facts presented, or of the career and proceedings of the principal characters that are passed in review. Nearly all the statements contained in the work rest upon the authority of Roman Catholic authors, and where the same facts are given by writers of opposite sympathies, the marginal references are to those who would be least suspected of partiality to the cause or doctrines of Huss.

The reader will find, in the fifteenth chapter of the second volume, some repetition of statements occurring elsewhere in the work. But as that chapter was designed to present a complete view of the Taborites and Calixtines, and necessarily took the form of a dissertation, I concluded not to strike out what seemed necessary to this end, even at the risk of repeating some statements that had preceded.

The task which I have endeavored to perform has been a labor of love. A field of investigation has been opened and explored, where it was a pleasure to linger. If, in the graveyard of History, the lettering on the tombstones of men whom the world should hold in grateful remembrance has been chiselled afresh, and shall be read with the veneration due to the memory of those whose career they record, I shall feel that my labors have not been in vain.

E. H. GILLETT.

Harlem, New York City, April 8, 1861.

CONTENTS.

CHAPTER I.

BOHEMIA AT THE CLOSE OF THE FOURTEENTH CENTURY. PREDECESSORS OF HUSS. 1347-1394.

CHAPTER II.

YOUTH OF HUSS. UNIVERSITY LIFE. WICKLIFFE. 1373-1398.

CHAPTER III.

PROGRESS OF THE NEW DOCTRINES AT PRAGUE. 1399-1407.

CHAPTER IV.

THE COUNCIL OF PISA. 1407–1409.

CHAPTER V.

HUSS AND THE ARCHBISHOP. 1409–1411.

CHAPTER VIII.

BULL FOR THE CRUSADE AT PRAGUE. JAN., 1412–JULY, 1412.

CHAPTER IX.

SECOND EXCOMMUNICATION OF HUSS. HE WITHDRAWS FROM PRAGUE. JULY, 1412–MAY, 1413.

CHAPTER X.

HUSS IN RETIREMENT. MAY, 1413–SEPT., 1414.

CHAPTER XI.

SERMONS, DOCTRINES, AND LETTERS OF HUSS. 1404–1414.

CHAPTER XII.

THE COUNCIL. SEPT., 1414–NOV., 1414.

CHAPTER XIII.

ARREST AND IMPRISONMENT OF HUSS. NOV. 3, 1414–DEC. 6, 1414.

CHAPTER XIV.

ANXIETIES OF THE POPE. THE ENGLISH AND FRENCH DEPUTATIONS. DEC. 7, 1414–DEC. 18, 1414.

CHAPTER XV.

PROCEEDINGS OF THE COUNCIL. HUSS ABANDONED BY THE EMPEROR. DEC. 25, 1414–FEB. 7, 1415.

CHAPTER XVI.

THE COUNCIL, UP TO THE TIME OF THE FLIGHT OF THE POPE. JAN. 8, 1415–MARCH 21, 1415.

CHAPTER XVII.

SUPREMACY OF THE COUNCIL. THE POPE SUSPENDED. TREATMENT OF HUSS. ARREST OF JEROME. MARCH 22, 1415–MAY 24, 1415.

CHAPTER XVIII.

THE COMMUNION OF THE CUP. THE BOHEMIANS AT CONSTANCE. MAY 14, 1415–MAY 18, 1415.

CHAPTER XIX.

THE POPE DEPOSED. MAY 19, 1415–MAY 31, 1415

CHAPTER XX.

HUSS AT GOTTLIEBEN. PRISON EXAMINATION. MAY 31, 1415-JUNE 1, 1415.

CHAPTER XXI.

FIRST AUDIENCE OF HUSS BEFORE THE COUNCIL. SECOND AUDIENCE. JUNE 1, 1415-JUNE 7, 1415.

CHAPTER XXII.

THIRD AUDIENCE OF HUSS BEFORE THE COUNCIL. ARTICLES OF ACCUSATION. JUNE 8, 1415.

CHAPTER XXIII.

THIRD AUDIENCE CONTINUED. JUNE 8, 1415.

THE

LIFE AND TIMES OF JOHN HUSS.

CHAPTER I.

BOHEMIA AT THE CLOSE OF THE FOURTEENTH CENTURY. PREDECESSORS OF HUSS.

CONDITION OF BOHEMIA. — NATIONAL FEELING. — THE INTRODUCTION OF THE USAGES OF THE ROMAN CHURCH. — THE WALDENSES. — PREDECESSORS OF HUSS. — CONRAD WALDHAUSER. — MILICZ OF KREMSIER. — MATTHIAS OF JANOW. — PETER OF DRESDEN. — FLOURISHING CONDITION OF BOHEMIA. — THOMAS OF STITNY. — DEATH OF ANNE OF LUXEMBOURG, QUEEN OF ENGLAND.

1347–1394.

DURING the latter half of the fourteenth century, (1350–1400,) Bohemia occupied a place among the nations of Europe somewhat correspondent to her local position in the heart of the continent. Her capital was the residence of the German emperor. Her university at Prague, though recently founded, was the oldest and most flourishing—indeed, almost the only one—in Eastern Europe. Her churches, cloisters, and palaces were remarked by the stranger with surprise and admiration, while through her connection with the German empire, her influence was widely felt. Petrarch could scarce resist the earnest and pressing invitation of Charles IV., who besought him to exchange his loved Vaucluse for a residence—in external beauty fully equal to any which his own Italy could afford—on the banks of the Moldau.

But if Prague lost the honor of sheltering the Italian poet and scholar, she was yet destined to be the centre of a movement which should agitate the entire Christian world. The cry of Reform which was to be heard in almost every country of Europe, demanding the removal of the papal schism, and a remedy for the evils of the church, was to find a memorable echo in her own university. In her bosom she was fondly to cherish one of her own sons, whose influence should be more enduring and extensive than that of Petrarch, and the fundamental principle of whose doctrines—the sole and supreme authority of the word of God—was to strike the key-note of the Great Reformation in the succeeding century. She was yet to witness, gathered on her surrounding hills and along her valleys, the mustered hosts of Christendom, whose defeat was to signalize the final struggle of crusading enthusiasm with the growing light and energy of the world's free thought.

As the capital of an enterprising nation, the residence of the German emperor, and the home of reviving art and literary culture, Prague was the foremost city of Eastern Europe. Her situation was one of the most beautiful and magnificent in the world. Around her on every side spread a broad region vitalized by her influence, and subsidiary to her prosperity and growth. Already upon that soil once possessed by barbarian hordes—the camping-ground of hosts which imperial Rome had regarded with trembling anxiety—a land of wild forests and streams and mountains, to which the ancient Boii had bequeathed their name—there had sprung up those institutions of law, government, and religion, which secured for Bohemia a fair reputation as a civilized and Christian state.

Her very position was one which seemed designed by nature to favor self-development. Situated in the heart of the European continent—bounded on her four sides by as many ranges of lofty mountains, while the angles of this gigantic diagram of rock were directed to the four points of the compass—with a fertile soil and a genial climate—with rivers bursting forth on every side from her mountain barriers, and meeting like rays about her central capital, thence to find their way by the Elbe to Hamburg and to the fourscore towns of the Hanseatic league rapidly rising in political and commercial importance—Bohemia seemed fitted by her location and general features to become one of the foremost states of Europe. She was at once sheltered and accessible, guarded from invasion, yet connected directly with the German towns by means of the Elbe, the great artery of European commerce. Her resources were sufficient to encourage enterprise and self-reliance. She was accessible enough to all that was good, useful, and improving, and yet so far secluded by nature as to encourage the patriotic purpose of maintaining and cherishing her own proper character, customs, and institutions.

But all this would have failed to give Bohemia

that important influence which she was destined to exert for at least the lifetime of a generation upon the condition, policy, and prosperity of Europe, if it had not been for other causes that at this juncture began to operate. The time had come when the force of free religious thought was to be manifested on a broader scale, and in a more conspicuous manner than ever before. During centuries past, the world had been losing faith in all but material forces. The German empire was built up and maintained by physical energy. Soldiers of fortune—mercenary chieftains—had become again and again the arbiters of national destiny. Faith in the papacy—no longer what it was antecedent to the "Babylonian Captivity"—had been sadly shaken. The appeal to the sword and to the right of the strongest had superseded every other. Even the popes had shown more faith in the temporal sword which they invoked, than in their own interdicts. Amid the clash of arms—the echoes of battle-fields like Poictiers and Cressy—other voices were drowned.

But the empire of ideas was now to be notably enlarged, if not inaugurated anew. Superficial observers might look with contempt on the utterances or writings of obscure priests or preachers. They might hope to find the key of destiny in the leaders of armies, in the hands of king or emperor. But it was soon to be seen that, on the great chessboard of European history, monarchs might be merely pawns, like Wenzel of Bohemia, or Charles VI. of France; while the real kings were the men of thought—pamphleteers, like Ullerston, Gerson, and Clemenges, or reformers, like Wickliffe, Janow, Jacobel, and Huss.

It is true, indeed, that the great reform movement, of which Huss was the leader, was, to human view, after a most desperate and prolonged struggle, crushed out—not, however, without leaving behind it most important results. But in its own day, it distinctly revealed the comparative impotence of mere material forces, employed to exterminate an idea that had become rooted in a nation's heart. Army after army, numbering scores of thousands of fierce and reckless men, was dashed to fragments in the attempt to subdue Bohemia to the papal obedience. The attention of Europe—of emperors, kings, popes, and councils—was riveted, for almost an entire generation, upon the progress and prospects of the movement originated by Huss at Prague. The interest of European history for this period centres mainly in the efforts that were made, by the combined forces of Christendom, to restore the old basis of things shaken and overthrown by the Hussite reform.

It is interesting and instructive to trace the origin of the forces from which this sprang, or by the alliance of which it was furthered and sustained. Huss himself did not call them into being. Some of them he found ready to his hand; of others, his own sagacity enabled him to take advantage. The patriotic spirit of the Bohemian people, their jealousy of foreign innovations, and the peculiar advantages which they enjoyed for assuming an independent position in respect to the usages and doctrines of the church, must all be taken into account, as well as the paramount influence of the novel exhibition and enforcement of scripture truth.

We find, indeed, at an earlier period than the one which we are about to consider, the development of a strong feeling of nationality. This feeling, in reality, had gained a remarkable development during the closing years of the fourteenth century—the period immediately preceding the entrance of Huss upon his public career. For the two preceding centuries it had been kept alive, and had even acquired strength in opposition to foreign innovations. The introduction of the usages of the Romish church, and the extended jurisdiction of Roman law, had not been gained without a struggle. The popular literature, meagre as it was, was warmly cherished, and gave place but slowly to Latin learning.

Still the policy of the rulers of the nation—especially of the last kings of the Premysl house—favored innovation and immigration.[1] The old jurisprudence was modified by the forced introduction of canon law. Artisans and merchants from abroad were encouraged to take up their residence within the kingdom. Colonies of German settlers were welcomed in the cities and the towns. In some cases they acquired a predominant influence. The nobility gave their castles German names. In many municipalities the German element was in the ascendant. The city records of Prague were written in German. Judicial proceedings were in the German language. German preachers occupied the pul-

[1] Helfert, 47, 48.

pits. German judges presided in the courts of justice, and the highest civil offices were filled by Germans. German manners and usages, German names and phrases, prevailed in social circles. The university was patronized by German students, who outnumbered the Bohemians in the proportion of five to one. The lucrative benefices of the church were filled by German priests and bishops; and for a time it seemed as if Bohemia was to become a German province.

Charles IV. encouraged the introduction of the usages of the Romish church, as well as German immigration. But already the national spirit had begun to react upon the innovations by which it was threatened to be overwhelmed. The first concession made to it was the erection of the archbishopric of Prague—a measure which the emperor successfully commended to the pope, on the ground that the Slavic tongue, peculiar to the Bohemians and Moravians, was strange to their diocesan, the archbishop of Mayence, and his clergy.[1] The second victory won by the national feeling was the enactment of a law that none should fill the office of a civil judge who could not understand and speak the Bohemian language.

Meanwhile, Bohemian literature had begun to revive. The scriptures were translated into Bohemian. The venerable Stitny—a patriot and scholar, to whom we shall again have occasion to refer—wrote numerous works in his native language, and labored in various ways to make the treasures of the Latin

[1] Helfert, 50, 51.

language accessible to his countrymen. "Before God," said he, "the Bohemian is just as good as the Latin." With much opposition, especially from the friends of "school-learning," he maintained his patriotic position, and endeared his name to every true Bohemian.

The struggle was at length transferred to the university. The Bohemian nation, outvoted by the other three, had seen the most honorable positions and offices held by strangers. Their first resistance to this usurpation of numbers, which denied them what they regarded as their rights, took place in 1384–5, under the rectorate of Konrad Soltow.[1] By the favor of the king and court, the archbishop and the native clergy, they gained their point. The foreign party appealed to the pope. The university was filled with confusion and discord. But the Bohemians won the victory, and at length (1399–1403) the "College of the Bohemian nation" was established, expressly for native Bohemians.

As we have already remarked, Huss commenced his university course at the very time when the struggle of patriotic feeling with foreign domination had been transferred to the scenes upon which he now entered. Bohemian by birth, and with a soul alive to the most generous impulses, he showed himself from the first a zealous champion of the nation's rights. From feeling and from principle, he put himself at the head of the popular movement, and his influence as a reformer was strengthened by his position as a patriot. In the latter character his

[1] Helfert, 53.

countrymen have never ceased to cherish his memory. In their eyes, the faults of the heretic are lost in the virtues of the patriot. Many a locality is even yet almost sacred, in popular esteem, from association with his name and memory. In the royal library of the great college-building at Prague, a Hussite hymn-book, written and illustrated with singular splendor, is still carefully preserved. This book, which must have cost many thousand florins, was the joint production of a large proportion of the citizens. Each guild and corporation had a few hymns written, and pictures painted to accompany them, and in this work they were joined by several noble families, each family or guild placing its own pictured arms or crest before its own portion of the book. Most of the pictures represent events in Biblical history, or incidents in the life of Huss. Among the latter are scenes of his disputes with the priests, and of his martyrdom, while the ecclesiastics in their robes are looking coldly on, and angels hover over the victim to comfort him in his agony.[1] Despite his *heresy*, the name of Huss is now spoken with veneration and affection even by those who would still feel constrained to pronounce him a heretic.

The same influences which nurtured a national and patriotic spirit, tended to counteract the aggrandizing and grasping policy of the court of Rome. It was foreign, anti-national, and odious.[2] The Bohemian noble was, moreover, proud-spirited and independent. His country itself lay sheltered in that deep basin which once held the waters of a primæval sea. On

[1] Kohl's Bohemia, p. 35. [2] Schröckh dwells largely on this point.

every side rose the mountain walls of its defence. It was indeed itself a fortress, and mythologic fancy might be excused if it ascribed the stupendous barriers and abutments that surrounded it to the hands of primæval Titans. The tide of foreign invasion broke as it dashed against the mountain fastness, and he who never had been conquered might cherish the pride that defied attack. A freedom of thought, less congenial to other lands, might find here a secure abode. By those rivers which spread like veins and arteries all over the land, and under the shadows of those forests and giant mountains which bounded the horizon, men felt but little awe or respect for ecclesiastical censure or persecuting edicts. The jests of the rough knights—often too much tainted, doubtless, with the vices of their kings—showed little regard for the assumed authority or sanctity of the Papal See. In the general assessment by which the avarice of the Roman court spread its huge dragnet over Europe, Bohemia, like England, was sheltered by her isolated situation. And besides all this, her attachment to her old usages, long cherished by the patriotic feeling of her citizens, had made her exceedingly reluctant to conform to the Romish ritual. Former sympathies and associations had connected her with the East. By the Greek church she had first been Christianized, and, until near the middle of the fourteenth century, a strong attachment to the rites and usages derived from this source had very generally prevailed.[1] The process by which the nation was brought to recognize the

[1] Schröckh xxxiv. 564, and xxxiii. 331.

authority of the See of Rome was slow and difficult. The celibacy of the clergy, and the withholding of the cup in the eucharist, were regarded as innovations. They excited a strong, bitter, and prolonged resistance. The attempt which was at length made, in the reign of the emperor Charles IV., to enforce them by laws and penalties, secured indeed an outward conformity, but among the masses of the nation, the work of reducing the church to Roman usages and ceremonial, could, as a general thing, only excite indignation.

Some of the Waldenses, moreover, driven out from their Piedmontese valleys, had found a refuge within the fortress-like walls of the Bohemian mountains, and there, in quiet and security, spread their doctrines and influence.[1] It was here that Peter Waldo, according to Maimbourg, the founder of that sect, was finally sheltered from the persecution which drove him first into Picardy, and then to Bohemia. Here, in a land where no papal police was as yet tolerated, he found, in all probability, a peaceful grave. Many of his disciples must have followed him. The inquisition drove them from their homes, and their only safety was in obscurity. Thirty-five of them perished in one fire at Bingen. At Strasbourg eighty were burned. The consequence was, that they were driven toward Bohemia. Reiner, in A. D. 1254, reckons the schools of the Leonists in the diocese of Passau at forty-one. Their influence in Bohemia must have been perceptibly felt, and their views

[1] Kohler's Johannes Huss und Seine Zeit draws a vivid picture of the caution and secresy of their worship in Bohemia.

were far enough from coinciding with the orthodoxy of Rome. They derided the clerical tonsure. They ridiculed those prevalent ecclesiastical promotions which filled the highest official stations of the church with successors to Simon Magus rather than the apostles. The vulgar tongue was as fitting for prayer, in their view, as the Latin, which they did not understand. Long before Laurentius Valla had exposed the spuriousness of the "false decretals," they had rejected them. They laughed at the legends of the saints. They reverenced "the traditions" of the church no more than Christ did the traditions of the Pharisees. They denied purgatory. They considered lights in churches needless. To them holy water was no better than any other, and the cross was but a piece of wood. But it was their veneration for, and their acquaintance with, the word of God, abundantly attested by their persecutors, that led them to dissent so emphatically from the Roman church. Of the purity of their lives, and the simple devotion which characterized their worship, their foes themselves leave us no room to doubt.

Nearly one hundred and forty years later, in 1391, we find, according to the testimony of a Roman inquisitor, that among their teachers were Hungarians and Bavarians, showing that on both sides of Bohemia the Waldensian doctrines had found a foothold. We cannot doubt that they were more generally held in the sheltered region that lay between Bavaria and Hungary.[1] We shall see hereafter the immediate connection between the Waldenses, and

[1] See Kohler's Huss und Seine Zeit.

the doctrines which brought the wrath of the Council of Constance upon the university of Prague, and the kingdom of Bohemia.

The views which had thus found their way into Bohemia, were never altogether rooted out. From time to time they were revived by men whose advocacy gave them an important influence upon the condition of the kingdom. There is no necessity, however, of attributing to a foreign source the origin of the reform movement in Bohemia. Whatever increment it may have received from foreign sources, it was undoubtedly in great part indigenous. The hereditary kingdom of the German emperor was really, at the close of the fourteenth century, (1370–1400,) in advance of the surrounding nations, in literary and industrial activity. The proof of this will be spread before us as we proceed. It was from the midst of this intellectual agitation and enterprise, that the religious movement sprang. It received an undesigned impulse from the enlarged views and even the aggrandizing policy of Charles IV. No one can trace his career of manifold activity[1]—using every art to extend and consolidate the empire,—discarding the sword and the warlike aims of his predecessors, but regaining by treaty and stratagem more than they had lost,—studiously avoiding all collision with the papacy, yet adroitly grasping every advantage which its necessities afforded him—and not perceive that under his liberal patronage the cause of learning and of letters would necessarily enter upon a career of brighter prospects. This was in fact the

[1] M. J. Schmidt's Geschichte Der Deutschen, iii. 562—619.

case. With the exception of the universities of Paris and Oxford, the university of Prague held the highest rank in Europe. It was natural that the attention of its teachers and students should be drawn to the scandalous state of the church, and that the facts which excited the indignation of Wickliffe at Oxford, should not be unnoted at Prague.

It was almost contemporaneously with the founding of the university, that the first notable criticism on the degeneracy of Christendom, and the first indignant protest against its corruptions, were put forth in Bohemia. The character, influence, and labors of those who gave utterance to these views and feelings, have been overshadowed by the more distinguished efforts of their successors, while their continued and professed adherence to the authority and usages of the church has saved them from the notoriety which their condemnation or rejection as heretics would have conferred.

But among the precursors of Huss, who anticipated him in the utterance of views of scriptural reform, there are three men worthy of special notice. These were, the Austrian, Conrad Waldhauser, or Conrad Steikna, as he has been improperly called; John Milicz, of Kremsier in Moravia; and Matthias of Janow.

The first of these, whose death was almost contemporaneous with the birth of Huss, belonged to the order of St. Augustine, and exerted a powerful influence in Vienna, where he preached for a space of fifteen years (1345–1360). During this period occurred the jubilee proclaimed by Clement VI.

(1350). Among the pilgrims to Rome on this occasion was Conrad himself. He had full opportunity to witness the effect of the papal bull of indulgence, and the mischievous results which followed its publication. The crowd that was assembled at Rome was immense.[1] "One would have thought," says Petrarch, who was present, "that the plague (1347) which had almost unpeopled the world had not so much as thinned it." The concourse of pilgrims was prodigious. It was estimated by the Romans themselves at over a million, and the number present at the end was equal to that at the beginning of the year.

It was impossible for an impartial observer to remain blind to the mischiefs attendant upon the scenes of the jubilee. A plenary absolution of all sins for a pilgrimage to Rome, or the pious donation of the amount of expense which such a pilgrimage would incur, could not be proclaimed, as it was by the papal bull, without producing results which would invite the reprehension of serious and thoughtful minds. The eyes of Conrad were opened by his visit to the capital of Christendom. He returned to Austria a preacher of repentance. The influence of his sermons may be gathered from the charge which his enemies, at a later period, brought against him, of disturbing everywhere the public peace.[2] He defended himself by referring to similar accusations brought against Christ himself.

But from the time of his visit to Rome he seems to have labored less at Vienna, and to have been en-

[1] Villani, as quoted by Bower, iii. 100. [2] Neander, v. 184.

gaged rather as an itinerant preacher. He taught "through all Austria," even to the city of Prague. Charles IV. appreciated the labors and the eloquence of the man. He endeavored to secure him for Bohemia, and in 1360 he was called as parish priest to the city of Leitmeritz. But the field was too narrow for his zeal. It was circumscribed, moreover, by opposition, and a controversy into which he was led with the Dominicans and Franciscans. The result was, that he determined to seek at Prague a broader and more inviting field.

For a year he preached in the church of St. Galli; but the edifice could not hold the throngs which pressed to hear him. Unwilling to have the word of God withheld from any who desired to hear it, and anxious to labor for the salvation of many, he went forth into the open market-place, and preached to immense audiences which there assembled. The spirit of his sermons may be gathered from his own words: "Not willing that the blood of souls should be required at my hands, I traced, as I was able, in the Holy Scripture, the future dangers impending over the souls of men." Upon the innovations that had been introduced into the church, and upon the monks, whom he regarded as the authors of them, he was especially severe. He exposed their vices, as well as their hypocrisy. He called them wolves in sheep's clothing. He showed from scripture that their peculiar dress and mode of life were unwarranted by the authority of the word of God, and could only have originated in monstrous fables; that their bodily mortifications were "vain and damnable"—without promise for the present life, or the hope of future recompense. Their notorious indolence and everlasting psalm-singing were frequent topics with him. The machinery of religion, which killed all true devotion, and measured its value, not by the feelings of the heart, but by bells and hour-glasses, was denounced. He protested against the perpetual vows to a monastic life which were imposed by parents upon their children. They only who were led by the Spirit of God, were the sons of God. Monasticism—against which he had nothing to say, when in itself considered—had become by its degeneracy a source of great mischief. One might as wisely embark in a leaky craft to cross the Danube, as repose in it for security. The monks themselves had become like the Pharisees of old; they had bound to men's shoulders burdens too heavy to be borne, which they would not touch themselves with one of their fingers; they had insolently set themselves up as teachers of the people; they had usurped to themselves the rights and privileges of the pastors, yet, in fact, shut men out of the kingdom of heaven by refusing them the Bible in their own language; they had encouraged superstition, and aggravated the prevalent corruption by their vain questions and controversies, their useless school-quarrels and nonsense. To carry out their designs, they made godliness a matter of traffic, introducing themselves into houses, and leading simple women astray. In this unsparing style he upbraided the monks.

It was natural that they should turn just as hotly upon their opponent. They exhausted their resources and exerted all their influence to secure his overthrow. But their efforts were unsuccessful. The king, Charles IV., is said to have favored him. He was perhaps unwilling to see a man, whose learning and sincerity won his respect, prostrated by such foes, and the rather that Conrad gave no occasion for reprehension in his faith or life.

But he poured the torrent of his rebukes not only upon the monks, but upon the general corruption of his times. His influence upon the minds of some of the richest women was such, that they gave away the proceeds of their most costly ornaments in charity to the poor.

Matthias of Janow characterizes both his predecessors, Conrad and Milicz, as men full of the spirit of Elijah. But Conrad was rather a John the Baptist. He was a powerful preacher of repentance. He spoke forth sharp warnings to flee from the wrath to come. No prevalent vice escaped his rebuke. Pride of dress, usury, lightness, and youthful vanities were rebuked, and a powerful impression was made. The usurer gave up his ill-gotten gains. The thoughtless and giddy became serious. Quite a number of Jews were drawn to listen to his sermons. A radical change was effected in the hearts of a large number of his hearers, while the purity of his own life exhibited an example of what he commended to them. In 1364 the hostility toward him came to a head. Twenty-nine articles were drawn up against him by the Dominicans and Franciscans, in concert; but when the day of trial came, no one dared to present them.

Conrad died while parish priest of the Teyn church, in the year 1369. The Jesuit Balbinus objects to his being considered a precursor of Huss. He confesses, however, that his writings against the monks betrayed a freedom of expression which might lead his readers to contemn their teachers and disobey their prelates. One of his treatises is entitled "Indictment of the Mendicants," and contains some severe charges against the bishops and the clergy. The Jesuit should have remembered that the unpardonable sin of Wickliffe was not venial in Conrad, unless Rome had two tribunals, one for England and another for Bohemia.

John Milicz was a native of Kremsier, in Moravia, and a contemporary of Conrad. He had studied theology and law at the university of Prague. By perusing the history of his native land, he had early perceived the superiority of the former and ancient constitution of the Greek church in Bohemia and Moravia.[1] Although a foreigner, he was, by the archbishop of Prague, appointed archdeacon and preacher of the cathedral church. Other offices of distinction were conferred upon him. But the bestowal of these dignities did not lull him into indolence. It only roused his energies anew to the inculcation of wholesome though unacceptable truths. He preached often against the introduction of the practice of administering the sacrament only under one form[2]—the use of an unknown tongue in the

[1] These statements are made on the authority of Schröckh.

[2] This statement, made on the authority of Schröckh, I cannot accept. See subsequent note.

public worship—the celibacy and wealth of the clergy—the vows of the religious orders—the false miracles and legends of the monks—and their self-invented sanctity. But his course was a disappointment to the hopes of the archbishop and the ecclesiastics. He saw that he was unacceptable to them, and resigned his office of archdeacon. This lucrative prebend he exchanged for the humble office of sacristan in the same church. It was in vain that several prelates urged him to accept, at their hands, the same dignity which he had previously held. He had always taught that a priest and monk should be poor. He was now completely so himself, and his whole worldly dependence was on the alms of his pious fellow-citizens.

To this condition he had not been brought without a severe inward struggle. He had to make a stern choice between popularity and promotion on one side, and poverty and reproach on the other. His acceptance as a preacher was such that he might almost command any position to which he might aspire. It had not indeed been so at the first. His natural and plain style of address had not been pleasing, especially to those who had been accustomed to that artistic inflation and bombast of the monks, which Milicz in his writings has criticised with caustic severity. But good sense at last carried the day. The tide turned in favor of the man whose sincerity of purpose and simplicity of speech stood in striking contrast with the conduct and manner of his opponents, for such the monks proved themselves to be. The people cherished toward him a strong affection. They would not suffer him to be silent, and sometimes he was constrained to preach three or four times the same day. Merchants and strangers from Germany visited Prague in large numbers, and to benefit them he learned the German language. Withdrawing for a while to Bishopteintz, in the circle of Pilsen, and engaging in a humble service as curate, he was not long content in retirement, and in a place where he seemed to himself to enjoy too much luxury, and soon returned to Prague.

Here his labors were abundant, and his self-denial was extreme. He preached twice every Sunday and holiday, and sometimes four or five times daily in different churches. His sermons were not unfrequently two or three hours long, and his only preparation—in many cases the only preparation possible—was prayer. His abstemiousness in eating and drinking was carried probably to an excess. He wore a rough hair shirt next to his skin; and, in his voluntary poverty, as well as in his writings, administered a severe rebuke to the mendicants who violated vows which he never had assumed.

His enthusiastic admirer and pupil, Matthias of Janow, said of him, "Having been a simple priest and secretary at the prince's court, before his experience of the visitation of the Spirit of Christ, he grew so rich in wisdom and all utterance of doctrine, that it was a light matter to him to preach five times a day,—once in Latin, once in German, and then again in the Bohemian tongue,—and this publicly, with a mighty force and a powerful voice; and he constantly brought forth from his treasure things old and new."

His preaching bore fruit in a striking reformation. Prague was noted for its depravity of manners. It abounded in brothels. Milicz directed his energies, among other things, to the reform of licentious women. At first twenty were converted, and a dwelling was procured for them. By enlisting the aid of devout women, the work was extended. Several hundreds were recovered from the paths of vice. "Little Venice," as it was called, the "Five Points" of Prague, was so transformed that it was thereafter known as "Little Jerusalem."[1] A Magdalene hospital was founded, and in the chapel annexed to it there was preaching every day. According to Janow, the very face of the city was transformed. "I confess," he says, "that I cannot enumerate even the tenth part of what my own eyes saw, my own ears heard, and my own hands handled, though I lived with him but a short time."

For six years Milicz continued to preach, unwearied in his efforts. But he was not satisfied with himself. His humility made him feel that he was unfit to preach. Only by the urgent persuasion of his friends, who represented to him the bad effects which would result from abandoning his field, was he restrained from adopting a more rigid and secluded life as a monk. But even their persuasions could not long restrain the impulse which he felt, urging him to solitary meditation. To this impulse he yielded. In seclusion from the world, and in the silence of his own thoughts, he reflected upon the condition of the church throughout the world. He

[1] Neander, v. 176.

seemed to see Antichrist embodied before him, in the variety of errors and abuses which stalked abroad under a Christian name.

Suddenly he felt called upon to visit the pope, narrate to him his visions, and utter his admonitions. He went at the command, as he supposed, of the Holy Spirit. He would have the pope originate a spiritual crusade for the overthrow of Antichrist. A general council should be called. The bishops should devise means for restoring discipline, and monks and secular priests should be exhorted to go forth as preachers.

Milicz went to Rome, when Urban, designing to return from Avignon (1367), was expected daily. For a month he gave himself up to fasting, prayer, and the reading of the scriptures. Still the pope did not arrive. Milicz could no longer restrain himself. He posted on the doors of St. Peter's that on a certain day he would appear and address the multitude. It is said, moreover, that he added, "The Antichrist is come; he has his seat in the church."[1] But the notification of the sermon alone was enough to excite suspicion. At the instigation of the mendicant monks, he was arrested by the inquisition, loaded with chains, given over to the Franciscans, and closely confined. But he endured all with uncomplaining meekness. Not a bitter word escaped his lips, and his persecutors were confounded by his patient submission.

After a prolonged imprisonment, he was asked what he had intended to preach. He replied by

[1] Gieseler, iii. 185.

asking his examiners to give him back his Bible, pen, ink, and paper, and they should have his discourse in writing. The request was granted, and Milicz's imprisonment was alleviated. Before a large assembly of prelates and learned men he delivered his discourse, and it made a profound impression. Still he was kept in prison, and there composed his celebrated work on Antichrist.[1] "The author writes this," he says, "a prisoner, and in chains, troubled in spirit, longing for the freedom of Christ's church, protesting that he has not kept back that which was in his heart, but has spoken it out to the church," &c.

On the arrival of Urban at Rome, Milicz was released, to the disappointment of the monks who had prophesied the fate of their old antagonist, but to the great joy of his friends at Prague, whom he hastened to rejoin.

With fresh zeal he now recommenced his labors. Not content with preaching himself, he wished to train others for the work. Often was he heard to say,[2] "Would that all were prophets." He established, in fact, what might be regarded as a Theological Seminary—a school of the prophets. Two or three hundred young men were gathered around him, under the same roof, who submitted themselves to his instruction and training. He copied books for them to study, and engaged them also in the work of transcription. His aim was to multiply and extend the circulation of devotional and instructive

[1] It is found among the writings of Matthias of Janow, contained in the last half of the first volume of the works of Huss.

[2] Neander, v. 181.

books. No external badge, no common discipline, rule, or vow, nor uniformity of dress, distinguished his pupils. They formed a unique brotherhood, bound together by common sympathies and common aims. No effort was spared by Milicz to promote their usefulness. When trained, he sought to find them spheres of labor,—with rare humility and fond affection, commending them as those who would surpass himself. Their exemplary, or perhaps we should say, puritanic conduct made them objects of reproach. They were nick-named "Miliczans," "Beghards," &c.

On the death of Conrad, Milicz succeeded to his office. Besides preaching daily, he drew up forms of prayer for public worship in the native language, which were extensively adopted. But his extraordinary course of activity, and reproof of sin, drew down upon him envy and persecution. The priests, whose disgraceful connections he rebuked, united against him. The archbishop, with great reluctance, was forced to call him to account for his street preaching. Twelve heads of accusation were drawn up against him, and sent to the pope (1374). Gregory XI., who then occupied the papal chair, wrote back to the archbishop, and the bishops of Breslau, Olmutz, and Leitomischel, expressing surprise at their negligence and that of the inquisitors, whereby this dangerous heretic had been permitted to spread his errors through Bohemia, Moravia, Silesia, and Poland, and urged them promptly to arrest the evil; provided, however, that the charges made should be found true. A similar admonition was likewise sent to the emperor Charles IV.

In these circumstances, Milicz, doubtless taught by past experience, preferred to submit his case to the pope himself, and, having made his appeal, set out for Avignon. Of the manner in which he was received, we are not informed; and while his cause was yet depending, he died in that city.

The influence exerted by Milicz directly, and through his pupils, must have been powerful and extensive. The archbishop, for many years at least, reposed great confidence in him, and treated him with much kindness. In many important commissions he was employed both by the archbishop and the emperor. Indeed, for a time he was imperial secretary and chancellor.[1]

The writings of Milicz were numerous, and all were written in the Latin language. Some of them still survive. Among them are his Fast sermons, Postilles, and especially his treatise on Antichrist, to which reference has been already made, and which is embodied in Janow's larger treatise on the same subject.[2] To Milicz unquestionably belongs the credit of having first boldly put forth those views on the subject of Antichrist, which are so largely extended and elucidated by Matthias of Janow, and which were substantially adopted by Huss himself.

In the footsteps of Conrad and Milicz, although eventually taking a position in advance of theirs, followed Matthias of Janow. He was born at Prague, but was generally called the Parisian, from having spent six years at the university of Paris, and having

[1] Palacky. Geschichte von Bohmen, iii. 1.

[2] Found in the first volume of the works of Huss.

there rceived his Doctor's degree. He was also called the Cracovian, from a temporary residence at Cracow. He was for a short time a pupil of Milicz, and perhaps through him became parish priest at Prague, and father confessor of the emperor Charles IV. For this post he was well fitted, both by talent and education. He had travelled much, and been a careful observer as well as close student.[1] He had a large acquaintance with the relations and customs of different countries. No one in his day had a clearer conception of the moral and religious condition of Christendom, and no one labored more diligently or zealousy for its reform.

The most decisive and important influence that shaped his career was exerted by the life and writings of Milicz. This penetrated him, as he expresses it, with that holy fire which left him no rest. It was through "the light of God's word" that the corruptions of the church were made manifest to him. "Once," says he, "my mind was encompassed by a thick wall; I thought of nothing but what delighted the eye and the ear, till it pleased the Lord Jesus to deliver me as a brand from the burning. And while I, worst slave to my passions, was resisting him in every way, he delivered me from the flames of Sodom, and brought me into the place of sorrow, of great adversities, and of much contempt. Then first I became poor and contrite, and searched with trembling the word of God."[2]

[1] Neander, v. 192.

[2] This forcible passage is found in Huss's works, vol. i., p. 399. After the passage above quoted, he adds, "Then did I begin to wonder at the exaltation of Satan, and the blindness with which he covered the eyes of men. And then did the most

In some respects Janow must be regarded as decidedly in advance of Conrad and Milicz. His familiarity with scripture is remarkable. His views of the necessity of reform are clear and comprehensive. He understands fully the difficulties with which it has to contend, and proposes to overcome them by sound and scriptural methods.

No one can peruse his writings without feeling that he has come in contact with a mind penetrated with the love of truth, and possessed of a clear insight into the spirit of the gospel. In an age when the worldly spirit was triumphant; when, with thousands of the priesthood, gain was godliness and promotion was success, he withstood the bribes which were extended to his selfishness and ambition. It was not without a bitter inward struggle that he finally was brought to the point of self-renunciation and self-denial. The record which he has left us of his experience is exceedingly vivid. It portrays the spiritual conflicts through which he was called to pass, in words which reveal the process by which he was prepared for his work.

"My feet," he says, "had almost gone; my steps had well-nigh slipped; and, unless a crucified Jesus

loving crucified Jesus, open my ear, that is, my understanding, that I might understand the scriptures appropriate to the present time; and he lifted my mind up to perceive how men were absorbed in vanity. And then reading, I clearly and distinctly perceived the abomination of desolation standing proudly in the holy place, and I was seized with horror and shuddering of heart. And I took up the lamentation of Jeremiah; and I went to them, and, between the porch and the altar, exhorted and admonished them to deplore the evils that had befallen Jerusalem, the daughter of my people." He then speaks of the fire in his bones which would not let him rest; but he was forced to dig through the wall into "the chamber of imagery," and write what he had seen.

had come to my rescue, my soul had sunk to hell. But he, my most faithful and loving Saviour, in whom is no guile, showed to me their counsels; and I knew the face of the harlot, by which she allures all that stand at the corners of the streets and the entrances of the paths. . . . Nevertheless, I prayed to God and the Father of Jesus Christ my Lord, holding up the Bible in my hands; and I cried out, with heart and voice, 'O Lord and Father, who ordainest my life, leave me not to their thoughts and counsels, and let me not be taken in their net, lest I fall under that reproachful sin which shall sting my conscience, and drive out wisdom from my soul!'[1] . . . I confess, before God and his Christ, that so alluring was this harlot Antichrist, that she so well feigned herself the true spouse of Jesus Christ, or rather, Satan by his arts so tricked her out, that from my early years I was long in doubt what I should choose, or what keep: whether I should seek out and chase after benefices, and thirstily grasp for honors, which to some extent I did, or rather, go forth without the camp, bearing the poverty and reproach of Christ: whether, with the many, I should live in quest of an easy and quiet life for the moment, or rather, cling to the faithful and holy truth of the gospel: whether to commend what almost all commend; lay my plans as many do; dispense with and gloss over the scriptures, as many of the great and learned and famous of this day do; or rather, manfully inculpate and accuse their unfruitful works of darkness, and so hold to the simple truth of the divine words, which

[1] Monumenta Hussi, i. 461.

plainly contravene the lives and morals of men of this age, and prove them false brethren: whether I should follow the spirit of wisdom with its suggestions, which I believe the divine Spirit of Jesus, or follow the sentiment of the great multitude, which, in their self-indulgence, without show of mercy or charity, while lovers of this world and full of carnal vanities, they claim to be safe. I confess that between these two courses I hung wavering in doubt; and unless our Lord Jesus be our keeper, none will escape the honeyed face and smile of this harlot—the tricks of Satan and the snares of Antichrist."

The man who had passed unscathed through such temptations, had been disciplined for future trials. He was one upon whom all the influences of gain and terror would be alike powerless.

His principal work is entitled, *De regulis veteris et Novi Testamenti.* Most of it still remains buried in manuscripts, the contents of which have been, in large extracts, set forth by P. Jordan,[1] in his "Predecessors of Hussism in Bohemia." It seems to be composed of a collection of independent treatises, written on different occasions, and hence, as might be expected, abounds in repetitions. Its title indicates its scope. It rejects the authority of human traditions and popish decretals, and substitutes in their place the supreme authority of the divine word. It tries everything by this test. The conduct of the bishops and the priests is severely arraigned. The Antichrist has already come. He is neither Jew, pagan, Saracen, nor worldly tyrant, but the "man who op-

[1] Neander, v. 194.

poses Christian truth and the Christian life by way of deception;—he is, and will be, the most wicked Christian, falsely styling himself by that name, assuming the highest station in the church, and possessing the highest consideration, arrogating dominion over all ecclesiastics and laymen;" one who, by the working of Satan, assumes to himself power and wealth and honor, and makes the church, with its goods and sacraments, subservient to his own carnal ends.

The kingdoms of Christ and Antichrist are to be slowly and gradually evolved, side by side. But the spiritual annihilation of the latter (1340) had already commenced. It was to be accomplished by God, "by the breath of his mouth," the utterance of his elect priests and preachers, who were to go forth in the spirit of Elias and Enoch. In his predecessor,—Milicz,—Janow recognizes one in whom Elias had reappeared. The work begun was to go forward, like the operation of the leaven, or the growth of the mustard-seed.

To expose Antichrist is with Janow an important object. He points out the arrogance and the worldly sympathies and connections of the bishops, their greed of wealth, their vain attempt to serve two masters. But worse than this, because more directly fatal to the spiritual improvement of the people, was the neglect of the parochial clergy. A secularized hierarchy was Antichrist embodied.

The causes of this apostasy are laid open. One of these is the transfer of reverence from the Holy Scriptures to the decretals and Clementines. Human ordinances are placed above the commandments of God. Another is, that men choose to seek salvation in sensible and corporeal things, rather than in the Crucified alone. Those who confess Christ are censured and persecuted. The false prophets extol their own stately ceremonies, and anathematize for their non-observance. Hereby the consciences of men are ensnared, and the devil acquires great power to involve men in guilt. But no multiplicity of human laws and ordinances can meet every contingency and relation. The Spirit of God alone can do this. Hence the multiplied laws of men are superfluous and inadequate. They should be called, not traditions, but superstitions. In view of this, Janow, with a Christian sagacity, assumes the tone of the prophet: "So have I gathered," he says, "from the Holy Scriptures; and I believe that all the above-named works of men, ordinances and ceremonies, will be utterly extirpated, cut up by the roots, and cease,—and God alone will be exalted, and his word will abide forever; and the time is close at hand when these ordinances shall be abolished."

The substitute for all these is God's word, "the common rule for all." But positive law has been ineffectual to recover fallen men, and Christ has left to them the law of the Spirit. To its sound and simple beginnings the Christian church should be brought back. Monastic orders are not needed for the governing of the church. The unity of this is found in its union with Christ. The priest and the layman alike are one in him. The first has peculiar duties, but the same great privileges are accessible to both.

In connection with this point, we should also consider Janow's views in regard to the sacrament. He had laid down the principles from which the doctrine of the communion of the cup for the laity was a plain and direct inference. Yet for this he was not called in question. His views in regard to *frequent* communion are those which seem to have been most obnoxious. On this point he spoke with great earnestness and warmth; and it deserves to be noticed that he uniformly expresses himself as if he thought the laity were also entitled, not only to frequent communion, but communion in both kinds; and it scarcely admits of question that his treatises or letters on this subject were the germ of Calixtine doctrine as developed subsequently by Jacobel.

A large portion of Janow's writings was for a period ascribed to Huss. Of the separate treatises from his pen, of which his larger work was composed, we have those on "Antichrist,"[1] on "The Kingdom, People, Life, and Manners of Antichrist," the "Abomination of Carnal Priests and Monks," "Abolishing Sects," "The Unity of the Church," and a few others less important.

The first, on Antichrist, is an "Anatomy of the Beast." It is indeed a literary curiosity, the product of a mind ingenious and somewhat fanciful, but penetrating, sagacious, scripturally enlightened, and

[1] I must confess myself at a loss to determine what portion of Janow's treatise on this subject is to be ascribed to Milicz. There is some evidence that additions have been made in some parts by a later hand; but the references made in successive treatises to those that preceded them, and some peculiarities of style and expression, would seem to indicate the same author throughout.

glowing with a fire of holy indignation against the monstrous corruptions of the church. The names of Antichrist are presented in alphabetical order—"Abomination of Desolation," "Babylon," "Bear of the Wood," &c. The various members of his mystical body are then described,—the head, hair, brow, eyes, nose, neck, breast, loins, &c. Most important are the three false principles which are formed from the tail of Antichrist. The first is, that as soon as one is elected pope of Rome, he becomes head of the whole militant church, and supreme vicar of Christ on earth. This is pronounced a bare lie. The second is, that what the pope determines in matters of faith is to be received as of equal authority with the gospel. This is likewise pronounced false; for we must believe him, who has so often erred in matters of faith, only when he is supported by the scriptures. The third,—that the laws of the pope are to be obeyed before the gospel,—is declared blasphemous; for it is blasphemy to believe the pope or any one else, or to accept his laws, in preference to Christ.[1]

The treatise on "The Abomination of Carnal Priests and Monks" is in the same vein with that on Antichrist. It is peculiarly severe upon the mendicants. Wickliffe at Oxford, or Gerson at Paris, could not have been more unsparing in their reprehensions. The lukewarmness of the prelates; their avarice, wealth, and simony; the negligence of the priesthood in the execution of their duties; the unseemly strifes between the monks and the regular clergy; the sacrilegious sale of sacred things; the bar-

[1] Mon. Hussi, i. 364.

ter of masses, indulgences, &c.; the false worship offered to the bones of dead saints, while God's poor but devoted children are contemned and despised,—are unsparingly exposed. The reign of hypocrisy had become universal. There were, indeed, not a few faithful still left, like the seven thousand in Israel, that had never bent the knee to Baal. But by the iniquity of the times they were proscribed or driven into solitude. No path was open for their promotion. Ambitious and worldly men, by disgraceful methods, attained places of power and influence in the church. Wickedness, if powerful and gilded with pomp, was flattered; while any mention or exhibition of the crucified Jesus in synodical assemblies was impatiently borne.

The various passages of scripture, both in the Old and New Testaments, in which the great apostasy of the church is foretold, or in which the iniquity of Antichrist is exhibited, are successively considered. Ezekiel's vision; Gog and Magog; he that sitteth in the temple of God; the locusts of Revelation; the beast with the seven heads and the ten horns; the woman seated upon the beast, with her cup of abomination in her hand, and her forehead branded "Babylon the great, the mother of harlots,"—are brought to view, and shown to be exact descriptions of the prevailing apostasy. Even now, Janow declares that the pious are persecuted. They are reproached as Beghards and Turpins, Picards and wretches. Schisms, fraternities, and orders abound. The "religious" eat and drink, and are drunken on the sins of the people. Blasphemous indulgences are published, which one can scarce credit. Donations are extorted by threats of hell, and the poor are robbed by the avarice of the monks.

But Antichrist is to be destroyed. Christ will destroy him by the breath of his mouth and the brightness of his coming. He will raise up those who shall proclaim his word, and thus consume the lies and errors of the great deceiver.

Janow protests that he does not write, directing his words against any individual, but at the general apostasy. Nothing is said in bitterness or pride; and if read as written, none will be injured. He declares that he would not have dared to write, but for the resistless impulse of truth.

The other treatises are in a similar strain. They are bold and fearless in utterance, but abound in gospel simplicity and charity.[1] Every point is enforced by scripture citations. At times, the treatise itself seems attenuated to a thread, upon which the admonitions, warnings, and truths of scripture are strung. Many passages soar to that height of moral rebuke, which reminds us of Christ scourging the money-changers from the sacred temple.

But Janow, although not prosecuted as a heretic,

[1] Something of their tone in the more spirited portions, may be gathered from the following passage: "How great is the abomination, and how damnable is the error, when an impious and polluted clerk is made priest; and still greater and more damnable, when this unworthy priest is set in the place of God in the temple, and in the holy of holies, in the sight of God and his angels, and is honored and adored, and the people run to him for all sacraments and sanctity. And how abominable is the abuse, that such a devil and son of iniquity should have the authority of the living and most high God on earth, and the power to dispose and dispense, according to his pride, the tremendous sacraments of God." *Mon. Hussi*, i. 445.

was regarded as an innovator. It was not long before his position began to attract attention. In 1381 he became a prebendary at Prague, and in 1389 he was arraigned before the synod of Prague, by whom his views were condemned. He is said to have been forced to a recantation, but his writings of a subsequent date clearly show that there had been no change in his views. For a time he was banished from the city, but through the favor of the emperor was soon permitted to return. He died in 1394, and in 1410 his writings were honored, with those of Wickliffe, in being committed to the flames.[1]

A mere glance at the lives and doctrines of these three men will suffice to show that already at Prague a work had commenced which could not pause, even when they should be called away. Seed had been sown: truth had been scattered abroad. The new ideas which they had thrown out, and which they had so earnestly vindicated, were to prove in the sequel a powerful leaven. The eyes of men are naturally attracted to the array of physical forces, to fleets and armies, and the extending bounds of empire. But at that day, it is beyond question that the more important results were staked on the teachings of these three men, than on all the territorial aggrandizements of the German empire. It is a shallow philosophy that overlooks the position of the public teacher of new doctrines. Ideas are mightier than swords or bayonets.

In connection with the names of Conrad, Milicz, and Janow, there are others that are worthy of at

[1] This has been called in question by later authorities.

least a passing notice. Some of them, less known by their writings, were scarcely less conspicuous in their own day in the cause of scriptural knowledge and reform. In one of his sermons,[1] Huss mentions, to their honor,—"Nicholas Biceps, the most acute logician; Adalbert, the flowing orator; Nicholas Litomischel, the most sagacious counsellor; Stephen of Colin, the most devoted patriot; John Steikna,[2] the noble preacher, whose voice was like the blast of a trumpet; and Peter Stupna, the sweetest singer and most glowing preacher." These belonged to the age then past, and he speaks of his audience as treading over their graves.

But besides these, the names of two laymen, who exerted an important influence upon the age, should not be passed unnoticed. Peter of Dresden was almost, if not quite, a Waldensian in sentiment, and to his influence over Jacobel is to be attributed, in large measure, the origin of that discussion in respect to the communion of the cup, which almost revolutionized Bohemia, and brought down upon it the energies of crusading Christendom. Peter had resided for a time at Prague. He went to Dresden and was there employed as a teacher. But his religious views rendered him obnoxious to persecution, and about the year 1400 he returned to Prague. He was evidently a man of superior ability, and one who possessed great power over the minds of others. At Prague, among the thousands congregated at its university, he would have large opportunities for insinuating

[1] Mon. Hussi, ii. 42.

[2] By some writers mistaken for Conrad, and incorrectly spoken of as Conrad Steikna.

his peculiar doctrines. The very fact that he was instrumental in shaping the enlarged views of Jacobel, suffices to rescue his name and memory from oblivion.[1]

Along with Conrad, Milicz, Janow, and Peter of Dresden, must be ranked a celebrated layman, Thomas Von Stitny, a Bohemian knight,[2] and a man of strong religious as well as patriotic feeling. He was, says Helfert, "a Christian philosopher, in the full meaning of the word." His early years had been spent at Prague. At the university he proved himself a diligent student. The stores of knowledge which he here acquired he bore back with him to the retirement of his father's castle. Here, exchanging the sword for the pen, he devoted himself to the education of his family and of his countrymen. Many was the book or treatise issued from his retreat, which found its way into the hands of the people, and was rapidly transcribed and widely circulated. In the agitating questions of the day,

[1] The practice of the communion of the cup previous to its introduction by Jacobel, is rejected by Gieseler. The strongest argument for his position, in my mind, is, that Jacobel, in defence of his course, makes no reference to any such practice in Bohemia previous to his own time. The other argument, that the Bohemian brethren, in their Apology, expressly state that Master Jacobel was first to introduce the practice, has less weight, as the Apology was written more than 100 years after the death of Huss. Still, as there is strong evidence that Bohemia largely felt the influence of the Græco-Slavonic church, I have not felt warranted to depart from the views presented by Schröckh and others. My impression is very decided, however, that Janow's urgency for a frequent participation in the eucharist has been mistaken for a zeal in behalf of the communion in both kinds. His strenuousness on the first point had its influence, no doubt, in drawing general attention to the manner of celebrating the Lord's supper, and thus indirectly prepared the way for Jacobel to advocate the communion of the cup, while some of his principles, in regard to the equal union of the priest and layman in Christ, would obviously lead to the conclusions reached by Jacobel.

[2] Helfert, 44.

Stitny took a deep interest. He was probably on intimate terms with Milicz, and his writings reflect the views of that reformer. Like Milicz, he reproves the prevalent vices and errors, reprimands the monks for their neglect and contempt of the rules of their several orders, and urges the claims of Christian purity and devotion. Devoted to the study of the scriptures, he had yet no thought of departing from the communion of the church, or of going further than the reform of its abuses. He loved his native land with all the affection of a patriot, and his writings, which indicate his zeal for reform, were written in the Bohemian tongue, and exerted an important influence.

If we consider, then, the connection of Bohemia with the Greek church—the seed sown by the Waldensian exiles—the sagacity, eloquence, and daring zeal of the men whom we have named as the predecessors of Huss—the influence which they, and others like them, exerted upon the mind and heart of the nation—the younger preachers and students of the university, who enjoyed their training, or aspired to tread in their steps; and if, in this same connection, we regard the condition of the papal government, already by protracted schism an object of scandal and contempt to all Christendom, and the reckless indifference to all religion shown by Wenzel, the Bohemian monarch,—as devoted to the wine-cask as his father, Charles IV., had been to the pope,—we shall see that the way was already prepared for the advent of a reformer such as Huss proved to be.

Other events, moreover, contributed to encourage

whatever aspirations or desires might find place in Bohemia, looking toward a purer state of the church. The founding of the university of Prague, in 1360, had given an intellectual impulse to the nation, and thousands of her young men were eager to improve the privileges now brought, as it were, to their own doors. The kingdom enjoyed, moreover, an unexampled prosperity. Charles IV., with all his arts of craft, and sometimes of meanness, was an able and sagacious sovereign. Under his wise policy the industry of the country was encouraged, and its resources were developed. Great privileges were granted to the cities as well as to the aristocracy. A new code of laws was drawn up and published. The Moldau was rendered navigable as far as the Elbe. Mining and agriculture were encouraged. German artificers were introduced into the country. New Prague sprang up by the side of Old Prague. Breslau was in like manner improved. The noble bridge that spans the Moldau was constructed. The king's passion for architecture was freely indulged, and his nobility aspired to imitate him. Magnificent churches and palaces were rising on every side, to attest the enterprise, wealth, and taste of the nation.[1]

On June 7th, 1394, Anne of Luxembourg, wife of Richard II. of England, and daughter of Charles IV., died. Her attendants returned to Bohemia; many of them, like their mistress, had imbibed the views of Wickliffe. They brought back with them from England to Prague, copies of his books. Oxford students, following the practice of the age, had

[1] Cochleius, Æneas Sylvius, and others.

visited the universities of the continent, and, among others, that of Prague. The new opinions found adherents. On all sides there were anxious curiosity, inquiry, discussion. University life had its privileges and freedoms. Upon these Rome had not yet ventured to lay her despotic hand. What was wanted was, a man who should use these privileges to investigate and publish the truth of the new opinions—a man who was able to think, able to speak, and not too timid to stand by his convictions; and such a man was found in John Huss.[1]

[1] In regard to the predecessors of Huss, quite a full though not the most reliable account is to be found in a work by Aug. Zitte, a secular priest, published at Prague in 1786. From this Schröckh has largely derived his account. Of the three prominent precursors of Huss, Zitte says: "Stiekna (Conrad) grasped the light and held it up; Milicz, more mighty in speech and act, placed this heavenly light in an evangelical candlestick; Janow showed it to all in God's house, so that many of the children of darkness turned back to the original brightness of the church, and came to see that it was far better to walk in the day than do works of darkness and pay regard to the pretences of the monks." Helfert also presents some valuable information. Jordan, on the Precursors of Huss, is most complete and satisfactory. Neander and Gieseler cite him mainly.

CHAPTER II.

YOUTH OF HUSS. UNIVERSITY LIFE. WICKLIFFE.

BIRTH AND EDUCATION OF HUSS. — HIS PARENTAGE. — DEATH OF HIS FATHER. — STUDIES AT PRACHATITZ. — GOES TO THE UNIVERSITY OF PRAGUE. — ACCOMPANIED BY HIS MOTHER. — HIS POVERTY. — STATE OF THE UNIVERSITY. — FOUNDED BY CHARLES IV. — MODELLED AFTER THE UNIVERSITY OF PARIS. — SEASONABLY FOUNDED. — THRONGED WITH STUDENTS. — ITS TEACHERS. — FAVOR SHOWN TO LEARNING BY THE EMPEROR CHARLES IV. — PROGRESS OF HUSS. — HIS ACQUAINTANCE WITH JACOBEL. — ACQUAINTANCE WITH JEROME. — MARTYROLOGY THE FAVORITE READING OF HUSS. — AFFECTED BY THE VICES OF THE AGE. — APPROVES THE SENTIMENTS OF WICKLIFFE ON CHRISTIAN REFORM. — WICKLIFFE. — SUPPORTED BY THE DUKE OF LANCASTER. — HIS CAREER. — OCCASION OF HIS FIRST WORK. — IT EXPRESSES THE TONE OF HIS LIFE. — THE MENDICANT ORDERS ATTACKED BY WICKLIFFE. — HIS TRANSLATION OF THE BIBLE. — HIS WRITINGS. — HIS OPINIONS. — THEIR PURITANIC CAST. — THEIR PREVALENCE AND SPREAD. — VAINLY CONDEMNED AT LONDON.

1373–1398.

JOHN HUSS, or John of Hussinitz, was born July 6th, 1373.[1] He derived his name from his native village, in the southern part of Bohemia, in the circle of Prachin. This was in accordance with the custom of the age. There is no ground for the slander of an obscure writer,[2] that Huss took the name of his village because he had no knowledge of his father. Among the most distinguished compeers of Huss, in his own and other lands, the greater number whom we shall be called to notice were men like himself, known by the name of the place where they were

[1] According to some authorities, however, are, in my judgment, in the date is 1369. The probabilities, favor of the year given above.

[2] Varillas.

born or educated. This was the case with that remarkable triumvirate of the university of Paris, John de Gerson, Nicholaus de Clemengiis, and Peter de Ailly. Among his own countrymen were James of Misa, or Jacobel, as he was called from his diminutive stature, John of Rokyzan, and numerous others, who, although like Huss of obscure birth, rose to eminence by their talent and diligence, and rescued the places of their birth from obscurity by the distinction which they themselves won.

According to Æneas Sylvius, who was afterwards raised to the papal chair, Huss might boast of an honest and worthy, although obscure parentage. His lot was one favored neither by fortune nor rank. His parents were poor peasants, kind and simple-hearted, who spared no pains to give their son a good education. There are few memorials left us of his childhood. But if we may judge of his training from the fruits it bore, it must have been characterized by affectionate anxiety and a severe purity of morals. We search in vain in any record, whether from friend or foe, for any trace of youthful vice or juvenile excess. Never was any character subjected to more severe or bitter scrutiny; but in the entire catalogue of accusations brought against him, not one is to be found affecting his character. We may reasonably suppose that in his own noble simplicity and unimpeached purity of life, were reflected the simple manners and the quiet virtues of his childhood's home. That home must have been the abode of peace, gentleness, and love.

His parents, we are told, bestowed great care on

his education.[1] He was at first sent to a school in his native place. This was kept at a monastery, not far from the residence of his parents. His quiet manners and quick intelligence made him soon a favorite with the monks. They were pleased with the company of the boy, and, to the disquiet of his parents, often took him with them when they went abroad. Upon his father's death, which occurred in his boyhood, he was left by his mother entirely to their charge. But such was her poverty that she could not provide him needful clothing. In this emergency, as also at a later period, the nobleman of the place, Nicholas of Hussinitz, came forward to his aid.

When placed in the monastery, Huss devoted himself zealously to study. With boyish curiosity he gazed upon the huge piles of manuscript stored in the monastery, and in vain assayed to read them. They were in the Latin language, and this he had not mastered. The monks, from their own ignorance, could render him but feeble aid, but such instruction as they could afford was freely given. His many questions sorely puzzled them. "If the boy wants to know more," they said, "let him go to the Prachatitz collegium."

To this, a school of higher grade in the neighboring village of Prachatitz, he was accordingly sent. Here he made rapid advances, and won the praise of his teachers. His remarkable progress gave high promise of future distinction.

His course here was at length completed, and he

[1] Becker, in his Life of Huss, does not give his authorities.

returned home to his widowed mother. "What shall we now do, my son?" she asked.[1] "I am going to Prague," was his reply. "Let us not be troubled on account of our poverty; God will care for us. The monks have promised that I shall certainly go."

Thus, at his own instance probably, it was determined that he should be sent to the university. His mother, impelled by maternal anxiety, accompanied him to the city. If the story of her journey is true, it affords a characteristic illustration of the simple manners of the age and country. She took with her, from her humble store, a goose (huss in Bohemian) and a cake as a present to the rector. Unfortunately the goose flew away while she was on her journey, and she could not recover it. The poor woman, associating perhaps the lost fowl with the fortunes of her son, received the accident as an ill omen. But if disturbed by susperstitious fears, she had yet that simple piety which taught her to trust in God. She fell at once upon her knees, and recommended her son to the care and protection of divine providence. She then continued her journey, much troubled to think that she had only the cake left to present to the rector.

Of the means by which Huss was supported at the university we have no reliable information. To his own early history he rarely refers in his writings. It is said that on his arrival in Prague he secured a place in the house of one of the professors, where he was employed in service, and received in return food and clothing, and at the same time enjoyed

[1] Becker.

access to a large and select library. The story is not improbable. John of Rokyzan, a few years younger than Huss, and afterwards archbishop of Prague, was, like him, of obscure parentage, and of extreme poverty. Yet as a charity student he received aid in the prosecution of his course, and by persevering exertion and obvious merit won admission to the "College of the Poor," of which Jacobel was professor. It would not be strange if the course of Huss was, in its early period, parallel to that of Rokyzan.

But if a charity student, and largely dependent on alms for support, the fortune of Huss was full as favored as that of thousands and tens of thousands gathered at the universities of Oxford, Paris, and Prague. Sometimes the pressure of want and hunger was so severe that talent was forced into the market, and genius sold its service for a piece of bread. The powerful Duke of Burgundy could descend to purchase the tribute of the venal learning and ability of Parisian scholars, to procure in them apologists for his crimes. But Huss, with abilities equal to any in the market, was never suspected of the guilt of any mercenary alliance. He had no powerful or wealthy friend whose patronage could warp his independence, or interfere with the freedom of his moral or intellectual development. If aided—as is not altogether improbable—by Nicholas of Hussinitz, it was with that generosity which studies to confer a favor without imposing an obligation.

The testimony borne to the character of Huss is uniformly favorable. His enemies themselves, who were ready to curse him as a heretic, speak of his manners and his morals almost in terms of eulogy. Æneas Sylvius describes him as "a powerful speaker, and distinguished for the reputation of a life of remarkable purity." The Jesuit Balbinus[1] says of him, that he was accounted even "more acute than eloquent; but his affability of manner, his life of austerity and self-denial, against which none could bring a charge, his features pale and melancholy, his body enfeebled, and his gentleness toward all, even of the humblest class, were more effective than any power of words." "Meanly born, but of no mean spirit," is the testimony of one of his opponents, and no doubt all would have responded to its truth.

With such abilities and tastes, the diligence of Huss soon secured for him eminence in literary attainment. His opportunities were diligently improved. An unprecedented spirit of enterprise and of intellectual activity characterized the period during which he was engaged in his academic pursuits. The university of Prague was now in its most flourishing state. It was founded in 1360 by the emperor Charles IV., a zealous friend of learning and of learned men. He was the son of John of Luxembourg, and grandson of the emperor Henry VII., and had ascended the throne in 1347. Had it not been for his blind, or perhaps we should rather say, politic submission to the popes, the events of the following reign might have illustrated his own. His energy and enterprise were directed into peaceful channels,

[1] L'Enfant, i. 20.

and he preferred the arts of diplomacy and intrigue to martial prowess. To his exertions Prague was greatly indebted. The prosperity and improvement of the kingdom were studiously promoted. Private citizens, moved by imperial example, devoted their wealth to public uses; and noble architectural structures for public worship, and other objects, sprang up to attest their zeal. Some of these were endowed with imperial munificence. Æneas Sylvius declares that no other kingdom of Europe could boast as numerous and splendid temples as Bohemia. The rites and usages of the church were invested with new pomp, and no expense was spared to add to their attractions.

Even after the desolations of the Hussite war, enough remained to testify to the taste, the munificent liberality, and devotion of the emperor. But Prague was the special object of his favor. He surrounded a portion of it,—the *kleine seite*,—with imposing walls, crowned here and there with towers which, by their names, perpetuated the builder's fame. He reared castles and temples of exceeding beauty. His course provoked the admiration and imitation of the citizens; and wealthy inhabitants of Prague expended their treasures in a like manner. The Bethlehem church, afterward famous as the one within whose spacious walls Huss addressed large assemblages of his fellow-citizens, was built at the expense of private individuals. Among the other labors of the emperor may be mentioned the stone bridge which he threw over the Moldau, uniting the two portions of the city. For that day it was a noble and imperial work. It was eighteen hundred feet in length, broad enough for three carriages to drive abreast, supported by sixteen arches, and adorned with twenty-eight statues of the saints. It still exists to attest the public spirit of the emperor to whom it owes its origin.

But the great work of Charles IV., and the one for which he deserves the highest praise, was his founding of the university of Prague. In undertaking it, he sought and received the sanction of the Roman pontiff, Innocent VI. The university of Paris furnished him a model. That institution, after the popes, had given law to Europe. In her schools the men had been trained who controlled the public opinion of the world, and became the teachers of kingdoms. She was, in fact, an *imperium in imperio.* Her word was respected and reverenced throughout Christendom. Even then, the hoar of centuries combined with her reputation for learning and piety to render her venerable. The emperor Charles IV. might well aspire to rival the reputation attributed, whether justly or not, to his great predecessor and namesake, Charlemagne, by becoming, like him, the founder of a university. The times were ripe for the enterprise. The ravages of the crusades, and the impending terror of the Turkish arms, had conspired to scatter the treasures of the Eastern empire over the kingdoms of the West. Those treasures were the learning and the learned men which had hitherto been resident within the walls of the city of Constantine. The intercourse between the East and West was once more renewed.

Frequent embassies sought to promote the long-deferred union of the Greek and Roman churches. Prelates of the first were received into the latter with distinguished honor. A new spirit of inquiry and a new thirst for knowledge had been diffused abroad. Popular movements had taken place in almost every kingdom in Europe, which showed that society, even to its lower strata, was restless, and ready for a change.

The labors of the emperor were attended with remarkable success. Scarcely had the university been completed before it was thronged with students. It seemed to reach maturity at a single stride. The zealous patronage of the emperor was, no doubt, one of the most important elements of its success. The most learned and skilful men, moreover, were sought out for instructors, and they were selected, without regard to land or language, for their fitness and ability.

Four nations were represented there,—Bavaria, Saxony, Poland, and Bohemia,—each of which had a vote in the affairs of the university. At an early period, over two thousand students belonged to it from the German nation alone. It was the practice of the emperor often to be present at the examinations and disputations. He came in his imperial robes, attended by his officers and nobles, sometimes remaining for three or four hours at a time. It is said that he would become frequently so absorbed in listening to the disputations, that, when reminded by his courtiers that it was meal-time, he would reply,[1] "Go, get

[1] Cochleius, p. 4.

your supper—my food is here." Circumstances like these could not fail to invest the university with great splendor and importance in the eyes of the nation, and kindle the ambition of the students to excel, and thus merit the notice and favor of the emperor.

Although Charles IV. died in November, 1378, the impulse of his influence still survived. The university continued to flourish. It must have been about the year 1389, and when Huss was sixteen years of age, that he was matriculated and became a member of that body. He pursued his studies with such application and success as to receive, in order, all the degrees of honor which the university could bestow, with the single exception of Doctor of Theology, of which we have no proof that it ever was conferred upon him. He received the degree of Bachelor in 1393, of Master of Arts in 1396; became priest and preacher of the Bethlehem church in 1400; dean of the Theological Faculty in 1401; and rector of the university in the following year. It was during his residence at the university as a student that his attention was first drawn to the subjects which afterwards so earnestly claimed his attention and his profound interest, for his convictions, moreover, in regard to which he was to lay down his life. He reached Prague in the same year in which Matthias of Janow died. It was in the year 1393 that he became intimate with a memorable man, James of Misa, or Jacobel (little James) as he was called,[1] from his diminutive bodily stature. This man was a native of the Circle of Pil-

[1] Some authorities speak of him as a fellow-student of Huss.

sen in Bohemia, and was at this time a teacher in the university. Though destitute of anything imposing in his personal appearance, his writings, and the influence he exerted upon the community and the nation, show him to have been a man of ability and energy. Like others of his countrymen before him, he had a strong leaning to the usages of the ancient Greek church. We shall see, in the course of this history, that he was a kindred spirit of Huss, and that their acquaintance of more than twenty years ripened into a friendship which led to the charge upon Huss of holding the peculiar views of his friend, though in this particular case the charge was false.

It was some years later (1398) that he became acquainted with Jerome of Prague, who, along with Jacobel, was accused of spreading the writings and opinions of Wickliffe in the university. Here was another friendship which reflects honor upon both the men whom it united while living, and associated in their deaths. Besides these, there must have been at Prague not a few others—disciples of Milicz and of Janow—whose influence was exerted in the direction of scriptural reform, and in whom Huss found those whose spirit sympathized with his own.

But we need not seek in external sources the impulse which shaped his career. From his earliest years, Huss had manifested a deep interest in the lives of distinguished and holy men deservedly eminent in the history of the Christian church. Upright in his whole conduct, and blameless in his morals and his devotion to religious duties, even by the confession of his bitterest enemies, his zeal for acquaintance with the career and pursuits of those to whom he might look as models, amounted almost to a passion.[1] His manner of life had always been plain, simple, and unostentatious. His tastes were pure and innocent. One might have read, in his pale and somewhat attenuated features, the earnestness of a meditative spirit. There was an air of gravity and reserve manifest in his countenance, which gave evidence of calm purpose and sedateness of thought. His demeanor toward all was friendly and unassuming. His ambition, if he had anything deserving an appellation of such equivocal meaning, was directed toward distinction in the paths of devotion and of Christian effort. He was poor, and yet scorned wealth. He loved truth, and cared little for the honors of men. But to write his name by the side of those who had adorned the history of the church by their exhibition of Christian virtues, was the high and lofty aim that possessed his soul. While a student, it was his delight to pore over the history of the martyrs, to trace the progress of their devotion, to contemplate their self-denials and their sufferings. Once, while reading the history of St. Laurentius, who was put to death by being roasted on a gridiron, he thrust his hand into the fire to test his own constancy and power of endurance, and see whether he would be able himself to endure the torture of a like martyrdom. A friend who was present interfered to prevent the full execution of his purpose.

In this incident we may perhaps discern, on the part of Huss, a morbid religious sensibility, a ten-

[1] Schröckh, xxxvi. 585.

dency to an ascetic fanaticism. But beyond question, his severe conscientiousness, his ardent feeling, and his quick susceptibilities especially fitted him to be impressed by the searching and powerful words of Milicz and of Janow. It is evident, from the record of their labors, that they had drawn to their side not a few who, amid the general apostasy of the church, were earnestly devoted to the purpose of a higher Christian life. At Prague, and especially in the university, Huss would come in contact with these. A common sympathy would bind him to them. Yet it was not without a severe inward struggle—as we learn from the record of his own experience—that he was brought to relinquish worldly ambitions, and commit himself to that course which was to bring upon him the reproach in which Milicz and Janow had shared.

But at a very early period his decision was taken, and he never faltered in his purpose. The circumstances in which he was placed, and the objects toward which his attention was necessarily directed, combined to add strength to his convictions and firmness to his resolve. He had of course, by his residence at the imperial capital and his connection at the university, large opportunities for information and observation. He was at one of the foci where the great interests of European Christendom converged. There especially he was brought to understand the real condition and the sad degeneracy of the church. There he heard, from teachers and students, not only from Bohemia and Germany, but in some instances from foreign countries, free expressions in regard to the evils of the times, and he could not fail to take a deep interest in the great questions that were agitating and dividing the Christian world. The great schism which had already endured for many years was the scandal of Christendom. The papacy had become an Augean stable, demanding for its cleansing a more than fabled Hercules. But the mischief was not merely one that was far remote. The church was enfeebled and diseased in all its members. In Bohemia, and within the walls of Prague, there was enough, and more than enough, to excite thoughtful minds to grave reflection. Huss saw on all sides an abounding and prevalent iniquity. He noted a degree of corruption in church and state that could not fail to excite at once grief and indignation. In the contrast between what he saw around him and a primitive Christianity, he seemed to behold the gospel travestied by the lives of those whose duty it was to expound it, but whose whole course was a libel upon Christianity itself. The money-changers had established themselves in the sacred temple. Bold bad men, intriguing aspirants, the profligate and the vicious, had usurped the province of pastors and the Sees of bishops. The scriptures gave place to the decretals, and secular passions were dominant in the most sacred spheres.

Huss was profoundly affected and afflicted by what he saw around him. In common with many others, he recognized the necessity of a thorough and radical reform. In the writings of Milicz and Janow, and in the fruits of their labors, he could not but have discerned signs of hope. There were, moreover, others conscientiously adhering to the old hierarchy, but demanding its renovation, whose voices must have reached him at Prague. But the words which seemed to his listening ear most earnest, hearty, and effective, came to him from beyond the British channel. In the Oxford professor, driven from his public post, but in his humble parish of Lutterworth scarcely escaping by a peaceful death the vengeance he had provoked, Huss recognized a man whose bold and daring views, extraordinary ability, and scriptural method of reform were powerfully to confirm the bent of his own mind. The influence of Wickliffe on the religious movement at Prague, and on the career of Huss, was most important. The death of the English queen in 1394, leaving her Bohemian attendants free to return to their own land, occurred before Huss had completed his university career; and through them, doubtless, the writings of Wickliffe were extensively published.

It is at this point that we are called to survey the connection of the Oxford professor with the student of Prague.

England had long maintained a jealous watchfulness against the usurpation of the See of Rome. From the time when the first Norman seized her sceptre, she seemed more deeply conscious of her individuality and independence. No king was ever more unpopular than John Lackland, who mortgaged the kingdom to the pope. The rude barons, extorting *Magna Charta* from their monarch, were little inclined to surrender rights, if possible still more precious, to a foreign potentate. English patriotism prepared the way for Wickliffe. Men regarded him as the champion of the nation's rights. For once religious reform was supported by the spirit of the nobles, and for some years, Wickliffe's protector, the Duke of Lancaster, virtually swayed the sceptre, and enabled him effectually to defy the priests and the monks, who were his most bitter opponents.

Wickliffe was born in 1324, in the small village of Wickliffe, in Yorkshire, of respectable and probably somewhat wealthy parents. He was educated at Merton college, Oxford. The title which he here won, in a college which produced Thomas Bradwardine, *the Profound Doctor*, Walter Burley, *the Perspicuous Doctor*, William Occam, *the Singular Doctor*, and others of eminence and merit, indicates his ability and success. Although a perfect master of the scholastic philosophy to which he applied himself, Wickliffe was honored with the appellation of *the Evangelical* or *Gospel Doctor*. His attention was early directed to the study and investigation of the Bible. In this respect his example had few precedents in the university. Fifty years before, Roger Bacon had said that scholastic studies were in higher repute than the knowledge of the scriptures. At first no exception seems to have been taken to Wickliffe's course. The language of his enemies attests his high standing. He is spoken of as a most eminent theological doctor, "accounted second to none in philosophy, and in scholastic attainments incomparable."

The first of his works which he made public, indicates his acquaintance, through the pages of the New Testament, with a Christianity compared with which what bore its name was a distorted and grotesque caricature. It is entitled "The Last Age of the Church,"[1] and seems to have been suggested by the general apprehension excited throughout Europe on account of the plague, and the strange phenomena by which it was accompanied. Fearful natural visitations and signs filled Christendom with alarm. When Wickliffe was in his fourteenth year, the great comet appeared. For several succeeding years the ravages of the locusts were fearfully destructive. An earthquake of unusual violence devastated Cyprus, Greece, Italy, and the valleys of the Alps as far as Basle. Mountains were swallowed up. In some places whole villages were overthrown. The air was thick, pestilential, stifling. Wine fermented in the casks. Fiery meteors appeared in the heavens. A gigantic pillar of flame was seen exactly over the papal palace of Avignon.[2] A second earthquake nearly destroyed Basle. At Avignon, (1334,) persons of every age and sex were said, in the heat and drought which prevailed, to have changed their skins like serpents. Scales fell from the face, the neck, the hands. The populace, seized with madness, scourged and lacerated their half-naked bodies as they ran howling through the streets.

But these self-inflictions were not to be compared with the excesses that the Flagellants were guilty of thirteen years later. The plague that now ravaged

[1] The authorship of this work is disputed. [2] Life of Petrarch.

Europe threatened to exterminate its inhabitants. It touched a sound and healthy body as fire touches tinder, and from the first moment all hope was abandoned. The victim was suddenly covered with black spots like burns, and not unfrequently dropped down dead almost before he was aware of the attack. At Basle, fourteen thousand people were destroyed by it; at Strasbourg and Erfurt, sixteen thousand; while in Italy its progress and desolations have been immortalized by the pen of Boccacio. The consternation was universal. Men that never prayed before, prayed now. Some few gave themselves up to voluptuous and luxurious indulgence; but the great mass trembled, and thousands went so far as to join the ranks of the Flagellants. Never had there been such seriousness, such alarm. Vice shrunk back abashed into the shade. Crime seemed paralyzed in its stronghold.[1]

All these things were familiar to Wickliffe. Some of them took place while he was yet a student at Oxford, and at Oxford he met students from the continent to whom the scenes themselves had been present, witnessed realities. He had not yet taken his second degree when the plague visited Europe. His own mind undoubtedly was deeply impressed; and while he wrote of "The Last Age of the Church," the impression had not passed from the minds of others. Indeed, it was not until August, 1348, that the destructive malady made its appearance at Dorchester in England. Its havoc was dreadful. It was regarded as the work of the destroying angel, pre-

[1] Life of Petrarch.

monitory to the final doom of the world. The gross and revolting corruptions of the church were, by men far less severe in their convictions than Wickliffe, accounted its procuring cause. Wickliffe seized the occasion to speak out words of solemn admonition and threatening. Worthless in its prophetic character, the treatise is valuable chiefly for the bold tone of utterance in which it denounces the prevalent sins of the age. It would be eagerly listened to, at least by many of his countrymen—as in the plague of 1666 even the Non-conformists were welcome to the pulpits of London, and thousands hung upon their words.

Never was a rebuke more plainly called for. The pictures left us of ecclesiastical vice and abuse are worthy of an original in Pandemonium. Petrarch, whose devotion sent him to Rome in the Jubilee of 1350, and carried him scrupulously through all the prescribed ritual of the pilgrims that he might attain the blessing, was shocked to observe the doings in the court of the pope. Avignon was to him "that Western Babylon, that he hated like Tartarus." He describes it as "a terrestrial hell, a residence of fiends and devils, a receptacle of all that is wicked and abominable." "Why," he asks, "should I speak of truth, where not only the houses, palaces, courts, churches, and the thrones of popes and cardinals, but the very earth and air appear to teem with lies? A future state, heaven, hell and judgment, are openly turned into ridicule as childish fables. . . . . Whatever perfidy and treachery; whatever barbarity and pride; whatever immodesty and unbridled lust you have ever heard or read of; in a word, whatever impiety and immorality either now is or ever was scattered over all the world, you may find here amassed in one heap." Rome was no better than Avignon, and the poison of the heart spread to the extremities of the ecclesiastical body.

What the state of England was can easily be gathered from the complaint of "Piers Plowman," and the pictures left us in Chaucer's rhymes. Wickliffe saw Antichrist around him on all sides, and his words, however stinging, were too palpably true to be gainsayed. His career was largely shaped by the influences already noted, and he pursued it unfaltering to the end. The mendicant monks, at first acceptable for their zeal and poverty, had now become the curse of Christendom. They were the militia of the pope—ecclesiastical robbers and banditti. At Paris and Prague, as well as Oxford, they had become a nuisance. But long before Gerson exposed them, they were arraigned by Wickliffe. His blows fell fast and heavy, and excited against him the envenomed rage of his foes. He succeeded, however, in greatly limiting their rapacity and turbulence. In the midst of this conflict, the pope revived his claim on England for tribute and homage. Edward III. laid the claim before parliament. It was resolved that it should be resisted; and the pen of Wickliffe was summoned to the task of its refutation.

But Wickliffe's great work was the translation of the Old and New Testaments—the first complete English version of the Bible. He employed his "poor priests" to multiply copies of it. These were widely circulated. The effect was wonderful. The germ of Protestantism was planted in English soil,—two centuries later to spring up to a vigorous growth. No episcopal scrutiny, espionage, or authority could root it out. "The Evangelical Doctor" vindicated the justice of his title. It was in vain that the attempt was made to silence or condemn him. To the English councils, and to the summons of the pope at Avignon, he paid little regard. From the first he was shielded by persons high in power; to the last he replied without the least trepidation, in plainer language than papal courts were wont to hear. Notwithstanding all the measures of persecution taken against him, driving him first from the headship of Canterbury Hall, and afterwards from Oxford, he died quietly in his own parish of Lutterworth, at the age of sixty-one years (1384).

The writings of Wickliffe were numerous; and though some of them were obscured with scholastic subtilties, yet others, in which he sets forth his religious doctrines based on the sole authority of scripture, are sufficiently perspicuous. Of his numerous treatises, many are of a practical character, adapted to the comprehension of the common people. Scattered among them are passages of exceeding beauty, and some in which we recognize the deep and fervent devotion of the author. It is his *Trialogos*, however, that has acquired most notoriety. It is in this work that he impugns the doctrine of transubstantiation, and presents what may be regarded as his theological system. This was the work which traversed Europe, and attracted most attention at

Prague. It is a compendious review of the religious questions of the age, and embraces the sum and substance of Wickliffe's religious opinions.

These opinions are nearly related to those held two centuries later, by the Puritans of the Elizabethan age. On the subject of justification by faith, his views are indistinct and ill-defined when compared with those of Luther. But the same is true of nearly all the reformers of the fourteenth and fifteenth centuries. His predestinarian notions fall little, if at all, short of those of Calvin. The prevalence of pilgrimages and image worship led him to denounce these abuses of devotion with unsparing severity. Of excommunication and papal interdict he stood in no fear. He treated them only with deserved contempt. Whatever an ideal pope might be, the actual pope was Antichrist. It was enough that the church had one Supreme Head in heaven. To give it another on earth was to make it a monster. The order of the hierarchy was odious and unscriptural. Presbyters and bishops, on New Testament authority, he accounted equal in rank. The church invisible was the *simple*, and the church visible the *mixed*, body of Christ. The seven sacraments of the church were all admitted, though in a qualified sense, by Wickliffe. It is evident that his exposition of their significance would strip them of all that peculiar importance which was attributed to them by the prevalent superstitions of the age. The fasts of the church, which substituted fish for flesh, were *fool fastings*. The cumbrous ceremonies which disfigured its services, he would have reduced to a simpler ritual. Church music had no charms for him, when it charmed the thoughts of men from the words sung to the manner of performance. Judicial astrology, which was strangely prevalent in his age, found in him an unsparing assailant. Some strange sentiments have been ascribed to him which are not to be found in his writings, but which, probably, were extorted from his scholastic propositions. One of his chief heresies, as charged upon him by his enemies, was the doctrine that "Dominion is founded in grace." Here, however, he seems to have merely followed the lead of the apostle Paul, when he said, "All things are yours;" for civil authority and jurisdiction found nowhere a more strenuous defender than Wickliffe. The fanaticism of the later Anabaptists had no place in his views or character. He did, indeed, maintain the supremacy of civil tribunals over the persons of ecclesiastics, as well as over the accumulated possessions of the church; but these views and theories were justified by the reformation, which, less than two centuries later, adopted them in England. Church endowments Wickliffe regarded as inconsistent with the purity and proper constitution of a spiritual body. He opposed the civil jurisdiction of ecclesiastics, and accounted tithes as the alms of the people, and not to be extorted against their free choice.

It is evident that most of Wickliffe's views were drawn from scripture. They were enforced by his own peculiar and impressive energy of language. In the university of Oxford, as well as in various parts of England, they took deep root. The minds of men were in a state to yield them a careful attention. The singular visitations of providence by earthquakes and the plague, the incredible and enormous corruptions of the church, the overgrown pretensions and claims of the popes, the sympathy of the Duke of Lancaster and of others high in power with the new opinions, and their admiration of Wickliffe, conspired to secure for his words a favorable reception, and to give them a powerful effect. His writings had acquired a notoriety that would secure them, after his death, a candid and careful perusal on the distant banks of the Moldau. It was all in vain that the bishops, in the council of London, condemned them. The seed was sown—it was taking root, and no ecclesiastical police could root it out.

CHAPTER III.

PROGRESS OF THE NEW DOCTRINES AT PRAGUE.

WICKLIFFE'S DOCTRINES DISSEMINATED AT PRAGUE. — CHARACTER AND COURSE OF JEROME. — WICKLIFFE'S BOOKS CIRCULATED. — THEY ARE CONDEMNED BY THE UNIVERSITY. — PART TAKEN BY HUSS. — HIS POSITION AND INFLUENCE. — HESITATION IN RECEIVING THE DOCTRINES OF WICKLIFFE. — BETHLEHEM CHAPEL FOUNDED. — HUSS APPOINTED PREACHER. — THE TWO ENGLISHMEN. — THEIR PICTURED SERMON. — PATRIOTIC FEELING OF THE BOHEMIANS IN THE UNIVERSITY. — THEIR OPPOSITION TO THE CLAIMS AND PRIVILEGES OF THE GERMANS. — HUSS AND WICKLIFFE. — LUTHER'S LANGUAGE IN REGARD TO HUSS. — CORRUPTION OF THE CHURCH. — GENERAL TESTIMONY. — PROGRESS OF HUSS IN APPROVING WICKLIFFE. — OTHERS UNITE WITH HIM. — TEMPTATION RESISTED. — THE MIRACLE AT WILSNACK. — HUSS EXPOSES IT. — THE PAPACY DURING THE FOURTEENTH CENTURY. — ORIGIN OF THE SCHISM. — ARCHBISHOP SBYNCO. — HE ADHERES TO GREGORY XII.

1399–1407.

THE spread of Wickliffe's doctrines could not be confined to England. There were various channels by which they would be sure, ere long, to reach Bohemia. One of these has been already noted. The attendants of Anne of Luxembourg, queen of England, returning upon her death (1394) to their native land, would naturally spread abroad a knowledge of the new opinions. Huss himself says (reply to John Stokes, 1411) that for twenty years they had been known in Bohemia.[1] Of course they must have been

[1] Mon. Hussi, i. 108.

brought to Prague before the death of Wickliffe. Nor was this all. It was a common practice with the scholars of that age to visit the different universities of Europe, disseminating their own philosophical and theological views, and at the same time imbibing those of others. By their means every novelty in the moral or religious world was soon ventilated and spread abroad.

But among these knights-errant of literature, no one in that age exhibited a more adventurous and enterprising spirit than Jerome Faulfisch,[1] or Jerome of Prague, as he is more commonly called. He was by several years the senior of Huss, full his equal in zeal for knowledge, far more impulsive in feeling, and remarkably enthusiastic in his devotion to whatever enterprise he undertook.

He had travelled through different lands, but made the longest stay in England. At Oxford he became acquainted with the writings of Wickliffe. The fame of the *Evangelical Doctor* was yet fresh within its halls, and his views were embraced or favored by a large number of the students. Jerome was struck with the ability with which they were presented, and was especially gratified by the manly tone in which they rebuked the errors and vices of the age. He transcribed several of his books, or caused to be transcribed, and bore them back with him on his return to Bohemia (1397–8).[2]

Jerome was not a man to conceal his sentiments or disguise his aims. He gave free expression to his

[1] Palacky denies that his family name was Faulfisch. The rightful bearer of this name has been mistaken for Jerome.

[2] Helfert.

opinions on the subjects discussed by the English reformer, and to his estimate of the man. He found himself at Prague surrounded by many inquiring minds, and the new views which he advanced could not fail to draw attention. But among the members of the university opinions were divided. Some were bitterly opposed to the positions taken by the "Evangelical Doctor," and few if any voices were raised decidedly in their favor.

At first—so we are assured by one historian[1]—Huss himself shared deeply in the popular prejudice. Shortly after his return from Oxford, in 1398, Jerome is said to have shown Huss one of the books of Wickliffe which he had brought back with him. Huss regarded it as heretical, and spoke severely against it. He advised Jerome either to burn it or throw it into the Moldau, lest it should fall into the hands of persons eager for innovation. The story at least is not improbable. To the last, there were some of Wickliffe's views which Huss never accepted, and at this early period he was probably acquainted with but a small portion of his writings.

But in the following years (previous to 1403) the books of Wickliffe seem to have been more extensively read and circulated at Prague. They began at least to attract in a special manner the attention of the university. A large number of his articles had been already condemned by the London synod, and it did not become the masters of Prague to be less orthodox than the English clergy. A still larger number was selected from the books of the English

[1] Theobald, i. 4. Quoted by Bonnechose.

reformer by John Hübner, who proposed their condemnation by the university.

To propose was to secure their sentence, especially after they had been interpolated, as is asserted, by Master Hübner. A blind prejudice existed against whatever bore the name of Wickliffe. It was enough that his views had been pronounced heretical by the English synod, and that his course had enraged the English clergy. To add a new impulse to the zeal of the German party in the university, Wickliffe's philosophy—for he was a Realist—greatly contributed. The Germans were Nominalists, while the Bohemians inclined to side with Wickliffe.

A convocation of the university was summoned (May 28, 1403) to examine and pronounce upon the controverted doctrines.[1] The theological faculty met also. A third and full assembly of the doctors, masters, bachelors, and all the students of the Bohemian portion of the university, was held at the church called Nigra Rosa. Huss himself is said to have been present. But few voices were lifted in favor of the obnoxious doctrines. Huss was not himself prepared to defend them, for, by his own account, there were certain portions of them which he could not accept. He sought, however, to prevent any decisive action.[2] But in spite of the opposition of him-

[1] Cochleius, p. 12.

[2] Helfert says, p. 64, that "Huss and his friends exerted themselves to their utmost to prevent the proposed sentence. They tried to show that the extracted articles were not fairly selected, and that a quite different sense was attributed to them than the author intended." A little before, two persons had been sentenced and burned in Prague for adulterating drugs. "Are not these," asked Huss, "more worthy of punishment who distort the sense of doctrines, than those who merely adulterate their wares?"

self and his friends, sentence against them was pronounced in the following words: "Know all men, that all the doctors and masters here assembled, with one consent, and with scarcely the show of objection, have rejected, refuted, and condemned the forty-five articles of Wickliffe, as in their sense heretical, erroneous, or scandalous." And they "charge all and each, subjects of this nation, that no one shall rashly presume to defend or teach, whether openly or secretly, any articles of such nature, and this under penalty of expulsion from the said nation."

Any one, moreover, who had not attained to the degree of master, was forbidden to read the books of Wickliffe, especially those on the Eucharist, his Dialogue and Trialogue, in which the aforesaid doctrines were more prominently and plainly brought forward."[1]

Whatever the views of Huss may have been—and undoubtedly he accepted some of the condemned articles—at this time he made no strenuous show of opposition to the sentence. He was probably aware that it would have been utterly ineffectual. But the decision may have been, and probably was, the means of drawing his attention to a closer examination of the whole subject. He at least, as a master of the university, was not prohibited from the perusal of Wickliffe's books. He might be willing to wait and improve future opportunities for pursuing the course that he should deem wisest after more mature deliberation.

[1] Cochleius.

Meanwhile the career of Huss was opening with bright promise. His position was one of high influence, and was becoming stronger and more important every day. He was popular not only in the university, but in the pulpit. In 1401 he had been selected, for his zeal and eloquence as well as his purity of life and religious devotion, to occupy one of the most important posts in the whole kingdom. He was made Confessor of Queen Sophia of Bavaria, second wife of King Wenzel. She was a woman of strong mind and high character. Through her influence Huss was received with favor at court, and acquired powerful friends.

Through one of these, the founder of Bethlehem chapel, then resident at Prague and present at court, he was soon called to occupy a position of still more commanding influence. It was in the pulpit of that chapel that the great work of Huss's life was to be achieved. We must trace the erection and endowment of this edifice to two causes,—one, the enterprise excited by the example of the emperor in his architectural improvements, and the other to that zeal for more popular religious instruction which had been enkindled by the labors of Conrad, Milicz, and Janow. To add to the architectural beauty of Prague by the erection of an elegant structure for public worship, and to afford facilities for the preaching of the word of God independent of the encumbrance of rites and ceremonies, were objects which combined to draw out the large liberality of the two men most concerned in the founding of the chapel.

It was built in the closing years of the fourteenth century. A rich merchant of Prague—Kreutz by name—gave the ground, and John of Mulheim founded the chapel. The intention of the latter is expressed in the deed of foundation. Anxious for the salvation of his own soul, and the spiritual refreshment of believers; and considering that, while in Prague there were many places suitable for purposes of divine worship, there was none specially provided simply for the preaching of the word of God, and that preachers in the Bohemian tongue especially were thus forced to go from place to place in private houses and secret conventicles, he determines to erect, on the ground granted by the merchant Krutz, a chapel in honor of the Holy Innocents, to be known by the name of Bethlehem, with the simple intent that common people and Christian believers might there "be refreshed by the bread of holy preaching."[1]

The erection of the building was commenced in the year 1391, but it was not completed till 1400. The first occupants of the pulpit were John Protiva, of Neudorf, and afterwards Stephen of Colin, both of them learned theologians and glowing patriots.[1] But at the court of the king the founder of the chapel became acquainted with Huss, and a warm friendship sprang up between the nobleman and the youthful preacher. The result was, that the founder himself selected Huss to fill the pulpit of Bethlehem chapel (1402). Doubtless he discerned in him those characteristics and qualifications which fitted him to carry

[1] The deed of foundation is given by Gieseler, iii. 415. [2] Helfert, p. 58.

out the original design of the endowment. A wiser choice could not have been made. It justified the sagacity of the nobleman, whose friendship was warmly reciprocated by Huss. The latter speaks of him frequently in his letters, and makes mention of him in terms of kindness and respect.

Thus the chapel becomes identified with the life and career of Huss.[1] Here for full twelve years[2] he occupied an independent position. The benefice, if such it must be called, was not the gift of prelatic favor, but left its possessor free from ecclesiastical restraint.

The recorded design of the founder of the chapel throws light upon the successful efforts of Milicz and Janow in bringing over others to their views. John of Mulheim was evidently one of a class at Prague who were zealous for the dissemination of scripture

[1] "In the chapel," says the Jesuit Balbinus, "were the arms and the triumphal chariot of Huss." He refers to the pulpit, and the pictures on the walls. In his prison at Constance Huss dreamed that he had painted Christ and his Apostles on the walls of his chapel. The pope came to erase them, but skilful painters appeared to restore what he erased. They defied the priests and bishops. "I thought," says Huss, "that I saw the people assembled, and exulting at the sight. For myself, when I woke up, I had a hearty laugh."

The friends of Huss gave his dream a favorable interpretation. By the image of Christ they understood his gospel, which should still be preached in the chapel. In fact the successors of Huss in his pulpit took the same ground with him, and this evangelical succession was for many years continued. Theobald, who wrote not far from two centuries later, speaks of Bethlehem chapel as still standing. He speaks of having seen the pulpit of Huss, which was made of pine covered with cloth. On the right of it was a picture of Jerome bound to the stake; in the centre of the pulpit Huss was seen, amid the flames kindling around him, while his bed, books, &c. are cast on the blazing pile to be consumed with him. On the left Huss is again exhibited, subjected to the torture. The executioner is pouring blazing oil on his head. In the vestry, the robe of Huss, of black silk, was carefully preserved. The pulpit had been mutilated to procure memorials of the reformer.

[2] So Huss says in his letters.

truth. Nor, unless he had been cognizant of a state of things which would warrant the measure, would he have made provision for the endowment of the chapel. He was confident that a preacher there would not lack for an audience, and he intended that the endowment should be a perpetual foundation. So long as the yearly income of the endowment did not exceed a certain amount, it was to be given to the support of the preacher. In case of an excess, provision was to be made for the care of the chapel and the purchasing of such books as the preacher might need. When it had increased so as to suffice for the support of two preachers, another was to be chosen as a colleague of the first. In case there was still an excess, the balance should be devoted to the support of charity students at the university.[1]

The preacher was, moreover, obligated to personal residence in the city. He was not to imitate those who sought their own and not the things of Christ, receiving the pay but not performing the labors; and he was to withdraw from his post of duty only in case of necessity, and with the permission of the archbishop or his vicar.

The election of the preacher, after the founder's death, was to be vested in the three senior masters of the Caroline college, belonging to the Bohemian nation, who were to sit and advise with the mayor of the old city. The last was to select one of three whom the first should nominate as most capable of discharging the duties of the office. The three masters, together with the preacher, should direct in re-

[1] Helfert.

gard to the disposition of the fund for charity students, and the conduct of those by whom it should be received.

The king sanctioned the endowment; Archbishop John of Jenstein laid the corner-stone of the edifice; and the pope, some years later, confirmed the foundation. The mayor and city council released the ground without requiring the payment of the customary tax paid on the transfer of property from municipal to ecclesiastical jurisdiction, and declared it free from all future city taxes and assessments.

Although the edifice was not completed till some years later, the first preacher, Protiva of Neudorf, commenced his labors as early as 1395. The merchant Kreutz, in the following year, appointed as altarist Matthias of Tucap, who probably remained at his post till 1403. But previous to this time Huss had commenced his labors as the preacher of the chapel. He was inducted by the vicar of the archbishop, March 14, 1402.[1]

His appointment seems to have been received with general favor. The archbishop was his warm and steadfast friend. He coöperated with him in several measures of reform, and manifested such confidence as to invite information from him in regard to the abuses and corruptions of the church.

From the first Huss was popular among the citizens, and his personal qualities combined with his eloquence to secure their love and attachment. Bethlehem chapel, notwithstanding its spaciousness, was crowded by throngs eager to hear the youthful

[1] Helfert, 270–275.

preacher expound the word of God. With honest zeal he set forth the divine commands, reprehending with just severity every departure from them. The excesses and vices of every class were faithfully, perhaps often sternly, rebuked. The blameless life of the preacher gave double force to his words. Men were forced to respect him in his conscientious discharge of official duty. They saw in him, not the actor nor the mere orator, but the devoted minister of Christ, who practised himself what he preached to others.

For several years he continued to fill the pulpit under no suspicion of heresy. Many, it is true, must have felt the severity of his admonitions—the indirect condemnation of their lives by the doctrines which he taught—and have been forced to regard him with secret hate. But, strong at court and in popular favor, it was only in whispers that dissatisfaction with him could be expressed.

Meanwhile he was himself taking enlarged views of the great question of reform. To this result he was brought in part, undoubtedly, by the perusal of Wickliffe's writings. The more he perused them, the more accordant they appeared to be with his own views. Speaking on this point at a later period, he says, himself, "I am drawn to him (Wickliffe) by the reputation he enjoys with the good, not the bad priests at the university of Oxford, and generally with the people, although not with bad, covetous, pomp-loving, dissipated prelates and priests. I am attracted by his writings, in which he expends every effort to conduct all men back to the law of Christ, and especially the clergy, inviting them to let go pomp and dominion of the world, and live, with the apostles, according to the law of Christ. I am attracted by the love he has for the law of Christ, maintaining the truth, and holding that not one jot or tittle of it could fail."[1]

We discern here the grounds upon which Huss sympathized with Wickliffe. His philosophical views were not matter that should afford charge for heresy, and throughout all his theological writings he conceded to scripture, and to scripture alone, the supreme authority. Huss felt, therefore, that he could not reject Wickliffe as a heretic, or condemn his fundamental position as heretical, without depriving himself of the very grounds upon which he rested his own views.

Wickliffe's writings had been condemned in 1403. In the following year two learned Englishmen, James and Conrad of Canterbury, came to Prague, and became members of the university. From policy, it may be, or under fear produced by the sentence of condemnation, they spoke but little of Wickliffe, while they maintained some of his most objectionable doctrines in public theses before the university. Among the questions they discussed were these: whether the pope is possessed of more power than any ordinary priest; whether the bread which he blesses in the mass, has any more efficacy than when blessed by any other priest? They professed it as their purpose in these discussions only to settle more firmly their attachment to the faith. Yet

[1] Monumenta i. 109.

silence was imposed upon them, and they were compelled to spread their views in secret. Even thus, many of the teachers of the university were found ranged upon their side. The method which they were driven to adopt to maintain their views was one certainly more effective with the populace than public disputation. The name of their host was Luke Welensky. They gained his consent to their spreading a painting on the walls of a room in his house in the outskirts of Prague. That picture was, in fact, the contrast of a pure with a corrupt Christianity, and spoke its lessons to every eye. It could be comprehended at a glance. Men crowded to see it, and heard a sermon while they gazed in silence and made their own comments. On one side of the picture was Christ, in his humble entrance into Jerusalem, seated upon an ass, while the people and children surrounded him, casting olive leaves and branches in his way; and his disciples, with their feet bare, followed after. On the other side was pictured the procession of the pope, mounted on a large charger which was covered with ornaments of gold, silver, and precious stones, while soldiers with drums and trumpets, spears and halberds, were in attendance; and behind followed the cardinals, mounted on horses in golden trappings. It was a pictured sermon. Huss spoke of it approvingly from the pulpit as the true antithetical representation of Christ and Antichrist. However he might as yet be disposed publicly to treat the *name* of Wickliffe, he admired at least some portions of his doctrines, when unveiled and brought out to popular comprehension. With his mind in such a state, several years passed on. He was highly respected, and almost idolized by the patriot feeling of the nation. He felt that his position justly pointed him out as the champion of its rights, the reformer of its abuses.

An occasion for his activity, in both these respects, was not wanting. The German party of the university, by mere numbers, possessed an overpowering strength and influence, and, united as they were with the more strenuous of the Bohemian clergy in their opposition to Wickliffe, carried all before them. Huss felt indignant at what, with a patriot's feelings, he could not but deem an usurpation. Each of the three foreign nations in the university possessed the same power with the Bohemian nation. He preferred that the university of Prague should be modelled more perfectly after the mother university at Paris, and that all the foreign nations, as in the latter institution, should have but one vote instead of three. He must have found a strong feeling in favor of the project, to warrant him in attempting to carry it out. But he did attempt it, and he finally succeeded. In this he was, no doubt, aided by his influence at court, the favor of the queen, and the anxiety of the Bohemian party to secure a larger share of the offices and honors of the university. To the progress of this struggle we shall again have occasion to refer.

During this period the views of Wickliffe continued steadily to gain new adherents. The public attention which had been drawn to them by their condemnation abroad as well as by the university, created a more extended curiosity and eagerness to peruse them, and many copies of his books were transcribed, and circulated from hand to hand. The labors of Milicz and Janow—the leavening influence of those in Prague, who, in large numbers, still cherished their memory—the repeated occasions upon which a true was held up in contrast with a false Christianity,—as in the sermons of Huss, and the picture of the two Englishmen—all contributed to the notoriety and spread of the obnoxious doctrines.

Huss himself lost all his horror at their heresy. A favorable change in his views of them was wrought by fuller acquaintance with them. His desire was simply to know the truth. No matter from what source it came, it was always acceptable. At a later period, in his treatise on the church, he says, "Often have I allowed myself to be set right, even by one of my own scholars, when I saw that the reasons were good; and I felt bound to thank him for the correction." This is not obstinacy, but the candor of a truth-loving spirit.

There is, it seems probable, a striking parallel between the manner in which the prejudices of Huss were overcome in favor of Wickliffe, and the manner in which those of Luther were overcome in favor of Huss. It was Luther who said of the works of Huss, "When I was studying at Erfurt, I found in a library of the convent a book entitled 'Sermons of John Huss.' I was seized with a curiosity to know what doctrines this heresiarch had taught. This reading filled me with incredible surprise. I could not comprehend why they should have burned so great a man, and one who explained scripture with so much discernment and wisdom. But inasmuch as the very name of Huss was such an abomination that I imagined that at the mention of it the heavens would fall and the sun be darkened, I shut the book with a sad heart. I consoled myself, however, by the thought that perhaps he wrote it before he fell into heresy; for, as yet, I knew nothing of the doings of the council of Constance."[1] Similar to this may have been, and doubtless was, the experience of Huss with regard to Wickliffe.

But the growing corruption of the Romish hierarchy, the identification of the foreign party to which he was opposed with the opposition to Wickliffe, and his own clearer convictions on the subjects of which the English reformer had treated, prepared Huss for an unprejudiced judgment of his writings. He was well aware that those writings must stand or fall on their own merits. He knew that few of those who pronounced sentence on them had ever read or examined them, that far less than himself were they qualified to condemn or approve, and that such a sentence as that which the university had pronounced could have but little weight with men of sound sense and sober judgment.

Meanwhile daily events were, to the eye of Huss, a running commentary on the truths he found so boldly stated and so ably maintained in the books of Wickliffe. Christendom was scandalized at the audacious impiety of the popes. Men could hardly believe their own eyes when they saw the length and breadth,

[1] Luther's Preface to Letters of Huss.

the height and depth, to which corruption had attained, in the very heart of the church. All the prominent historians of the age, of every class and party, are unanimous in their condemnation of the prevalent and abounding iniquity. The very men by whose influence and decision Huss at last perished, were those who exposed the evil with most unsparing severity. At this time they were speaking at once the language of his convictions and of their own. Any one who listened merely to their words and regarded their common anxieties, would have imagined that they would have rushed as brothers into one another's arms. Huss never used language more severely scathing and vindictive in regard to the corruptions of the Romish church than what remains to us from the pens of some of his most virulent opposers. The power of human expression is tasked to its utmost capacity to depict what Theodore Vrie calls the "arrogance and pomp, the tyranny and sacrilege, the pride and simony, of popes, cardinals, prelates, and bishops." Their iniquity is only paralleled by their ignorance and effrontery. The English Ullerston, the Italian Zabarella, and that remarkable triumvirate of the university of Paris,—Gerson, D'Ailly, and Clemengis—men to whom attached no taint of heresy—seem to vie with each other in the effort to exhibit the wickedness of the times, and hold it up to indignant rebuke. There is in existence a small pamphlet from the pen of Clemengis, in which he lashes, with blows that must have stung like scorpions, the vices of the whole ecclesiastical order. He spares no class of the clergy, to use his own words, from "the golden head of the image to the toes of clay." In a torrent of burning and indignant eloquence, he appeals to the facts of a corruption too notorious for denial; bids "the church look to the vision of the Apocalypse, there read the damnation of the great harlot that sitteth upon many waters, and then contemplate her own marked doings and the dire calamity that shall come upon her." We shall see, as we progress, that this language in all its severity was well merited. Men spoke thus because they were forced to it,—more in sorrow than in anger. They loved the church; and because they loved her, they could not bear to see her fondle in her bosom the viperous brood of iniquity.

Huss followed up the study of Wickliffe's writings, and he could not but recognize in the Englishman a brother reformer. His earlier prejudices gave way to the convictions produced by a more careful examination. The more he read, the more fully he was led to approve and commend. Some of his fellow-collegians detected him in the perusal of the works of the arch-heretic. In a reproachful way they remarked, that by a decree of the council his soul had been sent to hell. Huss replied, "I only wish that my soul, when it leaves this body, may reach the place where that of this excellent Briton now dwells." [1]

[1] This language was probably used under the impulse of the moment. The more deliberate judgment of Huss, pronounced some years later, was as follows: "I do not believe or grant that Wickliffe was a heretic, but neither do I deny it; but I hope that he was not; for, in doubtful matters, we ought of our neighbors to prefer the more charitable opinion." Mon. Hussi. i. 109. Again he says, (p. 169,) "Of no one should we mortal men assert, without revelation or sacred scripture, that he is eternally damned."

The minds of others were favorably impressed, as well as his own, by a perusal of the writings of Wickliffe. Stanislaus of Znoyma,[1] a former teacher of Huss, spoke out boldly in their favor, in disregard of the sentence of the university. He did this publicly, and offered to maintain his position against any who were disposed to impugn it.[2] From his chair in the university he praised Wickliffe; spoke of him as an "abused man," a profound theologian and philosopher; deprecated the detraction of those who would count him a heretic, declaring that from his writings "the most beautiful flowers might be gathered."[3]

Nor was he alone in this. Paletz—whom we shall meet again as the accuser of Huss, but now his companion and bosom friend—was equally outspoken. On a public occasion he had praised Wickliffe before the university, declaring that his argument was unanswerable, and throwing his book in full congregation, in the midst of the masters, exclaiming, "Let who will impugn a single word, I will defend it."

These men, along with Huss, embraced many of the views of Wickliffe and spoke in their defence. But persecution tried them and found them wanting. At the critical moment they abandoned their ground. But Huss uniformly and without wavering maintained his. He adopted the new views, not because they were Wickliffe's, or because they were plausibly set forth, but because he found them accordant with the word of God: by this he had already learned

[1] Oftener written Znaim.

[2] On one occasion, when Stanislaus was arguing with great vehemence in defence of Wickliffe, some of the older doctors could not endure it, and in consequence rose abruptly and left the assembly. *Mon. Hussi,* i. 267.

[3] Mon. Hussi. i. 267.

to put all human opinions and teachings to the test. In reply to Paletz, he afterwards said—and his whole career is a fitting comment on the truth of his words—"Though Wickliffe, or an angel from heaven taught otherwise than the scripture teaches, I could not follow him. I disobey the perverse mandates of my superiors, because scripture teaches me to obey God rather than man."[1]

Yet he had attained to this position not without a severe struggle. His age was just the one for a supple, adroit, and able man to achieve success. It was an age of temporizers—an age when the necessary capital for business, whether in secular or ecclesiastical spheres, was, in the judgment of most, first of all an easy conscience. The man of real ability, whose convictions were in the market, might aspire to almost any eminence he chose.

Huss was not blind to this fact. He had before him inviting avenues of ambition. He saw the most tempting prizes almost within his grasp, and luring him to betray his own convictions. To forego them, to scorn them, and, moreover, to incur reproach or hatred or persecution for the cause of truth—to stand independent of the corrupt influences around him, and abide fast by his convictions, was no easy task. Yet this task he achieved, in a strength which he ascribed to a higher than any human source.

Up to this time no suspicion of heresy had attached to Huss. He had indeed more than once already offended against the slavish and superstitious

[1] In his controversy with Paletz, Huss subsequently says, "I hold to the true opinions of Wickliffe, not because he says them, but because scripture, or infallible reason teaches them." *Mon. Hussi*, i. 264.

notions of a corrupt hierarchy. In 1403, Sigismund, king of Hungary, who took during Wenzel's imprisonment the title of Governor of Bohemia, and who afterwards became emperor, was at variance with the pope, Boniface IX. The latter had sustained and encouraged Ladislaus, king of Naples, as a rival claimant of the throne. In revenge, Sigismund forbade the levying of money for Rome within the precincts of the kingdom. Huss, on this occasion, preached boldly against the indulgences granted by the pope. But then it was neither crime nor heresy. Sigismund approved it. His brother Wenzel had his grievances with the pope also. Boniface had consented to his deposition, and both the royal brothers could not have disliked the severity of Huss, so fully warranted by the scandals of the popedom.

It must have been not long after this that he exposed to popular reprehension and derision a pretended miracle invented by clerical avarice. He went so far as to write a tract against it, and his course was approved by the archbishop. A priest at Wilsnack had declared that, in a conflagration which had taken place, he had found the host in the fire, unconsumed, and sprinkled with drops of blood, which he declared to be the blood of Jesus Christ. This was soon noised abroad. The story was spread that at a sight of the host miracles had been wrought. Throngs crowded to behold the wonderful object. The sick and maimed hoped to derive a benefit from their journey to Wilsnack. They came from every direction, even from as far as Prague Huss burned with indignation at the sacrilegious trick. He argued before the citizens that the whole thing was an imposture. The blood of Christ had been glorified with his body in the resurrection, and was quite inseparable from it. Hence none could adore it on the earth while it was not here. The wickedly avaricious priests would not hesitate to sprinkle their own blood on the host, to make fools believe it to be the blood of Christ. As to the objection that other relics of Christ—his crown of thorns, his robe, his cross—were preserved and seem to be stained with blood, he answers in a manner to show his incredulity: and as to the asserted preservation of the circumcised flesh of the Saviour, he says, "Let us have the proof of it; but sooner will the last trumpet sound for judgment than that proof will appear." "As to such deceptions, I see nothing more strange in them than what is practised here in Prague, of exhibiting the blood of Jesus Christ mingled with the milk of the Virgin Mary." As to the objection that the miracle might be wrought by God's omnipotence, he replies by drawing a distinction between what God can and what God will do. As to the miracles claimed to have been wrought, he denies them altogether, and asserts that a false priest would not hesitate to sustain his lying imposture with new lies. He then gives a list of false miracles, wrought by the pretended blood of Christ, which had been detected and exposed in Hungary, Germany, and elsewhere.[1]

It may have been in consequence of Huss's decided action and prompt exposure of the imposture

[1] Mon. Hussi, i., 154–163.

that a certain citizen of Prague, Peter Zicko, determined to visit Wilsnack. He had a shrunken hand; and taking with him a hand formed of silver, he communicated to the priests his intention of bestowing the latter on them, in case the former was restored to soundness. For three days he waited patiently to hear the result. At length it was thus announced by a priest to the assembled multitude: "Listen, my children, to a new miracle. A citizen of Prague has been healed, in virtue of Christ's blood, of a shrunken hand. In testimony of it he has presented this," holding up to them the hand of silver. Zicko,—who, till that moment, had probably remained concealed,—at once arose, and lifting up his hand, said in a loud tone of voice, "O you priest! why do you lie? Here is my withered hand just as it was before."[1]

He returned to Prague and told his story. It confirmed the words of Huss. The archbishop Sbynco, afterwards the open enemy of the reformer, commanded and ordered, under penalty of excommunication, directing that proclamation should be made by every priest in Prague, that no one should visit Wilsnack. Several works beside that of Huss appeared on the subject. The doctors of Erfurth also refuted this idolatry.

The cry against Huss for heresy was of nearly the same date with the struggle between the Bohemian and other nations in the university, and was no doubt very closely connected with it. But for the time it was disregarded. Other matters of more

[1] Mon. Hussi, i., 162.

importance absorbed the attention of the Christian world. The state of the papacy was such, that two popes possessed each a divided allegiance; while some nations, as France for a short period, were for withholding obedience from both. Huss held these views, and so accorded with many of the wisest and best men of Europe. He wished to have Bohemia withdraw herself from each party, and join with that portion of the cardinals who rejected both popes in the election of one whom all should recognize as the head of the church. But to understand his position, we must take a brief retrospect of the condition of the papacy for the previous century.

At the commencement of the fourteenth century the papal chair was occupied by a man who revived the spirit and pretensions of Gregory VII. and Innocent III. Boniface VIII. was a man whose unscrupulous character and great abilities were united with craft and arrogance, and "an ambition as boundless as his avarice." Interposing as mediator between the kings of France and England, he soon assumed the authority of a judge, and imposed conditions which aroused indignation. Philip the Fair soon had an opportunity to resent the wrong, although his course was dictated, probably, as much by the interests of his kingdom as by the spirit of revenge. Large sums of money were constantly levied in France, and under various pretences transmitted to Rome. The king, whose treasury stood in great need of funds, published an ordinance prohibiting the exportation of gold and silver, coined or uncoined, from the kingdom without his permission.

Boniface retaliated by his famous constitution, in which he forbade secular princes, save by his approval, to exact any sum or sums of money from ecclesiastical revenues. A war of manifestoes followed, which was temporarily closed by a hollow truce. New causes of complaint arose. The pope threatened to absolve Philip's subjects from their allegiance. The king, supported by the three estates of the kingdom and the advice of his barons, defied the threat. His excommunication followed. France was put under interdict, and the universities were deprived of their privileges. Philip retaliated by arresting the pope, who with his court was then at Anagni. One of those who seized him struck him with his gauntlet and drew blood. He was soon, however, rescued from the hands of the conspirators, but, overwhelmed with grief and shame at the violence offered him, he soon died delirious.

Benedict XI., who succeeded Boniface in 1303, was a man of milder temper, but his reign was short; and in the following year Clement V., a Frenchman, was chosen pope. He was crowned at Lyons, and as the creature of Philip took up his residence at Avignon. Thus commenced what the Italians called "the Babylonian captivity." For nearly seventy years the popes were the liegemen of the kings of France. One or two of them are deserving of honorable mention; but the names of John XXII., Clement VI., and Gregory XI. are covered with deserved infamy. The first was for many years at open feud with the German emperor, and in common with the others endeavored to satiate his avarice by a simony too notorious to allow of concealment. They all amassed prodigious wealth by the abuse of *Annates*, and the reservation and disposal of benefices. These were the men who converted Avignon into that "western Babylon" which Petrarch hated "like Tartarus." In 1376 Gregory XI. determined to return to Rome. The insurrections and disorders of that city, as well as of many parts of Italy, demanded his presence. But a short period sufficed to make him repent of his purpose. He resolved to return to France, but before he could execute his resolution he died (1378).

The cardinals assembled at Rome to elect a successor. Alarmed by the tumultuous cries of the mob, who were determined to have no Frenchman elected, their choice fell upon the archbishop of Bari, a Neapolitan, who assumed the title of Urban VI. The harshness and arrogance of Urban soon alienated from him the minds of his cardinals. Several of them, protesting that the former election had not been free, withdrew, and elected to the pontificate a Frenchman, who took the name of Clement VII., and established his court at Avignon.

Thus commenced the great schism of the Western church. Christendom was divided into two obediences, one acknowledging a pope at Rome, the other a pope at Avignon. For nearly forty years the church was thus presented as "a monster with two heads." The avarice, arrogance, and ambition of the pontificate were exposed to the scorn, and became the scandal of Europe. Boniface IX. succeeded Urban VI. at Rome in 1389, and Peter de

Luna, known as Benedict XIII., was elected in 1394, in place of Clement VII. at Avignon. Successive efforts were made to induce one or both to resign, and thus restore peace and unity to the church; but all proved futile. On the death of Boniface IX. at Rome, Innocent VII. was chosen his successor; and in 1406 he in his turn gave place to Gregory XII., whose pontificate continued to the assembling of the council at Constance. The great question that agitated Europe was, what measures should be adopted for giving peace and restoring unity to the church. At Oxford, at Paris, at Prague, men discussed the subject, and the majority seemed everywhere to incline to what was called "the way of cession." They would have both claimants to the tiara resign their pretensions, and a general council, summoned for the purpose, elect a new pontiff, in whose authority all might acquiesce. Each of the contending popes however had still his partisans, and wherever these were found the church was divided and convulsed. Archbishop Sbynco followed the obedience of Gregory. Huss rejected both popes, and, with the theologians of the university of Paris, preferred the way of cession. This fact must be taken into account, in order fully to understand the relations of Huss and the archbishop. Until about the time of the council of Pisa (1408) they seem to have been on the most friendly terms, and to have coöperated to some extent in promoting measures of reform. A few years later we find them antagonists. Sbynco was a man who paid some slight regard to the external proprieties and purity of the church. Huss looked to the reviving of a new and better spirit within it. Sbynco adhered to Gregory. Huss favored the action of the council.[1] Even the controversy of the different nations in the university was insufficient to throw the greater question of the peace and unity of Christendom into the shade.

[1] Mon. Hussi, i., 236.

CHAPTER IV.

THE COUNCIL OF PISA.[1]

State of Europe. — Anarchy and Violence. — Ecclesiastical Abuses. — Efforts for Union. — Ambition and Craft of Benedict. — France Withdraws her Allegiance. — Proposed Conference of the Popes. — Gregory's Protestation. — Benedict's Strategy. — Gregory's Cardinals Dissatisfied. — They Desert Him. — Their Appeal. — Circumstances of Benedict. — Royal Letter. — Cardinals of Gregory and Benedict Unite. — Gregory Summoned by his Cardinals to Lucca. — Council Summoned. — Regarded with General Favor. — Views Prevalent in Bohemia. — The King's Decision. — Opposition of the University. — Influences Arrayed Against the Council. — Benedict and his Adherents. — Benedict Appoints a Council. — Gregory Does the Same. — The Three Parties. — The Council in Germany. — Terrible Conflict at Liege. — General Alarm. — Benedict's Council. — Its Futile Issue. — Council of Pisa. — Position of the City. — Members in Attendance. — Opening of the Council. — Objections in the Council to its Proceedings. — Gerson's Vindication. — Ambassadors of Robert. — Ladislaus. — Sentence Against the Anti-Popes. — The Conclave. — Alexander V. Elected. — His Life and Character. — Coronation. — Close of the Council of Pisa. — Gregory's Council at Friuli. — Danger of his Arrest. — His Chamberlain Seized. — Gregory Escapes. — Alexander's Election Favorably Received. — Bohemia. — Dissappointment in the Results of the Council. — Views of Clemengis. — Of Boniface of Ferrara. — Lack of General Enthusiasm. — Theodore de Vrie. — Relative Authority of Popes and Councils. — Peter D'Ailly. — Alexander V. and the Mendicants. — Their Privileges and Arrogance. — Spread and Power of the Order. — Difficulties at Paris. — Gerson's Sermon on the Subject. — Unpopularity of Alexander. — Position of Sbynco at Prague.

1407–1409.

The best minds of Europe were fully convinced that the time had at length arrived when more vig-

[1] The materials for this sketch of the Council of Pisa have been drawn mainly from Monstrelet, "L'Enfant's History of the Council," "Schröckh's Church History," and the "Continuations of Fleury." The authorities on various incidental points where individual views are expressed, are "Gerson's Works," "Clemengis' Life and Letters," and the writings of De Neim, De Vrie, and Aretin. Some of the latter are found in Van der Hardt's Compilation.

orous efforts should be made to put an end to that scandal of Christendom,—the papal schism. It had already endured for thirty years, yet with no prospect that either of the rival pontiffs or conclaves would yield his claims.

Meanwhile violence and anarchy prevailed largely throughout Europe. Wenzel, the oldest son of the emperor Charles IV., though still the king of Bohemia, had been deposed from the imperial throne and deprived of his hereditary rights, and Robert had been elevated by the electors to the vacant dignity. Sigismund, the second son of the emperor, who, in the partition of the imperial domain, had secured Hungary for his portion, was pressed by the terror of Moslem invasion, while Ladislaus, king of Naples, contested as a rival his right to the Hungarian throne. Poland and the Teutonic knights stood in hostile attitude to one another, and a fierce and protracted conflict had spread desolation on all sides. The German princes were often at feud, involving the whole land in intestine commotions. France, under the authority of a weak and feeble monarch—sometimes so deranged as to leave the throne virtually vacant—was torn by contending factions. The rival dukes of Burgundy and Orleans grasped at and alternately secured the preponderating influence, till the unscrupulous violence of the former (1407) removed his competitor by the stroke of the assassin.

Everywhere there were turbulence, crime, lawlessness, and impunity. Nor was this all. Profligacy and corruption pervaded the hierarchy. The sacred offices of the church were bartered and sold. Priestly avarice and arrogance had assumed an unblushing front. Deeds of darkness, that disgraced the highest dignitaries of the church, were performed in the light of day, and shamelessly avowed; and the demand was almost universal that some limit should be set to these abuses.

Nearly all these mischiefs, political and ecclesiastical, were attributed to the schism of the church. Pontifical authority might have exercised a restraining and controlling influence, but the rival pontiffs fulminated against each other, and the corruption which made their courts the Augean stables of Christendom, destroyed all respect for the tiara.

Successive efforts were made to remedy the evil; but the kingdoms were divided in their allegiance. Some held with the French, and some with the Italian pope. At first there was hope that on the death of one, his cardinals would refuse to elect a successor, and join themselves to the conclave of the other. Yet this hope was disappointed. Benedict XIII. continued the French succession.

But his own ambition overshot its mark. He was too arrogant in his claims, and France began to waver in her allegiance. The university discussed the problem of peace and union. By its advice deputations were sent to Benedict, urging him to cede. He temporized—played his part as hypocrite with adroit skill; but finally, forced to show his hand, broke out in bold defiance, and declared that he would never betray the sacred trust of the flock of Christ by resigning his pretensions. This provoked indignation. France was exasperated, and withdrew her allegiance. Benedict was not terrified even by this. He issued his bull of excommunication against all who had been concerned in the act. The bull was introduced into the French parliament, and torn and cut with knives as the soldiers passed it from hand to hand; while the messengers who brought it were arrested, clad in ignominious robes, and marched through the streets amid the hootings of the rabble. Nor was this all. Marshal Boncicaut was ordered to arrest the pope. With his armed bands he proceeded to Avignon; but the wily pontiff had received timely warning, and managed to escape his hands.

But Gregory, as well as Benedict, had been elected under the solemn pledge to use his influence to give peace to the church. If necessary, he was to cede his office. It was urged that the two contendents should meet together and effect some compromise by which a union of the church should be secured. Both professed extreme readiness to do this. Each proclaimed himself eager to meet the other. Indeed, when professions were so cheap, and pontifical veracity had not altogether lost credit, it could scarcely be otherwise. Probably Gregory was, if not more sincere, at least less perfidious. Previous to his election he had sworn, and at his suggestion all the cardinals had sworn, with a solemn oath, to do whatever was practicable to effect peace and union in the church. In his sermon after his election, he had, to the great joy of his hearers, exhorted the cardinals to labor with him for this object. "To whatever place," said he, "it is possible that a union can be secured in, I am resolved to go. If destitute of gallies, I will embark in a skiff; and if the journey must be by land, and horses cannot be procured, I would sooner go staff in hand on foot, than fail to keep my word."

But the possession of power had begotten the love of it. The fingers that had grasped the sceptre as flesh, had been turned to iron, and would not relax their rigid hold. Nor was Benedict behind Gregory either in protestations or lack of performance. But in manæuvering against his antagonist he gained the weathergage. A place was appointed for the proposed conference, and Benedict was present at the time specified. Gregory was too late, and his cunning rival threw upon him the odium of the failure of a project which it was impossible should succeed. After this, neither would accede to the propositions of the other. One would not leave the sea-coast, and the other would not approach it. Gregory complained that he had no gallies; and Benedict would not venture into the heart of Italy, where he would be powerless and his person insecure. It was facetiously said of them, that one was a land-animal afraid of the sea, and the other a sea-animal afraid of the land.

Gregory's adherents began to mistrust him. His cardinals, and numerous ambassadors from different kingdoms and provinces, pressed him to active measures. But the old man was inflexible to all remonstrance. His oath was forgotten, or a construction, the reverse of the obvious one, was put upon it. Just at the critical moment, when it seemed that he must yield, he heard that his ally, Ladislaus of Naples, had made his triumphal entry into Rome. This was glad intelligence to the exiled pontiff, who, though an Italian pope, had been driven from its walls. He was inspired with fresh hopes. With Rome in his possession he felt that he might defy his rival. To increase the number of his partisans he created several new cardinals. The old ones vainly opposed his project. A Carmelite, who had withstood it in presence of the ambassadors, was thrown into prison, and would have perished but for the intercession of powerful friends. Gregory would allow no sermon to be preached before him that had not first been examined and approved. But such proceedings were suicidal. His old cardinals forsook him, some on one pretext, some on another. Some fled to Lucca, others to Naples. Only seven were left, and a majority of these of the new creation. The others vainly strove to bring him back to reason. Disappointed in the effort, they drew up an appeal from Gregory to a general council, and notified Christendom of the withdrawal of their allegiance.

The statement of the grounds of their appeal is instructive. They describe Gregory as an unscrupulous tyrant, in whose power they were always in fear of prison or of massacre. Some of them had been selected for assassination, and soldiers had been stationed in the papal palace to execute the deed. They were not allowed to meet except by the pope's express order. For these and other reasons they appealed "from the pope ill-informed to the pope better informed; from the pope to Jesus Christ, of whom he is vicar; from the pope to a general council, to whom it belongs to judge the sovereign pontiff; from the present pope to a future pope, who shall be authorized to redress what his predecessor has unwarrantably ordained."

Gregory answered the appeal, but he could not bring back his cardinals. He excommunicated them. He deprived them of their dignities and benefices. But his spiritual thunders had lost their terror. The cardinals responded with specific accusations, posted up on the church doors of Lucca. In these they exhausted the vocabulary of opprobrious epithets to describe "the monster." They summon him, as unworthy of his title, to appear before them at Lucca and hear his sentence of deposition.

Meanwhile it fared but little better with Benedict He had been forced to leave Avignon. At Paris his adherents were in personal danger. D'Ailly hid himself. Clemengis fled to his obscure retreat at Langres. The edict of neutrality was published. No hall or square could contain the crowd. The violence of the people could scarce exceed that of the university. The regent of theology used language on one occasion against the pope so vulgar and outrageous as to be unfit to be repeated. Some were disgusted by it and left the assembly, but there was no mistaking the current of the national feeling. It was in deadly opposition to Benedict.

Notification of the withdrawal of obedience was sent under the king's seal to different courts. The princes were exhorted to renounce allegiance both to Benedict and Gregory. Urged by the university, the king wrote to the cardinals of both popes exhorting them to unite and summon a general council. They did in fact unite. Four of Benedict's cardinals, who had followed him from Porto Venere to Perpignan, whither he had fled for security, left him and withdrew to Livorno. Here they were joined by the cardinals of Gregory, and both parties united to form one college.

They responded in approval to the letter of the king of France, and informed him that they were about to convoke a council. In this reply the popes are not spared, and the authors of the schism are represented as worse than the Jews and the pagan soldiers, who, though they crucified Christ, spared his seamless robe. The united college appointed the convocation of the council at Pisa for March 25, 1409. To this they invited the prelates and ambassadors of Christendom. The cardinals of each obedience summoned their chief to meet them there. Those of Gregory, however, refused to treat him any longer as pope. Their letter to him is full of bitter recriminations. They remind him of his oaths and perjuries, his violence and oppression. He had required them to violate their oaths, "as if in taking the keys of the kingdom of heaven he had acquired the authority to perjure himself and to give license to others to do the same." In justice to themselves and the church they withdraw from *his society and his tabernacles*, and close with warning him, under severe penalties, to be present for trial at the council.

Intelligence of the proposed council was received with very extensive and general approval. England and France were strongly in its favor. Germany inclined, though with less unanimity, in the same direction, for the emperor Robert was the partisan of Gregory, and was suspicious of a council convoked, in part, by his recusant and rebellious cardinals. Through the influence of that adroit and unscrupulous tactician, Balthasar Cossa, afterwards John XXIII., who had broken with Gregory, and as tyrant of Bologna defied his threats and interdict, Florence was led to decide in favor of the council. The university of Bologna took the same ground. The Venetians, though declining to declare against Gregory, sided with the council. Genoa and Milan were both subject to French influence, and could not be counted as doubtful. Even at Rome, though the cry still was *vive Ladislaus*, no one ventured to call Gregory, pope. His legate was driven from the city, and in spite of the residence of Gregory in Italy, the greater portion of the states was found ranged on the side of the council.

In Bohemia the proposed council excited a lively interest. Wenzel, deposed from the imperial throne, had never entirely abandoned the purpose to recover the lost dignity. He was, at this very time—when the message of the cardinals reached him, announcing the council, and inviting him to recognize it—engaged in forming an arrangement with Gregory by which the latter was no longer to sustain the cause of the emperor Robert, Wenzel's rival. But the pope hesitated, and Wenzel readily exchanged allies. He forbade the archbishop of Prague and his clergy any longer to obey Gregory, and devoted his energies to secure his own recognition by the approaching council. On the 24th of November, 1408, he replied to the cardinals, approving of their measures, engaging to send a deputation which should be received and treated as that of a German emperor. The university of Prague was summoned to a decision, accordant with the royal policy.[1]

Henning Von Baltenhagen, the then rector, called a general assembly of the four nations. The Bohemians manifested a ready and almost unanimous disposition to accede to the wishes of the king. The three other nations, however, were reluctant to withdraw allegiance from Gregory, and the archbishop Sbynco was on their side. The decision of the majority was adverse to the royal project.

The Bohemians in the university had long complained of the usurpations of the other nations. They objected that each of these, instead of all united, had the same vote with themselves, and that in this respect the university of Prague had departed from the Parisian model. The present occasion, therefore, seemed to them a favorable one for presenting to the king their request that the Bohemians might possess in the university at Prague the same powers and privileges which the French nation possessed in the university of Paris. The earnestness of their desire was not a little increased by the fact that the opposition to reform and to the doctrines of Wickliffe proceeded for the most part from the foreign nations. The Bohemians, with Huss, Stanislaus of Znoyma, and Paletz at their head, inclined to welcome many of the views, and to defend some, at least, of the

[1] Helfert, p. 75.

treatises of the English reformer. It was becoming more evident, every day, that the national feeling and the cause of church reform—or innovation as some called it—were becoming more closely allied.

The king was at Kuttenberg when the deputation from the university reached him. To the surprise of all, he received the representatives of the three nations with great favor, and assured them that he would not infringe upon their rights or privileges. The Bohemians, on the other hand, were harshly repulsed, and Huss especially was sharply reproached for the rumored heresy in which he, with his friend Jerome, had involved the orthodox reputation of Bohemia. The king bitterly complained of the trouble which the matter gave him, and declared that in case others to whom the duty more properly belonged did not attend to it, he would see if fire could not settle the matter.

The deputation returned to Prague. Huss, overwhelmed by the strange issue of a project of which he had entertained great hopes, was struck down by a severe sickness. Meanwhile, however, the king, ever fickle in purpose, had changed his views. One of his favorites,[1] a man high in office and of large experience, took the side of the Bohemians, and won the king over to his opinions. The consequence was, that soon after (January 18, 1409) Wenzel issued a royal decree, granting the request which had vainly been presented to him at Kuttenberg. The consequences that followed this measure, and its effect

[1] Niklas, Ahne der Lobkowize. Helfert.

upon the conditions and prospects of the university, will be noted hereafter.

On the 22d of January, 1409, little more than a month after the decree respecting the rights of the Bohemians, the royal order was proclaimed throughout the kingdom that henceforth Gregory XII. should be no longer recognized as pope, and that obedience to him was to be withdrawn. Bohemia thus saw itself ranged on the side of the cardinals, and of the friends of the approaching council. This policy was advocated by Huss, both on religious and national grounds. By Wenzel it was adopted from the merest self-interest. Although the archbishop opposed the measure, it met with general acceptance. The nobility and magistrates were empowered and directed to see that no subject of the kingdom received or acknowledged any document from Gregory, whether charitative or judicial. The prohibition extended to all classes,—prelates, monks, abbots, and priests, as well as the nobility and common people.

The general sentiment of the nation favored this measure. Although the university had condemned it, the national assembly, composed of the most distinguished princes and nobility of the kingdom, and at which the bishops and prelates were present, endorsed it with great unanimity. The king wrote to this effect to the cardinals, and in the closing paragraph of his letter, after expressing his purpose to assist honestly at the council, informed the cardinals that his ambassadors must be received as those of the lawful emperor, that thus his just title might receive recognition.

It was easy to perceive that the condition thus insisted on would not be unacceptable. The cardinals desired for their project the imperial sanction. This, Robert, as the ally of Gregory, would of course refuse to grant. Nor had the council anything to fear from his resentment, through the favor now extended to the rival claimant to the imperial crown. Robert's recent unfortunate expedition into Italy had already exposed his authority to contempt, while any opposition which he might make to the council would be neutralized by divisions which existed within the bounds of the empire, and over which he had but feeble control. Bohemia acceded to the project of the council, and Wenzel, as emperor *de jure*, extended to it the imperial sanction.

Still, there were powerful opposing influences which the convocation of the council had to encounter. In the various kingdoms, each of the popes had influential adherents. Though opposed to each other, they really coöperated as against the council. Benedict, especially, was far from idle. Indeed, he played his part with masterly skill. He had the art to secure and retain the confidence of men whose motives were above impeachment. Clemengis, who declined to serve him longer as secretary when he learned of the bull to be fulminated against France, still sided with him. Vincent of Ferrara—"the apostle of the West," and the Whitefield of his age—vindicated him as lawful pope. This alone was worth a kingdom to Benedict. Vincent preached publicly against the proposed mode of cession, and Benedict made him—venerated by all Western

Europe almost as another St. Paul—his confessor, and master of the sacred palace. Vincent's brother, Boniface, second in influence only to himself in the region south of the Pyrenees, was of the same mind with him. With such allegiance as Benedict still retained, he therefore determined on his part to hold a general council of his own. It was summoned to meet at Perpignan, November 1st, 1408.

Gregory, though less shrewd and sagacious, saw plainly enough that he too must labor to keep up appearances. He summoned his council also. At first, he was at a loss for a place. Rome was closed against him. Venice was more than half-persuaded to yield allegiance to the council of Pisa. Florence and its allies, leagued with Louis of Anjou in his rivalship with Ladislaus for the Neapolitan crown, were swayed by Frence influence. Genoa, moreover, had adopted a neutral position. Ladislaus, ostensibly opposed to Gregory, but really playing into his hands, dared not offer him an Italian city, from fear lest the council at Pisa should fulminate against him. Gregory at last settled on Friuli, in the Venetian territory, and, after tedious delays, his council met there, July 22d, 1409.

As preparation was now made for the assembling of three councils, it became an object with each party to secure for itself as large and powerful a representation as possible. The field which most invited attention was Germany. But the contest here lay not between Gregory and Benedict, but between Gregory and the council of Pisa. The emperor Robert favored Gregory; but the diet which was called to hear the statements of the ambassadors of the cardinals, leaned toward *neutrality* and adhesion to the council.

There was good reason for this. Germany had bitterly felt the evils of the schism. When each diocese had, as well as the popedom, its rival claimants, the mischief was no longer limited to Rome or Avignon. It reached to distant cities and humble homes. To the city of Liege it was especially disastrous. Two bishops claimed the See, each sanctioned by the pope of his allegiance. John of Bavaria, grandson of the emperor Lewis, had been confirmed by Urban VI., whom the Liegeois had recognized as pope as early as 1389. But Louis refused to take the order of the priesthood, and the aggrieved citizens rose against him and drove him to Mæstricht. On this occasion they were led on by Henry de Pervies, but on the condition that his son should be elected bishop in place of John. But distrusting Gregory, to whom Lewis adhered, they applied to Benedict to confirm the new incumbent. A legate was sent accordingly, and Liege was thus brought under the allegiance of Benedict.

A war ensued between the city and the expelled bishop. But the last had a powerful ally in the Duke of Burgundy, his brother-in-law. Somewhat tardily his army arrived at Mæstricht, where the bishop still held out, though the siege was pressed by an army of 50,000 men. A battle ensued, and the carnage was terrible. The duke led his own forces, largely composed of the finest portion of the nobility of his estates. The rout of the Liegeois was perfect. Their leader and bishop—father and son—were found among the dead, the hand of one clasped in the hand of the other. It is even said that none escaped to carry back the news of the disaster to the unfortunate city, or warn it of its fate. Sixty persons were executed. The legate of Benedict and the officers of the bishop were thrown into the Meuse. John was restored to his bishopric, and the people could appreciate the value of his benedictions.

But Germany took the alarm. Each city felt that the evil might soon be brought to its own doors. If the popes were tyrants, it was better, perhaps, after all, to have but one. This feeling was manifest at the diet held near the close of 1408, at Frankfort-on-the-Main. It was numerously attended. Gregory and the cardinals, England, France, Poland, Bohemia, and other states, were represented by their ambassadors. The emperor was almost alone in his adhesion to Gregory.

Thus the general sentiment of Christendom was settling down in favor of the council of Pisa. The popular conviction was confirmed by the futile hostility of Benedict. His council, summoned for November 1, 1408, was first to meet. There was but a meagre attendance. French soldiers guarded the roads and the passes of the Pyrenees, and a large proportion of the members could reach Perpignan only under strange disguise. But of these, not a few were anxious for the union of the church, and when they discovered the obstinacy and real designs of Benedict, forsook him in disgust. Those who still lingered with him were not agreed. But the opinion in favor of a delegation to Pisa preponderated. The delegation was sent, but with limited powers of negotiation. It was arrested on its way, and with some difficulty reached its destination. But even here it was exposed to danger. So strong was the public odium against it, the cardinals dared not speak with their old associates. The latter were exposed to violence and insult, and in the assembly at which they presented themselves, the marshal told them that it would be impossible to protect them unless they remained in their seats till the crowd dispersed. Threats of burning them were freely thrown out. The Podesta, with some of the chief men of the city, had to accompany them to their lodgings to prevent their being stoned. They could accomplish nothing, and were forced clandestinely to leave the city. Such was the issue of Benedict's attempt.

Meanwhile the council of Pisa had commenced its sessions. It was favored by the locality where it had been convoked. Pisa could be approached from every direction, by sea as well as by land. It was thus easy of access, and could be abundantly supplied with provisions with little difficulty. It stood in the midst of a large and fertile plain, watered by the Arno, on the banks of which it was built. A more eligible spot for the council could not have been selected. Pisa, moreover, was subject to Florence, by which it had been conquered during the previous year, and was thus secured alike against internal strifes and foreign foes. Ladislaus, the secret ally of Gregory, had been forced to retreat before the arms of Florence.

The number of members in attendance was large. France was well represented, and among her deputation stood prominent in position and ability the chancellor of the university, John Gerson. The English deputation had been addressed by him as they passed through Paris, and had imbibed the spirit kindled by the fiery logic of the great chancellor. Most historians[1] reckon as present at the council, either in person or by deputies, twenty-two cardinals, four patriarchs, nearly two hundred bishops, nearly three hundred abbots, besides priors, generals of orders, deputies of universities, and chapters of metropolitan churches and cathedrals, more than three hundred doctors in theology and canon law, and the ambassadors of six kings and numerous princes.

On the appointed day (March 25, 1409) the council assembled in the body of the fine and spacious cathedral of Pisa—the most splendid structure of the kind in Italy, with the exception of the cathedral at Milan. The scene was one of imposing pomp and grandeur. The prelates marched on toward the cathedral in procession, clothed in their official robes. They moved along the aisles, under the shadow of the massive pillars of oriental granite, to seats prepared for them before the altar. The sides of the nave were fitted up for the bishops and abbots, and the remaining space was occupied by the less distinguished members of the council.

The session was opened in the most solemn and imposing manner. Mass was celebrated by one of

[1] Maimbourg.

the cardinals after the pontifical form. The archbishop of Milan preached the sermon. He vividly depicted the evils under which Christendom mourned —the confusion and disorder of the church — the corruption of morals—the sufferings and oppressions endured by the good—and the power and triumph of the basest and vilest men. He urged upon the council the importance of their work, and the hopes inspired by their convocation. They were expected to give to the church "one sole, true, unquestioned pastor, so that no longer should men see with abhorrence two monstrous heads affixed to the mystic body of Christ." Both the contendents were considered heretical. It was significant of the action of the council.

It would be tedious to recite the ceremonies and proceedings of the successive sessions. The two contendents were cited, but did not appear. The citation was repeated, but with the same result; and the council proceeded to measures for the deposition of Benedict and Gregory.

These, however, had their secret adherents in the council, who obstructed its proceedings. They raised questions of order and privilege. They disputed the legitimacy of a council that had not been convoked by a pope. They scrupled the right of a pope to abdicate. They held that the relative merits of the two contendents were matters to be discussed.

But Gerson came forward in behalf of the council: with remorseless logic he drove his opponents from their strongest positions. He repeated the arguments of his favorite treatise, published before he left Paris, *De Auferibilitate Papæ.* He held that the unity of the church resides in Jesus Christ its spouse and head; that the church, by its assembled representatives in general council, may make all necessary provisions; that the mystic body of Christ, as well as any civil body, may provide itself a head; that, without inquiring into the origin of the schism, it may yet proceed to free the church from it; that, though some evils might follow decisive measures, yet that a part may be sacrificed to save the whole; that, disregarding the formalities of positive statute, the council may temper its rigor with equity, or even dispense with the law itself; and that, while all proper security should be assured to the contendents, yet, upon their non-appearance, the council might, notwithstanding, proceed to set them aside and elect a new pope.

These arguments prevailed with the council. The emperor Robert vainly strove to stay its proceedings. On the very day when action was to have been taken, his ambassadors appeared. They threw out questions and doubts respecting the authority and the legitimacy of the council. It had been convoked, they said, neither by pope nor emperor.

The old flame of controversy was enkindled anew. The people present were scandalized at the course taken by the ambassadors. Even the hostlers before the doors of the cathedral took part in the dispute. The council discussed their propositions, and prepared a reply; but before it was given in they had secretly left the city. They fully appreciated their own and their masters' unpopularity. The sermon preached at the first congregation held after they had left, was from the text, "The hireling fleeth." Robert's envoys, however, before leaving, nailed to the doors of the church his appeal to a general council, and his protest against the issuing of any decree against Gregory, whom he recognized as lawful pope.

Ladislaus in his turn was disposed to interrupt the council's proceedings. He attacked Sienna, subject, like Pisa, to Florentine authority. But his defeat, which soon followed at Arezzo, relieved them of their fears.

The council proceeded with its work. Testimony was taken and recited, and the definitive sentence against the popes was pronounced on the fifth of June. The doors of the cathedral were thrown open, and the large edifice was crowded to its full capacity. The decision of the council was read; and Benedict and Gregory, for their persistence in schism, their notorious heresy, their perjured violation of solemn oaths, and their wickedness and enormous excesses, were deposed from the pontificate. The Roman See was declared vacant. All persons, of what station soever, were absolved from allegiance to either of the contendents, and were forbidden to recognize their authority. All acts, bulls, excommunications, and processes of Benedict or Gregory, subsequent to the convocation of the council, were declared null and void. No member of the council was to leave the church till he had signed the sentence. It was a few days after this that the ambassadors of Benedict reached Pisa.

On the fifteenth of June the council proceeded to take measures for the election of a new pope. Towards evening twenty-three cardinals entered the conclave provided for their reception in the episcopal palace. Their session continued till the twenty-sixth of the month. According to the Monk of St. Denis, the conclave breathed nothing but disinterestedness, piety, and zeal for the church of God. But the more plain-spoken De Niem forces us to question somewhat the sincerity of their devotion. Each of the electors had promised, in case he should be elected, to remember the cardinals' friends, and grant their demands. Another witness speaks of the incredible efforts and promises of the French to the Italian cardinals, to secure the election of one of their own nation.

A pope was at length elected. It was Peter Philargi, cardinal of Milan, who assumed the title of Alexander V. His elevation is ascribed to Balthasar Cossa, his successor, by whom he was governed and controlled.

The new pope was as unexceptionable a man probably as the conclave could have selected. He was reputed to be a man of rare knowledge and eloquence, of correct habits, and business talent. He was sixty-six years of age at the time of his election —a capital qualification in the eyes of Cossa.

His life had been one of active industry and successful effort. He had studied at Oxford and Paris. At the latter place he had received a doctor's degree, and had taught theology and sacred literature. He became bishop of Vicenza, and afterwards of Milan. Innocent VII. raised him to the cardinalate. His testimony of himself is not to his disparagement. "I was," said he "a rich bishop, a poor cardinal, a mendicant pope."

On the seventh of July the ceremony of coronation took place. Alexander received the pontifical crown, standing on the steps of the cathedral, from the hands of Cardinal Saluces. The ordinary ceremonial was observed, and Alexander notified his election to all Europe. Just one month after the coronation came the closing session of the council. A few unimportant regulations were made, but the great subject of reform was referred to a more convenient season—a future council. The claim of Louis of Anjou, the rival of Ladislaus to the kingdom of Naples, was endorsed by the pope, and he was appointed grand-gonfalonier of the Romish church against the common enemy of both.

The council of Pisa was already drawing to its close, when that of Gregory assembled at Friuli, (July 22, 1409.) It simply denounced the action of that of Pisa, and decided, as might have been expected, in favor of the claims of Gregory. But the sentence of Gregory was already pronounced, and measures had been taken at Venice for his arrest. Aware of his danger, he resolved on flight, first, however, appointing legates in different kingdoms to strengthen his party. Among these was his faithful archbishop, Sbynco of Prague.

But the poor old man, who, before he set out for Friuli, looked more like the dead than the living, found that he was not safe even in the midst of his council. He had made the patriarch of Aquileia his bitter enemy by attempting to deprive him of his benefice. The time for vengeance had now come. The prelate gathered soldiers to cut off his retreat. Venice was only too ready to seize him on her own territories. Under the show of remaining some time longer at Friuli, in order to lull suspicion, he hurriedly prepared the means of escape. At his request Ladislaus sent two gallies and fifty horsemen to his relief. But the question was, how to reach the port where the gallies lay. Gregory assumed the disguise of a merchant, and, travelling on horseback, followed by two attendants on foot, passed safely and unsuspected through the guard of soldiers stationed by the patriarch to intercept him. In a little while his chamberlain followed, clothed in pontifical habits, with a considerable escort. The soldiers, naturally supposing that this must be the pope, seized him, his company, and baggage. Plundering the poor chamberlain, they drew him along with them several miles, bare-headed, and in most wretched plight. To their deep mortification, they learned, on reaching their place of rendezvous, from a domestic of the patriarch, that they had mistaken their man. They at once endeavored to correct their error, and started in full pursuit of Gregory. But they were too late. When they reached the port he had already found a skiff, and was on his way to the gallies. Enraged and disappointed, the soldiers vented their spite on the poor chamberlain. They stripped him of his rich dress, and left him only a poor doublet. Not yet content, they beat him with clubs. The blows revealed a secret. There was a ringing of metal. They stripped him and found concealed about his person five hundred florins of gold. This they seized, and divided among themselves. The next day one of them, in derision of Gregory, clothed himself in the pontifical robes of which they had despoiled the chamberlain, and walked through the streets dispensing his benedictions.

Gregory's adherents, members of the council, lingered yet at Friuli. At length, in October, under the escort of five hundred German knights hired for the purpose, they effected their escape. Gregory had already got safe to Gaeta.

Thus the issue of both the other councils exposed them to contempt, while that of Pisa had succeeded in elevating to the pontificate a respectable man. Had he lived, all Christendom might, in the course of a few years, have been united in his allegiance. The intelligence of his election was favorably received in various countries, and, in spite of the partisans of the anti-popes, who were everywhere to be found as legates or beneficiaries, his authority was generally acknowledged. The intelligence of his election caused great joy at Paris. The university looked upon him almost as her son. The people cried *Vive Alexander, our Pope!* His legate was received with great honors. The princes of the blood went to meet him, and escorted him into Paris. Florence and Sienna sent deputies to express their recognition of his authority. Germany for the most part, though Robert still adhered to Gregory, favored the council. Bohemia, by a strongly preponderating sentiment, ranged itself on the side of Alexander, and the influence of Sbynco was seriously affected by his adherence to Gregory, and his position as legate.

Huss, although not an active participant, was a careful observer of what was taking place before the eyes of Christendom. He favored the council of Pisa, and shared with the French theologians their indignation at the craft, duplicity, and ambition of the anti-popes. The age was itself a school to teach contempt of papal authority, and yet Huss transferred his honest allegiance to Alexander V. This simple act shows that he was not moved by faction, and that he had as yet no thought of coming into conflict with Christendom.

Still, the result fell short of what had been expected. A new pope had been elected, but this was all. The two anti-popes had been set aside, but the mischief of the schism in great part still remained. Huss had an illustration of this at Prague in the position and character of the archbishop, manifesting a hostile attitude towards the council, the Bohemian nation generally, and the expressed will and authority of the king. Nor was this all. The ardent hopes of the friends of peace and reform, which had been excited by the convocation of the council, had been doomed to disappointment. If a new pope had been elected, it added another claimant to the papacy. The emperor still recognized Gregory, and Spain continued, to some extent, her allegiance to Benedict. The corruptions of the church had received little if any check. The language of some of the most faithful and able men of the age, in speaking of it, is characterized by great severity. Clemengis,—a patriot, a scholar, and a Christian, once rector of the university of Paris, and afterward's Benedict's private secretary, —had now withdrawn into a retirement more congenial to his tastes, and in the quiet vale of Langres pursued his sacred studies. The Holy Scriptures were his daily companion. In these he found "the gold of wisdom, the silver of eloquence, the gems of virtue, lavishly poured forth from the fountain of supernal grace." Here he learned, as he assures us, more in a few days than he had before in as many years from the heathen poets and orators which he had now thrown aside.

The views of such a man, at such a crisis, are worthy of our notice. He saw with a clearer eye than most, the deep-seated malady of Christendom, and had sense enough to perceive that no remedy could avail, short of a thorough and entire reform.

"The assembly of Pisa," said he, "only deceived the church of God. It cried *Peace, peace*, when there was no peace. These carnal and avaricious men are so eager after their benefices, that, blinded by their passions, they have obstructed the reformation of the church, for which many are so anxious. Thus they first of all proceeded to a new election. When this was done, and they had obtained the promotions they asked, they cried *Peace and Union!* and so, after having dissolved the council, they returned with the *peace* they sought, that is to say, their own advancement." Could Huss have uttered more unpalatable truth?

Boniface of Ferrara, brother of Vincent, "not his

inferior in piety," speaks of the council as "a profane, heretical, cursed, seditious, absurd, scandalous, diabolical assembly." He charges its being summoned to violence and intrigue as well as the selfishness of the cardinals. He maintains, which is not improbable from the known character of Balthasar Cossa, that he had gained the doctors of Bologna by bribes, or overawed them by his authority, to approve the council.

The intelligence of the election was not everywhere received as it was in France. One of the cardinals was reported to have said to one of the ambassadors of the king of Arragon, the next day after the election, "Be assured, as long as the pope is elected from the Italians, we shall have one of their fancy." Several other cardinals, after the election, withdrew dissatisfied to their benefices, determined never to see Alexander V. again, or be members of his council. At Genoa there was no sign of satisfaction given at the receipt of the news; not a bell was struck.

Many learned men in Italy, France, Germany, and elsewhere, refused to give in their adherence to the council. Some maintained, and with much show of reason, that it had increased the schism rather than removed it. There were now three claimants to the popedom instead of two. All were not of the mind of Cardinal Chalant, who deserted Benedict and joined the council in hope of his own election. When Boniface of Ferrara remonstrated with him on his course, his reply was that of the reckless and ambitious partisan. "What will come of this," asked Boniface, "but the election of a third pope who will be only an anti-pope?" "What difference if we only make one?" answered the cardinal. "Be he anti-pope, or even devil, he will then become pure."

Clemengis disputed the authority of the council. Bad men, he admits and asserts, were there, but the Holy Spirit did not preside over it.

Theodore Vrie, a German monk, gives the history of the evils and corruptions of the age, in the form of a dialogue between Christ and his church. He makes the latter say: "Behold, I pray you, what union, or rather division! Yet it is an execrable schism. They have wished to elect only one supreme pastor, and have made three. I had two husbands, and they have given me a third."

The council had in fact opened an unlimited field for controversy. A large portion of Christendom regarded the pontificate as supreme *jure divino*, and above all subjection to any earthly tribunal. Gerson, and the French theologians generally, repudiated this view. With them the church itself was supreme, and its decisions, by its representatives in a general council, the law from which there could be no appeal. The very title of the treatise of the chancellor of the university, *De Auferibilitate Papæ*, was startling to all the partisans of papal infallibility. But Clemengis went further. Agreeing with Gerson in many points, he yet disputes the infallibility of councils, and especially that of Pisa. His argument on the subject is a masterpiece of skill and shrewdness, and evidently suggests, though in the form of dialogue, his real sentiments. We may fairly declare it unanswerable. One after another he hunts out every subterfuge of his opponent, and, under the show of the greatest docility, leaves the objector who presumes to teach him, a humble learner.

Peter D'Ailly, afterwards cardinal of Cambray, held positions not much discordant from those of Gerson, as was manifest at the council of Constance. Such disputes struck at the very root of papal authority. Yet they had spread over Christendom. Huss at Prague was but carrying out to their legitimate issue the principles of Gerson and Clemengis.

One of the first acts of the newly elected pope was a bull in favor of the mendicants. To say no worse of it, it was, in a political point of view, a gross blunder, which his successor found it necessary to correct. This order of monks had been established in the beginning of the thirteenth century. They had been favored by the popes, who bestowed upon them peculiar privileges and immunities. Freed from all secular and episcopal jurisdiction, privileged to demand alms wherever they roamed, these brethren of St. Dominic assumed the name of "preaching friars." They were authorized to preach everywhere, irrespective of the will or authority of the parish priest. They were privileged to hear confessions, read masses, and sell papal indulgences. Their influence soon became most extensive and efficient. They were justly called "The standing army of the pope." But their privileges and success awoke soon a jealousy against them on the part of the regular clergy. Spreading themselves all over Christendom, their early zeal and vows of poverty acquired for them a power that was considered dangerous in such irresponsible hands. Yet, in spite of a rising opposition, this hardy and devoted militia of the church did its work to perfection. Its numbers and efficiency increased. Fresh lifeblood seemed to be infused into a decaying system. Youthful activity succeeded to visible decrepitude. The mendicant was free to act wherever occasion offered. He intruded into the region of parochial duty. He seated himself in the chair of the confessional. He seized the honors of the university, or the crosier of the bishop. His influence was felt in each secular department. None understood better the secrets of diplomatic intrigue. None could avail himself more skilfully of every occasion, to serve at once himself and his master.

In the course of sixty years these holy beggars had increased to "extravagant swarms." Their early vows of poverty were forgotten. The barefooted brethren had become possessed of stately edifices and large domains. Their success was their corruption and disaster. Supported by the popes, they insulted the curates and bishops. Multitudes forsook their parish priests to follow the mendicants and confess to them.

The struggle continued. Sometimes their audacity forced the popes to revoke their privileges, soon however to be restored. Councils and synods differed, some approving and some condemning the order. The question of the mendicants agitated all Christendom. Even papal infallibility split upon this rock. The popes wavered in regard to the policy to be adopted. They dared not sustain them throughout, and would not dismiss them altogether. In

England the contest was sharp and protracted. We have seen the course of Wickliffe, and the bitter hostility with which he was regarded by the mendicants. In this contest, the better portion of the English nation sympathized with the reformer. To such an extent had the evil grown at one time, that the law records were "filled with warrants for the arrest of the sanctimonious vagrants."

A similar disturbance had been created by them in other parts of Christendom. While Janow and Huss opposed them at Prague, they were not suffered to enjoy at Paris an undisputed triumph. In 1408, one of their number, John Gozel, boldly maintained, in the college of Navarre, their impudent and assuming claims. Among other positions, he held that the curates, as such, were inferior to the mendicants, and were unauthorized to preach, to confess, to grant extreme unction or burial, or even to receive tithes. Such was the presumption inspired by their powerful influence and wonderful success. But such bold avowals were too offensive to be passed over in silence. The theological faculty of the university were incensed. They summoned the offender before them, and forced him to retract his proposition and publicly disavow it.

Things were in this state when Alexander's bull in favor of the mendicants arrived. It was addressed to all the prelates of Christendom, and contained a recapitulation of the bulls of previous popes in favor of the offending order. Either unwilling to credit the bull, or the more formally to express their dissent from its provisions, the university sent a deputation to Pisa to learn the facts in the case. They satisfied themselves that the bull was genuine, and examined it in the original. Observing that it professed to have been expedited "with the consent and by the advice of the cardinals," they visited them all individually to learn the facts. They all, without exception, denied any participation in the matter, and were perfectly agreed in condemning it as prejudicial to the rights of the regular clergy.[1] The report of the deputation kindled in France a flame of indignation and remonstrance. The act of the pope was evidently one of partiality and favoritism toward the mendicants, of which order he had been himself a member. The rector of the university of Paris assembled the doctors and regents to deliberate on the course to be adopted. It was resolved that all the mendicant monks should be expelled. They were forbidden to preach till they had renounced the bull. Some complied with the requisition; others, emboldened by the authority of the pope, resolved to brave the indignation and sentence of the university. They ran raving through the streets, with copies of the bull authorizing their privileges in their hands, insulting the regular clergy, and maintaining that to them properly belonged the right to preach, hear confessions, and receive tithes from parishes. The king, at the urgency of the university, and to repress this license, published a prohibition against them.

Gerson, chancellor of the university, was directed to preach a sermon on the subject. He maintained

[1] Council of Pisa, i. 316.

that if any one proposed to break up the established order of the hierarchy, he was to be resisted as Lucifer and the wicked angels. Coming to the question in hand, he asserted that the bull had been extorted from the pope by surprise, or been obtained through his inadvertence. The university had judged it to be "intolerable, incompatible with the welfare of the church, and that it must be rescinded before the preaching friars could be restored to their privileges."

The priests were required in their sermons to justify the course of the university. In every city small treatises were drawn up and circulated, containing in the French language an explanation of the matter, in order to instruct the common people on the subject.

The effect of all these measures was to render the pope unpopular. The joy that had been excited by the news of his election quickly subsided. He had lost the strength of allegiance on the part of France, which could enable him to defy his competitors. There were now three popes in the field. The council had rather aggravated than healed the schism of the church.

At Prague, Alexander V., elected at Pisa, was, if not fully acknowledged, at least preferred. Wenzel, from spite at Gregory, would at least give precedence to the claims of one whom he regarded as Gregory's antagonist. The result that had thus been reached left Sbynco, the archbishop, in a false position. His adherence to Gregory, while Bohemia ranged itself, though by no means with enthusiasm, on the side of Alexander, was of no little service in strengthening the position of Huss.

CHAPTER V.

HUSS AND THE ARCHBISHOP.[1]

MARTIAL OPERATIONS OF SBYNCO. — HIS SYNOD. — PATER ARRAIGNED. — BOHEMIANS ON WICKLIFFE. — PRIEST ABRAHAM. — SBYNCO SATISFIED. — WENZEL'S DECISION IN REGARD TO THE UNIVERSITY. — THE FOREIGN NATIONS REFUSE TO OBEY. — COMMAND OF THE KING. — THE SECESSION OF THE NATIONS. — HUSS CHOSEN RECTOR. — CHARACTER AND LIFE OF WENZEL. — SBYNCO. — TRANSUBSTANTIATION TO BE PREACHED. — HUSS IN HIS PULPIT. — SUBSTANCE OF HIS PREACHING. — ORDINANCE AIMED AT HUSS. — SBYNCO FORCED TO BE RECONCILED WITH ALEXANDER V. — HUSS CIRCULATES WICKLIFFE'S WRITINGS. — BRODA'S LETTER OF COMPLAINT TO THE ARCHBISHOP. — MEASURES TAKEN. — THE UNIVERSITY. — THE FIVE STUDENTS. — THE ARCHBISHOP CONDEMNED BY A PAPAL COMMISSION. — SUBMITS TO ALEXANDER V. — THE PAPAL BULL. — ITS RECEPTION. — OPPOSITION TO IT. — COURSE OF HUSS. — HIS APPEAL. — THE BURNING OF THE BOOKS. — PUBLIC INDIGNATION. — KNOWLEDGE OF THE SCRIPTURES. — SERMON OF HUSS. — CONTINUES TO PREACH. — WICKLIFFE DEFENDED. — SERMON OF HUSS.

1409–1411.

IT is now time for us to return and note the progress of affairs at Prague. We have already seen the national feeling allying itself with the cause of reform. The condemnation of Wickliffe's articles by the university in 1403 was regarded as specially obnoxious, from the fact that it had been brought about by a majority composed of the vote of the foreign nations. It was looked upon by the Bohemians as a victory over themselves, and increased that dissatis-

[1] The main authorities upon which I have relied for the materials of this chapter, are "The Life and Works of Huss," "Helfert's Life of Huss," "Anti-Hussus," by Stephen of Dola; "Godeau's History of the Church," "Æneas Sylvius," "Cochleius' Life of Huss," "Bonfinius' History of Bohemia," and such extracts from Pelzel, Palacky, Theobald, and Balbinus as I have met with in L'Enfant, Bonnechose, Van der Hardt, Neander, and others.

faction which issued in the petition addressed by the Bohemians to Wenzel. The tendencies of the two parties became continually more manifest. The patriotic feeling of the nation rejected the decision against Wickliffe's books, while the foreign influence was almost unanimously in its favor. Huss was the acknowledged leader of the former, and among his most powerful supporters were some who were afterwards his most virulent opponents. Undoubtedly the party which adhered to him was composed largely of members to whom theological questions were of minor importance.

At this time[1] the archbishop troubled himself but little with the affairs of the university, and was on good terms with Huss. His attention was directed more to his worldly than his spiritual possessions. His diocese was neglected, while he engaged, in the summer of 1404, in the siege of the fortress where the knight Nicholas Zul of Ostrodek had gathered his robber band. Zul was taken captive, given over to the civil authorities, and in his prison visited by Huss, whose words made such an impression upon his mind that he at least assumed the aspect of an humble penitent.

But no sooner had Sbynco subdued the fortress than his attention was directed to other martial operations. For the two succeeding years he was engaged, along with the provost of Choteschau, Sulek of Hradek, in an invasion of Moravia, and had no time or opportunity to note the progress of religious affairs at Prague.

[1] Helfert, 69, 70.

At length, aroused by the express admonitions of the pope, he summoned in 1406 a synod of his diocese clergy, and in conjunction with them issued his decree that henceforth no one, under severe penalty, should hold, teach, or, for purposes of academic debate, argue in favor of Wickliffe's doctrines. It was proposed to institute an investigation for the purpose of detecting any who might be the secret or open adherents of the English reformer.

But the measure proved futile. Either Sbynco was not prepared to break with Huss, who as queen's confessor and preacher in Bethlehem chapel was an opponent to be feared, or he felt, as is more probable, little interest in the questions at issue, which he failed fully to comprehend. Huss distinctly rejected the views of Wickliffe on the subject of transubstantiation, and was less obnoxious in this respect probably than some of his associates. [1]

The two years which followed were years of comparative quiet. But in the spring of 1408, Matthias of Knin, surnamed Pater, a master of arts in the university, was arraigned before the archiepiscopal court on the charge of John Eliä, one of the Bohemian friends of Huss. [2] He was accused of holding that the substance of the bread remains after the sacramental words have been pronounced. Pater was thrown into prison, and only secured his release by a solemn recantation. Scarcely, however, was he again at liberty, when, in presence of witnesses, he made affidavit that his recantation had been extorted by fear of prison and torture.

[1] Mon. Hussi, i. 164. [2] Helfert, 71.

The matter excited a deep interest, especially among the Bohemians, who were now seen to be divided among themselves. A meeting was speedily called to consult in regard to the doctrines of Wickliffe. Clemens of Mnichowic, pastor at Wran and the then rector, presided. Among those present were Huss, Jacobel, John Eliă, Stanislaus, Andrew Broda, and Stephen Paletz. The assembly consisted of sixty-four masters and doctors, one hundred and fifty graduates, and one thousand students. The decision was, that under penalty of expulsion no member of the Bohemian nation should teach or defend any of Wickliffe's articles. But the provision was added, that the prohibition referred to was only to the articles as understood in an heretical, erroneous, or scandalous sense. The issue of the matter was thus a compromise between the two wings of the national party. It enabled them yet a while longer to coöperate on patriotic grounds, and in opposition to the foreign influence.

It was not long after this before the explorations of John of Kbel, the vicar-general of the archbishop, detected another case of heresy. The criminal in this case was priest Abraham, pastor of the church of the Holy Ghost. One of the charges against him—probably not the only one—is quite significant. He asserted that laymen, as well as priests, might be allowed to preach the gospel. Huss took a deep interest in the case, and was present at the trial. He had a somewhat warm discussion with the vicar, but with no good result. Priest Abraham was given over to the inquisitor Jaroslow, bishop of Sarepta, by whom he was imprisoned and afterwards banished. Huss remonstrated on the matter with the archbishop. He pointed him to the indolent and worthless priests in the diocese whom he left unmolested, while he had banished as a heretic one who was exemplary in the discharge of every priestly duty.[1]

But Sbynco felt that he had done enough. He wearied of the troublous business of dealing with heretics, and readily—at the request of Wenzel—certified that after diligent investigation no further heresy or error was to be found in the land.[2]

Such was the state of things when the king, in the autumn of 1408, laid the subject of the withdrawal of obedience from Gregory before the university. The unanimity of the three foreign nations in opposing it, and of the national party in its favor, only added to the mutual alienation of feeling which had long existed; and when the king, under the influence of his favorite, granted the request of the Bohemians, and issued his decree giving the Bohemians an equal vote and control in the university with the three other nations, the long smouldering flames burst forth. Huss was still prostrate on his sick-bed, when John Eliä and Andrew Broda entered his chamber and announced the realization of his long-cherished hopes. He gave them his warmest thanks for the cheering intelligence, and charged them, in case he should not recover, to remain faithful to the popular cause.[3]

The foreign party were taken by surprise. They had not imagined that the king would have ventured

[1] Helfert, p. 72. [2] Ib. [3] Helfert, 77.

on so bold a step. In the security of their confidence they had made rash threats of what they would do in case of such an emergency. They had pledged one another, if the request of the Bohemians was granted and the decree was executed, to leave Prague in a body. Even when the decision of the king had been made public, they could scarce believe that it would be carried out. They employed all the means in their power to divert Wenzel from his purpose, but in vain.

At length the critical hour arrived. The annual elections were to take place. A new rector and dean of the faculty of arts were to be chosen. The three nations were proceeding after the old order, when the Bohemians interposed. The confusion and discord were such that the old officers made it an apology for putting off the election. Henning Von Baltenhagen, the rector, and Albert Warrentrappe, the dean, refused to yield up the insignia of their office.[1]

This state of things could not continue. The indolent monarch might have disregarded his own decrees, but the favorite, Nicholas Von Lobkowic, at whose instance it had been issued, had still the ear of the king, and urged him to decisive measures. On the 9th of May, 1409, while the council of Pisa was yet in its early sessions, Nicholas appeared before the university, and in the name of the king required the dean and rector to give up the insignia of their office, and by royal authority appointed Zdenek Von Labaun as rector, and Simon Von Tisnow as dean.

[1] Helfert, 77.

The defeated party were exasperated beyond measure, and prepared at once to execute their threatened purpose. Some of them burned down the theological college, and in a few days five thousand German students, with their doctors, masters, and bachelors, true to their vows, but with sad hearts, had left the city. Most of these belonged to the Saxon nation. The Bavarians, during the long alienation of emperor Robert and Wenzel, had experienced a marked decrease of numbers, while of the Polish nation only a portion were of German sympathies, and the Slavic masters and students were for the most part inclined to regard the Bohemians as brethren. The voluntary exiles, who went forth from the university at Prague, found a home at Leipsic, and laid there the foundations of a new university.

It was not difficult to determine, now that the foreign nations had left, upon whom the choice of rector would fall. Preëminent among his countrymen, *facile princeps*, by the concession of all, unless of some disappointed rivals—once his warmest friends, but soon to be his bitter enemies—John Huss was again called to fill the post of rector.

Such was the triumph of the reformer, at the critical moment when he was about to come in direct conflict with the archiepiscopal influence at Prague. Sbynco, opposed as legate of Gregory to the measures of the council of Pisa, found himself in an unenviable position. Although as yet he had not come to an open rupture with Huss, he had been made to feel the weight of his influence, and had grown restive under his censure and the reports of his sermons in Bethlehem chapel. The decisive conflict could not long be deferred.

But Sbynco still persisted—in spite of the council and its decisions—in adhering to the cause of Gregory XII. In this he was encouraged by hopes based on the uncertainty of the future and the fickleness of Wenzel. The character of the king,—a curious compound of indolence and passion, wilful caprice, and mischievous humor,—went far to deprive him of all respect. No man had possessed better opportunities to know what he was than the archbishop, and this acquaintance with his general imbecility, and his indifference towards all but the gratification of his appetites, undoubtedly encouraged him for a while to persist in his course as the legate of Gregory in the kingdom of Bohemia.

Wenzel's life had been marked by the most singular freaks of caprice, and the strangest vicissitudes of fortune.[1] The oldest son of Charles IV., he had ascended the imperial throne (1378) at the early age of fifteen. At this period, though his character was but partially developed, he was regarded with respect and confidence. He gave promise of the highest virtues for the ornament and glory of his throne. But it was not long before the hopes of his early years were obscured by debaucheries and excess. He became strangely reckless of his authority, studious only of his ease or amusement, and utterly void of all self-respect. He had no trace of the ambition or enterprise of a great sovereign, and only

[1] M. I. Schmidt's Geschicht Der Deutschen, iv. 1–40.

disgraced the imperial title which he bore. In 1395 he sold the dukedom of Milan to the Visconti for 100,000 florins. Twenty-six cities, embracing nearly the whole of Lombardy, and extending to the Lagune of Venice, were alienated from the empire by a stroke of the pen. It was but shortly after this that in a freak of fancy he resolved to visit the king of France, to consult with him on the union of the church. All attempts to dissuade him from his mad project were of no avail. In fact he proceeded to execute his purpose, and at Rheims followed up his course of imperial profligacy by the cession of Genoa to France. Not content with this, he excited the discontent and alarm of his subjects by recognizing Benedict at Avignon as lawful pope, and withdrawing his allegiance from Boniface IX., who then wore the tiara at Rome.

An act like this, worthy of the drunken frolic in which it originated, made the prelates of Germany tremble for the results that might follow the recklessness and incapacity of the emperor. The archbishop of Mayence was a zealous adherent of Boniface IX., and had no disposition to run the risk of losing his mitre. At his instigation, the princes of the empire cited Wenzel to appear before their tribunal. On his refusal to comply, he was formally deposed. When counselled to bring about a reconciliation with Boniface IX., he treated the matter with supreme indifference. He shut himself up in complete inactivity at Prague, and appeared to feel the loss of his empire less than he would have felt the loss of his wine. The citizens of Nuremberg could not be satisfied with the absolution from allegiance extended by the electoral college to the whole empire, and besought a release from Wenzel himself. He freely granted it, accepting, instead of the 20,000 crowns offered him, a certain number of cartloads of his favorite wine. Even his own brother, Sigismund, pronounced him unfit to rule, shut him up in prison, (the Spinka,) and at length incautiously entrusted him to the care of the Hapsburgs. By these he was set at liberty; and the Bohemians, preferring him with all his freaks and debaucheries to his brother Sigismund, acknowledged him as their sovereign, and restored him to his throne as king of Bohemia.

Still he felt, at least occasionally, a sense of his degradation, and was willing to attempt to regain the imperial crown when it did not cost too great effort. Boniface IX. had consented to his deposition, and had covered it with his pontifical sanction. As the successor of Boniface, Gregory was by no means acceptable to Wenzel; and it was at least something to be still recognized as emperor by a general council which had deposed, along with Benedict, the successor of his old antagonist.

It was evident, therefore, that Huss had little to hope, and Sbynco little to fear, from the king. On the whole, however, he sided with Huss. The writhings of the aggrieved ecclesiastics rather amused him. It has been said of him that "he united in his character all the extravagance of Anthony, the infamous cowardice of Heliogabalus, and the bloody passions of Tiberius." This is a severe judgment, and should be qualified by the addition of another vice, which, in such connection, assumes the phase almost of a virtue—his constitutional indolence.

Huss could place but little reliance upon the support of Wenzel; yet it was something to be left unmolested. From his pulpit in Bethlehem chapel he wielded an influence which was more powerfully felt throughout Bohemia than that either of the archbishop or the king. Sbynco, indeed, was not a man of any remarkable ability. He was almost unlettered, utterly destitute of all claim to be ranked as a theologian, and, with no little natural shrewdness, a most contemptible opponent in argument when pitted against Huss. His strength was simply in the exalted position which he occupied, and the facility with which the party he represented could make him its instrument.

The action of the council must have been felt by him as a sore grievance. The opposition between him and Huss had already become quite fully developed, and on other questions than that of the papacy they were at issue. Two years before the council, the archbishop had directed the clergy to preach the doctrine of transubstantiation, impugned in Wickliffe's writings, and threatened to punish as a heretic any one who should refuse obedience. The doctrine itself was one to which Huss did not object,—nay, it was one which he devoutly held; but the order which required it was in reality directed against the writings both of Wickliffe and his defenders. Huss was regarded as the foremost of these, and could not but feel that he was aimed at in the mandate of the archbishop, especially as at the same time the clergy united in complaints against him.[1] By the action of the council, however, his position in regard to the papacy was approved, and that of Sbynco was condemned. There was no reason, in any respect which he entertained for the archbishop, why he should longer be silent. Indeed, a necessity seemed laid upon him to speak out, and controvert the position taken by Sbynco as Gregory's legate.

He did speak out, freely, boldly, and without respect of persons. He vindicated the course which the council had pursued. Opposition was overborne. The enemies of Huss had dexterously excited prejudice against him for the part which he had taken in vindicating the rights of Bohemians in the university, and which had led to the withdrawal of the Germans. The city had been deprived of their presence, and the merchants had lost their patronage. It was easy, in these circumstances, to spread abroad misrepresentations and calumnies against Huss. But he rose above them all, and still maintained his influence unimpaired in the pulpit of Bethlehem chapel.

This, indeed, was his throne. For seven years he had here wielded the sceptre of his powerful eloquence. The whole city was moved by his words. For the greater part of this period no one had attempted to interfere with him. Only the Germans and a few of his own countrymen had cried out against his heresy in favoring Wickliffe. The schism of the papacy had utterly paralyzed pontifical influence in Bohemia, and while many of the clergy favored the cause of Gregory, the king rather inclined

[1] Neander, v. 258.

to the support of Benedict. Thus Huss was allowed the exercise of an almost unrestricted freedom, and now that the council of Pisa had virtually condemned Sbynco, his position was stronger than ever before.

At no period in these last centuries has the power of the pulpit been more strikingly exhibited than in the case of Huss and his Bethlehem chapel at Prague. Luther, a little more than a century later, found a most powerful ally in the press, which then for the first time began to be employed for popular effect. But Huss was dependent, for the most part, upon the pulpit alone. And here it was that he stood forth without a peer or a rival in the kingdom.

He occupied his post under a solemn sense of responsibility, not to popes and prelates, but to God alone. He was not burdened by the duty of saying masses, or by ceremonial observances of any kind. His attention was directed to the simple preaching of the word of God, and its application to the evils of the times. The extended commentaries on scripture which are found in his works, as well as his sermons which are still preserved, show what composed the staple of his pulpit utterances. He did not cease to testify publicly his respect for the memory of Wickliffe, though he disavowed him as authority, and declined to accept his opinions save so far as they were sustained by the word of God.

Huss was at least passively supported by the king. He had powerful friends both at the court and in the university, of which he was again rector. Among the nobility he numbered some staunch supporters. Jerome seems to have been a favorite of the dissolute monarch, whom he sometimes accompanied on his forays and hunting parties. His influence was effectually exerted upon the side of the reformer, and he treated the plans and projects of the archbishop with undisguised contempt.

But the latter was not disposed quietly to acquiesce in the policy of the court. As the legate of Gregory, he had the presumption to impose silence upon all who questioned his claims as lawful pontiff, or who professed adherence to the council of Pisa. Spurning the royal mandate, he set himself in the attitude of open and avowed opposition. He issued an ordinance forbidding all teachers of the university who had joined the party of the cardinals against the schismatic popes, and had thus abandoned the cause of Gregory, the discharge of all priestly duties within his diocese.[1]

This ordinance was especially aimed at Huss. Its force would have been but slight and contemptible, but for the members of the clergy who hated him for his scathing rebukes of their vices and immoralities. These joined themselves to the archbishop, and made his opposition more serious.

But, strong in his convictions and the consciousness of his own integrity, Huss refused to obey the episcopal mandate. He was sincere in his advocacy of the council of Pisa, exhorting the nobility and common people to abandon the cause of Gregory. He referred to the subject from the pulpit, and the clergy who sustained the archbishop did not escape reprehension.

[1] Helfert, 85. Mon. Hussi, i. 93.

Sbynco carried his complaints to the king. But it was to no purpose. Wenzel had little sympathy with the archbishop. He was rather amused than otherwise to have Huss rebuke men whom he himself had no cause to love. "So long," he replied, "as Master Huss preached against us of the laity, you were very much pleased with it; your turn has come now, and you had better be content." An old Bohemian chronicler observes, to the same effect, that "While Huss rebuked the vices of the laity he was only praised. Men said the Spirit of God spoke through him. But just as soon as he attacked the pope and the higher and lower clergy, rebuking their pride, avarice, simony, and other vices, and claiming that they should not accumulate property, the entire priesthood rose up against him saying, He is an incarnate devil—a heretic."

The archbishop found himself powerless. He could accomplish nothing. Gregory, moreover, was not in circumstances to enforce the ordinances of his legate. His secret ally, Ladislaus of Naples, had just lost his grasp upon Rome. The general in command, Paolo Orsini, to whom with two thousand cuirassiers he had entrusted the city, was seduced by Florentine gold, and, passing into the pay of the republic, admitted the allies into the castle of St. Angelo.[1]

This was a sore blow to Gregory. It admitted the Pisan pope, Alexander V., to the gates of the eternal city. This was enough to decide the policy of Sbynco, who had no disposition to adhere to the fortunes of a sinking cause. He now withdrew his

[1] Proctor's Italy, 139.

allegiance from Gregory, or at least initiated measures for reconciliation with Alexander V.

But before these measures could ripen to their results, and while they were yet inchoate, the power and authority of the archbishop had become almost annihilated at Prague. This did not tend to soothe his ruffled spirit. He was spurred on by those who wished to make him their instrument of revenge on Huss, and he was only too willing to render them his aid.

His bitterness against Huss was doubtless sharpened by events that soon followed. The latter did not disguise or conceal his high esteem of Wickliffe's writings. He manifested it by his actions as well as words. Not content with expressing his views from the pulpit, he determined that others should read this proscribed heretic for themselves. He translated several of his treatises into the Bohemian tongue. These he sent to some of the most distinguished nobles, by whom they were read and widely circulated. But not only did he provide for their diffusion in his native land. He sent some of them into Moravia, and gave to the margrave of that land, who was Wenzel's uncle, a copy of Wickliffe's Trialogue, which he had translated—a work which was accounted, above all his others, most poisonous and heretical.

Huss himself, in the midst of his sermons, is said to have commended them to his hearers as containing most important truth, and fitted to produce a deep and lasting impression—adding, it is said, repeatedly, that he only wished for himself, after death, that he might go where that good and holy man had gone.

The report of all this produced in various quarters great alarm. Some of the teachers of the university remonstrated with Huss, and warned him to desist from what they considered his heretical course. The archbishop was at this time absent from Prague. He was residing at his archiepiscopal palace at Raudnitz.[1] Andrew of Broda, master of arts and bachelor of theology, a former friend of Huss, and a zealous Bohemian, was among the first to separate from the reformer. He wrote to the archbishop of what was occurring at Prague, and besought him to provide against the growing evil. His letter shows that he had cause for apprehension from the spread of Wickliffe's views. "I think," so he proceeds, "that you should regard that terrible truth of God by Ezekiel, where he says, 'I will call my pastors to account for the flock that has been committed to their hand.' Let your fatherly reverence consider that your unsuspicious lambs are in danger of being seized. The shepherd rushes to meet the tiger when one of his flock is assaulted, and rescues him again. But consider that one soul is worth more than a thousand such flocks. Let us watch the more vigilantly against the poisonous arts and the snares of our great foe. This is our duty as pastors. We are to correct the erring, and bring them back, even by compulsion, into the way of truth. But to come to the matter in hand, I wish to inform your fatherly reverence that various books of that pestilent Eng-

[1] Cochleius, 16.

lishman, Wickliffe, are multiplied in your diocese; books full of damnable errors, and errors that have been already condemned. Of these works are his 'Dialogue and Trialogue,' his 'Treatise on the Body of Christ,' and many others, as I hear, by which, and their poisonous doctrines, the flock is greatly endangered. I beseech you, therefore, by the blood of Christ, by your salvation, for which I hope and pray, by the protection of Christ's faithful ones, all of whom I would to God may be saved; yea, on my bended knee most earnestly do I beseech you to be on your guard, lest by the multiplication of these pestilent books your flock shall drink in that infidel poison which will destroy their souls. For neither pestilence, famine, or sword can inflict such evils as will spring from this perfidious depravity of heretical men."[1]

The archbishop became alarmed. Scarce a year before, after a careful examination as he said, he had found Bohemia free from heresy. But Broda's letter aroused him. He determined to meet the evil promptly. Scarcely had the reply reached Prague, when the summons went forth that all heretical writings should be brought to the archbishop. But now the definition of heresy had grown suddenly more broad. It included not only the writings of Wickliffe, but of Huss and Jerome, as well as their predecessors, Milicz and Janow.[2] The books were

[1] The letter is given in full by Cochleius.

[2] This is questioned by some writers, nor can I find it supported by any contemporaneous testimony. The statement is probably based on inferences from the bad repute into which these writings fell on account of the favor extended to them by the followers of Huss. The assertion, substantially as given above, is made in so many instances, that I have not felt at liberty to reject it.

brought. Huss himself came to the archbishop, bearing with him Wickliffe's writings, in which he wished the errors pointed out. 'Let him know the heresy and he would reject it.' At a previous interview with the archbishop he had offered to disavow everything he had done which could be shown to be in opposition to Christian truth. He wished to be satisfied from reason and scripture. He could not yield till convinced by argument. But argument was not the archbishop's forte. Nor were his learned assessors, who subsequently by the pope's direction were to act conjointly with him, any more ready to discuss. Though four of them were teachers of theology, and two doctors of the canon law, they considered fire the most effective logic. It shows how widely the views of Wickliffe had spread, that more than two hundred carefully written and splendidly bound volumes were gathered to be committed to the flames.[1]

But the work of the archbishop could not be executed without a remonstrance. His decree requiring the possessors of Wickliffe's books to give them into his hands, had extended to include the members of the university. This was very generally regarded by the masters and students as an usurpation of their privileges.[2] The university claimed to be independent of the archbishop, and to hold its rights immediately of the pope. The requirement which denied them the privilege of retaining Wickliffe's writings was in fact an infringement upon the rights of the university.

[1] Godeau xxxvi. 288.

[2] Helfert, 91.

Most of the masters and students, however, complied with the decree of the archbishop. Only five refused utterly to obey it.[1] They laid their complaint before the pope, representing the decree as unwise, and an unwarranted usurpation of power. They sent their procurator, Marcus of Koniggratz, to Bologna, and through his efforts the matter gave promise of a favorable issue. The university of Bologna pronounced in favor of the rights of the university of Prague, and the pope decided that Sbynco must appear before him to justify himself for the course which he had pursued. Till he had done this, his proceedings against Huss and his party were to be null and void.

Sbynco, on the other hand, was not idle. As legate of Gregory, he had enjoined silence on Huss and others who had refused to acknowledge Gregory as pope. But the condition of things was such that unless he could have the support of the pope elected by the council of Pisa, his case was desperate. Abandoning Gregory without a scruple, he now sent a deputation to Bologna to counteract the influence of the appeal of the students, and the representation of the friends of Huss. His deputation consisted of Jaroslaw the inquisitor, and a canon of Prague. They set forth in glowing colors the dangerous spread of Wickliffe's doctrines in Bohemia, and secured a revocation of the decision in favor of the students' appeal. A papal bull was issued,[2] condemning the articles of Wickliffe, forbidding preach-

[1] Helfert, 85.

[2] It was proclaimed at Prague, March 9, 1410, ten weeks after it was issued.

ing in private chapels, and authorizing the archbishop to appoint a commission of four masters in theology and two doctors of laws, to prevent the spread of errors and enforce the measures adopted by the archbishop. The students and their procurator, under pain of excommunication, were to make solemn declaration of their subjecting themselves to the papal order, and of their accepting the judgment of the archbishop.

By the advice of the commission Sbynco summoned a synod of the clergy, before whom the results of their investigation were laid. It was numerously attended. Many doctors, masters, students, and others were present. Wickliffe's books were condemned, and it was declared the safest course to burn them. The five recusant students were required to deliver up their books; no one was to venture to hold, teach, or defend an article of Wickliffe, under severe penalty, including the loss of his benefice and imprisonment by the civil power, and no more preaching was to be allowed, except in cathedral, cloister, and parish churches.[1]

The archbishop, reconciled now to Pope Alexander and fortified by his authority, resolved to execute his purpose. The books were collected, and preparation was made to burn them. The archbishop might now act not only with the support of the synod of his own clergy, but under cover of the bull of the pope. His former demand for the books was renewed.

Meanwhile Alexander V., the author of the obnoxious bull, had died, and the friends of Wickliffe

[1] Helfert, 89.

seized upon this as an argument for a stay of proceedings. It was argued that the authority of the bull expired with its author. Nor was this all. The university objected to the wholesale condemnation of Wickliffe's books, some of which were purely philosophical. The prohibition to preach in Bethlehem chapel, which had been established by archiepiscopal, papal, and royal briefs, was opposed to scripture, which taught that Christ preached in the temple, on the mountain, on the sea, in the fields and streets, and bade his disciples go everywhere preaching the gospel.[1]

These views were urged by Huss, Zdislaw of Wartenberg, and three of the five recusant students, who embodied them in a protest, and thus incurred the sentence of archiepiscopal excommunication.

The king was now appealed to, to prevent the burning of the books. The university, with a good degree of unanimity, declared itself opposed to the archbishop's project.[2] (June 15, 1410.) Wenzel promised that he would not allow it to be executed. He secured from the archbishop a pledge to defer any action in the matter until the arrival in Prague of Jost, margave of Moravia.

In these circumstances, with the ban of the church impending over him, what course was Huss to take? The papal bull, proclaimed by the archbishop, and endorsing his own previous decree, absolutely forbade his preaching in Bethlehem chapel.

But Huss did not hesitate for a moment what course to take. He did not ask what is prudence,

[1] Helfert, 89. [2] Helfert, 90.

but what is duty. He opposed the prohibition on two grounds. First: it was in conflict with the original deed of endowment sanctioned by archiepiscopal, papal, and royal briefs, by which Bethlehem chapel had been expressly devoted to the preaching of the word of God. Secondly: it was in conflict with scripture, which taught that Jesus preached in the temple, in the streets and fields, on the sea and on the mountain, and had bidden his disciples to go everywhere preaching the gospel. Thus the effect of the prohibition would tend only to the injury of the church, and was not to be obeyed.

In arguing the case more fully, he says, "Where is there any authority of Holy Writ, or where are there any rational grounds for forbidding preaching in so public a place, fitted up for that very purpose, in the midst of the great city of Prague? Nothing else can be at the bottom of this but the jealousy of Antichrist." The pope himself had travestied the history of the apostles by his incongruous course. When he "heard at his court that Bohemia received the word of God, he did not send Peter and John to pray for the Bohemians, and to lay their hands on them, that in hearing the word of God they might receive the Holy Ghost; but he sent back some ill-disposed persons belonging to Bohemia, and commanded, in his bull, that the word of God should not be preached in private chapels."[1]

But Huss felt that he had been called of God to preach, and he could not be silent. He maintained

[1] The history of these proceedings is found in the controversial writings of Huss, and the account of his trial before the council of Constance.

that one whose life is conformed to Christ's law—who seeks the glory of God and the salvation of men,—preaching not lies, not ribaldry, not fables, but the law of Christ and the doctrines of the holy fathers of the church—opposing heretics and false teachers,—such a person never arrogates to himself the call to preach without authority. Huss felt the full force of the words of Paul—"Woe is me if I preach not the gospel." Subsequently he declared his purpose to continue to preach, in the following memorable and well-weighed words: "In order that I may not make myself guilty by my silence, forsaking the truth for a piece of bread, or through fear of man, I avow it to be my purpose to defend the truth which God has enabled me to know, and especially the truth of the Holy Scriptures, even to death; since I know that the truth stands, and is forever mighty, and abides eternally; and with her there is no respect of persons. And if the fear of death should terrify me, still I hope in my God, and in the assistance of the Holy Spirit, that the Lord himself will give me firmness. And if I have found favor in his sight, he will crown me with martyrdom. But what more glorious triumph is there than this? Inciting his faithful ones to this victory, our Lord says, 'Fear not them that kill the body.'"[1]

These were not words of vainglorious boasting, as the sequel shows. Huss had weighed carefully the question of duty. He had come to his decision in full view of the consequences which it might involve. Enthusiastic, indeed, in devotion to what he regarded

[1] Mon. Hussi, i. 106.

as the cause of truth, he was yet calm and self-possessed, clear in his views, and firm in his purpose. The zeal of his earlier years has been chastened by fuller knowledge and larger experience; but the martyr-spirit still glowed within him. He could not submit to the prohibition that would exclude him from the pulpit of Bethlehem chapel. He resolved on an appeal, and did in fact appeal, previous to the burning of the books, from the pope ill-informed to the pope well-informed.

This appeal of Huss so thoroughly reviews the ground upon which he justified his course, that it deserves to be presented at length. It was made on the 25th of June, 1410, and represented the position of himself and his friends who joined with him in it.[1] The act took place, in a formal and public manner, in Bethlehem chapel, before a notary public, and in the presence of seven witnesses, who represented all those members of the university and nobility who wished to be regarded as adhering to him in the matter. The grounds of the appeal were as follows:— First: that the sentence of the archbishop, authorized by the pope, is opposed to the privileges of the university, sanctioning an act which tramples on them, inasmuch as the said university is exempt from all other jurisdiction save that of the pope alone, even from that of legates, deputies, and sub-deputies of the Roman See. Secondly: that the burning of the books was an act of disobedience to the order that the archbishop had received from Alexander V., not

[1] Huss made the appeal in conjunction with many other masters and teachers. Monumenta, i. 89.

to attempt anything, either by himself or others, against these books and against the university, before the matter had been judged of at Rome, and to revoke whatever had been done to the prejudice of the privileges of the university, as far as possible. Thirdly: that instead of obeying this order, he had intrigued at the court of Rome against the university and against John Huss; he had published abroad that Huss was spreading errors at Prague in the kingdom of Bohemia, in the marquisate of Moravia, and in other provinces; and he had, moreover, surreptitiously obtained a bull for the condemnation of these pretended errors. Fourthly: that we are not required to obey commands that are scandalous, contrary to common law, to the public welfare, and especially to the gospel; such as are the pretended commands of the pope, and the sentence of Sbynco passed in consequence of these supposed commands, since it is well known that in the whole kingdom of Bohemia and in Moravia there is neither heresy nor error, and it is a capital sin to interdict the preaching of the gospel. Fifthly: that there is no heresy in Bohemia is proved by the document published by the archbishop himself (July 17, 1408) in the assembled synod of that year. This document states that the archbishop, at the king's order, had made, by his prelates and officials, a careful inquisition, and had found no heretic in his diocese. Sixthly: that though all this were otherwise, the sentences and proceedings of Sbynco were utterly null and void, because they took place after the death of Alexander V.; and because, according to the common law, when he is dead who has commanded anything, his authority expires with him, except so far as it has been carried into effect during his life. Seventhly: that none can be so ignorant in Holy Scripture and canon law, as not to know that books of logic, philosophy, morality, mathematics, &c., such as most of Wickliffe's are, are incapable of heresy, nor, consequently, can they be subject to ecclesiastical condemnation. Moses and Daniel were learned in the knowledge of the Egyptians and Chaldeans. The church ordained, when the necessity arose and the circumstances of the time required, that heretical books should be read, not to sustain their errors, but to refute them, and to draw out of them whatever good they contained. St. Paul had read, and quoted passages from heathen authors; moreover, it was necessary that students of the university should read the books of Aristotle, Averröes, and other unbelieving philosophers; and for the same reason that would justify the condemnation of Wickliffe's works, the book of the 'master of sentences' (Peter Lombard) and those of Origen, which contained many errors, must be burned. Yet Huss protests that he has no wish to maintain any error, wheresoever he may find it. Eighthly: that this condemnation of Wickliffe's books, in short, is opposed to the honor of the kingdom of Bohemia, of Moravia, and other provinces, and especially of the university of Prague; since, on the fourteenth of June of the present year, it had decided solemnly, in full assembly of masters, doctors, licentiates, bachelors, and students, that it was opposed to the sentence of Sbynco in regard to the books of Wickliffe.

Ninthly: that it belongs to the Apostolic See, and to no other, to explain and interpret its own orders; and that Sbynco was not authorized to interpret, as he had done, the pretended bull of the pope. Tenthly: that between the arrival of the bull, and the sentence pronounced by Sbynco, sufficient time had not elapsed to examine such a large number of books and writings on matters so important. Eleventhly: that the Bethlehem chapel was founded expressly for preaching the word of God in the vulgar tongue, for though there were churches enough in Prague for the worship of God, there was none but this for preaching. Twelfthly: that its establishment had been confirmed by the Apostolic See, by the king of Bohemia, and by a former archbishop of Prague.

Such was the appeal of Huss. It indicated that he had calmly and deliberately surveyed the ground upon which he stood, and was prepared to maintain it.

The appeal of Huss was made June 25th, 1410. Less than three weeks after, (July 15,) the archbishop, who grew impatient over the delay of the margrave of Moravia, and who wished to anticipate any opposition from the new pope, proceeded to execute sentence upon Wickliffe's books. Bands of armed soldiers were stationed around the court of his palace to prevent any disturbance, and in his presence and that of several prelates and a large number of the clergy the fire was kindled, and about two hundred volumes, some of them in elegant and costly binding, were devoted to the flames.[1]

[1] Helfert, 90.

The bells tolled from all the towers of the city, as for a solemn funeral. An old chronicler remarks that it was meant to indicate the end of trouble, while by God's providence it proved the beginning of sorrows. Three days later, Huss, Zdislaw of Wartenberg, and those of the recusant students and others who had signed the protest against the archbishop's order and the papal bull, were solemnly excommunicated.

The deed was done. The books were burned. The ban of the church rested on those who had dared to object. Doubtless the archbishop felt that he had secured a triumph. He had executed the papal sentence, and proved himself an able instrument of the church party who had instigated him to the bold deed.

But it provoked more than it overawed. The king, the court, and a large proportion of the citizens of Prague were enraged and embittered by it. A cry of indignation ran throughout Bohemia. Some of the priests, but the nobility especially, protested against this vandal act. The queen wept, and Wenzel cursed aloud. Some acts of violence were committed by the enraged populace. The archbishop trembled in his fortified palace. His name was covered with disgrace by his insulting and bigoted course. Songs in derision of him were sung in the streets. So far was this carried, that the king found it necessary to prohibit it under severe penalties.

But his work was only half executed.[1] Not all of

[1] Cochleius, p. 18.

Wickliffe's books were burned. Some refused to give them up. They scorned the archbishop's mandate, and required a more convincing logic than that of fagots and bonfires. Though the art of printing was not yet invented, so great, says Cochleius, was the zeal of the people against the clergy, and their anxiety for the writings of Wickliffe, inflamed as they were by the frequent harangues of the new dogmatists, that in a short time a large number of the forbidden books had been transcribed. This was a work of secrecy, for the act, if discovered, would have been treated as a crime.

Meanwhile the suppression of derisive songs by the king, forced the people to invent some new expression of their disgust with the proceedings of the archbishop and his clergy. Many of the people had acquired such a knowledge of the scriptures, which had been translated for them into the Bohemian language, as to be able to refute and silence the priests in argument. We may perhaps trace some elements of the rapid success of the principles of reform to the fact that the Bible had already been given to the Bohemian nation in their own tongue. There still exists, in the imperial library of Vienna, an index of a translation of the Bible bearing date A. D. 1382. The author of it, Zadislaus Bathori, was a monk of the order of St. Paul. He withdrew to a cavern in the mountains, and, excluding every human being, labored for twenty years at his solitary task. Cochleius, an inveterate enemy of the Hussites, testifies to the thorough acquaintance of many of the common people with the doctrines of the Bible.

"Furriers, shoemakers, tailors, and that class of mechanics, by their frequent attendance on sermons, and *their zealous reading of the scriptures that had been translated for them into the vernacular tongue*, were led to open discussion with the priests before the people. And not men only, but women also, reached such a measure of audacity and impudence as to venture to dispute in regard to the doctrines of the scripture, and maintain themselves against the priests. Some of them moreover composed books, one of which is thus characterized by a countryman. 'Its Jezebel author, mad with rage in her threatenings against the servant of God, and from the Holy Scriptures extolling not the church of God but her own sect, thus deals out her lies: She says, that 'in every class, especially among the ecclesiastics, not an individual can be found, with the exception of the Hussites, whose life is truly pure and spiritual, and who can preach the word of God by the Holy Spirit.' And yet, this work was received and treated with the highest regard by the sect, of both sexes; and its author was looked upon as a woman of wonderful subtilty in the Holy Scriptures, and an able defender of Master Huss and his sectaries."

It was impossible that convictions which had taken so strong a hold upon their minds, and which the study of the Bible had confirmed, should easily be eradicated. It is no wonder that the argument of fire should exasperate them. They could see through the smoke of Wickliffe's books nothing clearer than before, except the ignorance and malice of their persecutors. In such a state of mind they might easily be excited to deeds of violence or imprudence, which in their cooler moments they would condemn. The whole history of Huss shows that with such excesses he had no sympathy, however much some of his followers might think to find a warrant for their action in his words. We are rather surprised that in such a state of the community, and while the authority was in Wenzel's feeble hands, such order should have been observed. It certainly shows that the influence of Huss's doctrines restrained as well as impelled.

On the Sunday following the burning of the books, Huss referred in his sermon to the events of the preceding week. He condemned, unhesitatingly, the conduct of the archbishop—maintained that by his burning he had rooted no sin out of the hearts of men, but rather had destroyed many treatises and arguments that contained important truths and excellent morals—had given occasion for disorder, altercations, and hatreds among the people, as well as acts of violence and crime—and had dishonored the king in the eyes of foreign nations by this foolish, senseless act.[1] The course of the king in this emergency seems to have been characterized by a more than usual share of discretion. While he prohibited the derisive and insulting songs of the people against the archbishop, he yet complained of his conduct to the pope, John XXIII., and asked him to impose some check upon his license.

The rash haste of the archbishop brought with it another evil. The former possessors of the burnt

[1] For a fuller view of Huss's position, see Mon. Hussi, i. 106.

books were dissatisfied at their loss, as well as the insulting course of the prelate. Their books were very costly, laboriously transcribed, and beautifully bound. They asked and obtained permission of the king to demand back of the archbishop an equivalent of their value. He rejected the demand. The king, willing to see justice done, authorized two of his nobles, with the old city council, to bring the claim before the abbots, deans, and other ecclesiastics, who had advised the prelate to burn the books. They also refused to entertain it, and violence followed. The people were indignant at the wrong insultingly done them, and would have redress. Three Carmelite monks, who had preached against Wickliffe, were seized and harshly treated. One of them was thrown into the river, and would have been drowned if a knight had not come to his help. In this act of violence Jerome was implicated. But Huss continued to preach. Indeed, he dared not be silent. And the power of his sermons over the throngs which pressed to hear him in Bethlehem chapel was incalculable. His words thrilled the hearts of his hearers, as he exclaimed, "Fire does not consume truth. It is always a mark of a little mind to vent anger on inanimate and uninjurious objects. The books which are burnt are a loss to the whole nation." Huss sent his appeal to Rome; and shortly after, Sbynco despatched a deputation who were to instruct the Roman court as to the real state of affairs at Prague, vindicate the proceedings of the archbishop, and present charges against Huss.

The matter came, as was inevitable, before the

university.[1] The cause of Huss, as excommunicate, was identified with that of Wickliffe. The real question was, whether the works of the latter should have been burned as heretical. If not, Huss was unjustly excommunicate. But the university, by an immense majority, condemned the measure of the archbishop. Philosophical works, at least, were not to be accounted heretical. Every student was at liberty to read the works of the heathen Aristotle, much more of learned Christian men, who, like Origen, had erred on some points. Why, then, should the perusal of Wickliffe's writings be prohibited, especially when the greater portion of them had not as yet been shown to be heretical?

For five successive days (July 27–Aug. 2, 1410)[2] the disputation was continued before the assembled university. Several masters took up, each, one of the treatises of Wickliffe, and defended it. Huss took that on the Trinity; Jacobel that on the Decalogue; Simon, of Tisnow, that on the Proofs of Propositions (*De Probationibus Propositionum*); Zdislaw of Wartenberg that on Universals (*De Universalibus*); and Procop of Pilsen that on Ideas (*De Ideis*).

At the same time, probably, and more fully at a later period, Huss defended those articles of Wickliffe in which he was himself personally interested. The first one selected for vindication was, "They who for excommunication by men only refuse to preach, are thereby excommunicate of God, and in the judgment will be found among the foes of Christ." Another was, "Any deacon or priest may preach the

[1] Helfert, 92. [2] It may have commenced a day or two earlier.

word of God without being dependent on bishop or pope."

While both parties were looking anxiously for the decision which was to be pronounced at Rome, the mutual exasperation at Prague was steadily increasing. The authority and the learning of the archbishop were alike contemned. The people in the streets called him the "A B C D" bishop. Meanwhile Huss from the pulpit gave his version of the matter. As he exposed the misrepresentations of the opposite party, who complained to the pope that the whole land was infected with heresy, and charged it to his account, the people cried out, as with one voice, "They lie, they lie."[1]

With the sentence of excommunication hanging over him, Huss was more earnest and eloquent than ever before. He had no longer any disposition to curb the spirit which impelled him to expose the vices of the ecclesiastical orders. They had complained of him to the archbishop, and still pursued him with calumny and malice. He heeded not their slanders or opposition. "Mark," said he to his vast audience, "what is written in scripture of the Pharisees, 'All that they bid you do, that observe and do, but do ye not after their works.' The same language might apply to our ecclesiastics now, whose conduct exhibits little conformity to the law." "What these men find in the gospel of Christ to their taste, they willingly receive; but when they meet with anything requiring labor and self-denial, they pass it by. What Jesus said to Peter—'I will

[1] Helfert, 92.

give to them the keys of the kingdom of heaven'—that they grasp at for the aggrandizement of their authority; but that other sentence addressed by Christ to Peter—'Follow me, and feed my sheep'—they eschew like poison. So, too, what Christ said to the disciples—'Whatsoever ye shall bind on earth shall be bound in heaven'—they accept gladly and comfort themselves with it; but when he says, 'Possess neither gold nor silver,' they decline it as offensive. If Christ says, 'Whoso heareth you, heareth me'—they use it as an argument for obedience to them; but they wrestle hard against what he again says—'Ye know that the princes of the Gentiles exercise dominion over them, and they that are great exercise authority upon them; but it shall not be so among you,'"[1] etc.

The evils which Huss rebuked were too glaring to be denied. He held up to view the purity and holiness required by Christ, and in this mirror exposed the avarice, ambition, luxury, sensuality, and violence of the profligate ecclesiastics. He could not compromise with his convictions; and with a high consciousness of his solemn responsibility to God rather than men, he aimed to discharge his whole duty. The lines that defined the two opposing parties were rapidly becoming more distinct.

[1] The language above cited is to be found in Helfert, while much more to the same purpose is to be met with in the works of Huss.

CHAPTER VI.

HUSS EXCOMMUNICATED. THE COMPROMISE.

Case of Huss at Rome. — Cardinal Colonna. — His Decision. — Its Reception at Prague. — Royal Embassy to the Pope, Praying that Huss may be Released from Personal Appearance at Rome. — Procurators of Huss. — Their Treatment. — Sentence of Excommunication. — Published at Prague. — Huss Justifies Himself in Preaching. — Interdict. — The King Interposes. — A Commission. — Compromise. — Letter of Sbynco. — Its Futility. — Sbynco's Conference with Huss. — Huss Preaches on the Subject. — Disgrace of Sbynco. — He Leaves Prague. — His Letter to the King. — His Death.

1411.

The appeal of Huss to John XXIII. was referred by the latter to a commission of four cardinals, of whom Otho de Colonna was one. The commission were authorized to invite to conference with them the doctors and masters of the theological faculties of Bologna, Paris, and Oxford, who might be present in Rome, and to advise with them what course was to be pursued with respect to Wickliffe's writings.[1]

The majority of the conference were opposed to the project of the archbishop in burning the books, but before they had reached any definite conclusion the deputation from the archbishop arrived in the city. They represented the case to John XXIII. in such a manner that he was induced to dissolve the

[1] Mon. Hussi, i. 87.

commission, and give the whole matter over to the sole charge of the cardinal, Otho de Colonna.

The cardinal gave a ready ear to Sbynco's representations. He sanctioned what he had done, urged him to the further prosecution of his measures, and directed him, if necessary, to call to his aid the secular arm. Huss was required within a certain specified time to appear and justify himself before the tribunal of the pope.

The intelligence of this decision reached Prague and produced much dissatisfaction. All classes, from the king to the peasant, including the nobility and the university, exclaimed against the injustice that required the personal appearance of Huss at Rome. It was only at the risk of his life that he could undertake the journey. Bands of Germans infested the roads, and, sympathizing with their exiled countrymen, they would have exulted in seizing Huss and putting him to death. Besides, the question was asked, Why cannot the matter be settled here in Prague?

Apprehension of the danger to be incurred induced the king, his queen, of whom Huss was confessor, the university of Prague, and a large number of the lords and barons of Bohemia and Moravia, to send an embassy[1] to the pope to pray him to dispense with the personal appearance of Huss, to suffer him to preach in the privileged chapels, to prevent Bohemia from being defamed by false accusations of heresy, and to send legates at the expense of the

[1] The embassy consisted of Dr. John Nas, and John, Cardinal of Reinstein. Helfert, p. 135.

kingdom, to examine the whole matter at Prague.[1] Huss on his side sent three procurators to Bologna to defend his cause and urge the reasons that prevented his personal appearance.

These procurators—at the head of whom was John of Jesenitz, an able man and a warm friend of Huss—proceeded on their journey. They appeared before Cardinal Colonna at Rome, but he refused to listen to their exculpation of Huss.[2] When the term fixed for his personal appearance had expired, the cardinal issued the decree of excommunication against him. It was based, not on an examination of the merits of the case, but on the imputed disobedience of Huss in refusing to appear. The request of the king, queen, nobles, and university that a legate might be sent to Prague, was treated with contempt.[3]

The sentence of excommunication was published (March 15, 1411) in all the parish churches of Prague with the exception of two, that of St. Michael in the old city, of which Christiann of Prachatic was pastor, and that of St. Benedict. But the procurators of Huss were still prosecuting his cause at Rome, and he refused to desert his pulpit in Bethlehem chapel. Dissatisfied at the futility of the measures hitherto adopted, Sbynco laid the city of Prague under inter-

[1] Fleury, xxv. 284. Palacky, iii. 258. Mon. Hussi, i. 87.

[2] Mon. Hussi, i. 87.

[3] The application of the king was not only that Huss might be released from appearing personally before the pope, but that he might be left free to preach in Bethlehem chapel. "It is our will also," he wrote, "that Bethlehem chapel, which, for the glory of God and the saving good of the people, we have endowed with franchises for the preaching of the gospel, should stand, and should be confirmed in its privileges, so that its patrons may not be deprived of their rights of patronage, and that Master Huss (whom the king styles loyal, devout, and beloved) may be established over this chapel, and preach the word of God in peace."

dict, and closed the churches to all public worship.[1]

Huss regarded this proceeding as the fruit of personal malice. He saw in it a manœuvre of the archiepiscopal party—the monks and curates—to drive him from his pulpit and render him powerless. The success of Sbynco's deputation at Rome he ascribed to the influence of the gifts with which he bribed the commission. We shall see, hereafter, that there was only too much ground for this charge.

Before the people, Huss justified himself boldly. Was it objected to him that he had been forbidden to preach? He replied, that it was better to obey God than men.[2] Was he under the ban of the church? Then the pope was its head and the cardinals its members; but where were the bishops and priests and all the rest of Christendom? Was he charged with favoring Wickliffe? He did not believe him to have been a heretic, and of every man, as far as possible, we are to think good rather than evil.[3] He held himself still as a dutiful son of the church, and felt no awe of an unrighteous excommunication.

In declining to obey the papal citation to appear personally at Rome, he felt that he was justified by sufficient reasons. These were afterwards presented more at length in his treatise on the church. Here he explains the origin of the troubles. "The priests of Christ," he says, "preached against the vices of a corrupt clergy. Hence arose the schism, and hence that clergy sought to suppress such preaching." "After the manner of the Pharisees, they trouble

[1] Helfert, 99. [2] Mon. Hussi. i. 239. [3] Ib. 139.

and excommunicate those who acknowledge Christ. It was because I preached Christ and the gospel, and exposed Antichrist, anxious that the clergy should live according to the law of Christ, that the prelates first, with the archbishop, contrived to get a bull from Alexander V. to prohibit preaching in the chapels before the people, from which bull I appealed; but I never was able to get a hearing. On good and reasonable grounds, I did not appear when I was cited. As to his apparent contempt of the citation, he asks:[1] "What reason had I for obedience—a man summoned from a distance of 1200 miles! What reason that I, a man unknown to the pope, informed against by my enemies, should be so very solicitous, and put myself to extraordinary pains to pass through the midst of my enemies, and place myself before judges and witnesses who are my enemies; that I should use up the property of the poor to defray the enormous expenses, or if I could not meet the expenses, miserably perish from hunger and thirst? And what was to be gained by my appearance? One consequence certainly would be, neglect of the work which God gave me to do, for my own salvation and that of others. There I should be learning, not what to believe, but how to conduct a process, a thing not permitted to a servant of God. There I should be robbed by the consistory of cardinals—made lukewarm in holy living; be betrayed into impatience by oppression; and if I had nothing to give, must be condemned, let my cause be ever so good; and what is still worse, I should be compelled

[1] Mon. Hussi, i. 245; also i. 88.

to worship the pope on my bended knees." Moreover, the journey would not only be a long one, but it would necessarily place him on the road in circumstances in which he would be surrounded by his enemies, the Germans. Hence he declined to appear, and continued to preach.[1]

This of course necessitated the imposition of the interdict upon the city. But matters were thus brought to a crisis. Either Huss must obey the citation, or the churches must be closed. The people would not endure the latter. They complained, and the king was forced to interfere. The archbishop himself had grown weary in what threatened to be a hopeless and interminable struggle. He manifested a disposition to compromise. The king appointed a commissioner, to whom the controversy on both sides should be referred, and to whose decision both parties should submit.[2] It was composed on one side of the elector of Saxony, Prince Stibor of Stiboric, and Lacek of Krawar, as laymen; and of ecclesiastics, the patriarch of Antioch, Conrad, bishop of Olmutz, provost Sulek of Chotestchau, and others. On the other side, of adherents to the anti-episcopal party, were Simon of Tisnow, rector of the university, John Huss, Stephen Paletz, Marcus of Koniggratz, and others. After careful deliberation, the conclusions of the commission were reached on the 6th of June, 1411. It was decided that both parties should desist from all legal prosecutions or measures, and should recall their procurators from Rome, while the archbishop should withdraw the

[1] Mart. Anec. iv. 46–45. [2] Helfert, 102, 103.

sentence of excommunication and remove the interdict.[1] The university was to remain in the possession and exercise of all its rights and privileges, unprejudiced by the precedent of the burning of the books.

Another condition of the compromise which was thus effected was, that Sbynco should write to John XXIII. that the difficulty between him and Huss was composed; that no more errors prevailed in Bohemia; and that it were wisdom to revoke the sentence issued against Huss, and dispense with his personal appearance at Rome.[2] The letter was actually written, and no doubt forwarded. That it was virtually extorted from the archbishop, and that it did not express his real sentiments, must at least have been suspected by those to whom it was addressed.

The letter, whether willingly or unwillingly written, is worthy of notice.[3] "Most holy father, Alexander V., of blessed memory, gave forth a bull which imported that in the kingdom of Bohemia at Prague, and in the marquisate of Moravia, heretical and schismatic doctrines were spread abroad, especially that damnable error in regard to the sacrament of the eucharist, with which many were infected; and that it was necessary to arrest the course of these novelties before they had infected the whole flock. To this end he ordained in the same bull that there should be an inquisition in regard to these errors, in order to their extirpation. But having executed this order conjointly with the professors of theology, the

[1] Helfert, 103. [2] Ib. [3] Mon. Hussi, i., 88.

doctors of canon law, and my other vicars, I have found no heretical errors, either in the kingdom of Bohemia, or at Prague, or in the marquisate of Moravia. No person could be found whom we could convict of opinions deserving ecclesiastical punishment. Likewise, at the instance of Wenzel, king of the Romans and Bohemia, as well as of his council, we have been fully reconciled to John Huss and the other doctors and masters of the university; so that the troubles that we had together are thoroughly settled. Therefore desiring, most holy father, according to the duty of my pastoral office, to maintain the kingdom of Bohemia in its good reputation, I have recourse to the clemency of your holiness, praying you to take compassion on this kingdom, and remove from it and annul the excommunication and consequent censures that have been laid upon it, and to dispense with the appearance before you in person of the honorable master, John Huss, Bachelor of Theology."

This letter of the archbishop, we are told, was never received. It may have been intercepted on the way by banditti, or by the enemies of Huss, with the archbishop's connivance. If it reached its destination, the circumstances in which it was written would deprive it of much of its weight. It would stand in opposition to Sbynco's previous representations. Certainly it did not avail to stay the proceedings against Huss. The pope, out of complaisance perhaps to the royal intercession, appointed a new commission, to whom the case of Huss was referred. Among the members of it was Cardinal Zabarella, one of the most liberal of the whole college, and most favorably disposed to the cause of reform. But through some unknown influence, the cause was again transferred to Cardinal Brancas alone, who, in spite of all the remonstrances of the procurators of Huss, who sought a prompt decision, kept the whole affair in suspense for a period of a year and a half.[1]

The archbishop had, in reality, capitulated to the friends of the reformer and the authority of the king. He had exhausted his resources of resistance as well as of offence. His spirit seemed fairly subdued by the unsuccessful issue of the conflict, and he never again came into open collision with Huss. To the complaints of his clergy he was compelled to listen; but the most which he attempted for their relief was to administer to Huss a gentle reprimand. On one occasion he cited him to his palace to answer for certain obnoxious views which he had presented from the pulpit. Huss promptly responded to the summons. But he must have felt rather amused than otherwise at the result of the interview. The scholar, the powerful logician, and orator stood before the ignorant "A B C D" bishop. Huss was informed that he was charged with preaching false and dangerous doctrines from the pulpit. He had taught,—so it was reported,—that there was no necessity of burying the dead in consecrated grounds, and that they might just as well be interred in the fields or woods. "You are aware, my son," said the archbishop, "that St. Adelbert had great difficulty in dissuading the Bohemians from these profane

[1] Mon. Hussi, i. 87.

burials; that often he was obliged to fulminate against them on the subject; and that, in answer to his prayers, God often chastised them with severity, till, in 1039, Bozelislaus, duke of Bohemia, engaged by oath that he and his posterity would hold the Christian faith inviolate, and have the dead interred in places consecrated to this purpose."[1] Huss humbly replied, that if anything had escaped him, either through forgetfulness or error, opposed to the Christian faith, he would correct it of his own accord. The archbishop seemed satisfied. "God give you grace; go, and sin no more," was the answer with which he dismissed him.

Huss probably felt that the principal matter of remonstrance was in itself comparatively unimportant. Greater truths filled his mind. It was only as this was connected with other things that it demanded specific notice. He had no desire to offend the archbishop, and yet he could not belie his convictions. The next Sabbath he preached openly on the subject, indirectly at least referring to the mandate of the archbishop. "It is a strange thing, my dear Bohemians," said he, "that we are to be forbidden to teach manifest truths, and especially those that shine forth so brightly in England and elsewhere in many places. These burials especially, and these great bells, serve merely to fill the purses of miserly priests. What they call *order*, is nothing else but confusion. Believe me, they wish to enslave you by this disorderly order. But if you will have courage, you may easily break your chains, and give yourselves a free-

[1] L'Enfant's Council of Pisa, ii. 47.

dom, the value of which cannot be told. Is it not a shameful thing and an enormous sin against God, opposed to all law and sense, to have burned books that are the depositaries of truth, and that were written only for your good?"[1]

A report of the sermon reached the archbishop. He complained of it to the king; but no notice was taken of his complaint. A stronger and abler man than Sbynco might have felt the burden which he had to bear too heavy for prolonged endurance. His reconciliation to Huss did not conciliate favor to himself. He could not fail to perceive that instead of an object of fear he had become an object of contempt. He and the priests who adhered to him were hooted at by the populace, and found no sympathy in Prague. His name was coupled with whatever was ridiculous in the fancies of the people. The derisive songs which were heard in the streets and the thoroughfares, which were aimed at the archbishop and his party, and which the king was forced by an express decree to suppress, showed the degree of contempt to which the party had fallen. The people assumed a defiant tone. They said, "Let the archbishop again bid us deliver up the books, and see whether we will obey him."[2]

Sbynco appealed to the king for a hearing, but his request was declined. His patience was exhausted by this unexpected refusal. He could no longer make his residence in Prague tolerable. Despairing of help from Wenzel, he determined to apply to his royal brother, Sigismund of Hungary. With a

[1] L'Enfant, ii. 48. [2] Mart. Anec., iv. 386.

troubled heart he left the city, and from Leitomischel wrote back to Wenzel his bitter complaint: "Five weeks long," he says, "I lingered with my attendants in the city, and exhausted all means to obtain a hearing of your grace, but to no purpose, even while my enemies had access as often as they desired. I would have spoken and explained my difficulties to your grace, as to my gracious Lord; but not only was this prevented, but in every way, and in more respects than one, was I publicly wronged. On this account I am forced to turn to Hungary, to beseech the brother of your grace that he will intercede with you on my behalf, and no longer allow my enemies to cast contempt upon my office."[1]

In a pitiful tone the archbishop recounts his grievances. Erroneous teachers were left unmolested. Some without authority heard confessions, claiming for themselves the same power as the pope. A wicked priest, whom he had commanded to arrest, had been taken out of his hands. Persons summoned before his tribunal had refused to appear, and been sustained in their contumacy by favorites of the king. Shameful and calumnious letters against himself had been written and circulated, of which he had complained to no purpose. The priest of St. Nicholas had been shamefully imprisoned and robbed of his goods, although innocent of wrong. Many of the clergy were still deprived of their goods and salaries. The king had charged him to write to the pope, exculpating those who had disregarded the interdict—a thing which his conscience forbade. He had been

[1] Helfert, 104.

hindered in the prosecution of ecclesiastical discipline. He had been defamed by gross falsehoods, and charged with the whole responsibility for the interdict. In vain had he sought to exculpate himself. The king had threatened to bring the clergy into subjection, and had rejected every application for relief. Such were the grievances of the archbishop.

The heart of Sbynco was broken. He had overrated his strength in attempting to deal with the reform movement at Prague. He had overtasked his powers; and we need not, as some have done,[1] impute his death to poison. He died at Presburg, on his journey to the court of Sigismund, September 28, 1411. His body was brought back to Prague for burial.

Evidently Sbynco was not the man for the difficult post which he was called to fill. He had neither the learning of a theologian, nor the strong will and energy of an inquisitor. Of the strength of principle he had none. He adhered to Gregory till his struggle with Huss forced him, in self-defence, to abandon a sinking cause; and when he had taken the position of a judge, and imposed the interdict on Prague, he still regarded it in the light of a politic manœuvre by which a foe was to be defeated, rather than as a punishment for wrong. A man of expedients, he was fitted by nature only to be a martyr to his own vacillation.

[1] Mart. Anec., iv. 418–19; Fleury, xxv. 312; Godeau, xxxvi. 292.

CHAPTER VII.

HUSS AND THE PAPAL POLICY.

Archbishop Albic. — His Infamous Character. — Crusade Against Ladislaus, a New Firebrand. — New Position of Huss. — Cannot Depend on Wenzel for Support. — His Decision. — Ladislaus and Alexander V. — Succession of Balthasar Cossa to the Pontificate. — His Education. — His Infamous Life. — Excommunicated by Gregory. — Promotes the Council of Pisa in Revenge. — Rules the Council. — His Notorious Character. — His Coronation. — His Proceedings. — General Acquiescence in the Decisions of the Council of Pisa. — Death of the Emperor Robert. — Plans of John XXIII. — Seeks the Alliance of Sigismund. — Crusade Proclaimed Against Ladislaus. — Huss Opposes it. — Condition of Ladislaus. — His Attack on Rome. — Crusade Published.

Sep., 1411–Jan., 1412.

The death of Sbynco left the archbishopric of Prague vacant. The man who was selected as his successor was Albic of Unitzow, a Moravian by birth, who had been the king's physician, and who, after attaining some reputation as a medical author, had but recently aspired after ecclesiastical promotion. He was already at an advanced period of life, and was a man by no means either fitted or disposed for controversy.[1] Indeed, the character of a new dignitary was such as to reduce his influence to a mere cypher.

The king, without waiting for orders from Rome, had elevated him to the vacant post. He wanted one to fill it who would give him no trouble; one

[1] Fleury, xxv. 312; L'Enfant's Pisa, ii. 92.

who would not venture to come into collision with the royal policy. But in the selection which he made he overshot the mark. Albic was too contemptible to stand even as a *nominis umbra*. All the writers who mention him speak of him in the same terms. His ignorance of theology was gross in the extreme, and yet his avarice was more gross than his ignorance. He seemed to embody in himself all that was mean and sordid. His miserly spirit made him mistrustful, and rather than leave the keys of his cellar in the hands of a butler, he carried them about with him. The cooks whom Sbynco had left in the episcopal palace were somewhat too profuse in their expenditures. Fearful of becoming impoverished, he discharged them. A toothless old woman, who ate only vegetables and drank no wine, was found to preside over his kitchen. His greedy avarice made the sight of a loaded table obnoxious. He grudged the expense of it. The music he loved best was that made by the picking and crushing of bones, for in this there could be no waste. He had rather hear a cry, than the noise of the cattle feeding the whole night long.

And yet his house was like a tavern or market. He sold wine, meat, provisions, game, in fact the best he had, for the large price it could bring him, hoarding the money in his coffers, and leaving the poorest and most meagre portion of his produce for his table and the few servants who could be induced to live with him. His stable and equipage were reduced to conformity with the style of his table.

Albic is said to have purchased his office of the

king. The known character of Wenzel renders the report not improbable. Galeazzo of Milan bargained with him for a dukedom, and the citizens of Nuremburg purchased release from allegiance to him by a few hogsheads of his favorite wine. Certainly he would not be troubled with conscientious scruples in a less secular traffic, in which popes and prelates furnished him authoritative precedents. It is only the avarice of Albic that tends to redeem the character of Wenzel from the charge. But Albic was too contemptible to both parties to be of any account in the estimation of either. Nobody respected him. His enemies had nothing to fear from him if they simply left him to himself. His friends, if he ever had any, would be shamed and burdened by his alliance. The office of archbishop of Prague, which ranked him as primate of the kingdom, prince of the empire, and legate of the See of Rome, was so inefficiently discharged, and so evidently and scandalously disgraced, that it became an absolute necessity to put it into more capable hands. The pope selected Conrad of Westphalia, dean of the Vissehrad, sub-chamberlain of the kingdom, and bishop of Olmutz in Moravia, to take the oversight of ecclesiastical affairs at Prague. It was not many months before Albic sold out his rights to Conrad, and relieved himself from the notoriety of a position that served merely as a pedestal for his infamy.

Meanwhile events had occurred which were to give a new aspect and a deeper interest to the struggle in which Huss was engaged. On September 9th, 1411, John XXIII. published a bull of no little significance,[1] which was to kindle anew the smouldering fires of controversy at Prague. The papal legate, who bore with him to the newly appointed primate the sacred *pallium*, was directed also to publish this bull upon his arrival. In this celebrated document, John XXIII. poured out the vials of his bitterest wrath and vengeance upon his political and ecclesiastical foe, King Ladislaus of Naples, and ally of Gregory XII. The curse of the ban, in its most awful forms, was pronounced upon him. He was declared to be a heretic, a schismatic, a man guilty of high treason against the majesty of God. As such, a crusade is proclaimed for the destruction of his party, and full indulgence is granted to all who should take part in it. Those who bear arms personally are to be assured, on repentance and confession, of full forgiveness of their sins; and those who should contribute in money the amount which they, if actively engaged, would have expended themselves in the course of a month, are to share the same favor.

The papal legate was suspicious lest Huss should oppose the bull. He requested Albic to summon Huss before him, and, in the archbishop's presence, demanded whether he would obey the apostolical mandates?[2] Huss did not hesitate for a reply. He declared himself perfectly ready to obey them. "Do you see," said the legate, turning to the archbishop, "the Master is quite ready to obey the apostolical mandates." "My lord," rejoined Huss, "understand me well; I said I am ready with all my heart to

[1] Mon. Hussi. i. 171. [2] L'Enfant. iii. 93.

obey the *apostolical* mandates; but I call *apostolical* mandates the doctrines of the apostles of Christ; and so far as the *papal* mandates agree with these, so far will I obey them most willingly. But if I see any thing in them at variance with these, I shall not obey, even though the stake were staring me in the face."[1]

Other questions, it was clearly evident, were now, for a time at least, to be overshadowed by the more engrossing one excited by the publication of the papal bull. It was plain that Huss was not disposed to pass it over in silence. From his pulpit in Bethlehem chapel he would take his full share in a discussion that was to agitate the kingdom.

We are now, therefore, to consider Huss as occupying a new position, and one more arduous than any which he had ever occupied before. He was to come in direct conflict with the papal authority, and the issue was to be the refutation of pontifical logic and morality, the exposure of pontifical baseness and iniquity. Up to this time, notwithstanding his excommunication and the bitter opposition of the clerical party, he had been sustained in part by powerful external aid. He was strong not only in the affections of the people, but his cause had received at least the silent support of the king. So long as there were but two rivals to contend for the popedom, and Gregory, whose party Wenzel had to thank for his deposition from the imperial throne, was one of them, it was easy to divine that the course of Huss, so far at least as the king was concerned, was sufficiently safe. But the aspect of the ecclesiastical

[1] Mon. Hussi, i. 293.

world was now changed. The contest was no longer with Sbynco. It was no longer with Gregory. It was with the pope who represented the council of Pisa, and who had been acknowledged by the king, the nation, and Huss himself. It was a contest in which, not the vices of the laity, the avarice or luxury of the inferior clergy, or the follies of an archbishop were to be arraigned, but the very authority of the acknowledged head of the church was to be disputed. The feebleness and vacillation of Sbynco had given place to the sagacity and vigor of Conrad, and for politic reasons of his own—as we shall soon see—the king was not disposed to extend Huss any special favor.

The archbishop and the king therefore were now ranged together, and Huss himself stood committed to the policy that had advised the assembling of the council of Pisa, and that recognized Alexander V. and John XXIII. as legitimate popes. In these circumstances, so different from any in which he had been previously placed, his courage was to be put more severely to the test. Should he speak, or keep silence; should he silently approve, or openly rebuke the iniquity of the pontiff himself? Should he venture to raise his single voice of protest against pontifical vice and impiety, when all, or nearly all his former powerful supporters were, by their fears or the necessity of their position, arrayed in the ranks of his adversaries? In the emergency that arose, Huss did not hesitate—did not tremble to speak his convictions. No ordinary courage would suffice for an emergency like this. The boldness and consistency of many who had hitherto stood by him were to be put to the test and found wanting. Those toward whom he had looked with deference—some who had hitherto been his bosom friends—were now to desert him. They could not be relied upon in the present crisis. Perhaps the one on whom he had placed the greatest reliance was his teacher at the university, Stanislaus of Znaim. For years he had been foremost in expressing his sympathy with Wickliffe. He had commended his writings. He had volunteered to defend them in public disputation. Indeed, the estimation in which the writings of the English reformer were held by Huss, had been ascribed to the influence and teaching of Stanislaus. At a mock mass got up by the Germans in contempt of the Bohemian party, the genealogy of Christ was thus travestied: "Peter of Znaim begat Stanislaus of Znaim; Stanislaus begat Stephen Paletz; Paletz begat Huss,"[1] thus intimating the spread of Wickliffism from one to another.

But the time had come when these, his most trusted associates, were first to waver, and then desert him.[2] Most men would have felt it a matter of prudence to fall back in their company. But Huss could not do it. He would not even keep silence. Boldly did he speak out. A crusade! What was it? Huss asked himself the question. And he gave the answer to it in Bethlehem chapel. He dared to say what he thought of a measure which travestied the fundamental principles of the gospel, and scandalized all Christian minds.

[1] Mon. Hussi, i. 256. [2] Ibid, 265, 289.

But to understand fully the circumstances of the crusade, and the position of Huss, we must trace the progress of events at the papal court, and note some of the prominent characters that now appear upon the stage.

While the intelligence of the election of Alexander V. was spreading over Europe, and was received according to the various views and feelings of parties in the church, Ladislaus of Naples, the ally of Gregory and the enemy of Alexander, was not idle. The new pope was disquieted by his movements and intrigues. Before leaving Pisa he fulminated a bull against the Neapolitan monarch. It bore date November 1, 1409. In this document he inveighs with severity against "Ladislaus, son of Charles of Durazzo, who dared to call himself king of Sicily." "Nourished by the milk and fed by the substance of the Romish church, he was crowned by Boniface IX. king of Naples and Sicily. Having abused his power to the prejudice of the church, he was excommunicated by Innocent VII., with whom, in the hope of his being converted from his evil ways, he was afterwards reconciled. But his usurpations still continued. In spite of his oath, and under pain of excommunication and deposition, he violated his promise not to lay hands on the patrimony of the church and the neighboring states. He had, moreover, rejected the council of Pisa, legitimately convoked: instead of returning to his duty, he had become the greatest enemy to the peace of the church, as well as a most dangerous favorer of heresy, by his adherence to Gregory; offering continued molestations to the papacy and the church, and traversing in every way the designs of the council." The bull then recounts his still more grievous occupation of Rome, and regions belonging to the patrimony of St. Peter. Under severe penalties he had forbidden his subjects to recognize Alexander as lawful pope, or render him any aid whatever. He had taken Gregory from the Venetian territory to conduct him to Rome, there to have him recognized. In view, therefore, of the grievous crimes of Ladislaus, his violation of his oath, his invasion of the territory of the church, and his conspiracy and intrigues against the council of Pisa, he is summoned on a fixed day to hear his sentence, by which he is deprived of his kingdom and of all other goods and rights.

The plague raged now at Pisa, and Alexander left it for Pistoia. Here he received the welcome news of the victory won by Louis of Anjou—on whom he had bestowed the investiture of the kingdom—over his hated rival. The league which had been planned at the council to crush Ladislaus, was taking effect. The armies of France were strengthened by the alliance of Florence and Sienna, as well as of Bologna, where Balthasar Cossa ruled with supreme authority. In Rome the allies had secret adherents. Paolo Orsini was at their head, and by his timely treachery Ladislaus was driven from Rome. Alexander received the grateful intelligence, and was exceedingly anxious to take immediate possession of the city. From this he was dissuaded by the cardinal, Balthasar Cossa, who urgently insisted that he should tarry with him at Bologna. Alexander reluctantly complied, for he owed his election at Pisa—so it was said—mainly to the artifice and intrigue of the subtle Cossa. At length, however, Alexander resolved to set out for Rome. This was not agreeable to the plans and policy of Balthasar Cossa, who had played the tyrant long enough at Bologna, and was ready to supersede Alexander by putting the tiara on his own head. Two things, at least, are evident: first, that Alexander did not visit Rome, but died at Bologna, at the politic moment for the election of Balthasar Cossa as his successor; and secondly, that the latter, at the council of Constance, was openly and publicly charged with having poisoned Alexander V. to make way for his own election.

Balthasar Cossa, better known by his title of John XXIII., had been the ruling spirit of the conclave by which his predecessor had been elected.[1] His own name had been mentioned for that high office, and it was undoubtedly, even then, the fixed object of his ambition. But with well-feigned humility he commended to the choice of the cardinals a man who, already advanced in years, was, in spite of his reputation for learning and piety, his pliant tool, and who would hold the popedom as his lieutenant till he was ready to occupy it himself.

On the 14th day of May, 1410, the cardinal electors entered the conclave to choose a successor to Alexander V. The choice resulted, as might have been foreseen, in the elevation of Balthasar Cossa to the vacant office.

[1] Godeau, xxxvi., 299–309.

This man was the son of a Neapolitan noble, of high rank but of limited wealth.[1] From his youth he was destined to the church, but his enterprising and adventurous spirit turned from it with disgust. The stirring scenes of a secular ambition were more to his taste. He thirsted for worldly power, pleasure, and distinction, and preferred the battle-field and the sword to the cloister and breviary. The occasion which he sought was not long in offering itself. In the wars that had arisen between Ladislaus of Naples and the rival claimant to that crown, Louis of Anjou, his active disposition found a sphere for its enterprise. With some of his brothers, who shared his tastes, he equipped a vessel of war, and became a rover of the sea. In these piratical excursions, in which friend and foe stood much the same chance, he indulged those tastes and habits which clung to him ever after, and made his name an object of awe and terror. He is said here to have acquired the habit of wakefulness by night and of sleeping by day, which was confirmed by his nocturnal debaucheries, and which clung to him even after his election to the pontificate. At length, weary of this mode of life, or driven from it by the close of the war, he was forced to choose some new object of ambition. His attention was directed to his original destination. Ecclesiastical eminence offered a school for his aspiring efforts, and, with characteristic recklessness, he determined to pursue it. It made little difference to him whether he was a prince of the world, or a prince of the church. In fact, stripping off the ecclesiastical badges

[1] Fleury, xxv., 265–7.

by which the latter was distinguished, one might be mistaken for the other, and in either sphere might be found equal means to gratify the passions. At the age of twenty-five he repaired to Bologna, under pretence of pursuing his studies at the university, but in fact[1] with the design of making an academical degree his stepping-stone to ecclesiastical dignities.

But the reputation of scholarship he soon found to be too laborious an acquisition. His passions led him to the study of men rather than books. He was more fond of intrigues than the writings of the Fathers. As might be supposed, his literary progress was slow. Pontifical favor, he soon discovered, would open an easier path to promotion. He studiously gained the favor of Boniface IX., who rewarded his assiduous flattery and politic obsequiousness with the archdeaconate of Bologna.

The station was important not only for its large revenues, but as the rectorship of the university was connected with it. Still Balthasar's ambition was not satisfied. What he had tasted of pontifical favor gave him a keener relish for more. His appetite grew by what it fed on. The walls of Bologna furnished him too limited a sphere of effort, and he determined to visit Rome to see what his personal influence could effect with the pope. As he mounted his horse to go, some of his friends[2] asked him whither he was going. "To the popedom," was the reply. Boniface made him one of his cubicularii, or waiters at his chamber-door. This admitted him on terms of intimacy to the pope. It was the very post

[1] Fleury, xxv., 267.

[2] Platina.

which he would have preferred, for it made him largely a dispenser of pontifical favor. His recommendations were sought and amply remunerated. He urged the sale of indulgences to bring money into the pontifical treasury. He drove a thriving trade in simony, and enriched himself by his gains. He soon became apostolical proto-notary, and in 1402 was made cardinal. His abilities were acknowledged, and the next year he was selected by the pope as the fittest and ablest man to recover Bologna from the usurpations of John Galeazzo of Milan. Other reasons, not improbable, are assigned for the selection. His mistress was the wife of a Neapolitan, and Boniface wished to improve the occasion to send her back to her husband. The mission of Balthasar justified the pope's selection of him, by its successful issue. Bologna was recovered to the popedom. But she found that she had only exchanged one tyrant for another, if possible, more severe. Balthasar was by no means inferior to Galeazzo in the greediness of his passions or the intolerance of his oppressions, and he was full as able and politic a despot. The oppressed citizens complained to Innocent VII., who had, meanwhile, succeeded Boniface. Balthasar discovered the applicants who accused his tyranny, and confiscated their property to his own use.

To Innocent VII. succeeded Gregory XII. Balthasar was not regarded by the new pope with a friendly eye. The legate had prevented the pope's nephew from taking possession of a benefice which Gregory had conferred upon him in Bologna. Excommunication and interdict followed. But the disobedient legate maintained his ground. He reigned supreme in Bologna, and defied the pope. He scorned the excommunication, and resolved to brave the interdict. He commanded that all the sacred rites should be performed as usual. None dared to disobey.

Gregory and Balthasar were now sworn enemies. The latter had nothing further to hope from the former, and was ready to take the first opportunity to repay his hate. The council of Pisa furnished the opportunity. But as parties seemed so evenly balanced that a slight weight might turn the scale, Balthasar determined to see what he could do with Gregory. The pope met his advances and rejected his overtures with scorn. The die was now cast, and the tyrant of Bologna was to be reckoned among the reformers of Christendom. His influence contributed no small share to the favor with which the council was regarded. He induced Florence to permit the council to be held at Pisa—a most favorable position—which contributed much to the large attendance upon the council, and the respect with which its decisions were regarded. He not only secured the place of the Florentines, to whom it was subject, but gained their approval of the project, as well as that of the university of Bologna. At the council he contributed largely to the final result—the deposition of Gregory and Benedict, and the election of Alexander V. The last was his friend, and the man of his own choice. Already near the grave, death would spare him long enough, as Balthasar might imagine, for himself to perfect his plans of succession.

The result justified his expectations, although suspicions were awakened against him of having by foul means contributed to their fulfilment. In the council of Constance he was accused of having been of a wicked disposition from his youth—lewd, dissolute, a liar, disobedient to his father and mother, and addicted to almost every vice.[1] Among all the various enormities with which he was charged, that of poisoning his predecessor to make room for himself was almost overlooked. Alexander V. died on the fourth of May, 1410, after having held the pontificate less than a year. On the seventeenth of the same month Balthasar Cossa was elected, and took the title of John XXIII.

The character and past course of the new pope were so notorious that many apprehended what would follow. As described by his secretaries, the character of John XXIII. was a monstrous compound of all the vices that can make a man detestable and odious. While his great talents are admitted, they serve merely as a magnificent frame to a picture of correspondently enormous depravity. Neim speaks of him as "a monster of avarice, ambition, cruelty, violence, injustice, and the most horrid sensuality." A pirate in his youth, he was fitter for the trade of a bandit than the office of a pope. He made himself, in fact, Pontifex Maximus of the banditti of Christendom. "Many were scandalized at his election," says one who was present at his coronation.

This ceremony was observed in a style of ostentatious magnificence better befitting the lord of Bo-

[1] Bower, iii. 187.

logna than the chief pastor of the church. Monstrelet describes it with all the enthusiasm that might be excited by the coronation of an emperor.[1] The procession on the occasion was composed of twenty-four cardinals, two patriarchs, three archbishops, twenty-five abbots, beside an almost innumerable multitude of ecclesiastics. All were present in the chapel of Alexander V. when his successor received the holy orders of priest. The mitre of the pope was of vermilion, with a white border. The next day the pope celebrated mass, directed by one of the cardinals, who showed him the service—with which he was less acquainted than with the use of carnal weapons—while the marquis of Ferrara and the lord of Malatesta held the basin in which he washed his hands. The first of these had brought with him in his train fifty-four knights, clothed in vermilion and azure, and was accompanied by martial music. When the mass was celebrated, the pope was borne out of the church, and, on a platform that had been erected for the occasion, was crowned in presence of the immense assemblage. Seated in a chair covered with drapery of gold, the triple-crown was placed by the hands of the cardinals upon his head. When this ceremony was complete, he descended from the platform, was placed on a horse richly caparisoned, and, followed by all the dignitaries of the church, he marched in procession through the streets of the city. The Jews met him on the way as he approached their quarter, and presented him with a copy of the Old Testament. He took it, looked at it, and then

[1] Monstrelet, i. 146.

threw it behind him, exclaiming, "Your law is good, but this of ours is better." Wherever the pope went, he had money scattered in the streets for the people to gather up. The Jews pressed near, but the two hundred men-at-arms that followed, armed with clubs, beat them, says Monstrelet, "in such a way as it was a pleasure to see." Music accompanied them on their march. They then returned to the papal palace, where each, in his order, received the pontifical benediction and a dispensation for four months.

The election of the pope is said to have been nearly unanimous. It is easy to account for this. John XXIII. had dissuaded Alexander from returning to Rome, and upon his death at Bologna, where Balthasar was all-powerful, the latter knew that the election could be swayed in great measure by his will. An author of that age reports that when a dissension arose in the conclave as to the person who should be elected, they turned to him and requested him to say whom he would choose to have elected. "Give me the robe of St. Peter," was the reply, "and I will give it to him who ought to be pope." It was given him, and, throwing it over his own shoulders, he exclaimed, "I am pope." The cardinals found it wiser to dissemble their dissatisfaction than bring down upon themselves the power of a master.

Unquestionably the election was a forced one. Platina reports that soon after the death of Alexander, Balthasar gained over a large number of the cardinals by bribes, especially the poorer members of the college. He adds, that it was a current rumor that this election was the result of violent measures, and that Balthasar had stationed troops in the city and in the neighboring country, to ensure his election by force if it could be secured in no other way. His object was now attained—the object avowed by the archdeacon of Bologna when, mounting his horse to visit Boniface at Rome, he declared, "I am going to the popedom."

John XXIII. did not neglect matters proper to secure and extend his allegiance. He wrote a circular letter, and despatched it throughout Christendom, to notify all of his election. He renewed the sentence of the council of Pisa against the two rival claimants to the popedom, as well as their adherents, giving the last, however, six months' grace in which to return to his own allegiance. He sent an embassage to Benedict, to sound his views on the subject of cession. But that inflexible rival would listen to no terms. He claimed that the church universal resided in the fortress of Peniscola, where he had shut himself up and maintained his court.[1]

One of the first measures of John XXIII. was to revoke the obnoxious bull of his predecessor in favor of the mendicants.[2] The bull by which this was done bears date June 27th, 1410—scarcely more than one month from his accession to the pontificate. He knew how important it was at the commencement of his reign to make a favorable impression, especially in France, where the bull of his predecessor had effectually cooled the enthusiasm with which his election had been at first received. But the plans of the pope did not succeed. The university was dissatis-

[1] Godeau, xxxvi. 312. [2] Fleury, xxv. 247, 275.

fied at the moderate censure passed on the bull of his predecessor, and both were alike rejected.

At Rome the news of the election was received by the people with demonstrations of joy. They banished the enemies of the newly-elected pope, and defeated the invading army of Ladislaus. John XXIII. might now return and resume his dominion in the eternal city. The first year of his pontificate was eminently auspicious. Notwithstanding local dissatisfactions, as in the university of Paris, he was recognized by the greater part of Europe. The allegiance of Benedict and Gregory, respectively, was very limited. It seemed that at last the schism was in a fair way to be extinguished. The dissatisfaction which existed in Germany was limited, for the most part, to the emperor Robert and his personal adherents. We have already seen that Bohemia had regarded with favor the council of Pisa. To this result the influence of Huss had largely contributed. Of this he in fact afterward reminded the pope and cardinals, in his letter of remonstrance addressed to them from his retreat at Hussinitz, while the city of Prague was laid under interdict on his account.

At this opportune moment, death removed the emperor Robert from the scene. He was a prince not altogether destitute of merit. He was the son of Rodolph, elector of the Palatinate. By the death of his father, he became elector in 1398, and in 1400, on the deposition of Wenzel, was elected to the imperial crown. The adherents of Wenzel at Aix-la-Chapelle would not admit him to the city, where the Roman emperors were usually crowned, and the ceremony took place at Cologne. His reign was eminently peaceable, and he was regarded as a lover of peace. The ill success of his invasion of Italy, at the commencement of his reign, may have had some influence in contributing to the result. His death occurred within a few days after the election of John XXIII. to the popedom.[1]

It was at this time, also, that a victory was obtained over the king of Naples by the armies of Rome. The intelligence of the victory was most agreeable to the pontiff, and helped to swell the tide of his prosperity. But, though once defeated, Ladislaus was still a formidable foe. John XXIII. was too shrewd and experienced in policy not to guard against the recurring danger. He sought to strengthen the Italian league against Ladislaus, and draw into the alliance Louis of Anjou and Sigismund of Hungary, both of them rivals of the king of Naples. The former of these was already gained. It remained to secure the latter.

It was while these things were pending that the case of Huss was committed, as we have seen, to the Cardinal Otho de Colonna, who had cited Huss to appear at Bologna. The pope had now too many things on his hands to pay it special attention. Italy was a scene of anarchy and conflict. The Venetians were dissatisfied with the course of Sigismund, and traversed his designs. John Maria Galeazzo, Duke of Milan, a monster of cruelty, and one of the most terrible scourges under which an oppressed people ever groaned, had been cut off by a conspiracy, the

[1] Fleury, xxv. 272.

conflicting elements of which coälesced long enough to strike down by the hand of violence a common foe, whose severity was more horrible than their rival ambitions. The party of the Guelphs siding with the pope, and of the Ghibelines inclining to the emperor, enough at least to give the appearance of principle to a faction whose object was power and plunder, added to the general confusion. Bands of marauders and armed banditti, mostly soldiers of fortune, ravaged the impoverished country without restraint, while Ladislaus from Naples menaced the states of the church with the terror of his arms. Italy was a caldron of civil tumult. The seething elements invited the necromantic skill of the depraved wretches who sought to control them. The resource of John XXIII. was in the terrors of excommunication, which he had himself braved while governor of Bologna. He proclaimed a crusade against Ladislaus, and put his kingdom under interdict. Is this, asked Huss, an act worthy of the common pastor of all Christendom? Bishops are required every Sabbath to read the bull of excommunication against Ladislaus. Christians are summoned, in this personal quarrel between the pope and king, to march against the latter and dethrone him. For this they are promised the forgiveness of their sins, and eternal salvation. Is the shedding of blood then to procure the remission of sins? Is it Christianity, is it gospel, to incite Christians to war upon Christians?[1] Such was the language of Huss in Bethlehem chapel. Jerome powerfully supported him. For a time a large num

[1] Mon. Hussi, i. 190.

ber of the teachers of the university urged the same views. But the interests of Wenzel allied him to the pope, and his hope to recover the imperial throne through pontifical influence would not allow him to resist the measures taken by John XXIII. to promote the crusade. His decision silenced the opposition of the university. Few dared to speak what they thought, while king and pope were both against them. But Huss, if he felt the restraints of the magistrates in the discharge of his public duties, was busy with his pen. Indeed, the course of the pontiff himself would not allow him to rest. It was not enough that one crusade had been proclaimed. Another, more bitterly provoked, was soon to follow, as if to keep up the agitation.[1]

In the commencement of hostilities between Ladislaus and the pope, the king of Naples had been simply excommunicated. In these circumstances the war had continued, with intervals of inaction, for many months. Ladislaus seemed to bear his sentence with great equanimity. With the lawlessness of a bandit and the faithlessness of a pagan, he was a fair match for the pontiff. But for the mischiefs of the war, it might not have been a bad spectacle to see the two men cope with one another. The excommunicated king, however, was a standing monument of the weakness and disgrace into which the papacy had fallen. He illustrated in his own person the degradation of its authority.

Two centuries earlier his case would have probably been a hopeless one. And, indeed, now the

[1] Mon. Hussi, i. 173.

terrible scenes of the crusade against the Albigenses had hardly passed from the memory of men. At that time the word of a pope had changed the South of France from a garden to a desert. Raymond, Count of Toulouse, suffered the humiliation of a public flogging in the church of St. Giles. His whole province was given up to pillage. His subjects were murdered by the wholesale, in almost unresisting submission. The fanaticism and cruelty of such a crusade were terrible.

Ladislaus had not indeed the same grounds for fear as the prince of Toulouse. The papal schism had largely broken the spell of pontifical authority. But yet he much preferred a warfare in which army could be measured against army, steel against steel. The weapons of excommunication and crusade were of a kind he had no disposition to provoke, till he was able effectually to defy them. He was reduced to the necessity of a forced peace—a humiliating reconciliation which only covered the purpose of a bitter revenge, for the time deferred.

Watching his opportunity, he acquired a new ally. Genoa, impatient of the French yoke, revolted, expelled its garrison, restored the republic, and joined the Neapolitan party. The scale was now turned. The prince of Anjou, the ally of John XXIII., was defeated, and the pope was left exposed to a vengeance which he had bitterly provoked. Under pretence of subduing a rebellious subject, Ladislaus gathered a powerful army on the confines of his kingdom, and placed himself at its head. He began his march, but suddenly turned aside and presented himself before the gates of Rome. His galleys had already entered the Tiber, and the pope, struck with consternation at the sudden and well-concerted attack, had scarcely time to escape from his capitol, when it passed into the hands of his foe. The Neapolitan army entered, and a frightful scene ensued. Rome was sacked. For several days she experienced all the horrors which mercenary bands of soldiers could inflict.[1]

As soon as the pope could get his spiritual battery in order, he opened anew a terrible broadside in the shape of another "crusade" against Ladislaus. He summoned Christendom to his aid to crush the king of Naples, and ravage his dominions with fire and sword. Plenary indulgence was extended to all who should engage in the holy warfare. Those who should contribute money to assist the pope were assured of a full recompense in spiritual privileges. Some of the indulgences promised would vie in absurdity and blasphemy with any which, a century later, were offered by Tetzel.

To many, there was nothing surprising in all this. It was accordant with the usages of the papacy. But in the eyes of Huss it was a sin to be rebuked.

[1] Proctor's Italy, 140.

CHAPTER VIII.

BULL FOR THE CRUSADE AT PRAGUE.

The Constancy of Huss Tried. — His Procurators. — His Petition for Release from the Summons to Appear in Person at Rome. — The Crusade. — Controversy with John Stokes. — Affairs at Prague. — Disputation at the University. — Dean of Passau and Bulls of Indulgences. — Decision of the Theological Faculty. — Huss's View of the Crusade. — Wenzel Tolerates the Proclamation. — Preaching of Huss. — Meeting Before the Council. — Admonition of the Archbishop. — Notice of the Proposed Dispute Affixed to the Doors of the Churches. — The Discussion. — Jerome's Speech. — Second Meeting of the University. — Indulgences Derided: a Practical Joke. — Interruption in the Churches. — The Offenders Before the Council. — Huss Intercedes for Them. — Reply. — Popular Commotion. — The Execution. — The Funeral. — Depression of Huss. — He is Enjoined Silence. — A Trying Period. — Anxieties of Huss. — Change in the Views of the King. — Reasons of it. — Sigismund's Position. — His Aspirations for the Imperial Crown. — His Election. — Anecdote. — His Character. — His Aims. — Wenzel's Exclusion from the Imperial Throne. — Other Reasons for his Change of Policy.

Jan., 1412–July, 1412.

It was in such circumstances,—a crusade proclaimed by the supreme pontiff against Ladislaus—the imperial throne vacant by the death of Robert—Wenzel anxious to recover, in part through the influence of the pope, his lost sceptre,—that the courage and constancy of Huss were put to the test. The policy of Wenzel forbade opposition to the papal measures. To risk the imperial crown by allowing too free criticism of the proclamation of the crusade, was, in his view, an act of folly. Huss could no longer depend upon the royal favor.

His cause was still in the hands of the papal commission. Some of his procurators had been arrested and thrown into prison. One of them, Jessenitz, had managed to escape. Another, a former teacher, and subsequently an opponent of Huss, Stanislaus of Znaim, had been suspected of heresy for his former defence of Wickliffe, and a tract which he had written on the subject, and was compelled to justify himself before he was released.[1] The other procurator was Stephen Paletz. Both of them appear to have been thoroughly frightened by their imprisonment, and they were set at liberty only after a period of eighteen months, during which they were kept in duress, and then even only through the urgent remonstrances of the king and of the university.

It was soon after this (September 1, 1411) that Huss made a solemn declaration of his views and intentions, or perhaps it might be called a confession of his faith, and, in a tone of becoming humility, petitioned the Holy See to be released from the summons of personal presence at Rome, as well as from the consequences of the process against him. This declaration was read before a full meeting of the university.[2] In it Huss maintained that not one jot or iota of the law of Christ could pass away—that Christ's holy church is founded on the rock; and he solemnly declared that it had never entered his mind to wish to do or teach any thing in opposition to the law of Christ or the holy Catholic church. He

[1] Huss says that Stanislaus was vexed and spoiled by the Roman court, and was forced to write out a refutation of his own views before he was released from his imprisonment. *Mon. Hussi*, i. 287.

[2] Helfert, 105. Neander, v. 274, gives the substance of this confession.

finally disculpated himself from various errors which he said had been falsely imputed to him, and which no one was further from approving than himself.

This declaration and petition was on its way to Rome, when it was met by the proclamation of the crusade issued by the pope a few days later. (September 9, 1411.) It might have been supposed that at such a juncture, and anxiously desiring a favorable response to his petition, Huss would have been more than usually cautious or reserved. So far from this, in less than two weeks after the meeting of the university, we find Huss in a spirited controversy with the Englishman, John Stokes, in regard to the writings of Wickliffe.[1] Stokes was not particularly successful in his part of the discussion, if we may judge from his proposal that the scene of debate should be transferred from Prague to Paris, Rome, or Oxford. The friends of Huss, on the other hand, held that if Stokes had anything to say or produce against Huss, he should bring his evidence or arguments against him in the place where he resided.

Intelligence of the crusade must have reached Prague about the last of September (1411). Huss at once freely and boldly discussed the papal iniquity. Paletz as yet adhered to him. He admitted that there were "palpable errors" in the papal bull.[2] The minds of men were shocked at the summons from Rome to Christian nations to take the field against their brethren. In the choice between John XXIII. and Ladislaus, good men would have found

[1] Mon. Hussi, i. 108.

[2] Ibid. 265. Huss says that in his controversy with Paletz, "Jam rebus dismissis conversus es ad signa vel terminos, retrocidens sicut cancer."

it hard to decide. It was difficult to say which was the more selfish, unprincipled, and abandoned. It is probable, however, that John XXIII. would have won the palm of audacious wickedness, on the simple ground that Ladislaus wore only a crown, while he disgraced the tiara.

Early in 1412 it was manifest that the spirit of Huss was fully aroused. At one of the regular disputations of the university, Huss maintained that the great Antichrist, which according to the word of God was to come at the end of the world, was even now in possession of the highest dignity of Christendom, and exercised transcendent authority over all Christian people, clerical and lay, and that he is in fact no other than the pope of Rome. Hence Christians are not to obey him, but, as the chief enemy and grand opponent of Christ, they are rather to resist him. Huss subsequently published his argument.

In the month of May, the dean of Passau, the papal legate, reached Prague.[1] He brought with him the papal bulls of indulgences. Neither the worthless Albic, who had received the pallium from Rome, nor the king, placed any obstructions in the way of the legate. Albic merely stipulated—and his very sordidness on this occasion appears almost as a redeeming feature in his character—that it should not be prescribed at the confessional what portion of his property each should give, but the matter should be left to the free will of the individual. The bulls were read from the pulpits in the various

[1] Helfert, 109.

churches of Prague; the crusade and indulgence preachers gathered the people at beat of drum, in public places in the city, and three boxes were placed,—one at the cathedral, another at the Tein church, and another at the Vissehrad,—to receive the money that might be contributed by the faithful.

The theological faculty of the university could not entirely ignore what was taking place around them. They met and deliberated, but came to the sage and safe conclusion to obey the orders of the king and the directions of the archbishop, receiving the papal bull without committing themselves to any decision in regard to it—a matter to which they were not called. This was the view of Paletz, who at this juncture separated from Huss.[1]

This tame and cowardly conclusion dissatisfied Huss. He felt for the honor of the law of God, for the cause of his native land, and the souls of his countrymen. His spirit within him glowed with the resolute purpose to unmask the false pretensions and iniquitous principles, not only of the crusade, but the bull of indulgences.

He regarded with indignation this unscrupulous act of the pope. He saw in it the prostitution of sacred interests to the interests of a personal ambition. He pronounced it an act of malignant and antichristian usurpation, and he felt called upon to meet it with a public rebuke.

[1] "Nolumus nec attendimus attentare aliquid contra Dom. Apostol. aut suas literas, aut eas quovis modo judicare vel definire, cum ad hoc nullam auctoritatem habeamus." This was the position—a non-committal one—first taken by Paletz, according to Huss. —*Mon.* i. 175.

Nor could it be objected to him that, as a foreign matter, it was one in which he had no interest. It was brought home to his own city and his own doors. The pope's bull, which he sent through Europe, required, as we have seen, every bishop on the same day to make proclamation of the excommunication against Ladislaus. It summoned, moreover, all Christians to march to his help, or assist him with levies and gold, in return for which he promised the plenary remission of sin, and eternal salvation. It was in consequence of this command that the boxes were placed at commodious places to receive contributions of money in behalf of the crusade. The preachers exhorted the people to liberality the more earnestly, that they did it under the eyes of the papal legate. Several of the university disapproved these measures till the king had extended them his sanction. This was not long wanting. The motives that led to it may easily be understood.

The acquiescence of the king gave a new strength to the papal party. Wavering minds were decided by it. But Huss and Jerome looked to the will of a higher monarch. The permission granted by the king, on their views and plans of action had no effect. In the lecture-room of the university, as well as in Bethlehem chapel, Huss denounced the papal measures. He maintained that it was an antichristian procedure to spur Christians on to war with Christians, and, with a view to shedding of blood, to sell indulgences for money. The course of Huss, as might have been expected, made him bitter enemies. The city was divided into opposite and hostile parties. The council of the king summoned before it the antagonist leaders—among them Huss and Stephen Paletz. Huss disputed before the council, and manfully maintained his views. His enemies could not deny the honesty of his convictions, or refute his arguments. But the council were not prepared for any decisive action. They dismissed the parties merely with the charge to treat one another kindly. The archbishop admonished Huss to obey the pope.[1] He received for answer, that he would do this only so long as the commands of the pope were in accordance with the teachings of Christ and his apostles. Huss demanded to be met by other arguments than counsels to a blind obedience. With the feelings of a patriot and a Christian, he could not see his countrymen betrayed to death and the gospel trodden under foot without remonstrance. The blood of his friends and neighbors was required to be shed. The small revenue of an impoverished people was to be exhausted for the foreign interests of an individual.

In June, 1412, he affixed to the doors of several churches and cloisters the notice that on a certain day, June 7th, he would publicly dispute on the following question: "Whether it is according to the law of Christ, and a profitable thing, that Christian believers, with God's glory, the salvation of souls, and the welfare of the kingdom in view, should give their support to the bull of the pope, proclaiming a crusade against Ladislaus, king of Naples?" He likewise challenged all the teachers of the university,

[1] This may have been on the occasion previously mentioned.

priests and monks, to meet him with their objections.[1] The concourse to the discussion was immense. The common people crowded in to listen, in spite of the effort of the authorities of the university to exclude them under the pretext that they could not understand the matter.[2] Huss began by asseverating that he had commenced his investigations simply with a view to the glory of God and the good of the church, impelled by his conscientious convictions. For his authority he should abide strictly by the teachings of Christ and his apostles. He then adduces the grounds on which an affirmative answer might be given to the question. "It seems," he says, "that we are to approve the bull of the pope because he is one of Christ's vicars on earth, to whom he has said, 'He that heareth you heareth me,' because he has 'the power of binding and loosing on earth;' because he has the keys of the kingdom of heaven, and is the supreme interpreter of the law of Christ; because such bulls have always been received, and the present is intended for the support of the church, to reduce whose authority is to hinder the salvation of souls," etc.

He then turns to the negative side of the question, and finds still more weighty the arguments for rejecting the bull. First of all, the putting of men to death which it requires, and the exhaustion of nations which it occasions, cannot well be reconciled with the love of Christ. As to the remission of sins promised, he admits the priest has power to absolve the true penitent, but by no means in the man-

[1] Mon. Hussi, i., 173.
[2] L'Enfant's Pisa, iii., 94.

ner prescribed by the pope. He that is wise holds not merely that whoever confesses is absolved, but that he is absolved on condition of repentance, sinning no more, relying on God's mercy and the purpose of future obedience to God's commands. Of such a conversion of the sinner the priest has no means to judge but by a revelation; for none can attain forgiveness of sin but he who has attained from God, who alone can bestow pardon, the necessary grace. Huss holds, moreover, that neither the pope nor any of the clergy may bear arms and fight for the sake of riches or worldly dominion; for Christ forbade his disciples to do this; and such, moreover, was the view of the apostles and of the fathers of the church. "Tears and prayer are the arms of a bishop." The passage, Luke xxii. 38, commonly cited to show that the church has two swords, a spiritual and a temporal, can import no more than this, that these swords belong to the whole church, which is composed of laity as well as clergy, and the latter of whom are to use only the spiritual, or the word of God. It is ignorance to believe that we must obey the pope in all things, especially in regard to a bull expedited from such selfish views. One should rather, after the example of Christ and his apostles, endure wrong patiently, than spur on Christians to exterminate one another. Does any one say that these commands belong only to those that are perfect? Then the pope should be the most perfect among the clergy. After commenting on many monstrous passages of the bull, Huss replies to the grounds adduced for an affirmative answer. When, for example, the keys of heaven are promised to Peter, this means only a limited authority, while the loosing and binding must be performed of God, before, as spoken by men, it can have any validity. How could ignorant, licentious, and covetous priests, who, for a specified sum, receive indulgences from the commissary, really impart the same to the poor and the rich in proportion to this tax? How can Christians doubt that these robbers are thieves of Antichrist; and if such an one is the doorkeeper, how can he open the door to those that would enter into Christ? We can find nowhere in scripture that any holy man said to another, I have forgiven you your sins; I have absolved you: nor are they holy men who have granted absolution from punishment and guilt for so many years and days that we cannot even learn the time when indulgences sprung up. Among other remarks, he adds, that we are no more to fear unrighteous papal excommunication than the apostles were terrified by the ban of the synagogue. Nor does he leave any one in doubt that he altogether rejects the doctrine of papal infallibility.[1]

As Huss proceeded with his argument, some of the older doctors, Wolf, Goebel, and Leo, sought to convince him, by citations out of ecclesiastical and imperial law, that he was in the wrong. They prophesied disorder and murders as the result of his course. They advised him rather to go to Rome to dispute with the pope in person, and objected to his ingratitude for setting himself in opposition to him whom he might thank for his office as priest. Dr. Leo inveighed against Huss as too young a man to handle

[1] Mon. Hussi, i., 173–191.

such grave matters. At this the people began to murmur. Huss quieted them. But Jerome made a long speech in which he supported the reformer throughout, and closed with these words: "Whoever holds with us, let him follow us. Huss and myself will go to the council-house, and tell the council boldly to their face, that the papal bull and indulgence are iniquitous."[1]

The speech of Jerome was energetic, and made a deep impression. The attendant knights and citizens interrupted him with their applause. "This man speaks truth. Right is on his side," was the cry from every quarter.

It would have needed but a word to procure an immediate attack by the multitude on the council-house, where the friends of indulgences were deliberating. But, through the influence of their leaders, the disposition which might so easily have resulted in violence was with some difficulty restrained.

A second meeting of the university was soon called, somewhat less numerously attended than the first. It was more peaceably conducted. Huss and Jerome were urged to consider the danger into which the city would be thrown by popular insurrection or commotion. Both promised to guard against giving any occasion for it, although Huss added,[2] "Shall I then keep silence when I ought to speak? Will not the truth inculpate me—me who knew it, and out of fear abandoned it? Should my life be dearer to me than my duty?"[3]

[1] L'Enfant, iii. 95.

[2] Becker, p. 51.

[3] L'Enfant states that many Hussites engaged by mutual oaths to visit

Such was the position taken by Huss. He could not violate conscience or abandon principle. Yet he was anxious to prevent any popular tumult. As the congregation dispersed, admiring crowds followed him to the door of his dwelling. As they left him there, they cried out, at parting, "Huss, abandon us not. Remain firm."

Firmness was indeed necessary. The king could not be relied upon in the emergency. Even yet he dared not break entirely with the pope. The enemies of Huss were many and powerful, and bitterly exasperated. Some occasion for this was given perhaps by the imprudence of Jerome, urged on by his own impulsive nature. A few days after the disputation in the university,[1] one of the royal favorites, Wok Woksa of Waldstein, encouraged, as it seems, by Jerome and other masters, had got up a procession through the streets of the city designed to manifest the popular contempt for the papal bulls. Prostitutes, with certificates of indulgences hung around their necks, were made to head the procession, which moved, amid the shouts and cheers of the citizens, till it reached a pile of faggots heaped up beneath the gallows. Here, in contempt of the boxes designed to receive the money paid for indulgences, an iron box was placed, into which, while the indulgences

all the churches in which the indulgences were published, and withstand the priests while engaged in the publication; that the magistrates feared lest an insurrection should be the result; and that the rector of the university sent for Huss and Jerome, to urge them strenuously to guard against the violence and carnage which might result from their measures. It is said that both promised no longer to oppose the indulgences, but to observe greater moderation. Becker's account seems to me more in keeping with the character of Huss.

[1] Helfert, 119.

thrown upon the lighted faggots were consumed, were cast, as contributions, not gold or silver, but the most nauseous things, together with a satirical writing against indulgences.

The effect of this singular scene was scarcely such as Huss could have desired; but it perfectly suited the taste of Jerome, and doubtless of thousands of others. Still, it was not a little exasperating to the papal party. It tended to fan the flame which was already kindled to a fiercer heat.

Nor was this all. The very next day after the discussion had taken place, several of the young men most zealous in opposition to the papal bulls, determined that the ignorance and iniquity of the papal clergy should be exposed. There were multitudes among them who felt themselves capable of silencing the priests by arguments drawn from scripture. They resolved to visit the churches generally, and contradict every priest who should preach the indulgence.[1]

On one of the following Sundays, the preachers in several of the churches were rudely interrupted by students and artisans. They were boldly called liars and deceivers.[2] The pope was denominated Antichrist for having proclaimed a crusade against a Christian people. In the castle church, whilst the preacher assailed Huss with unmeasured abuse in the hope of restoring the doctrine of indulgences to its former reputation, a shoemaker from Poland, named Stasseck—or, as given by L'Enfant, Stanislaus Passec

[1] Helfert, 119, 120.

[2] So says Cochleius, 37, 38. His partisan prejudice must be taken into account.

—came forward and gave the priest the lie. A great uproar at once ensued. The offended party prevailed on the warden of the castle to take the offender into custody, and deliver him over to the civil magistrates. Similar disturbances occurred the same day at the Thein church, as well as at the convent of St. James. In the church, while the priest was commending the papal bull, he was interrupted by a student named Martin Krschidesco crying out, "Now it is plain that the pope is truly Antichrist, since he has proclaimed a crusade against Christians." In the convent, the vender of indulgences was expelled by another student named John Hudek. Both offenders were arrested, and, with the shoemaker, committed to the city prison.

From the known opinions of most of the members of the council, the worst was to be feared. There was no doubt that the prisoners would be punished with extreme severity. They were in fact sentenced to death as disturbers of the peace.[1] Intelligence of this was at once communicated to Huss. He hastened from the college to the council-house. Having obtained admittance, accompained by a large number of the professors and students, he earnestly entreated the magistrates not to punish the three inconsiderate youths with death. Their crime, he asserted, might be excused in some measure by their zeal for the gospel, and the great offence occasioned by indulgences, for if they deserved to be punished for the sake of the indulgences, he deserved it far more

[1] The sentence was based ostensibly on a decree of Wenzel, forbidding any to speak against the papal bull under pain of death.

himself. But the council had been wrought upon by the priests, and were deaf to his entreaties. They objected to him that this was no concern of his, and that he was mixing himself up in matters that did not belong to him. They suggested that it was his aim to set the city in an uproar, and that he had already injured it enough by the expulsion of the Germans. They said the question now was not in regard to indulgences, but concerning open violators of the public peace who had sought to produce bloodshed. Still they encouraged him to hope that favor would be shown them. They told him that as to the prisoners 'he and his friends might set their minds at ease. Their petitions would, either the following morning, or possibly the same day, be of some service to them.'

The report of the danger that menaced the prisoners had already spread through the city. More than two thousand armed men were in a short time assembled around the council-house. They were ready at a word to offer powerful and effectual aid for the release of the prisoners. But Huss was averse to violence. He only wished to save the lives of the three young men. Whether he understood the irony of the answer of the council or not, he suppressed the bitterness that he must have felt. He humbly thanked the senate for the promised favor, and, communicating it to the people, persuaded them to disperse. Scarcely was the danger passed, and Huss gone, than the scornful laugh was raised at his expense. The lords of the council declared him to be a deluded and credulous fool. Doubtless a bold bad man would have shown less scruple, and cut the knot by decisive measures. But Huss would not countenance violence, although he had been threatened with it himself.

He would by no means take the offenders out of the hands of justice. His own love of peace and order would not permit him to sanction their disturbance, and yet he could not willingly consent to a penalty so unjust as a capital infliction. He returned to his house in the cherished expectation that a just measure of penalty might satisfy all parties, and make a salutary impression.

But his hopes were doomed to disappointment. Scarcely had the crowd withdrawn and the streets been cleared, when the council, left unmolested, proceeded with its work. The executioner was admitted through a back door, and the prisoners were beheaded. But the foul deed could not long remain a secret. The blood of the murdered men flowed from the place where they were beheaded out into the open street, and told the story of their fate. In every part of the city old and young flew to arms. Grief and vengeance possessed all hearts. Nobility and students led on the people. The council-house fell into the hands of the assailants; but the principal object of their vengeance—the guilty judges—had fled.

The people's thirst for vengeance now gave place to bitter expressions of their grief. They sought out the place where the young men were executed, broke open the vaults which concealed the bodies, and into which they had hurriedly been thrown, wrapped them in rich shrouds, and, placing them on a gilded bier, bore them in solemn procession to the Bethlehem church. An innumerable train of mourners followed them, with waving banners and funeral hymns. They could not but regard the victims of this summary injustice somewhat in the light of martyrs.

Huss was deeply grieved at this melancholy issue of the affair. He felt the blow as a personal injury. Two of the victims were his own students. For eight days he was completely unmanned, and gave himself up to retirement and sorrow. Reviving at length from his depression, he preached a funeral sermon on the fate of the three youths.[1] In this he declared that such a death had more than compensated for all that was sinful and earthly in them, and had exalted them to the rank of immortal martyrs for the sake of gospel truth. "Henceforth," said he, "no communion can exist between the adherents of Rome and the Bohemian Christians;" but he conjured the weeping people to beware of using violence toward the enemy, leaving God to deal with their wicked malice and remorseless cruelty.

Notwithstanding this touching and Christian appeal, the magistrates forbade the preacher, under pain of severe punishment, to make even any distant allusion in public to those who had recently been beheaded. But if Huss was ready to comply, the seed he had sown in the cause of truth had been watered by the blood of its victims, and its harvest was sure.

[1] Helfert gives a somewhat different account of the execution. He represents it as public. The other accounts are as stated in the text.

The cause of reform could not die. The very rashness of the enemy had given it its martyrs.

But there were causes at work which were soon destined to operate in favor of Huss. Popular indignation at the extortions of Rome made itself manifest, and came to the knowledge of the king, while abroad the changed aspect of affairs destroyed in Wenzel the hope of recovering the empire, and indisposed him any longer to temporize with the pope. In order to understand the change which now took place in the royal policy, our attention must be directed to another quarter, from which new actors appear upon the troubled scene. Sigismund, second son of the emperor Charles IV., had received, in right of his wife Mary, daughter of Louis, king of Hungary, the throne of that kingdom. The position of Hungary made it the Thermopylæ of Christendom, and destined it to receive the first shock of Moslem invasion. In the terrible battle of Nicopolis, (1396,) where the proudest nobility of Europe, gathering to the standard of the Hungarian monarch, sustained so terrible a defeat, his hopes seemed to be blasted. But when, six years after, the arms of the invader yielded to the prowess of Tamerlane, and Bajazet was forced, in his iron cage, to grace the triumphant progress of the Asiatic conqueror, the good fortune of Sigismund seemed to be restored. Yet the course of events had caused him to take a deep interest in the affairs of Italy. The ambition of Ladislaus was insatiable. He is said, not improbably, to have aspired to the imperial crown. With some show of justice he claimed the crown of Hungary, where his childhood had been spent, and where he had been favorably regarded by Louis, the previous monarch. The debaucheries and cruelty of Sigismund, who at this time seems to have been no unworthy relative of his royal brother, had disgusted and alienated his subjects (1401). His person was seized, and a general revolt spread through the kingdom. At this opportune moment, Ladislaus, previously instructed no doubt by his partisans, appeared with a fleet off the shores of Dalmatia. Zara and several other maritime cities acknowledged his authority. He even received at the former place the Hungarian crown. But in the meantime Sigismund had recovered his liberty. His fickle palatines renewed their allegiance, and Ladislaus, defeated in his attempt, withdrew, and sold to the grasping ambition of Venice his recent conquests in maritime Dalmatia. Sigismund could not regard with favor either the spoiler or his jackals. The necessity of his position made him the friend of the enemies of the king of Naples.

Meanwhile John XXIII. had been placed by Ladislaus in difficult circumstances, and Sigismund and John XXIII. alike complained of his violence. The interests of the king and pope were the same. On the accession of the latter to the pontificate, Sigismund sent him ambassadors, the burden of whose complaint was the usurpations of Venice. The pope, anxious to secure the favor of the king, answered him by the promise of his influence in his behalf.

But the occasion had already come when that influence was to be exerted in another direction than the one proposed, and with a large measure of success. By the death of Robert the imperial throne was vacant. To the pope it was of immense importance that it should be occupied by one who would sympathize with him in his opposition to the king of Naples. He wrote to the electors, urging them to make choice of Sigismund for emperor. He represented to them his fitness for the place at the present crisis. The enmity of Sigismund to Ladislaus was, however, his chief merit in the eyes of the pope.

The persuasions of the pope were not without effect. They were powerfully seconded, however, by other motives. After the deposition of Wenzel, Sigismund, as the second son of Charles IV., seemed to have the clearest right to the imperial crown. Notwithstanding his dissolute habits, he had given proof of capacity and energy. When Wenzel, in 1393, was making himself at once the laughing-stock and curse of the empire, Sigismund, conspiring with several others, had seized and imprisoned him. In spite of a rival claimant, he had grasped and retained the dominion of Hungary. He had distinguished himself in his conflicts with the Turks, and had aspired to draw around him the strength of Christendom for their defeat. France had sent him her gallant knights, and those of them who survived returned to declare the shame of their own rashness and defeat in not listening to the wiser counsels of the Hungarian monarch.

The result of the election was the elevation of Sigismund to the imperial throne. It is said that, when the electors were assembled, and Sigismund was asked, first of all, in quality of king of Hungary, to make his nomination, he named himself. "I know myself," said he, "others I do not; I do not know that they would be as capable as I am to govern the empire, especially in this period of the schism of the church."[1] The electors, admiring the frankness of the king, or possibly overawed by his audacious impudence, unanimously gave him their suffrages. This must however have been after the death of Jodicus, who for ten months was a rival claimant of the imperial crown.

The character of Sigismund seemed to be a singular compound of that of his father and that of his brother, Wenzel. He had the subtility of the first, and the license of the last, except that his shrine was that of Venus rather than of Bacchus. Endowed with eloquence and energy, as well as possessed of a fine personal appearance, he lacked the more important qualities necessary to a perfect statesmanship. He was a man for the emergency, not for a settled and consistent policy. He sought to ride the wave, rather than provide for the voyage. He settled his disputes with Venice by the sale of Zara, thus imitating the policy of his foe. He compromised his disputes in other quarters in order to set himself at the task, toward which his ambition seems to have been more directed even than to the imperial crown, of giving peace to the church. We shall see in the sequel with what success.

[1] His language on this occasion, as given by Menzel, is, "There is no prince in the empire whom I know better than myself. No one surpasses me in power or in the art of governing, whether in prosperity or adversity. I, therefore, as elector of Brandenburg, give Sigismund, king of Hungary, my vote, and herewith elect myself emperor."

The schism stood in fact in the way of the execution of the great design which he had long cherished. So long as the church was divided by the dissensions which prevailed, Christendom was endangered by the Turk. If the anti-popes could be removed, and one be elected in their place who should be universally recognized, the mighty torrent of Moslem invasion might be met and turned back. Such a result would crown the name of Sigismund with imperishable fame, and wipe out the shame of the defeat of Nicopolis. If we see the emperor therefore turning against the pope, to whom in part he owed his election, and who promised to be his firmest ally; if we see him using his influence to dethrone him, and afterward shutting him up for years in prison, we may be prepared to understand the policy to which such results were due. It was this which led him to attempt the reconciliation of the knights of the Teutonic Order, and the king of Poland, by whom the former in several battles had been almost entirely prostrated in the year 1410. It was with a similar purpose, as well as undoubtedly to win the glory of having restored peace to the church, that a few months later he extorted from the reluctant pope the summoning, in conjunction with himself, of the famous council of Constance.

But Sigismund's election effectually excluded Wenzel from the imperial throne. He saw himself at once and effectually bereft of his last hope of recovering the Roman crown—the object for which he had intrigued with the council, and for which he had put forth all the energy which his feeble, irresolute, and self-indulgent nature allowed him to exert. It was no longer his interest to favor, in any special manner, the pontiff who had conspired with his brother to rob him of what he considered his hereditary right.

There were other causes, moreover, now contributing to a reaction in favor of Huss. The king, who was always the creature of circumstance, had at first accepted, or rather tolerated the papal bull. But he grew dissatisfied when he was told what streams of gold it was draining off to Rome—how the poor peasant who had no money sold his cow, till the popular genius of the country seized upon these facts and gave them expression in the street songs. He brought before him men who could testify to the truth of these things, and then dispatched them to Rome with a complaint against this traffic in indulgences. "Your dealers," says he to the pope, "where they are offered a span, take an ell; they promise heaven to all that will yield up their gold, and preach much else little likely to promote the salvation of the faithful. But while they deceive simple minds, they heap up great stores of wealth."

With all his faults, the king was not disposed to have his subjects abused by any but himself; and above all, he disliked to be troubled with petitions and complaints. The election of Sigismund removed the last chance for his recovery of the empire, and he had no longer any motive to treat the papal measures with any studied forbearance. In these circumstances, and with the influences of national feeling brought to bear strongly upon him, he abandoned the cause of the pope, or at least ceased to manifest any zeal in its behalf.

CHAPTER IX.

SECOND EXCOMMUNICATION OF HUSS. HE WITHDRAWS FROM PRAGUE.

EXCOMMUNICATION OF HUSS. — HOW HE WAS TO BE DEALT WITH. — BETHLEHEM CHAPEL TO BE TORN DOWN. — THE ATTEMPT DEFEATED. — THE CITY COUNCIL DIVIDED. — THE INTERDICT. — ITS LEGITIMATE EFFECT. — WENZEL'S DECREE REQUIRING DIVINE SERVICE TO BE PERFORMED AS USUAL. — THE DIVISION IN THE UNIVERSITY. — THEOLOGICAL FACULTY. — THE EIGHT DOCTORS. — HUSS STILL PREACHES. — LETTER FROM ENGLAND. — REPLY OF HUSS. — HE LEAVES PRAGUE. —HIS APPEAL TO JESUS CHRIST. — SUBSTANCE OF HIS COMPLAINTS. — MARTIN V. AND THE COUNCIL OF CONSTANCE. — GERSON ON APPEAL FROM THE POPE. — HUSS PREACHES IN THE CITIES AND VILLAGES IN THE OPEN AIR. — HIS VINDICATION. — AN INTERRUPTION. — LETTER TO THE CARDINALS. — REASONS FOR LEAVING PRAGUE. — BUSY WITH HIS PEN.

JULY, 1412–MAY, 1413.

THE time was at hand when Huss was specially to feel the need of the support of the king. There was no longer any hope of mercy at Rome for a man who had unscrupulously exposed the iniquity of the papacy and had sinned against its avarice. The issue of his case could not long remain doubtful. In July, 1412, John XXIII. committed the matter into the hands of the cardinal, Peter de Angelis, who decided finally to confirm the excommunication of Huss. To this conclusion he had been brought in part by the representations of the priest of St. Adalbert, in New Prague, Michael of Deutschbrod, or, as he is better known, Michael de Causis. No fitter tool of malice and intrigue could be found. He had defrauded the king and fled his country, and his character was that of a knave and a profligate. We shall meet him again at the council of Constance.

The terrible bull of excommunication was launched against Huss in the summer of 1412.[1] None might give him food or drink. None might buy of him, or sell to him. None might converse or hold intercourse with him. None might give him lodging, or allow him fire or water. Every city, village, or castle where he might reside was put under interdict. The sacraments could not be administered there. All religious worship was suspended there. If Huss persevered in his obduracy, his curse of excommunication was to be published in every parish church on every Sunday and feast day, with solemn tolling of the bells and the casting of lighted torches to the earth. If he died excommunicate, he was to be denied church burial; or, if buried in consecrated ground, his body was to be dug up again from its grave.

Nor was this all. John XXIII. gave significant expression of his bitter purpose to crush the reformer, in a bull proceeding directly from himself, in virtue of which the person of Huss was to be seized and brought before the archbishop of Prague or the bishop of Leitomischel, while the Bethlehem chapel was to be torn down and levelled to the ground, that it might no longer continue a den of heretics. No wonder that Paletz now broke entirely with Huss, and turned pale before such an array of spiritual terrors; that his course was such that Huss could say,

[1] Helfert, 122.

"he turned and walked backward like a crab." A worldly prudence invited him to abandon what seemed a desperate cause.

The Germans of Prague, bitterly opposed to Huss, undertook the execution of that part of the bull which had respect to Bethlehem chapel. On one of the festivals of the church, they assembled, provided with arms, and under the lead of a certain Bohemian, Bernhart Chotek, marched toward the chapel, where they found Huss occupying the pulpit. But here their new-born zeal was suddenly cooled by the sight of the immense assembly, which, although unarmed, inspired a healthful respect.

In the city council, whither they turned back to report their failure, a bitter discussion ensued as to what should be done. The Germans, who were in the majority, held that there never would be peace till the chapel was pulled down; but they dared not take the initiative in the bold measure. The Bohemian members were too resolute in spirit, although in the minority, to allow their opponents the hope of a peaceful issue. The two parties were forced to content themselves with mutual reproaches. The church party called the chapel, in derision, "The Church of the Three Saints," while the friends of Huss invented a new street-song to express their contempt.[1]

The ecclesiastical authorities adhering to John XXIII. endeavored to enforce the interdict. The bull of excommunication against Huss had been published, as far as possible, in all the parish churches;

[1] Helfert, 123.

but he still refused to leave the city, or abandon his pulpit. Nothing remained but to attempt to drive him forth by the most extreme terrors that spiritual tyranny ever devised.

It is true that this final weapon of pontifical vengeance was not what it had been centuries before. But even now it was not rashly to be braved. It was still formidable. Kings had bowed submissive before its terrors; and although the schism of the church and the views which Huss disseminated at Prague had, in many minds, deprived it of much of its authority, it was still not lightly to be contemned. We regard it now as the outrageous stretch of papal tyranny, a monument of that intensely vindictive malice which, for the offence of an individual, doomed a whole city or kingdom to the bitterest infliction. Aided by the superstitions of men, it seemed to grasp at once the powers not only of the present life, but of the life to come. During an interdict, the churches were closed, the bells were silent, the dead were left unburied, and no rites but those of baptism and extreme unction could be performed. All the economy of social and civil life seemed struck with a palsy; the wheels of enterprise and labor stood still, waiting for the guilty to depart, or die. Some few of the clergy of Prague may have had boldness to imitate the conduct of him by whom it was imposed, when, seven years before, as tyrant of Bologna, he had defied the interdict of Gregory. The greater number, however, would be awed to obedience by the papal authority.

It was at this critical moment that Wenzel interposed. Huss, from a sense of duty, refused to abandon his post or yield to an unjust excommunication. In fact, it is doubtful whether his friends, in the circumstances, would have allowed him to depart. Heedless of the interdict themselves, they experienced but little inconvenience from it. It did not close Bethlehem chapel, or seal the lips of Huss. Indeed, the blow was more severely felt by the papal than the reform party. The priests of the former, it is true, were, for the most part, well content with a state of things that did not much molest their indolence; but the people complained.

Wenzel issued a decree enjoining upon the parish priests attendance upon their spiritual duties, in spite of the presence of Huss within the walls. Any neglect of this order should be visited by a forfeit of salary. The decree wrought wonders. It counterworked the papal bull. The priests, many of them, returned to the discharge of their duties, although Huss still remained unmolested within the walls of the city.

Meanwhile, however, a division had sprung up in the university which threatened serious consequences. The students and masters were nearly unanimous in sustaining Huss; but the theological faculty had taken ground against him almost to a man.[1] The faculty was composed of the doctors of theology, several of whom had been, but a year or two before, his most intimate friends or his firmest supporters. Among them were Stanislaus, Paletz, Andrew Broda,

[1] Huss, however, complains that his eight principal opponents assumed to speak in behalf of the whole theological faculty.

and John Eliă. The time of danger had come. Stanislaus and Paletz had felt the claws of the lion. The others also had proved too timid to stand by their convictions in the hour of trial. Repeated conferences were held, but the division of sentiment was becoming more marked. Several discussions were held at Zebrak,[1] at which Huss was present, but with no favorable issue. A controversy commenced, which is to be noted hereafter, and which continued for quite a period, between the eight doctors, or a portion of them, on one side, and Huss on the other.[2] No Protestant reader at the present day will hesitate in his decision as to which side victory inclined.

Huss still kept his place in Bethlehem chapel, cheering the hearts and inspiring the zeal of his adherents. At this difficult and troubled moment, (autumn of 1412,) he received an encouraging letter from England. It was written by a Wickliffite named Richard, and spoke cheering words. Huss took it with him into the pulpit, and read it to his hearers. "See," said he, "our dearly beloved brother Richard has written you a letter full of cheer and encouragement."[3] Huss replied to it "in the name of the church of Christ in Bohemia, and in the name of the church of Christ in England," assuring its author that the king, queen, lords, knights, and common people in the cities and throughout the land, were holding fast by the true doctrine.[4]

It was not without some scruples that Huss had continued to remain at Prague. He felt that it was

[1] Helfert, 137.
[2] Mon. Hussi, 256–323.
[3] Helfert, 116.
[4] Helfert, 131.

perhaps wiser for him, for a time at least, to withdraw from its walls. To some extent, no doubt, the interdict was still enforced, and Huss bore it ill that any should suffer on his account. The king at length allowed, if he did not advise him to leave. There was no doubt that the cause he loved would still have able advocates. It would at least be manifest, if he withdrew, that it was not bound up in the person of one man, and was not dependent on his presence. At any moment when it seemed advisable, it was in his power to return, while the correspondence of his friends would keep him informed of whatever might occur in his absence. He therefore, toward the close of 1412, left the city, and Master Hawlik supplied his place in Bethlehem chapel.

He was not willing to depart, however, without clearly defining his position. He did not go from any regard for usurped papal authority, or unjust excommunication. On leaving the city, he drew up his third and final appeal from the sentence of the pope. His former appeals had proved vain. John XXIII. had excommunicated him. But there was another court left to which he might look, and one to which popes and emperors were amenable. "Almighty God, one essence in three persons, is the first and final refuge of all who are oppressed. He is the Lord, who keepeth truth forever, doing justice for those who suffer wrong, near to those who call upon him in truth, and condemning to destruction incorrigible transgressors. Our Lord Jesus Christ, true God and true man, surrounded by high priests, scribes, and Pharisees, his judges and their partisans, and willing to ransom by a bloody and shameful death from eternal condemnation, his children chosen from the foundation of the world, has given his disciples a noble example for committing their cause to the judgment of that God who has all power and knowledge, and who doeth whatsoever he will. Imitating his holy and great example, I appeal to God, who sees me oppressed by this unjust sentence and by the pretended excommunication of high priests, scribes, Pharisees, and judges occupying Moses' seat. I follow likewise the example of Chrysostom, who appealed from two councils; of the blessed bishop, Andrew of Prague, and of Robert of Lincoln, who appealed with all humility and devotion to the sovereign and infinitely just Judge, who can neither be intimidated by any fear, nor corrupted by gifts, nor deceived by false testimony. I desire that all Christian believers, especially princes, barons, gentlemen, vassals, and all the inhabitants of our Bohemian kingdom, should be informed, and moved to sympathy for the pretended excommunication launched against me by Peter, Cardinal Deacon of St. Ange, commissioned to do it by Pope John XXIII., at the instigation of my enemy, Michael de Causis, and with the approval of the canons of Prague. This cardinal, for nearly two years, has utterly refused audience to my advocates and procurators, though he ought not to have refused it to a Jew, a pagan, or a heretic. This same cardinal has been unwilling to accept my reasonable excuses that I alleged for a dispensation from appearing personally before him, nor has he made any account of the authentic testimony of the university of Prague. Whence it is evident that I have not incurred the guilt of contumacy, since it is not through scorn, but for valid reasons, that I did not appear at Rome when I was cited, as, first, because my enemies would lie in ambush for me on the road; then, because the dangers of others serve me for an example; again, because my procurators are engaged to submit to the trial by fire, against whomsoever at the court of Rome; and finally, because they have imprisoned my procurators, without any reason for it, so far as I am aware. So also, as it is established by all ancient laws as well as by the sacred books of the Old and New Testaments, and by canon law, that the judges are to visit the places where the crime has been committed, and there take evidence of the facts bearing on the accusation, of persons who are acquainted with the accused, and are neither his ill-wishers nor his enemies, men who are not impelled by malice, but by zeal for the law of God; and finally, as it is ordained by the same laws, that he who is cited or accused may appear in a safe place where he may be free to defend himself, and that the judge be not one of his enemies any more than the witnesses—it is plain that, all these conditions having been wanting, I am absolved before God from the guilt of contumacy, and discharged from this pretended and frivolous excommunication. I, John Huss, present this appeal to Jesus Christ, my Master, who knows, protects, and judges the righteous cause of every individual whomsoever."[1]

[1] Mon. Hussi, i. 236, etc. Also, L'Enfant's Pisa, iii. 85, 86.

This appeal of Huss speaks for itself. It shows us a man conscious of the wrong done him, calmly yet decidedly exposing it, and resting, in a faith which nothing could shake, on that final refuge of oppressed innocence—the justice of God. Some of his enemies objected to his appeal as unwarranted and impertinent. But no one can put himself in the circumstances of Huss, conscious of the honest integrity of his own heart, and not feel that it is the noble expression of a character and faith worthy of all honor.

Nor could it in that day be justly regarded as heresy to appeal from the pope. Urban VI. was pronounced by the cardinals who elected him to be apostate, excommunicate, Antichrist, ursurper, anathematized, the destroyer of Christianity. The cardinals of Gregory, but a few months before, had appealed from him to a general council. They called him a worthy co-laborer of his rival the anti-pope Benedict, his compeer in acts of violent outrage and iniquity against all Christendom. How different from the calm, unvindictive, but solemn appeal of Huss!

In the council of Constance, some years later, the declaration of the newly-elected pope, Martin V., that it was not permissible to appeal from the decision of a pope, was promptly met and sharply answered. John Gerson, ex-chancellor of the university of Paris, and a bitter enemy of Huss, could not suffer the declaration to pass in silence, or even seem to have the approval of the council. He asserts that others beside himself regarded the papal document in which it was inserted as tending to overthrow not only all the authority of the council of Pisa, but of that of Constance, and to render null all that they had done in deposing the intruding popes, or electing Martin V. himself.[1]

This declaration of the pope gave Gerson occasion for writing a treatise on the subject. He discusses the question, *whether it is permissible to appeal from the judgment of the pope, and in what case.* He opposes to the constitution of the pope the decree of the fifth session of the council, which makes the pope himself, as well as all others, in matters pertaining to faith, the extirpation of schism, and the reformation of the church in head and members, subject to the council. This decree Gerson supports on various grounds, some from scripture and some from reason. But the same reasons that exist for appealing from a pope to a general council equally fallible, might much better apply to an appeal from a pope or a general council to the unerring Judge, or at least to his revealed will. In the case of Huss there was no other resource. From the archbishop and the pope he appealed for the justice of his cause to the Judge of all.

But the expulsion of Huss from Prague only removed him to another sphere of action, where his influence was felt in the end as powerfully perhaps as in that city. He did not forget in his exile the principles he had avowed before the archbishop, and which had induced him to persist in preaching in Bethlehem chapel. They were equally powerful with him now. No place for him was too profane or sacred for holding forth the word of God. Throngs crowded

[1] Gerson. Op.

to hear, and were curious to see, a man who had been excommunicated, yet who spoke with the earnestness and fervor of an apostle; who had been driven out of Prague by the interdict, yet whose holy and blameless life shamed his persecutors. His eloquence was as effective in the open fields as in Bethlehem chapel. Poor peasants and proud nobles gathered around him, in the forests and the highways, to hear his forcible expositions and applications of the word of God. The rector of the university of Prague left the lecture-room and the academic halls to talk to the ignorant multitudes scattered over the land. Some might think of him as of Paul, "Much learning hath made thee mad;" but it was a learning that the humblest could appreciate; a learning that consisted in a thorough acquaintance with the word of God and the duties which it enjoined. From city to city, and from village to village, Huss pursued his apostolic mission. His hearers came in crowds from their homes, fields, and workshops. The impression made was in many cases deep and abiding. Years did not efface it. When Huss afterward was enclosed by prison walls in the city of Constance, there were thousands of his Bohemian countrymen, far distant from Prague, on whose hearts his memory was deeply engraven by the experience wrought within them through the words that were uttered now.

In his treatise on the church he has presented us with the vindication of his present course.[1] "The command that forbids me to preach is opposed to the words and example both of Christ and his apostles.

[1] Cochleius, 19; Mon. Hussi, i. 197–240.

Christ preached to the people on the sea, in the desert, in the open fields, in houses, in synagogues, in villages, in the streets; and the apostles preached everywhere, the Lord helping them. The command, moreover, is opposed to the interests of the church, in forbidding the word to have free course. It was for these reasons," says he, "that I appealed against the bull intended to silence me."

Removed from the immediate neighborhood of his most virulent and violent foes, the life of Huss was one of comparative quiet. Yet thrown, as he necessarily was, among such vast and incongruous multitudes, some among them acting as the spies of his persecutors, his words were not always received with unanimous applause. On one occasion[1] he was speaking in severe terms of the pope and cardinals, in the castle of a certain lord, when an old man, supposed to have been a priestly spy, assuming the appearance of great simplicity, asked him what those words *popes and cardinals* meant in the Bohemian language, and if he had ever seen one of them. "I never have seen them, and I have no wish to see them," said Huss. "But how comes it," asked the old man, "that you speak such bad things of people you have never seen or examined? For myself," said he, "I was a long time ago in Rome with my father; and I have seen the pope and some of the cardinals, and I found in them a remarkable piety." "Very well," replied Huss, "if they are so much to your taste, go back and spend the rest of your life with them." The old man shaking his head, answered,

[1] L'Enfant's Pisa, iii. 87.

"My Master, I am too old to undertake so long a journey, but do you, who are yet a young man, go and tell them to their face what you have said so comfortably of them in their absence, and you will see what answer they will give you." The lord of the castle, who had Huss under his protection, took him away with him, and imposed silence on the intruder.

In the works of Huss are found several treatises and letters that were written during this period of his retreat. One of the latter is addressed to the cardinals. In this he sets forth to them, with much mildness and modesty, that the occasion of his misfortunes and reproach must be his apology for addressing them and John XXIII. "At the time," says he, "when obedience was withdrawn from Gregory, and men joined themselves to the college of cardinals in order to give peace to the church, I urged this union in my preaching before the nobility, the clergy, and the people, with energy and success. But Sbynco, archbishop of Prague, then an enemy of the sacred college of cardinals, caused a prohibition to be affixed to the doors of the churches, forbidding all the doctors of the university, and me in particular, from performing any sacerdotal function, and alleging as the reason, that we had unadvisedly and wickedly abandoned Gregory. In consequence of this he was compelled, after the council of Pisa, to change his party and adhere to the decisions of the council." After having thus set forth facts which were incontestible, he prays the cardinals to remember the promise they had made, of according protection and favor to those who should unite with them;

and engages to give reasons for his faith, even at the peril of fire, before the university, all the prelates, and those who had been his hearers. He sends to them, moreover, the favorable testimony that the university of Prague had borne of him.

His letter was one well adapted to secure him a favorable hearing. But there was scarcely time for its perusal before affairs took a new shape, and Huss had nothing left to hope for from the pope or cardinals.

In some of his letters he states the reasons that had led to his withdrawal from Prague, and his retreat to his native village. "I feared," says he, "that my presence there would be the means of drawing down persecution on the faithful, and increasing the animosity and grievances of my persecutors." "My enemies reproach me," says he, "for having fled; but I have done so in imitation of Christ's example, and in obedience to his precept not to abandon the truth, for which I am ready to suffer death, God helping me, but from fear of being the occasion of the eternal damnation of the wicked and the affliction of the good." In his retreat he did not forget that example which taught him not only when persecuted in one city to flee to another, but in all places to speak as he was able, "all the words of this life."

It was during this retreat of Huss from Prague, that his pen was most busy. Released from the duties which occupied him in the university, and from the distractions which disturbed his mind at Prague, he had leisure for a more careful investigation and exposition of his views.[1] This leisure he improved by the use of his pen, and in all probability he thus effected as much or more than he would have done by remaining at Prague. In the after days of his persecution, the friends that clustered around him, that remonstrated in his behalf, that were ready to take up arms and risk their lives to defend his memory, were the country lords and knights, some of whom had, doubtless, become attached to him as their teacher at the university, while others had learned to love and revere the man, as they read in their feudal castles circulating copies of treatises from his pen.

The first portion of the period during which Huss was absent from Prague was spent chiefly at the castle Kozi-Hrádek, which belonged to the lords of Astie.[2] Here his work on the church, with the controversial treatises in its defence against Stanislaus and Paletz, was written. Much of his subsequent correspondence dates from Kozi. It was from this place that he wrote numerous letters to his fast friend, Christiann· of Prachatitz, rector of the university. Subsequently the noble knight, Henry of Lazau, offered him his castle, the stronghold of Cracowec, as a place of refuge. From this, as a centre, he went forth in various directions as an itinerant apostle, and tens of thousands improved the opportunity to hear the gospel from his lips.

[1] Helfert, 145. [2] Helfert, 148.

CHAPTER X.

HUSS IN RETIREMENT.

Foreign Prejudice Against Huss. — Council of Rome. — Incident of the Owl. — Complaints Against the Archbishop. — Futility of the Measures Against Huss. — His Work on the Church. — Question in Regard to the Validity of the Excommunication of Huss. — Jessenitz. — The Royal Court of France. — Views of Gerson. — Views of D'Ailly. — Appeal to Scripture. — Disturbances. — Derisive Songs. — Contemptuous Treatment of the Monks. — The Friar and his Relics. — Jerome and the Papal Indulgences. — The Provocation Given. — Three Antagonists of Huss. — Broda. — Stephen of Dola. — His Work Against Wickliffe. — Its Covert Attack on Huss. — Letter of Huss. — Treatise of Stephen, or "Anti-Hussus." — His Motives. — Conrad and the University of Paris. — "Counsel" of the Latter. — Synod of Prague. — Counter "Counsel" of Huss — "Counsel" of the Doctors. — The Theological Faculty. — Conrad Consults the Bishop of Leitomischel. — His Answer. — Futility of the Synod's Action. — Wenzel and his Measures of Reform. — Their Effect upon the Enemies of Huss. — His Absence from Prague. — His Language on the Humiliation of his Enemies. — The Cause of Reform Advances. — "The Missionaries" of Huss. — Demand in Bohemia for a General Council. — Other Reasons for it. — The Schism. — Doubts of D'Ailly. — Their Solution by Gerson. — Corruption of the Church. — Hungary and the Turks. — The Terror Inspired by Them. — A Council Summoned.

May, 1413–Sept., 1414.

The popular movement at Prague in favor of reform had now begun to attract attention generally throughout Christendom. It was discussed at Paris and Oxford as well as Rome. Everywhere Huss was reputed a heretic. His enemies, and they were many, had industriously circulated the most exaggerated reports in regard to his proceedings. With most his cause was already prejudged. Undoubtedly it contributed greatly to this result that his views were everywhere identified with those of Wickliffe.

To this impression the decisions of the council of Rome, held in 1412, gave renewed strength. John XXIII. was a shrewd tactitian, and readily perceived the advantage which he might derive from convoking at Rome the general council which that of Pisa had declared should be held within three years. He might preside over it himself in the very capital of the Christian world, and gain the prestige over his rivals.[1] Although its results disappointed his hopes, and a meagre representation of the church attended its sessions, the popular odium attached to the doctrines of Wickliffe invited the sentence which condemned them and all who favored them as heretical. The sentence carried indeed the less weight with it, that so few of the higher dignitaries of the church gave their countenance to the council, while those who followed the allegiance of the rival pontiffs found in its proceedings abundant matter for ridicule. During its session, according to Clemengis, an owl had made its appearance in the place of convocation, and, alighting on one of the rafters, could not be dislodged by sticks and stones thrown at it by the grave fathers of the council. Great was the consternation produced by its appearance, and the assembly broke up in strange confusion.[2] It was said by some, who relished an incident so ridiculous, that the Holy Ghost had come to attend the sessions, only he had taken the form of an owl instead of a dove. Still

[1] Fleury, xxv. 327.

[2] Fleury relates the story of the owl, with some embellishments, xxv. 329.

the decisions of the council in regard to the doctrines of Wickliffe had given them new notoriety, and the time and occasion of their condemnation aided to cast the odium of their heresy upon the proceedings of Huss. The commotions at Prague were ascribed to his teachings. The violence and insults offered to the clergy were exaggerated by report; and D'Ailly, who attended the council, testifies that he heard of them on his return from Rome, from the lips of some of the countrymen of Huss whom he fell in with on his journey. Foreign prejudice thus came to the aid of the party at Prague opposed to reform. John XXIII., moreover, wrote a letter to the king, in which, referring to the sentence of the council of Rome against Wickliffe, he urged the extermination from Bohemia of all who adhered to his doctrines.

But all these measures failed to secure their object. Huss[1] had left Prague; but he seems, on several successive occasions, to have returned, whenever he judged that duty required or safety would permit.[2] His absence, however, only provoked and exasperated the popular feeling. His friends complained that the pope and the archbishop had forbidden the preaching of the word of God and the gospel of Christ, and, by the indulgences issued by the Roman court and sanctioned by the bishop's consistory, sought their own selfish interests, and not those of Jesus Christ; that they took from Christ's sheep the wool and the milk, but fed them neither with the word of God nor holy examples. They insisted, moreover, that the commands of the pope and his

[1] L'Enfant. Council of Constance, 24. [2] Helfert, 145.

prelates were not to be obeyed unless they accorded with the doctrine and life of Christ and his apostles; that the laity ought to judge of the doings of the priesthood, for Peter was reprehended by Paul because he was to be blamed; and they laid down the rules by which, in any case, it might be determined whether the prelates were to be obeyed. As to papal jurisdiction, they treated it with scornful derision, pointing to the schismatic popes, each condemning the others, and condemned by them, yet unable to subject them to his obedience. In such circumstances, the processes of the papal court were powerless and nugatory.[1] They could not be enforced at Prague. Nor did the absence of Huss help to restore quiet. It only provoked to a bolder reprehension of ecclesiastical corruption and injustice, and aggravated the popular hostility to the measures of Rome. Nor did the friends of Huss shrink from discussion with the ablest members of the opposite party. Cochleius complains that the latter were assaulted by shrewd and various questionings on the part of men who were prepared to judge of doctrine for themselves, and paid little heed to judicial (ecclesiastical) decisions.

Meanwhile Huss, in his retirement, was busy with his pen. His enemies had driven him from Prague, but they had only forced him into a new sphere of activity where his influence was to be, if possible, more widely, at least more permanently felt.

His treatise on the church is the most elaborate and systematic of his works, and it was written

[1] Cochleius, p. 24.

at this period. The germs of it had long existed in his mind, and had been presented in his sermons in Bethlehem chapel.[1] But he now proceeded to develop them in a more concise and connected method. It is from this work mainly that his enemies drew the materials upon which to base their charges against him; and it was of this that cardinal D'Ailly remarked, at the council of Constance, that, through an endless multitude of arguments, it attacked the papal authority, and the plenitude of the papal power, as much as the Koran did the Catholic faith.[2]

Huss showed in this work the strong influence exerted over him by the writings of Augustine. He divides the human race into two classes, with reference to their final destiny,—the elect and non-elect, or the saved and lost. The elect or predestinate, of all times, compose the one true Catholic church. Of this body Christ alone is the one and all-sufficient head. He is himself the rock, as he declared to Peter, on which he would build his church. The church is his mystic body, his bride, ransomed by his blood, that it might be blameless, without stain or wrinkle. The living who are predestinate, compose the church militant so long as they are here on earth. They strive against the world, the flesh, and the devil. Those in purgatory compose the sleeping church, and the saints in their eternal home in glory the church triumphant.

The visible church, or the church as to its external aspect, embraces two classes. There are those in it who are not of it, just as the human body may have its wens, excrescences, or parts superfluous. There are

[1] Mon. Hussi, i., 297–255. [2] Gerson, Op.

some who are truly predestinate, real believers, obedient to Christ. There are some who are thrust out of the visible church by the power of Antichrist, who are yet members of it. Others are nominally members, but yet are hypocrites; others still, neither in name nor reality, pertain to it.

The church, externally viewed, has in it good and bad, predestinate and reprobate, wheat and tares. Some are to be gathered to the heavenly country, others are to be burned with the fire unquenchable. The reprobate are symbolized by the foolish virgins, by the guests who refuse the invitation to the marriage, the barren tree, the worthless fishes.

Christ is the sole supreme head of the church, the true pontifix, high priest, and bishop of souls. The apostles did not call themselves the heads of the church, but servants of Christ and of the church. Even Gregory would not allow himself to be called universal bishop.

But after this came a change. Till the donation of Constantine, the bishop of Rome was but the peer of his brethren. Later emperors confirmed the donation, and the pope has since claimed to be the head of the church militant, and vicar of Christ on earth, so that, in a certain sense, the church on earth has three heads,—Christ as God, Christ as incarnate, and his vicar for the time being.

But in truth the pope is no more a successor of Peter, than the cardinals are successors of the apostles. He is only to be considered Christ's and Peter's successor and vicar, when he resembles Peter in faith, humility, and love; and cardinals are successors of the apostles only when they emulate their virtues and devotion. But this same might be said of others who have never been popes or cardinals. St. Augustine was of more service to the church than many popes, and than all the cardinals from the beginning until now. Were not Jerome, Gregory, Ambrose, and men of that sort truer and better successors and vicars of the apostles, than the present pope with his cardinals, who, neither by a holy life, doctrine, or wisdom, enlighten the people? If, instead of fulfilling their calling, and having Christ's example before them, they rather strive for worldly things, splendor and pomp, and excite avarice and envy in believers, then are they successors, not of Christ, of Peter, or of the apostles, but of Satan, Antichrist, Judas Iscariot.

It cannot therefore be said that the pope, as such, is the head of the church. The pope can know, in regard to himself, with absolute certainty, whether he can be saved, no more than any other man. In case he is not predestinate, he is not only not the head of the church, but not even a member of it. Peter, as Paul testifies, fell into error. Pope Leo was a heretic. All may see what pope Gregory XII. is, condemned, together with his rival, at the council of Pisa.

The popedom is not essential to the well-being and edification of the church. If it is said, that for Christians spread over the whole earth there *must* be a pope, the *must* is only to be understood in the sense in which it is said in scripture, that "offences must needs come; but woe to him by whom they come."

In the early church there were but two grades of office, deacon and presbyter; all beside are of later and of human invention. But God can bring back his church to the old pattern, just as the apostles and true priests took oversight of the church in all matters essential to its well-being, before the office of pope was introduced. So it may be again; and it were possible that there should be no more a pope till the last day. God be praised, who sent his only begotten Son to be the head of the church militant, for he is able to preside over it, lead it, infuse into it energy and grace, even though there were no pope, or though a woman were seated in the papal chair.

As of the pope and cardinals, so of the prelates and clergy. Here, too, there is a clergy of Christ and a clergy of Antichrist. The former is built on Christ and his laws, labors constantly for the glory of God, and seeks simply to follow Christ. The latter, though wearing the robes of Christ's clergy, rests upon privileges savoring of pride and avarice, finds itself obliged to defend human ordinances, strives after a proud, splendid equipage. Not the office makes the priest, but the priest the office. The place does not sanctify the man, but the man the place. Not every priest is a saint, but every saint is a priest. Faithful Christians keeping the commandments are the magnates of the church, but prelates who break them are least, and if reprobates, have no part in the kingdom of God. It is false to say that the laity are to depend on the prelates for what they believe. The divine mission of pope, bishop, priest, etc., is determined by the fact that he seeks not his own glory, but the glory of God; not his own advantage, but the edification and peace of the church. Hence, if an inferior does not discern in his superior a becoming conduct, he is not bound to hold him in a state of present justification, or even among the predestinate.

And as to obedience, it is the voluntary act of a reasonable creature, by which he subjects himself to the decision of those above him. Hence each subject must prove the command of his superior, whether it is permissible and to be respected. For in case it tends to the injury of the church and of souls, he must not comply with, but oppose it. Every true Christian must, hence, when a command issues to him from the pope, deliberate whence it originates—whether it is an apostolic ordinance and a law of Christ, or mediately such, and he is then to regard and honor it; but if the opposite is the case, he must not honor, but rather firmly oppose it, and not by subjection incur guilt. Opposition in such a case is true obedience. *Devianti Papæ rebellare, est Christo domino obedire.*

Nor is this all. "If thy brother sin against thee, rebuke him." If spiritual superiors err in life and conduct, the laity may chide them; and if it is ill-endured, and the question is asked, How come you to judge us? the laity may reply, How does it happen that you seek alms and tithes of us?

The power of the keys, that is, the power to receive the worthy, and reject the unworthy, belongs to God alone, who ordains salvation, or foreknows perdition. The priest has no power to release from guilt and eternal punishment; the pope even has not this power; then would he be sinless and infallible, but this belongs to God only. The priest has only the churchly office of declaring, (*ministerium denunciationis,*) not of binding or loosing, unless this is already done of God. And God is governed, not by the human sentence of loosing or binding, but the absolution must follow the grace of God and the sinner's repentance. Intellectual knowledge is not essential to the soul's salvation, but true contrition and confession of the heart.

Such in substance were the main positions taken by Huss, in this the most able and systematic of his writings. Cochleius confesses the remarkable ability displayed in its production. He saw, more clearly perhaps than Huss himself, the broad scope and the full bearing of the argument. It reduced the whole cumbrous mass of the dominant hierarchy to a heap of rubbish. It annihilated papal authority. It made the simple priest the peer of the pope. It dissipated at once the arrogant pretensions of the church of Rome. It made the faith that works by love, and not organic connection with the hierarchy, the condition of membership in the spiritual church of Christ. It stripped the priesthood of that superstitious terror with which they were invested, as the sole dispensers of salvation. It made the simple layman, if a true believer, a king and priest unto God. All human distinctions of rank and office were seen to shrink into insignificance before the ennobling relation which the humblest member of Christ might sustain to him as the great head of the church. Excommunication, and all the fulminations of papal authority, if unjust, or in conflict with the law of Christ, became, *ipso facto*, null and void.

Here was a basis for the most sweeping reforms. Huss had reached a point where he could not logically pause. He was evidently unaware of the radical divergence of his own views from those of the dominant hierarchy. He was in spirit a Protestant —a Puritan—before these terms were known. And yet he held fast to certain so-called Catholic dogmas,—confession, purgatory, transubstantiation, etc., —and really believed himself, rightfully, a member still of the church that had cast him out.

But the church party, with men like Paletz and Stanislaus at its head, were not blind to the logical consequences that followed from the fundamental principle of the argument of Huss; and against this, the sole and supreme authority of scripture, they directed their attacks. The treatise of Huss opened the field for controversy. It gave precision to the views of the party he represented, and exasperated their opponents. The dividing lines were more closely drawn, and the mutual repulsion and antagonism were aggravated. The treatise of Huss was attacked by the doctors, and he was prompt to repel the attack. Each new collision brought the combatants back to this old battle-ground. The real question at issue was between the authority of the pope and the authority of the scriptures.

The treatise of Huss bore, in a very obvious manner, upon the important question now agitated in his absence at Prague—the validity of his excommunication. The friends of the papacy were strenuous in defending it, while those who adhered to Huss were equally zealous in its refutation. The former maintained that Huss, as excommunicate, had no longer the right or authority to preach, and they insisted and urged that he should be silenced. They asserted that he was not at liberty to disregard or contemn the papal sentence. It was enough that that sentence had been pronounced.

But it so happened that the excommunication of Huss was subsequently extended to embrace persons who had adopted his views, and who never had been brought to trial or heard in their own defence.[1] A new phase was thus given to the question of the validity of the papal sentence, which those who impugned it were not slow to perceive. If excommunication was unjust in one instance, it might be in another. The pope was no longer infallible. His decisions might be called in question, and it mattered little what the merits of the case of Huss might be, if the author of his excommunication was shown to have committed a gross blunder as well as gross injustice. Jessenitz, a preacher at Prague, and one of the procurators of Huss at Rome, took up the matter, and argued the nullity of the sentence on principles which were evidently in advance of the age, and which, however consonant to justice, were utterly repudiated by the papal party.[2] And yet, the most enlightened and able members of the Catholic church—some most

[1] Mon. Hussi, i. 87. "Scholares et familares Hussi," were included in the sentence of excommunication.

[2] See his treatise included in Mon. Hussi, vol. i, 329.

bitterly prejudiced against Huss—might be cited in defence of his view of excommunication. The royal court of France had but recently declared the excommunications of Benedict to be no longer binding, and, even at the ensuing council of Constance, the French embassadors maintained that the fulminations, sentences, and censures pronounced against those who refused the payment of annates, were not to be feared, nor did those against whom they had been directed need to be absolved.[1] Gerson himself had written but a few months previous,[2] "We ought not to be compelled to obey those whose conduct is notoriously vile, and scandalizes the whole church. . . . . If we should withdraw ourselves from every brother who walketh disorderly, how much more from a perverse and unjust superior, by whose example the commonwealth is corrupted and the church disgraced." If Huss appealed moreover to a council, then from the treatise of D'Ailly "On the Difficulty of Reform," he might have drawn abundant materials, equally pertinent in defence of his cause. That able writer had maintained, just after the close of the Pisan council, that in authority, dignity, and official superintendence, a pope is subject to a general council representing the universal church. Their decisions were like the gospel of Christ. A pope could not change or dispense with them, for over them he had no jurisdiction.[3] He held, moreover, that the pope as a man might sin, might err. And what else is he but human? "Man of men, clay of clay, a sinner, and peccable; two days before, the son of a poor rustic."

[1] Van der Hardt, i. 146. [2] Ibid, i. 127. [3] Ibid, i. 88.

He is not above the gospel—then his authority would be greater than Christ's, and could not be derived from him as its source.[1] Of the church Catholic, moreover, the pope is not the head, but Christ only.[2] Surely, with such authorities upon his side, Huss might well venture the lists with any of his antagonists, for the church of that age could not boast two abler champions than Gerson and D'Ailly.

But to such authority Huss did not appeal. We find no trace in his writings to show that he was even acquainted with the writings of the Paris theologians. It was to the gospel—to scripture alone—that he looked for the warrant and sanction of his course. Here, indeed, was the strength of his cause. The plain common-sense of the citizens of Prague could not comprehend the force or conclusiveness of that logic which placed the decisions of men, or even the decretals of the popes, on a level with, much more above, the plain doctrine of the word of God. At every step in their arguments, the papal party were met by some troublesome citation from scripture, some plain and direct declaration, which could be met by no visionary theory or scholastic subtlety. So far had the simplicity of scriptural doctrine and worship prevailed, that ecclesiastical decisions and sacerdotal authority were utterly powerless, unless they could allege in their favor some indisputable evidence from the sacred writings.

It was indeed to be expected that in such a state of things occasional acts of violence should occur. The cupidity and impudence of those who favored

[1] Van der Hardt, i. 77. [2] Ibid, 70.

the cause of indulgences, especially of those who trafficked in them, afforded a standing provocation to a populace not all of whom were capable of the same self-restraint. Stephen of Dola, in his controversial writings,[1] complains of those whom he describes as missionaries of Huss, and, curiously enough, recounts the results of their labors in the same language which Christ employed when he foretold the divisions that should arise from his teachings. The scriptural knowledge of the people and their increased intelligence, as well as jealousy of the clergy, led them to look with deep indignation upon those ecclesiastical impositions, the manifest and perhaps sole object of which was to rob them of their money. When Gerson could speak as he did on the subject of indulgences, and expose the futility of so many *Ave Marias* before an image, it is not surprising that men, who had studied the subject only in the light of the gospel, should resent the claims of the papal agents as an insult to reason itself. And with all this intelligent resistance to the usurpation of Roman cupidity, there was often joined much of that party zeal which must necessarily spring up where a community is arrayed in opposing sections. Huss expressly disowns and condemns the conduct of some of his followers, who resorted to the low and disgraceful measure of applying to their antagonists abusive epithets.[2] Three years before, the conduct of Sbynco had been such that it was impossible to restrain that popular contempt for him

[1] Mart. Anec. Anti Hussus, iv. p. 383. Gerson. Opera. ii. 406.

[2] Mon. Hussi, i. 264.

and his course, which had found expression in derisive songs and ballads sung along the streets; and, notwithstanding the decree of the king and the influence of Huss to the contrary, ballads of a similar character, directed against the priests of the papal party, were still in common use. The monks, as they passed along the streets, were sometimes insulted and hooted at by the promiscuous crowds of men and boys, who regarded them with any other feelings than those of reverence or respect. That popular odium against them which in England had made the words of Wickliffe so effective, was equally strong at Prague, where they were scorned for their vices and hated for their impudence. "Go, lay off your cowls; thresh in the barns; get you wives; go to work farming;"[1] such were the greetings which they received from the populace as they passed by.

On one occasion a friar was sitting with his relics in the church of the Carmelites, exhibiting his treasures and begging for money for the building of a church, when one of the disciples of Huss came up. In somewhat rude phrase he demanded of the mendicant, "What are you about here, friar?" "Seeking alms, while I exhibit my relics," was the reply. "You speak false," said the disciple of Huss, "if you call these the relics of saints. You keep here the bones of dead carcasses, and deceive Christians by your greedy begging." Suiting the action to the word, he kicked over the table on which the relics lay, and tumbled them to the earth. The friar caught the offender, put him under arrest, and had him called

[1] Anti-Hussus, Mart. Anec., iv. 557.

upon to answer the charge against him, when the prisoner's friends learning what had taken place, assembled in large numbers, deeply indignant, and armed for the rescue. The residence of the friars, probably not without a good degree of resistance both by the arm and tongue, was sacked and ravaged, and the poor mendicants, after revilings and beatings, were left to mend their broken relics.

That similar scenes not unfrequently occurred, is most probable. Among the charges brought against Jerome at the council of Constance, are some which imply that his conduct in this respect had been far from unexceptionable. Some of these are denied; but the evidence is strong, if not decisive, in regard to his course on the reception of the papal bulls for the crusade. On another occasion he is said to have thrown a priest into the Moldau, who, but for timely aid, would have been drowned. But such violence was bitterly provoked. The burning of the books by Sbynco, the execution of the three men for asserting the falsehood of the indulgences, the excommunication of Huss, to say nothing of the course pursued by his assailants, had excited a strong feeling against the patrons of papal fraud and ecclesiastical corruption. We are only surprised that the deep resentment felt was confined in its expression within such limits.

Among the antagonists of Huss were four men who had been numbered among his most intimate friends. These were Stanislaus of Znoyma, his former teacher, Stephen, prior of Dola, Stephen Paletz, and Andrew Broda, the two latter once his fellow-students, sharers of his table and his bed. Broda deserted him from the moment that he was excommunicated, but he still corresponded with him by letter, in the hope of inducing him to return again, as he phrased it, to the unity of the church. A man of kindly disposition, but of no remarkable ability, and terrified at the very name of papal fulminations, Broda shrunk from Huss as from the touch of leprosy, yet still addressed him in terms dictated by the memories of former intercourse and affection. Stephen of Dola, however, was less scrupulous. His first assault upon Huss was under cover of an attack against the articles of Wickliffe.[1] He calls the English reformer, "Thou son, not of man, but the devil;" and asks, "Why do you love vanity and seek after a lie?" As he proceeds his vocabulary of abuse is enlarged, and he speaks of him as "a tricky fox with deep holes," "a worse traitor than Judas." He arraigns Wickliffe for maintaining that the decretals are apocryphal, and that the clergy who waste time in their study are fools, while papal and episcopal indulgences are warmly defended.

That Huss felt that the treatise was aimed at him is manifest from his letter to the monks of Dola, where the author of the work had been prior, before his removal to Olmutz. This letter is inserted by Stephen in his preface to his "Anti-Hussus," in which he throws off the mask and comes out boldly against

[1] The treatises of "Anti-Wicklefus," "Anti-Hussus," etc., are to be found in Mart. Anecdota., tom. iv. Cochleius identifies their author, Stephen of Dola, with Stephen Paletz. This is obviously an error. The date of the first treatise alone is sufficient to refute it. It was written a year or two before Paletz became an antagonist of Huss, and at that time Paletz was as much a Wickliffite as Huss.

Huss himself. In this letter[1] Huss complains of Stephen for the slanders which he had uttered against himself and others. He was unwilling to be so fully identified with Wickliffe. "Though Wickliffe, or an angel from heaven, taught otherwise than scripture teaches, I would not follow him—my heart abhors the errors ascribed to me." Such is his language. As to his disregard of excommunication, he claims that he has not shown contempt for any just authority. "I disobey," he says, "the *de-ordination* of my superiors, because scripture teaches me to obey God rather than man. The apostles preached Jesus Christ when forbidden by the chief priests." After giving his reasons for non-compliance with the papal citation, he cautions his antagonist how he judges others.

But Stephen, in his reply, seems to pay small heed to such wise counsel. He begins his treatise by a play upon Huss' name, bidding him beware lest he fly too high and scorch his wings. He charges him with having made his pulpit, in Bethlehem church, a chair not of preaching, but of prevarication. His temple was turned into an ensnaring den of Wickliffites, where he spoke against his fathers and brethren and the common pastor of the church, to the grave scandal of the people. A just sentence had, therefore, overtaken him. It was but right that, by the force of the interdict, he should be made a vagabond, driven from place to place to conceal himself. But the great crime of Huss, in the eyes of Stephen, was his contempt for ecclesi-

[1] Mart. Anect., iv. 363.

astical authority. The evils that had followed his teachings were frightful, in the view of his accuser. "So far has Huss prevailed," says Stephen, "that I have heard and understood that many of the laity say, 'What so great need is there that we should confess to a mortal man, when with contrite heart we confess to the High Priest, God Almighty, alone?'"

To this treatise of the monk of Dola, Huss replied. The issue was such that the author found little encouragement to renew the attack in a direct manner. In his "Dialogus Volatilis," addressed to the bishop of Leitomischel, he takes occasion again to reprehend the course of Huss, complaining mainly of his disobedience and disregard of the sentence of excommunication.

It is not difficult, from the knowledge of the course of Paletz, and his former relations, and subsequent treatment of Huss, to divine some at least of the motives that incited him to assail a former friend and companion. Huss and Paletz were both men of marked ability, and, to a considerable extent, their aims had harmonized. But when Huss braved the fulminations of the papal court, Paletz, whose convictions on the subject in dispute were the same with those of his associate, shrunk back with a craven fear. It was now that jealousy of his rival's influence gave a sting to the malice of his treachery. Stephen of Dola had dilated upon the large salary which Huss received,[1] and Paletz, probably judging from after-disclosures at the council of Constance,

[1] Mart. Anec., iv. 558.

shared the same feelings. Moreover, having committed himself to a cause which demanded first of all the sacrifice of conscience, the pride of Paletz forbade his withdrawal from a conflict which he had himself challenged. Henceforth with him it was war, without truce or compromise, till one or the other was forced to submission.

Meanwhile the enemies of Huss at Prague and in the university were not idle. Conrad, who had acted as administrator of the archiepiscopal office, and who now, in name as well as in reality, was archbishop of Prague, was a man of a different temper from his predecessor Sbynco. Less rash and hasty, he proceeded in his measures with a cautious deliberation. He sent to the university of Paris to procure an authentic copy of the counsel which they had given to his predecessor in regard to the steps to be taken for extirpating heresy from Bohemia.[1] This counsel, notwithstanding the schism, and the liberality of the Paris theologians, was after the most approved pattern of church orthodoxy. It directed that the doctors and masters of the university should be assembled by the archbishop along with his clergy at his palace, and that each should be required to declare, under oath, that he neither holds nor wishes to maintain any of the forty-five articles of Wickliffe; that in regard to relics, indulgences, and the ceremonies, customs, and censures of the church, he believes as the church believes of which the pope is the head, and the cardinals, the

[1] The various "Counsels" connected with this matter are to be found in Cochleius, and in Helfert's Appendix.

manifest successors of the apostles, are the body; that each should profess obedience to the Roman See; and that it should be announced to all the members of the university that no one should maintain any of the forty-five articles, under pain of anathema, or banishment from the kingdom. These measures were, moreover, to be published throughout the diocese, and any one who transgressed should be proceeded against according to canonical sanctions. The derisive songs which were sung in the streets and taverns were to be suppressed, and Huss was not to be allowed to preach until he had obtained absolution from the court of Rome.

This counsel of the university of Paris was submitted by the archbishop to a synod, summoned to meet at Bömischbrod, but afterwards transferred to Prague. Huss, aware of the proposed measure, came[1] with a "counsel" of his own, which he was prepared to lay before them. "For the honor of God, the salvation of the people, the good name of Bohemia and Moravia, as well as of Prague and the university, and for the restoration of peace and unity:"—such was the object, according to Huss, to be promoted by the measures he proposed. These were, that the former edict of conciliation between the archbishop and the barons and Huss should be solemnly confirmed; that Bohemia should be allowed to retain its rights, liberties, and privileges, in the same manner with other kingdoms; that Huss, against whom Sbynco had brought no charge when

[1] It is doubtful whether he was present in person. Jessenitz was his procurator.

he consented to the compromise, should be present to meet any charges whenever they were made, and that none should be allowed to make any which he was not prepared to substantiate, under pain of a sentence such as his charge against Huss implied; that public notice should be given that any who wished to accuse Huss should inscribe their names upon the archbishop's chancellor's book; that such as spread reports that were merely slanderous, should be punished; that the doctors of theology and of canon law should be required, if they knew of any heretic, to name him,—and if they should say they knew of none, should be forbidden, under penalties, to circulate charges of heresy; that in case this was done, a deputation should be sent to the Roman court to vindicate the fair name and honor of the kingdom; and that for the present the interdict should not be enforced, notwithstanding the presence of Huss.

But Paletz and Stanislaus, in the name of other masters of the theological faculty, had their "counsel" to present. As the king and barons had directed an investigation of the causes of the troubles, they propose to point them out. In their view, they were threefold, viz: the opposition made to the condemnation of Wickliffe's articles; the contempt shown the pope and cardinals, as well as their authority, by appeals to Holy Scripture as their judge, while the appellants interpret it as they please; and the general disregard of ecclesiastical authority, both that of prelates and of the Apostolic See, by inferiors. The doctors held that the clergy were not to judge of the validity or justice of the excommunication of Huss, and that consequently, accepting it, they must observe the interdict. Papal and prelatical authority was exalted above that of the scriptures. The doctors would have it enjoined, under severe penalties, that no one in Bohemia should hold or teach other than as the Romish church holds and teaches; and, in case any should offend by speaking in favor of Wickliffe's articles, or resisting the ecclesiastical authority, he should be given over for judgment to the ecclesiastical courts, or, in case this did not avail, to the secular arm. The excommunication of Huss, without any discussion of its justice or injustice, was to be accounted valid in virtue of the authority of the Apostolic See.

The theological faculty also presented a separate "counsel."[1] It agreed mainly with that of Paletz and Stanislaus. It proposed, however, a meeting of all the doctors and masters of the university at the archbishop's palace, where each should be required, under solemn oath, to declare that he accepted none of Wickliffe's forty-five articles as true; that, as to the seven sacraments and all matters of faith, he believed in accordance with the Romish church, whose head is the pope and whose body is the college of cardinals; and that he recognized the duty of obedience to the Apostolic See and the prelates of the church. This oath was to be required of all, under penalty of excommunication and banishment. The archbishop also was to summon a synod, and by it enjoin

[1] A fuller account of the synod is given in Tomek's "History of the University of Prague," quoted by Helfert, 280–284.

that no error should be preached throughout the land. And as to Huss, he should be utterly forbidden to preach till he had received absolution from the pope; nor was he any longer to be allowed, by his secret presence in Prague, to put obstacles in the way of the observance of the divine offices.

With such diverse counsels before it, it was impossible for the convocation to effect a compromise. The position of Huss was utterly irreconcilable with that of the doctors, and the archbishop was at a loss what course to pursue. He had not the Quixotic zeal that would lead him to repeat the blunders of his predecessor, or tilt at the shadow of heresy at the risk of his position, as well as honor and peace. He sent, therefore, the various "counsels," including that of Huss as well as those of the universities of Paris and Prague, to the martial bishop of Leitomischel—"John the Iron," as he was most appropriately called—asking his advice. The stern prelate—whom we again meet at the council of Constance—more fitted both by taste and experience to wield the sword than the crosier, was most ferociously orthodox. He was opposed to all compromise, and favored the execution, to the letter, of the "counsel" of the university of Paris. His advice was, that the vice-chancellor should take careful supervision of the masters and students of the university, investigating and correcting their errors; that, as the controversies which found place among them were ventilated among the people by the public preaching from the pulpit, care should be taken that Huss and his followers should be silenced—especially were they to be excluded from Bethlehem chapel; that the papal mandates on the subject should be enforced, and that heretical books, and those who owned or read them, should be anathematized. The bishop then attempts to refute the counsel of Huss, and closes by exhorting archbishop Conrad to a zealous prosecution of measures for extirpating heresy from Bohemia.

The synod had met, Feb. 6, 1413. The bishop's letter dates four days later, Feb. 10,[1]—so that his response must have been prompt at least. But there was yet another who was to take part in the discussion. This was Jacobel, or James of Misa, a friend of Huss. Whether his views were presented at the synod, or subsequently, as in the case of the bishop, is somewhat uncertain. It appears probable, however, that they were urged before the synod.[2]

The object of the convocation was a compromise that should promote peace. "But," inquired Jacobel, "what sort of a peace is meant? Is it peace with the world, or peace with God? If the latter, it could be secured only by keeping the divine commandments. The very origin of the strife was in the unholy and violent resistance offered to those who wished to establish this peace. Without it, moreover, the peace of the world would be of no avail; but let it be first secured, and the other would follow of itself."

Whether in consequence of this discussion or not, Wenzel was led to issue a decree which seemed intended for the support of the ecclesiastical authori-

[1] Cochleius.

[2] Helfert's extract from Tomek's "History of the University of Prague" would seem to indicate that this was the case.

ties, although he advised the doctors to refute error by arguments rather than by edicts. The decree, however, was publicly proclaimed in the council-house of the city. But it was evidently designed more to keep up appearances, than to throw any obstruction in the way of the friends of Huss. Indeed, viewed in this light, it was but a dam of straw thrown across the tide of popular feeling. It was impossible that the decree should be enforced. Nor was it long before a refutation of the positions taken by the doctors appeared. Two of the procurators of Huss, who had answered his citation at the Roman court, John of Jessenitz, and Frederic Epinge, the first a doctor, and the last a bachelor of canon law, had already come forward publicly in his defence,—and this defence overthrew the main points on which the doctors based their conclusions. To this Huss refers the doctors. Jessenitz had shown that no prelate should excommunicate any one, unless he knows that he is first excommunicate of God; and in several respects had argued the nullity of Huss' sentence. But Huss himself went further. He reprehends those excommunications which are unjustly prelatic, or rather *Pilatic*, and maintains that the curse of the wicked is rather a benediction. The scriptural knowledge that had already become diffused among the people, enabled them to vindicate this view of the matter, and meet even the doctors with arguments not easy to be confuted. In vain were the decretals cited, or the authority of the church adduced. "Laity, butchers, shoemakers, tailors, and humble mechanics," says Stephen of Dola, "rise up proudly, and contemn authority." Cochleius[1] has preserved a brief summary of the arguments employed by the Hussite party to refute the doctors. As to the first cause of the troubles, they deny utterly the truth of the charge that the nation generally are heretical, and denominate the imputation of erroneous views in regard to the sacraments a mere slander. They hold, that not the pope and his cardinals, but that all priests and bishops are successors of the apostles. The head of the church is not the pope, but Christ. The body is not the cardinals, but all believers. Such is the testimony of scripture and of the fathers. They deny, moreover, the competent authority, on the part of bishops and archbishops, for condemning the articles of Wickliffe. These were substantially the views presented by Huss in his work on the church.

As to the second cause of discord urged by the doctors, Huss himself refers to the schismatic state of the church, divided under the allegiance of three several popes, and shows how futile the effort to obtain from them decisions of doubtful questions, in regard to which they could not agree, and especially if these should be found contrary to the scriptures of the Old and New Testaments, from which the fathers themselves deduced their authority. Besides, he remarks how the doctors stultify themselves in citing scripture, (Deut. xvii.,) to show that not scripture, but the prelates are to decide doubtful questions! He appeals to scripture for the support of his position, yet they make the pope supreme. As

[1] P. 50.

to the place where the decision is to be solicited—in accordance with the passage cited from Deuteronomy—why is it to be sought at Bologna, Perusia, or Avignon, where the pope resides, rather than at Jerusalem, Antioch, or Rome? The doctors, moreover, had asserted that the pope was in all things to be obeyed. This was putting a contempt upon the Holy Scriptures and the sacred canons; for some popes had been heretical, and one was a woman, and these not only should not be obeyed, but should not be communed with or favored—so at least the rubrics and canons taught. The true causes of the troubles in Bohemia are traced to the preaching of the gospel, with the reproofs and admonitions of which the clergy are enraged, on account of the exposure which is thus made of their simony and heretical practices.

As to the argument of the doctors that the excommunication of Huss was to be considered valid because the papal mandates to that effect had been issued and had been generally received, the same argument might be employed to show that because Adam and Eve complied with the temptations of the devil, and obeyed him, therefore their descendants should do the same; or that, inasmuch as our fathers were pagans, we should have remained pagan still. Besides, various reasons might be adduced to show that the sentence against Huss was null and void.

But the doctors were not content even yet to let the matter rest. To the arguments of Huss they make a lengthy and minute reply. They do not hesitate to maintain, in an almost unqualified manner, the most objectionable of their former doctrines, although upon some points they could not agree among themselves. Huss shows, in his reply to them, how Paletz and Stanislaus could not accord on the subject of the headship of the church. Paletz, however, seems to have been supported by most of the other six doctors, and to have carried the day over the more enlightened and scriptural views of Stanislaus. A large part of the argument is taken up in showing that the headship of the church is in the pope, and in reducing the authority of scripture to a *minimum*, while that of the prelates and the pope and cardinals is exalted above all other authority on earth. They maintain that so long as it could not manifestly be known or shown that John XXIII. was a heretic, his commands were to be obeyed. Could they have looked forward to the trial and deposition of that pontiff two years later, they would probably have modified or kept back that proposition.

These views were urged in behalf of others more obscure, by eight doctors, of whom Paletz, Stanislaus, and Andrew Broda are the most prominent. The names of the others were Peter de Ikoyma, John Eliă, John Hildesis, Matthew the Monk, and Herman the Eremite; beside whom, we find the names of George Bota and Simon Wenda mentioned.[1] All of these no doubt sympathized together in the general opposition to the reform party; but as the reply of Huss is denominated "The Refutation of the Eight Theological Doctors," it is most probable that only eight of them appended their names to the docu-

[1] Mon. Hussi, i. 265.

ment.[1] Notwithstanding their united effort, Huss did not shrink from the encounter to which they had thus challenged him. In the most merciless manner he exposes the inconsistency of their positions, and quotes them—as his knowledge of their former views enabled him to do—against themselves. But it scarcely needed that Huss should throw his pen into the scale, to determine how it should preponderate. The argument of the doctors had only exposed the weakness of a cause which their united ability could not even render plausible. Some of their statements were so evidently subversive of the whole doctrine of scriptural Christianity, that the only choice left was between the word of God and the decretals or constitutions of the popes. It was in vain that the doctors attempted to recommend the latter. Popular opinion spurned such counsel. The reasons given for this by Cochleius are, that the followers of Huss were loud in their demand for the reform of the clergy, "whose vices, as simony, concubinage, avarice, luxury, and worldly pride, they accused with bitterness in their frequent sermons and harangues to the people," and that for this the laity encouraged and sustained them. It is evident, therefore, that in the popular conviction there must have been a large basis of truth at the bottom of the charges.

It must now have become evident to the archbishop that to adopt the counsel which the university of Paris had extended to his predecessor was no longer practicable. The reform party had become

[1] Huss represents it as a piece of arrogance on the part of the eight doctors, that they assumed as they did to speak for the whole theological faculty.

too numerous and powerful to be thus summarily dealt with. There was a prospect that the conflict would be more bitterly renewed, and the king felt that it was time for him to interpose. The synod had accomplished nothing. No compromise could be effected by it. The king therefore tried another expedient. He appointed a commission, consisting of the archbishop, the Vissehrad dean, Jacob, the provost of All-Saints, Zdenek of Labaun, and Christiann of Prachatitz, rector of the university, as well as a fast friend of Huss. The two parties were bound, under penalty of fine and banishment, to abide by the decision of this commission. For two days both parties were heard, but agreement was impossible. Four doctors entered their protest and withdrew from the conference. The king, exasperated at their course, banished them.[1] Shortly after, the party suffered another defeat.[2] The German element had hitherto predominated in the city council; but at this juncture, one of its members, for some cause, was executed. The king, by new appointments, gave the Bohemians the ascendency.

Nor was this all. The king followed up the matter by measures for reforming the clergy. He kept back the salary of unworthy priests, and thus practically adopted one of the principles for which Huss had contended, namely, that the secular power is authorized to resort to forcible measures, and the control of the temporalities of the church, for the reform of clerical corruption. This step of the king was de-

[1] Stanislaus, one of them, died soon after. Paletz, who was another, had leisure now to prepare his accusations.

[2] Helfert, 140.

cisive in securing the predominance of the reform party. It struck terror into the ranks of its opponents. The priests who had opposed Huss were less anxious to see the sentence against him executed than to retain their salaries. A thousand eyes were watching them; a thousand witnesses were ready to testify against them, whenever they rendered themselves obnoxious to the cause of reform. Rather than be harrassed by frequent accusations and constant risks, some of them openly joined the party which they had opposed, and others, for the time at least, were constrained to moderation, if not to silence.[1] The abandonment of the papal cause, in many cases no doubt, was a cover to past delinquencies, so that the very vices and excesses of the clergy were forced for the time being to strengthen the cause which had been hitherto an object of mortal hatred. It was no longer dangerous for Huss to visit Prague. His enemies did not dare to molest him, and he might safely challenge his accusers to present their charges.

During the period of these discussions, which continued from the time of the publication of the crusade to the spring of 1414, it is difficult to trace the course of Huss except from his writings. That he was during a portion of the time absent from Prague, is evident from his letters. That he frequently returned, or was present in Prague, in spite of the interdict, is attested not only by the royal decree which required the priests to perform the divine offices as usual, notwithstanding the presence of Huss, but from the writings of Paletz and of Broda. According to

[1] Cochleius, p. 62. See Helfert, also, as well as Huss *vs.* The Doctors.

the latter, Huss boasted that he walked openly in the city and in the sight of all, and yet the interdict was disregarded. The only reply which Broda can make is, that his presence was not always known, and that he was in fact seen by very few. It was therefore the ignorance of the clergy as to the presence of Huss—so he would represent—which led them to continue in the discharge of their duties.

Yet, if not in the city, he was at least not far distant. The demand which was made by his friends, that in case accusations were presented against him he should be allowed to be present and confront his accusers, would seem to imply this. But after the royal measures taken upon the subject of clerical reform, in the summer and autumn of the year 1413, most of the difficulties which drove him from the city would be removed. Opposition was for the most part silenced, and Huss was at liberty to return to Prague. In these circumstances, his enemies found themselves disappointed and defeated. Huss openly disregarded the papal sentence; while many questioned even whether any had ever been pronounced against him. The interdict was a mere nullity. Those who had sought to enforce it, cringed as suppliants of the royal favor and bounty. They were no longer the bold accusers, but trembled at the charges to which on every side they were exposed. There was now occasion for Huss in his turn to exult, if he had been so disposed. The humiliation of his enemies was in fact so ludicrous in some of its aspects, that he could not but refer to it. With Wickliffe, he had accounted tithes mere alms, or voluntary grants, and as such they might be withheld if the neglect or vice of the ecclesiastics furnished occasion. His enemies had virulently assailed a position so fatal to the security and integrity of their gains, nor did they spare its author in the venom of their malice. Now they came to the town hall to present their petitions for their tithes. "Ah!" said the lords, "you said before that tithes were not purely alms; but you assert now that they are, and so condemn yourselves." Huss noticed this absurd course of the clergy.[1] "I wonder," says he, with stinging sarcasm, "I wonder that the doctors do not now teach in the town hall the putting into execution of that article on the withholding of temporalities from the delinquent clergy by the secular lords! Now, like the chief priests and Pharisees, they are silent; they no more assemble to condemn that article. Surely, what they feared has come upon them, and will come again. For they will lose their temporalities, but God grant that they may save their souls! The doctors said that if the articles were comdemned, there would be peace and concord; but their prophecy has turned out the reverse. They were exultant in the condemnation, but now they mourn as they give up their salaries. They condemned the article that tithes were alms; now they beg that their salaries, which are alms, may not be taken away."[2]

Resistance to Huss was no longer offered. Only Paletz and Broda still kept up the controversy by their letters, reproaching Huss mainly for his contumacy, and for what they denominated his slanders against the clergy

[1] Cochleius, p. 63. [2] Ibid.

For several months affairs remained quiet at Prague. The adherents of Huss were no longer molested, and the heat of controversy died away. The archbishop seemed to have given up all thought of any further proceedings against Huss. Meanwhile the cause of reform steadily advanced. Its adherents, in their study of the scriptures, were attaining views more and more evangelical. They were publicly known as the *evangelical* party. Huss no longer approved of the worship of a wooden cross.[1] He condemned the adoration paid to the pictures of the saints in the churches. On the subject of confession he appeals to Chrysostom as sustaining him in his teachings upon that subject. "I do not bid you present yourselves in public, or accuse yourselves before others; I only wish you to obey the prophet where he says, Lay your way open before the Lord, confess your sins to the true judge, declare your faults, not with the tongue, but the conscience, and then hope to obtain mercy."

The seed which Huss had sown was ripening to its harvest. Many had adopted his views, and with a zeal equal to his own, though not always as discreet, disseminated them abroad. Even while the measures for the reform of the clergy had not yet been adopted, the adherents of Huss had been active and diligent in their work. "You send your messengers," says Stephen of Dola, "everywhere,—to nobles, soldiers, common people, women." The present period allowed them larger and freer scope for their labors. They quoted scripture largely in defence of their

[1] Mart. Anec. 550.

course." The word of God, they maintained, should not be bound. "Go ye into all the world, and preach the gospel." This was the commission which furnished them their warrant. "If persecuted in one city, flee ye into another," justified them in shunning dangers which they did not feel called to meet. Things done in secret they were ready "to proclaim upon the housetops;" and if it was objected to them that they were violating ecclesiastical ordinances, they were ready with the reply, "It is better to obey God than man." Such was the method and justification of the missionaries which Huss sent out, according to Stephen. The evangelical party was manifestly in the ascendant. Bohemia might almost be considered as hopelessly lost to the church. Something must be done to check the spreading heresy. But there was no hope in the king: he could not be relied on, but was rather amused with the complaints of the clergy. There was no hope in the barons: they strongly sympathized with Huss. There was no hope in the archbishop: even now there may have been ground to suspect the orthodoxy of his intentions in regard to rooting out heretical views. The university was already lost to the church party. Help, if any was to be found, must come from abroad. There was a conviction becoming deeper and more general on every side, among the papal party, that Huss could only be managed, and his heresy restrained, by a general council. Might not one be convoked?

This was a question not only agitated in Bohemia, but all over Europe. There were many reasons which conspired to urge its convocation. The scandalous condition of Christendom, divided in allegiance to three rival pontiffs, was a problem which, by general consent, demanded the assembled wisdom of the church for its solution. There was, moreover, on all sides a loud demand for ecclesiastical reform. How could measures which had this for their object be initiated, except by the action of a general council?

There were, indeed, other reasons for such a convocation, which rested upon the emperor's mind with peculiar weight. His hereditary kingdom of Hungary was peculiarly exposed to Moslem invasion. Already he had experienced the effects of the power, valor, and fanatical energy of his terrible neighbors. In the fearful battle of Nicopolis (1396) an army of 100,000 men, drawn from every part of Europe, and among whom were some of the highest nobility of France, had been routed in utter and almost annihilating defeat. Yet it had been their proud boast that if the sky should fall they would uphold it upon their lances. Few escaped from the field of battle, and for these, enormous ransoms were demanded. Sigismund himself experienced great difficulty and danger in attempting to return to Hungary, which he only reached after a twelve months' absence, and even then to find in Ladislaus of Naples a dangerous competitor for his crown. The danger to Europe was indeed menacing. The Eastern empire could only serve as a temporary barrier to the flashing vengeance of Ilderim, or the lightning, as Bajazet, the Turkish sultan, was called. It might well be that he would soon execute his exultant threat of marching to Rome, and feeding his horse with a bushel of oats upon the altar of St. Peter. But an attack of the gout accomplished what armies were weak to achieve. It stayed the day of Moslem vengeance, and granted Europe a brief reprieve. Meanwhile the weak emperor of the East made his way to the Western courts supplicating aid. None could be afforded; but help was to come from another source. A strange ally appeared, invited by the diplomacy of the Eastern empire and the negociations of Christian monarchs. It was the victorious Tamerlane—the Napoleon of his age—whose ambition had already grasped the larger part of Asia, and could brook no rival empire. More than 1,000,000 men met on the battle-field of Angoura, in Natolia, (July 26th, 1402,) and Tamerlane was victorious. His victim, the sultan, is said to have dashed out his brains against the bars of the iron cage in which he was confined and exhibited by his conqueror.

But the danger had only been deferred. A few years passed, and the Turkish power again assumed a threatening aspect. Sigismund had peculiar reason to beware of its invasions. Yet how could he hope to meet the tide and roll it back, unless he could receive the united support of Christendom? But the prospects of such support, while the church was rent by schism and the nations were arrayed against one another, or rent by internal dissensions, was dark and dubious. The troubles and discords of Bohemia, moreover, required attention, and the emperor was not unmindful of the glory which he might secure as guardian of the church in defending her against foes within as well as without.

All these motives and considerations conspired to enforce the policy of convoking a council. The demand for it came from diverse and distant quarters. By the persuasions of the emperor—persuasions pointed with threats and terror—John XXIII. reluctantly consented to join the emperor in taking measures for its convocation. It was to meet at Constance, an imperial city, on the third day of October, 1414. Huss was cited to appear before it and answer the charges to be brought against him. The emperor directed Wenzel to see that Huss was escorted thither properly attended.

CHAPTER XI.

SERMONS, DOCTRINES, AND LETTERS OF HUSS.

GERSON'S LETTER. — SERMONS OF HUSS. — A LULL OF THE STORM. — CONFIDENCE OF HUSS. — HIS INFLUENCE. — HIS ACTIVITY DURING THIS PERIOD. — HIS WRITINGS. — REPLY TO THE EIGHT DOCTORS. — OTHER WRITINGS OF HUSS. — THEIR EVANGELICAL CHARACTER. — AUTHORITY OF SCRIPTURE WITH HUSS. — THE SECRET OF HIS STRENGTH. — LETTERS DURING HIS ABSENCE FROM PRAGUE. — HIS INDECISION ABOUT HIS RETURN. — LETTER OF SYMPATHY FROM ENGLAND. — PERIOD OF TRIAL.

1404-1414.

THE course of Huss had made him many enemies beyond the limits of Bohemia. The Germans were enraged at the part he had taken in vindicating the rights of the Bohemian nation in the university. His defence of Wickliffe was regarded as an adoption of all his objectionable views, though the inference was in fact unwarranted. England, France, and Germany were ready to lend their influence to silence the reformer.

John Gerson was at this time the chancellor of the university of Paris. He was probably the most powerful subject in France, the Duke of Burgundy excepted. Born of poor parents, he had raised himself by his genius and application to a position in which he exerted a greater sway over the mind of Christendom than any private man in Europe. We cannot but respect his ability, and acknowledge the general integrity of his course. The whole vigor and energy of his manhood were devoted to the interests of the church, and the removal of the papal schism. He was dismayed at the intelligence that reached him from Bohemia. Some of the German students who left Prague would doubtless visit the university of Paris, and report, with all necessary exaggeration, every story that could be devised or distorted to his prejudice. And yet Gerson's bosom friend, Clemengis, had uttered truths and expostulations full as fervid and stinging as any that fell from the lips of the Bohemian reformer. Could these two men have laid aside their opposite philosophies—for Gerson was a Nominalist, and Huss a Realist—and have become acquainted with one another, we can well imagine that all their antagonism would have been laid aside, and they have rushed with mutual admiration into each other's arms.

But this result was not to take place. Opposite philosophical views embittered in Gerson's mind the prejudice which he had already conceived against Huss. He regarded him only as a heretic, a dangerous champion of Wickliffe, to be punished with severity. A historian, opposed to Huss,[1] has preserved us the letter which he wrote to the archbishop of Prague, during the absence of Huss in the year 1413. Assuming as unquestioned the heresy of Huss, he speaks of the methods of extirpating it. These he finds to have been in past times various: "by miracles in the times of the apostles; by argumentative disputations of learned men afterward;

[1] Cochleius.

and when these failed, by general councils, held under the favor of emperors. Last of all, when the evil became desperate, the arm of the secular power was invoked to cut off heresies, with those that favored them, and cast them into the fire, thus guarding against *their word eating like a canker*, to their own and others' destruction." He suggests to the archbishop that his path of duty is plain. "If false teachers sowing heresy demand miracles, let them know that their object has been attained, and they are passed and gone. Our faith is not now a novel thing to be confirmed by them. These men may have not only Moses and the prophets, but the apostles and ancient doctors, as well as the holy councils. They have also modern doctors, gathered in the universities, especially that mother of them, the university of Paris, which has been free of heresy hitherto, and, with God's protection, shall be for ever. Having all these things, let them believe them. Otherwise they would not believe, though one rose from the dead. There will be no end to disputing with such men, who contend with persevering animosity, and lean on their own conceit. Moreover, by too much altercation truth suffers, the common people are scandalized, and charity is violated. Such perversity of obstinate men comes to this of the poet, *Ægrescit Medendo*.[1] If, then, none of the previously mentioned remedies avails, it only remains that the axe of the secular arm be laid at the root of the barren and cursed tree. That arm you are to invoke by all methods; and you are required to do it by a

[1] Is sickened by remedies.

regard for the salvation of those committed to your hands."

The university of Paris, doubtless at the instigation of Gerson, had already pronounced sentence upon some of the more obnoxious doctrines advocated by Huss.[1] His enemies were busy abroad as well as at home, and the prospect of the approaching council would not slacken their diligence.

Yet an examination of the sermons of Huss, preached in the earlier years of his ministry, will show that at that time, when no suspicion of his orthodoxy existed, he had really held the same views which were subsequently charged as heretical. In them we find those ideas advanced which were the germ of his treatise on the church, and in the utterance of his rebukes he is full as free and earnest as at any subsequent period. He had commenced his labors in Bethlehem chapel a year before Sbynco was elevated to the archbishopric of Prague. From his reputation for integrity and ability, as well as from his distinguished position, it was not strange that he should have been selected during successive years to preach the synodical sermon. On the first occasion upon which he discharged this duty—probably in 1404—he took occasion to rebuke the tyrannic exercise of ecclesiastical authority by which worldly-minded priests exulted over the poor, in the infliction of censures. He holds up to reprehension their drunkenness, luxury, and lascivious connections, and

[1] A list of these may be found in the volume of Ecclesiastical History, by P. Natalis Alexander. Some seventeen propositions of Huss are condemned, mainly those which seemed most allied to Wickliffe's views.

calls attention to their avarice, extortion, and ambition to secure plurality of benefices.[1]

In his synodical sermon of the following year, (1405,) he distinctly teaches that Christ, and not Peter, is the rock on which the church is built; that the church of the predestinate is the mystic body of Christ; that every priest in mortal sin is an enemy of God; and that the extortions of the ecclesiastics are detestable. He rebukes the monks for their robbery, and the violation of their vows of poverty, and exposes the simony that trafficked in sacred things.[2] In his discourse in 1407, he is especially severe upon the corrupt and shameful life of the clergy, their licentiousness, disobedience, quarrels, and greed of gain; and he does not fail to strike a heavy blow at the gainful frauds practised in the sale of indulgences. He sees worldly prosperity, but spiritual misery on all sides. "The church shines in its walls, but starves in its poor saints; it clothes its stones with gold, but leaves its children naked."[3] His picture of priestly luxury[4] is drawn in a masterly manner. Almost everything had become matter of traffic. All the offices of the church were for sale. Pride, simony, and thirst for promotion were almost universal. Yet he holds that none but he who "puts on the Lord Jesus Christ" can put on any moral virtue, and declares the danger lest he who is a pluralist in benefices shall be a pluralist in torments.[5]

In 1410, (March 4,) Huss preached before the university; and another sermon bears date Aug. 28th of the same year. In these he refers largely to cur-

[1] Mon. Hussi, ii. 27. [2] Ibid, 29–32. [3] Ibid, 36. [4] Ibid, 38. [5] Ibid, 39.

rent events. He complains of those doctors who persecute the preachers of the gospel by their slanders. "To silence them they invent lies, put forth innuendoes, say that by their love of error they have driven out the foreign nations from the university. They falsely accuse them of thinking ill of the body of Christ, and of saying that the pope is of no account." It seems, therefore, by this sermon, that he recognizes the authority of the popes, since he calls Alexander V., and John XXIII. who had just been elected his successor, vicars of the apostles. He prays for the soul of one in case of his having committed any venial sin, and for the sanctification of the other.

About the close of the same year he preached on the words of Luke, xiii. 23—"Compel them to come in."[1] In this sermon are some things worthy of special notice. He holds that the civil power extends to clergy as well as laity. Christ subjected himself to the authority of human rulers. A prelate should be feared, not like a lay prince, for corporeal inflictions, but for the spiritual terrors which he threatens against the guilty. In this same sermon the course of the king is commended in requiring the priests to preach and discharge their office under penalty of losing their revenues. This shows that the interdict was disregarded by the king, and that at this time he did not approve of the measures of the pope.

In the following year Huss preached on All-Saints day on the words of John xi. 21, where Martha says to Jesus, "Lord, if thou hadst been here my brother

[1] Mon. Hussi, ii. 47.

had not died." In this sermon he treats on the different practices of commemorating the lives of the saints, or the festivals dedicated to their memory. Some of these he approves, and others he condemns. Those which he approves are meditation on the misery of man subjected to death by sin, and on the death of Christ on account of our sins. This meditation leads us, he says, to enter into our own hearts, so that we may be convertud and die happily. We should pray, moreover, for the dead, and thus procure aid for the *sleeping church*, that is, for souls in purgatory.

That which he reprehends in these solemnities is the pomp and show that accompany them, the false eulogies of the dead, and the profit which thereby accrues to the priests. On this subject he quotes a Latin verse:—

De morbo medicus quadet, de morte Sacerdos.[1]

"To what serves the multiplication of vigils in the houses of those who have died rich, except for vain praises? There is no great anxiety to chaunt the appointed psalms, either on the part of him who pays or the priest who is paid. He that pays only asks that numerous vigils be performed in honor of the dead; and he that is paid is only anxious to be done with them. To this end he hurries through his duty as fast as he can. To what end is this pompous gathering of the rich to the processions of the dead? Is it not laughable and quite ridiculous to see the priests comfortably seated on their cushioned chairs,

[1] Disease gratifies the physician, death the priest.

while Christ wept over the tomb of Lazarus? What is the use of the ceaseless tolling of so many bells, but needlessly to lavish out money that might be better employed? And as to the feasts that are made after the burial, in what do they end, but gluttony, drunkenness, and vain conversations?"[1]

Although it appears by this sermon that Huss still believed in purgatory, he did not regard the prayers of the living for the dead as any very effectual aid: "because,"[2] says he, "the matter is not spoken of in the whole scripture, except in the second book of Maccabees, which is not reckoned by the Jews in the canon of the Old Testament. Neither the prophets, nor Jesus Christ, nor his apostles, nor the saints that followed them, ever taught explicitly that we should pray for the dead; but they have said that he that lived a holy life should be saved. For myself, I believe that this practice has been introduced first of all by the avarice of the priests, who take little trouble to exhort the people as the prophets, Christ, and his apostles did, to an holy life; but who take particular pains to persuade them to make rich offerings, in the hope of blessedness and a speedy deliverance from purgatory." He then accuses the priests of supporting this delusion by many falsehoods, and among others, by this: of attributing to St. Gregory, in his *Stella Clericorum*, the words, "Oh! what a marvellous gift of divine mercy, that a mass is never celebrated which does not result in these two things—the conversion of a sinner, and the deliverance of at least one soul from the pains of pur-

[1] Mon. Hussi, ii. 49.

[2] Mon. Hussi, ii. 52.

gatory." He maintains, moreover, that the mass of a wicked priest is an abomination in the sight of God, and can be of no service either to the living or the dead.

The abuses of saint's-days, of which Huss complained in his sermons, were by no means exaggerated. The evil throughout Christendom had grown to an enormous magnitude. Almost at the same time that Huss was calling for a reform at Prague, Clemengis, studying the scriptures at Langres, had his attention forcibly drawn to the same subject. The ex-rector of the university of Paris is not one whit behind the ex-rector of the university of Prague in the severity of his rebuke. "From sunrise to midnight, they (they multitude) loiter, swear, blaspheme, curse God and all the saints, shouting, disputing, quarrelling. With their clamor, tumult, and excess, they seem to rave like madmen. They strive to see who can drink the most, pledge one another in their cups, become drunk, and fall to violence and bloodshed. Passions are roused, threats uttered, injuries inflicted. The wretched criminals are brought before the courts, found guilty, and fined so heavily that the loss of one day cannot be made good by a month's labor.

"What heathen, acquainted with the old sacrilegious ritual, would not suppose, if he could be present on these occasions, that they were rather the florals of Venus on the orgies of Bacchus, than the festival of a saint, especially when he saw such enormities practised as was customary in their idolatrous rites? That festival is even accounted tame and uninteresting which is not spiced with a fight and bloodshed. Now need we be surprised that Mars should become the associate of Bacchus and Venus. Minds impelled by wine and lust are readily led into contention, as by the poets Venus is figured united to Mars by a subtile and indissoluble bond.

"Who does not see how much more honest and healthful it would be not to observe these festivals at all, than to observe them in this manner? Whose heart is so alien to all that is reasonable, so led astray by the perversity of error, as not to perceive that there is less evil on these festivals of the saints in ploughing, herding flocks, sowing, and other rustic occupations, than to,—not celebrate,—but profane them by such horrid and heathen rites? And yet if any one pressed by extreme poverty should have been found to have done any work in his field or vineyard, he is at once summoned to answer for a violation of the day, and is harshly dealt with. But he who shall commit these grosser transgressions against the law and commandments of God, may go free of punishment, and even of accusation."

In regard to the vigils with which Huss finds fault, the language of Clemengis is no less severe. He declares the observance of them in many cases to be base and shameful. Some, in the very churches, spend the night in dances, and singing wanton songs, playing at dice, and using impious and profane language; and in these things the priests joined, furnishing their flocks a fitting example.

Clemengis reprehends the rites of some of the festivals more recently introduced. The lessons that were read were almost all of them apocryphal; the formula of the service was itself deformed, utterly unfitted to excite devotional feeling, of trivial meaning, and uncouth expression; by the puerilities of rhythm ministering to a vain and barren curiosity. Such is the testimony of a man whose learning, character, and standing give his words the greatest weight.[1] The language of Huss is temperate and calm by the side of that of the learned Frenchman, and his opportunities for observation in Bohemia, great as they were, did not surpass those of Clemengis in France. Surely, with such grievous corruptions obtruding themselves everywhere upon the notice of Christendom, it was time that the voice of remonstrance was loudly and effectually raised.

It thus appears that from the first Huss had adopted the principles which he maintained to the end. His earliest sermons are as earnest and severe as those which were preached at a later period. If he was a heretic in 1412, when the bulls of the pope were published in Prague, he was equally so when he preached his first sermon in Bethlehem chapel. Uniformly he had appealed to scripture as the supreme authority for Christian doctrine.

It is thus seen that Huss had grounds of confidence in the consistency of his course and the justice of his cause. He felt ready, therefore, to submit them to the judgment of a body answering to his ideal of the convocated wisdom and piety of the church. Imperfectly did he comprehend the effectiveness of those powerful influences which were conspiring to

[1] Clemeng. Op.

crush him. So clear was he in his own convictions, so sanguine in the belief that the simple statement of the grounds of his faith would vindicate him from any charge of heresy, that he only asked the privilege of a free audience before the general council which it was proposed to convoke. Upon this he insisted in his letter to Sigismund, asking for a safe-conduct.

Nor was he without encouragement in the affection of his fellow-citizens. From the time when, on the withdrawal of the Germans, he had been elevated to the rectorship of the university, the sympathy of the nation had rallied to his side. A large number of the educated men of the country had been brought under his influence, as exerted both in the lecture-room and in the pulpit, while the patriotic feeling, both of the nobility and of the common people, was strongly enlisted in his support.

Indeed, for the four years from 1409 to 1413, there was not another man in the kingdom whose influence was equal to his own. His character, ability, position, and doctrines, and even the persecution which had driven him into temporary exile, had conspired to elevate him in popular esteem, and to give publicity and effect to his uttered sentiments.

This period, moreover, had been one characterized on his part by unwearied effort and incessant industry. Most of his writings, now preserved in his "*Monumenta*," were produced during these four years. Among these, the first in importance, and among the earliest in date, is his work on the church, the substance of which has already been given. This work—the extraordinary ability of which is conceded by his opponents[1]—gave occasion for repeated and prolonged controversy, and some of the ablest efforts of Huss were produced in defence of its positions. Stanislaus and Paletz had united to assail it. To them he replied with overwhelming force. Both of them had, at the time of the interdict, been excommunicated along with Huss. Terrified by the bull, they had, in the most humiliating manner, abandoned their former ground. When Huss was informed of Paletz's desertion, he replied, "Paletz is my friend, and truth is my friend; but both being my friends, the truth I must honor in preference." Indeed, to appreciate the relative position of the two men, and the course which Paletz afterwards took as the persecutor of his friend, we need to know what Huss has stated in his writings as to the origin of the difficulty. He says, "On the publication of the bull of crusade and indulgences, he presented me with a paper, in his own hand-writing, stating the palpable errors of the bull. I keep this paper still in my hands, as evidence of what I say. It was on his consultation with another colleague, that he changed his course and went back."[2] With such facts in hand, it was not difficult for Huss to place his old associate in a most unenviable light.

Still more important in some respects was the controversy of Huss, already mentioned, with "The Eight Doctors." From his treatise[3] in connection with it, it appears that Paletz, stung by the cutting reply and scathing exposure administered by Huss,

[1] Cochleius. [2] Mon. Hussi, 228, 265. [3] Ibid, 293.

had urged upon a clerical assemblage at Zebrak, a more active prosecution of the process against the reputed heretic. Others shared his zeal, and Huss, for reasons more obvious in his age than in ours, offered to submit himself—as Savanarola afterwards did—to the ordeal by fire. But with the good sense that must have characterized his estimate of a barbarous and absurd custom, he insisted that to make the terms equal all his accusers should submit to the same ordeal. To this, however, they very naturally objected. They had not sufficient confidence, either in the justice of their cause, or the harmlessness of the flames, to warrant them in walking one after another into the midst of the blazing fagots. They proposed that one of the accusers should be selected, and that he and Huss together should undergo the ordeal. Huss insisted—we can scarcely believe without something of a grave waggery—on his own proposition. It was too much for his clerical opponents. They were affrighted, and declined the terms. But, not altogether to be defeated, the eight doctors assail Huss with the pen.

It was a most unfortunate measure. The eight combined are no match for Huss, single-handed and alone. His treatise is one of the ablest arguments in controversial divinity that was ever penned. Huss and the doctors remind us of Milton and Salmasius. For keenness of reply, vigor of retort, and caustic irony, the Bohemian and the Englishman might be accounted peers; and surely, in the old blind poet of England there could not have been a more devoted love of truth, a more ardent and fearless chivalry in its defence, or a greater readiness to risk all in a holy cause, than were to be found in Huss.

Other works of the reformer, worthy of more extended notice than can now be given them, are his treatises on "The Three Doubts," on "The Body of Christ," etc., and his "Commentaries" on different portions of scripture, as well as several smaller works, in which his views on important subjects are clearly defined.

Throughout these writings the sentiments and doctrines are for the most part such as would now be termed Evangelical. Occasionally he gives utterance to views which betray the lingering influence of tradition and authority. Transubstantiation he maintains,[1] in as firm a tone as Luther employed when he met Zwingle with the repeated citation, "This is my body." He allows, though very cautiously, and with qualification, of prayers for the dead. He was as yet satisfied with the old observance of the eucharist in which bread only was administered. He allowed confession to a priest, and a qualified absolution, although he contended that none could forgive sins but God only.

But in the most explicit manner he maintains that the scriptures are the only supreme authority in matters of faith, and vindicates "The sufficiency of the law of Christ for the rule of the church." False decretals, traditions, and priestly superstitions are thus swept away at a single stroke. Christ is the sole head of the church, and no bull or excommunication is to be regarded which conflicts with justice

[1] Mon. Hussi, i. 164.

or with the cause of Christian truth. It is first of all to be tried by the word of God. In his reprobation of the sale of indulgences, and masses for the dead, he was most severe. While not as distinct as later reformers on the doctrine of justification by faith, he holds that "Christ is the basis of all merit of the members of the church," and that works without faith are of no avail.

But in the exposition of the claims of the law of God in setting forth its condemnation of all sin and wickedness,—the venality, avarice, ambition, extortion, sensuality, and vice of the ecclesiastical orders, and indeed of all classes,—he expended his strength. His own life was above reproach, and his vehement rebukes did not lose their force by being made to recoil upon himself.

This was one great secret of his strength. In a corrupt and venal age he refused the bribes of ambition, and stood unawed by the terrors of power. He was known as one set for the defence of truth. The strength of his convictions contributed to make him strong.

And in his letters, written during his exile from Prague, we gather instructive views of his aims and character, as well as of the earnestness of his purpose. An active correspondence was kept up with his friends in the capital. Throughout this correspondence there breathes the spirit of a most ardent and glowing devotion, while the deep and apostolic anxiety with which he watched over the spiritual welfare and progress of his absent flock, is betrayed in almost every line. The reasons of his withdrawal from Prague are discussed. "'The hireling fleeth.' I have thought of that. But we must pray for guidance. We can do nothing better. Tell me whether my absence gives occasion for scandal. Are sacraments administered? Pray God to direct me what to do."

Again, he writes to the friend who had succeeded to his place as rector: "Your letter consoles me, where you say that the righteous will not be overwhelmed with sadness, let what will happen, and all that will live godly must suffer persecution. What to me are riches, honors, or disgrace? My sins alone grieve me. What if the just man lose his life; it is only to find the true life. God will yet destroy Antichrist. Be prepared for the conflict. Woe is me if I do not expose the abomination of desolation by preaching, teaching, and writing." Again, in another letter, he says, "I count it all joy that I am called a heretic, and so am excommunicated as disobedient. With Peter and John, it is better to obey God than man. The word of God is to be preached." He cites the examples of ancient saints to confirm his own faith under his harsh experience.

But his enforced separation from his beloved flock bore heavily upon his spirits. His heart was still with them. He did not forget to admonish and encourage them in his absence. Personal consequences to himself alone would not have kept him from them. "I have withdrawn myself," he says, "that I may not prove to the wicked an occasion of everlasting damnation, and to the good, cause of oppression and trouble."[1] Again he writes: "I say to you, my be-

[1] Epis. xi.

loved, though I am not in prison, yet I would gladly, for Christ's sake, die and be with him; and yet I would gladly, too, for your good, preach to you God's word; but I am in a strait betwixt two, and know not which to choose. For I await God's mercy, and I fear again lest something bad be done among you, so as to expose the faithful to persecution, and the unbelieving to eternal deatn."

He reminds his Bethlehem congregation of his many years of service among them,[1] and its fruits, and says, "For this, as God is my witness, I have labored more than twelve years among you preaching the divine word; and in this, my greatest consolation was to observe your earnest diligence in hearing God's word, and to witness the true and sincere repentance of many." He bids them beware of fickleness, and "have no regard for those persons walking a crooked path, who have turned about, and are now the most violent enemies of God, and our enemies." For himself, he asks their prayers, that God would give him good success in preaching his word. "In all the places where a need exists—in cities, in villages, in castles, in the fields, in the forests, wherever I can be of any use—pray for me that the word of God may not be kept back in me."

To the citizens of Prague he writes, (Christmas of 1413,) urging them to be constant in hearing the word of God. With scriptural admonitions he exhorts and encourages them, reminding them how Christ was treated. "I hear," he says, "of the plan in agitation for tearing down or invading the

[1] Epis. xiii.

churches where the gospel is preached, Bethlehem chapel especially. I am confident that God will not suffer them to accomplish anything. They tried to catch the goose (Huss) in the net of citations and anathemas, and now they are having designs upon some of you. But, instead of a single swallow, the truth has sent forth many eagles, that fly high in the strength of Christ. Pray for me, that I may write and preach more abundantly against the wickedness of Antichrist.[1] . . . If I came to Prague, my enemies would lie in wait for me, and would persecute you. But we will pray for them, that the elect among them may be saved."

In another letter, he says, "I am at a loss what to do; if I return to Prague, my presence might bring trouble. . . . Do not be disturbed for my absence; I trust in God that all will yet turn out well. Let them sing their ribaldry, or crucify me with their blasphemies, or stone the church doors, if they will."[2]

From these letters it is evident that some, during his absence, were urgent for his return to Prague. This, however, was at the time contrary to his own judgment. He desired to return, both on his own account and for the sake of his friends, but he did not deem it wise. He consoles them with encouragements drawn from the prophecies of Christ's second coming. "I fled," he says, "because Christ bids those that are persecuted in one city to flee into another. He did so himself. Some of your priests would be glad to have me back at Prague, to bring the inter-

[1] Mon. Hussi, 98. [2] Epis. vi.

dict in force, only that they might be relieved of saying masses at the canonical hours. They however are stung by the gospel. I should be glad indeed to come back and see you, and preach the gospel."

To the citizens of a neighboring town,[1] to which it appears the reform movement had extended, Huss writes an encouraging letter: "I have never seen you, but I have heard of your faith. I am unknown to you by face, but in Christ I would be faithful for your salvation."

Of the letters which he received during this period of his exile, but one has been preserved. It came from England, and it bore to Huss the expression of the sympathy and consolations of a Christian brother, "unknown by face, but not by faith and love, for space cannot separate those whom the love of Christ unites." How precious and cheering to him such sympathy and brotherhood from the land of Wickliffe! Bohemia had caught the echo of reform from England, and now Prague was prepared to respond in the person of one not unworthy to rank as Wickliffe's peer.

Yet the period from the first publication of the interdict until final return of Huss to Prague, had been one, to him, of severe trial. His enemies were not disposed to leave him at peace. His anxieties in behalf of what he regarded as the sacred cause of truth, knew no intermission. His warfare with error and with abounding iniquity was vigorous and incessant. Yet if he had been willing to abandon

[1] Epis. xiv.

his ground and belie his own convictions, he could almost have imposed his own terms. But he was not a man to be bought or sold. His conscience was made of sterner stuff.

From his own declarations, we know that his inward conflicts were severe. Yet, so far as we can judge from the course of his public career, he never wavered. Not for a single moment did he so far forget his position or duty, as to yield to guilty compromise. Amid the surging agitations around him he stands ever firm, like the rock amid the billows. Power has no terrors, and honor has no bribes, that can sway him from the straightforward path of duty.

Such is the man who, in the calm confidence of his own innocence and of the justice of his cause, patiently awaits the assembling of a general council, to which he will carry his appeal.

CHAPTER XII.

THE COUNCIL.

Assembling of the Council of Constance. — Selection of the Place. — Its Situation. — Its Present Condition. — Memorials of the Council. — The Summons of the Emperor and Pope Calling it. — Death of Ladislaus. — Reluctance of the Pope to go to Constance. — The Emperor Yields to the Demands of the Pope. — The Pope on his Journey. — The Princes. — Sigismund and his Position in Regard to the Council. — Huss at Prague.— Prepares to Leave. — Vindications of his Innocence. — Challenges Accusation. — Parting of Huss and Jerome. — Emperor's Letter. — Huss' Protectors. — Farewell Letter. — Forebodings of Huss. — His Firmness. — Letter to Martin. — The Martyr Spirit. — The Journey. — Kindly Receptions of Huss. — Letter from Nuremburg. — Reaches Constance. — Scenes In and Without the City. — Their Contrast with Christian Simplicity.— Learning Represented at the Council. — Poggio. — Niem. — Æneas Sylvius. — Zabarella. — Manuel Chrysoloras. — Gerson. — D'Ailly. — The Universities. — Humble Position of Huss amid these Scenes.

Sept., 1414–Nov., 1414.

The time had at length arrived for the assembling of the council of Constance. Never had any similar event occurred in the history of the church which excited a deeper or more general interest throughout the Christian world. The schism which had rent the church in pieces, and arrayed one portion against the other—the profligacy and reckless ambition of the rival popes—the wide and fearful corruption which had spread from the highest to the lowest dignitaries of the hierarchy—the alleged heresies of Huss and Petit—and the almost utter neglect into which ecclesiastical authority had fallen, combined to render the assembling of the council an event from which no ordinary results were anticipated. The emperor himself postponed regard for the interests of his kingdom to promote the convocation and the success of the council. It was in his view a greater glory to restore Christendom to the unity of a common head, than achieve victory or conquest on the field of battle. By his exertions the great obstacles to the convoking of a council had been met and removed,[1] and at the appointed time throngs from every portion of Christendom began to pour into the ancient city of Constance.

This city had been chosen by the emperor as the place for the assembling of the council. Reluctantly had the pope receded from his resolution not to allow its convocation where his power and authority would not be paramount.[2] The position of Constance was central, and comparatively easy of access. It was within the circle of Swabia, and subject to the imperial authority. Neither of the popes could here hope to control, or restrain the freedom of, the adherents of the other.

The city of Constance is situated upon the borders of the lake to which it gives it name. At the time of the council, and in the most flourishing period of its history, it contained little short of fifty thousand inhabitants. The traveller now finds scarcely a tithe of its former population within its walls. Old and curious houses, still standing, meet his eye as he walks the streets, but many of them untenanted. On the shores of the lake, and but a few feet from

[1] Fleury xxv. 350, 351. [2] Ib. 349.

the landing, he sees the *Kaufhaus*, or market, memorable still as the place where the sessions of the council were held. It was built A. D. 1338, and, at the time of the assembling of the council three-quarters of a century later, offered the best accommodations for a large audience-chamber to be found within the city. As the traveller walks up the solid steps of the edifice, once so thronged but now comparatively deserted, he enters the second story—a wide, low room, supported by heavy wooden pillars, and with a rough plank floor, like that of a barn. More than four hundred years ago this room was occupied by an assembly such as Christendom had never seen convoked before. The chair of the emperor, and the one in which the pope for a short time presided over the sessions of the council, together with other relics, form a museum of curiosities which are carefully preserved.

The summons to the council had been issued by the emperor, with the constrained assent[1] of John XXIII., in October 1413. The cardinals more readily united in the summons, at least a portion of them. Full assurances of security for person and property were given to all who should attend. The emperor pledged himself not to interfere with the respect claimed for the pope, or to put hindrances in the way of his exercising his authority.

In December the pope issued his proclamation also, directing all prelates to be present in person at the council, and all princes who could not attend to send[2] deputies, who should be authorized to act in

[1] Fleury, xxv. 349, gives the statements of Aretin. [2] Fleury, xxv. 357.

their name. In the vast crowd that obeyed the summons, we find nearly all the men of the age who were eminent in learning, station, and authority. In some cases they were freely elected, as at Paris, by provincial or national councils; and a fixed rate was allowed for their expenses, that nothing might interfere with their presence and their regular attendance upon the sessions of the council.

The only one of the rival popes who personally appeared at Constance was John XXIII. The hostility of Ladislaus in Italy had contributed greatly to induce him to consent that the council should be summoned to meet in a city beyond the limits of his government; but at the last moment, when he was about to set out for Constance, he heard the welcome intelligence of Ladislaus' death. This man, his bitter foe, had gathered an army for the siege of Bologna, when he was arrested by the hand of disease, and forced to withdraw, first to Rome and then to Naples, where he breathed his last.[1] The pope's former reluctance to leave Italy returned.[2] He stood no longer in pressing need of Sigismund's aid. In his anxiety to secure Rome again, he sent his general, Isolani, to seize and take possession of it. He would have been glad to have followed himself. It is amusing to see the efforts of the pope and emperor to elude and deceive one another. Sigismund was afraid that now, after all, the pope would not appear at Constance. Some of his friends warned him of the danger he incurred of going thither as pope and

[1] Monstrelet, i., 316, relates the horrid manner of his death, poisoned by the daughter of his physician. Another authority makes John XXIII. responsible for the deed.

[2] Fleury, xxv. 388.

coming back a private man. But the counsel of the cardinals, more anxious for the union of the church, prevailed.[1] John determined, before he set out, to secure of the emperor the most advantageous terms possible. Sigismund, on his part, dared not refuse the pope's demands, lest his absence should defeat the design of the council. The emperor's commissary at Constance was to accept, in the emperor's name, the pope's terms, and the magistrates and burgesses of Constance were exhorted and commanded to swear, on their part, to their faithful observance. No pretext was to be left the pope for non-appearance. The emperor knew the man with whom he had to deal, and, with a policy which matched the pope's, conceded everything. John XXIII. was to be received at Constance with all the honors due to the papal dignity: he should be recognized as true and sole pontiff; he should be at perfect freedom to come or go, and should exercise his authority over his dependents and all that appertained to him, without restriction. The city was bound to see that justice was done him, and his safe-conducts were to be recognized and respected. Such were the terms sworn to and signed, by order of the emperor, before the pope would set out for the council.

At length, with many fears and forebodings, he commenced his journey.[2] On the first of October, 1414, he left Bologna. His equipage and attendance were splendid and imposing. Gold, silver, gems, and costly raiment added to the pomp and magnificence of a princely retinue of cardinals, nobles, and their

[1] Fleury, xxv. 389.

[2] Godeau, xxxvi. 408.

attendants. At Merau he paused in his journey to confirm his alliance with Frederic, Duke of Austria, by which each was bound to support the other in his designs. On the twenty-eighth of October the pope reached Constance. Nine cardinals only, of the thirty-three who should have been present, were in his train. With these, however, and a large number of bishops and archbishops, and with the servants of his court, he made his entrance on horseback into the city. His reception was all that he could have claimed or expected. The clergy and magistrates met and escorted him with imposing pomp to the episcopal palace.

Already the streets were thronged with strangers from every part of Christendom, and more were on their way. There came thither to this celebrated council thirty cardinals, twenty archbishops, one hundred and fifty bishops, as many prelates, a multitude of abbots and doctors, and eighteen hundred priests. Among the sovereigns who attended in person, could be distinguished the Elector Palatine, the Electors of Mentz and of Saxony, and the Dukes of Austria, of Bavaria, and of Silesia. There were, besides, a vast number of margraves, counts, and barons, and a great crowd of noblemen and knights. At one time there might have been counted, as we are told,[1] thirty thousand horses within the circuit of the city. Each prince, nobleman, and knight was attended by his train,[2] and the number of persons present from abroad is estimated to have been not

[1] Fleury, xxv. 393.

[2] Helfert states that the escort of the Duke of Warwick was 500 horsemen; that of the Pope 600; and that of the Emperor 1000. P. 167.

less than forty or fifty thousand. Among these were reckoned almost every trade and profession, and some whose profession was their disgrace, but whose instincts and tastes made them seek the welcome they found among the miscellaneous crowd.

The pope had already reached Constance, "the pit for catching foxes," as he called it,[1] while observing it on his approach from a neighboring hill. The emperor was more tardily to make his appearance. Among the feeble monarchs of that day, in Europe, he towered conspicuous. Active, enterprising, intrepid, inexhaustible in resources, he owed the imperial sceptre mainly to his own exertions. Often unsuccessful, his reverses were never suffered to repress his spirit or damp his energies. All the varieties of his experience had conspired to make him a shrewd and able politician, while his devotion to the interests of the church had gained him an influence and reputation that veiled the selfishness of his aims.

At the period of the assembling of the council, Sigismund was in the full strength and vigor of a mature manhood, with a prestige and power that restrained, if they could not suppress, the dissatisfactions of enemies and rivals. He was forty-seven years of age, and to the respect which he claimed for the vigor and energy of his measures, must be added the impression of his personal appearance. His manners were noble and engaging. His look and walk bespoke the emperor. He could converse with facility in several languages, nor as the son of Charles IV. was he wanting in that regard for litera-

[1] L'Enfant, i. 19. Godeau, xxxvi. 410.

ture which honored at once his father's memory and his own tastes. "I can in a single day make a thousand noblemen," he used to say, "but in a thousand years I cannot make a single scholar."[1] The fierce and often sanguinary impulses of his youth had been checked by his own discretion, as well as by the lessons of experience. The example of his brother served as a warning against the indulgence of his lusts; and though his impetuous temper, even on the throne, sometimes gained the mastery, it was only for the moment that the cooler dictates of reason and policy were forced to give way. His brother's ruling passion was for wine and revelry, and it made him reckless of expenditure; but Sigismund, by his aspiration for the honor of restoring peace and union to the church, and in the pursuance of this design, was also liberal even to a degree of prodigality. With much that was grand and chivalrous in his nature, his life shows that he could, when necessary, adopt the arts of fraud and dissimulation to promote his purpose, and his memory will never lose the stain which his shameful breach of trust toward the Bohemian reformer has made indelible. With such station, talents, and reputation, the influence of Sigismund in the council was more controlling and decisive than that of any other member.

On the eleventh of October, while the pope was yet midway on his journey, John Huss left Prague for Constance. Before quitting the Bohemian capital, he took occasion to make a full declaration of his doctrinal views. Although his mind must at

[1] Æneas Sylvius, 45. Quoted by L'Enfant, i. 48.

times have been filled by melancholy presentiments, his heart did not quail, nor did he neglect any legitimate means of vindicating his innocence. He openly declared his purpose to render at Constance, before the assembled representatives of the Christian world, a testimony of his faith. A few days before his departure,[1] in a paper affixed to the gates of the palace, he announced that he was about to depart in order to justify himself before the council; "so that," said he, "if any one suspects me of heresy, let him proceed thither and prove, in presence of the pope and the doctors, if I ever entertained or taught any false or mistaken doctrine. If any man can convict me of having inculcated any doctrine contrary to the Christian faith, I will consent to undergo all the penalty to which heretics are liable. But I trust that God will not grant the victory to unbelievers—to men who outrage the truth."

Huss next announced his readiness to render an account of his faith in presence of the archbishop of Prague and his clergy.[2] He then boldly applied for a certificate of his orthodoxy from the very person who, in virtue of his office, should have been most anxious to condemn him if he had believed him guilty,—the bishop of Nazareth, grand inquisitor of the diocese of Prague. The certificate was granted,[3] though we can only surmise the influences which must have virtually extorted it. It seems most probable that the popular feeling enlisted on the side of the reformer constrained the inquisitor to sign a doc-

[1] Mon. Hussi, i. 2. Godeau, xxxvi. 413.

[2] Mon. Hussi, i. 2.

[3] Ib. i. 3. Godeau, xxxvi. 414.

ument which he would willingly have withheld. An authentic copy of it, as drawn up before a notary, was in substance as follows:—"By these presents, we make known to all men that we have often held converse with the honorable Master John Huss, bachelor in theology of the celebrated university of Prague; that we have had several serious conferences with him relative to the Holy Scriptures, and other matters; and that we have always considered him to be a faithful and good Catholic, not finding in him up to this day any evil or error. We certify besides, that the said John Huss has declared that he was ready to render reason for his faith in presence of the archbishop and his clergy against any one that might come forward to accuse him of error or heresy; but that no one presented himself to support the charge. In faith of which we have delivered to him this letter, sealed with our great seal, this 30th August, 1414."

Armed with this paper, Huss proceeded to the abbey of St. James, where the barons and the archbishop of Prague were assembled for public business.[1] There he besought the prelate to declare openly, if he either accused or suspected him of heresy; and in case he did not, he conjured him to give a public testimony of the fact, which he might find of service in his journey to Constance. By another account, contained in a document subsequently drawn up by the nobles of Bohemia, it would appear that the question of the orthodoxy of Huss was put to the archbishop by the nobles themselves, and that his

[1] Mon. Hussi, i. 4.

reply was, that he had never "known of any erroneous word on the part of Huss;" and that this answer was given of his own free-will, and under no constraint; though it was added by the archbishop, that he thought "that Huss should purge himself from the excommunication which he had incurred." It is undoubtedly true that such was the reply of the archbishop. Seven years after this he openly favored the Hussites.

A few days later, Huss asked permission to appear before a general assembly of the clergy of Prague, presided over by the archbishop. He offered to establish his innocence by scripture, by the holy canons of the church, and by the fathers; but his application was refused.[1]

The motives which must have influenced the clergy in this matter are obvious. Undoubtedly they preferred to have Huss leave the city without such testimony as they would be constrained to give, and they hoped by means of the council to be permanently relieved of his presence. Some of them doubtless imagined that it would be much easier to deal with him in the distant city of Constance, where they could secretly magnify his errors, than in Prague, where his friends were at once so numerous and so powerful.[2]

In the month of October, 1414, Huss bade adieu to his chapel at Bethlehem, where his voice was

[1] Fleury, xxv. 403.

[2] Paletz says, "No one ventured to call the followers of Huss by their proper names, for fear of danger to property or person.—*Mon. Hussi,* i. 255. It is not probable that the danger was less when the Inquisitor was forced to give his certificate, and the most politic course for the clergy was to have nothing to do with the matter.

never more to be heard, and to his faithful friends and disciples, some of whom were to follow him in his path of self-denial, suffering, and martyrdom. He left behind him his faithful companion and bosom friend, Jerome, and the scene of parting was one of deep emotion on the part of each. "Dear Master," said Jerome, "be firm; maintain intrepidly what thou hast written and preached against the pride, avarice, and other vices of the churchmen, with arguments drawn from the Holy Scriptures. Should this task become too severe for thee,—should I learn that thou hast fallen into any peril,—I shall fly at once to thy assistance."[1]

The diet had demanded of the emperor a safe-conduct for Huss. This was readily granted him by Sigismund, in the usual form; and the document, dated "Spires, October 18," was forwarded to him, so as to meet him on the road,—not, however, till he had passed the borders of Bohemia, where the safe-conduct of Wenzel which he had received would cease to have validity. By the king, two staunch and faithful knights, the Lords of Chlum and Duba, were appointed as companions and protectors of Huss.[2] Several other noble barons joined the escort. John de Chlum was one of the most devoted adherents of the reformer, and his life offers a pure model of the most touching and devoted friendship. His name in the eyes of posterity is inseparably associated with that of Huss.

Previously to his departure the master would have addressed a farewell sermon to his beloved follow-

[1] L'Enfant, xiii. [2] Mon. Hussi, i. 4.

ers, but time, or probably his own tender and sympathetic spirit, would not allow of it. His written valediction shows that he was not unmindful of the danger which he incurred. "My brethren,"[1] said he, "do not suppose that I am provoking for myself unworthy treatment for any false doctrine. . . . I am departing with a safe-conduct from the king to meet my many and mortal enemies. . . . I confide altogether in the all-powerful God, in my Saviour. I trust that he will listen to your ardent prayers that he will put his wisdom and prudence into my mouth, in order that I may resist them; and that he will accord me his Holy Spirit, to fortify me in his truth, so that I may face with courage, temptations, prison, and if necessary, a cruel death. Jesus Christ suffered for his well-beloved; and ought we then to be astonished that he has left us his example, in order that we may ourselves endure with patience all things for our own salvation? He is God, and we are his creatures; he is the Lord, and we are his servants; he is Master of the world, and we are contemptible mortals; yet he suffered! Why then should we not suffer also, particularly when suffering is for us a purification? Therefore, beloved, if my death ought to contribute to his glory, pray that it may come quickly, and that he may enable me to support all my calamities with constancy. But if it be better that I return among you, let us pray to God that I may return without stain,—that is, that I may not suppress one tittle of the truth of the gospel, in order to leave my brethren an excellent

[1] Ib. 57. Ep. ii.

example to follow. Probably, therefore, you will never more behold my face at Prague; but should the will of the all-powerful God deign to restore me to you, let us then advance with a firmer heart in the knowledge and the love of his law."

It is not strange that Huss should have felt oppressed by the presentiment that he would never return to the scene of his past labors. While thoroughly conscious of his own integrity and honesty of purpose—an integrity and honesty which his enemies could not deny—he was to some extent aware of the unscrupulous means which a bigoted malice stood ready to employ. He deemed his return to Prague, at the best, doubtful.[1] He knew that some of his most bitter foes would be present at the council, and that their whole influence would be exerted to secure his condemnation. He knew that his former friend and associate, who had once been almost a brother, with whom he had studied, ate, and slept, but now his most violent persecutor,—Stephen Paletz,—and a former curé of a church in Old Prague, Michael De Causis, along with several others, his bitter antagonists, had preceded him to Constance, and were determined on his ruin. He knew that the German nation, as represented in the council, would not forget their old

[1] In the midst of his trials at Constance, the parting words of one of his congregation, a Polish tailor, came to his mind, "God be with thee, for hardly do I think you will get back again unharmed, dearest Master John, and most steadfast in the truth. Not the king of Hungary, but the King of heaven reward thee with all good, for the good and true instruction that I have received from thee."—*Ep.* 33. Others told him to beware of the emperor's treachery, and evidently apprehended that he would never return.—*Ep.* 34, p. 59.

grudge of virtual expulsion, as they considered it, from the university. And when we add to this his knowledge of the general corruption of the clergy, whom he had offended by his rebukes, and their readiness to become instruments in a transaction which could be covered with the veil of pious and devout zeal, we see that Huss may have well commenced his journey with the presentiment of imprisonment, if not of martyrdom.

But his spirit did not quail before the danger. He met it with no presumptuous rashness, but with the calm constancy and courage of a Christian hero. There was, indeed, one hope that contributed much to cheer and sustain him, and that was, that he would be privileged freely and fully to state and explain his views before the council, and show their accordance with what he still deemed the standards of the church,—the scriptures and the fathers. In this hope he was doomed to disappointment; yet his faith in God humbled him to such a degree in his own esteem, while it forbade all fear of man, that the thought of turning aside or shunning the ordeal to which he was summoned seems never to have entered his mind.

In a letter which he wrote to one of his disciples, Priest Martin,[1] at his setting out for the council, he speaks of himself with the greatest humility, and we seem to read the reformer's heart while he unbosoms himself to his friend. He accuses himself, as if they were grave offences, of faults which most would have deemed too trifling to be noticed,[2]—of having

[1] Mon. Hussi, i. Epis. ii. p. 57. [2] Playing chess.

felt pleasure in wearing rich apparel, and of having wasted hours in frivolous occupations. His own severe and enlightened conscience made him his own accuser where others could not bring the first charge of guilt. He adds these affecting instructions:

"May the glory of God and the salvation of souls occupy thy mind, and not the possession of benefices and estates. Beware of adorning thy house more than thy soul; and above all, give thy care to the spiritual edifice. Be pious and humble with the poor; and consume not thy substance in feasting. Shouldest thou not amend thy life, and refrain from superfluities, I fear thou will be severely chastised, as I am myself—I, who also made use of such things, led away by custom, and troubled by a spirit of pride. Thou knowest my doctrine, for thou hast received my instructions from thy childhood; it is useless therefore for me to write to thee any further. But I conjure thee by the mercy of our Lord, not to imitate me in any of the vanities into which thou hast seen me fall." He concludes by making some bequests, and disposing, as if by will, of several articles which belonged to him; and then, on the cover of the letter, he adds this prophetic phrase, "I conjure thee, my friend, not to break this seal until thou art fully certified of my death."

The spirit of the martyr glows brighter and more brightly in the farewell letters of Huss. We see him rising above all the influences of the fear or of the applause of men. His soul, always pure and upright, soars to a heavenly atmosphere of holy, elevated purpose. There is less of the impetuosity and the passion of former days, yet the torrent of zeal flows in a deper, a calmer, but stronger current. We discern, if possible, less than ever of the partisan, or of the popular orator fed on the public acclamations. He shuns the parting scene of a public leave-taking, where he knew that the strong affection which was felt for him would burst forth in turbulent grief. He needed no assurance of the attachment of the people or of the nobility to sustain him. A firmer support he found in the promises of the divine Word, and in solitary communings with his own heart and with God. Henceforward he is to be thrown almost alone among bitter and implacable enemies. Strange faces will meet his, and prejudice will misrepresent the man and pervert his words. He stands already in presence of a cruel fate. But his soul is unmoved, unshaken by human terrors. Conscious of his own integrity, he plants his feet on the Rock of Ages. Bereft in great measure of human resource, he looks up to heaven for aid. Grace confers upon the reformer now a calm majesty of soul, such as we failed to discern while we saw him controlling others by his eloquence, or imbuing their minds with the deep sincerity and earnestness of his own convictions. With no attendant pomp—without bravado—with no disgusting exhibition of self-confidence—but with the lowliness, meekness, patience, and courage of a martyr, Huss sets out for the city where few will be found of spirit kindred to his own.

The reformer's journey to Constance was quiet, orderly, and uninterrupted.[1] His fame had preceded

[1] The kind reception of Huss on his journey is the more surprising from

him, and all malice seemed lost in curiosity to see or hear the man of whom such stories had been told.[1] The simple earnestness of his speech, and the reasonableness of his views as he presented them, bespoke the favor of his auditors. The common people, and the humbler priests and curates, who had themselves suffered in some cases bitterly from the despotism and avarice of the higher ecclesiastics, would scarce find fault with a man who had really been fighting their battles, and was now suffering in their cause. There was, in fact, throughout the whole Christian world, a conviction of the need of reformation, but a conviction most deeply rooted in the minds of those whose sympathies would lead them to adopt for their leader some Piers Ploughman—some one of themselves, whose honest and straightforward speech spared neither princely arrogance nor prelatical corruption. In Huss they saw one whom the persecuting rage of the priests had forced into notoriety, but who, in stigmatizing their hypocrisy, arrogance, and avarice, had really shown himself the friend of the poor, humble, and oppressed. Throughout his journey he experienced only respect and kindness. Even when he had crossed the Bohemian frontier, and entered the German territory where he expected to meet the malice instigated by the expelled students, he was happily disappointed. He was greeted with favor instead of scorn.

the fact that he was preceded by the Bishop of Lubeck, who attempted to poison the minds of the common people against him. Huss says, Epis. vi., "Habui unum precursorum, Episcopum Lubicensem, qui uno nocturno, nos semper precessit, et divulgavit quod me ducerent catenatum in curru, et quod caverent me, quia ego cognoscerem mentem hominum."

[1] Mon. Hussi, i. 58. Ep. iii.

From Nuremberg, which he had reached on the twentieth day of October, he writes back to his friends, giving an account of his journey up to that time. In his own characteristic language the reformer says,[1] "Be it known to you, beloved brethren, that I have not found it necessary to travel once *in incognito*, since the day of my departure, but have ridden freely, and without disguise. I have travelled on horseback, and with my features exposed to public view. On my drawing near Bernau, I found the curé and his vicars waiting for me; when I came up to them, he drank to my health in a cup of wine, and also, when we reached the inn, presented me with a large flagon of wine. He and his people gladly expressed their satisfaction with my opinions, and the good man called himself my old but unknown friend. I was afterwards joyfully received by all the Germans in Neustadt. As we travelled through Weiden, a very considerable crowd eyed us with the astonishment of admiration, and when we arrived at Sultzbach, we stopped at the house where the district session was that day held. The assembly being not yet dispersed, I thus addressed the consuls and notables of the town: 'Behold, I am that John Huss of whom you have doubtless heard much evil. Here I am: ascertain the real state of the case by interrogating me yourselves.' We conversed together for some time, and they approved of all I said. We next passed through Hersbruck, and spent the night in the town of Lauf, where the curé, a great jurist, and his vicars had come to see me, with whom I con-

[1] Epis. iii.

versed, much to their satisfaction." Huss next proceeded to Nuremburg, the chief city of Franconia, where the independent spirit of the citizens, which has since been subdued in the lapse of centuries, then boldly defied the imperial fortress, and claimed the free exercise of municipal rights. Some merchants having ridden forward, and given notice that Huss was approaching the city, the people came thronging to the streets and public places looking eagerly for his coming. They gazed on the Bohemian escort as it passed by, anxiously inquiring which was John Huss. As soon as they discovered him, they surrounded and accompanied him to the inn, with many encouraging assurances that the council would not dare to injure him. During his repast, some priests were announced. He rose from the table to meet them, but finding that they wished for private conversation with him, Huss replied, "that he was unwilling to whisper his doctrines in the ears of only a few individuals, but would rather proclaim them on the housetop." "I speak only in public, and they who wish to hear me have only to listen." By means of placards on the doors of the churches, these men, and all who felt disposed to come, were invited to a religious conference, on the afternoon of the following day. A large number assembled. Besides the townspeople, the magistrates of the city were present. The discussion continued till evening. Among others, a Carthusian doctor presented himself, and displayed much subtlety in argument. But the popular voice was on the side of the reformer. When in the evening Huss concluded the defence of his opinions, the mayor, councillors, magistrates, and people overwhelmed him with clamors of applause. "At last they said to me," writes Huss, "Master, all that we have just heard is Catholic; we have taught those things for many, many years, looking on them as true; and such we consider them still. Undoubtedly you will return from this council with honor." "Learn," says Huss, "that I have not hitherto met with a single enemy, but that in every place where I have stopped I have been excellently received. In fact, the bitterest enemies I have are certain obscure persons from Bohemia. What more shall I say to you? The Lords Wenceslaus Duba and John Chlum act piously and nobly toward me. They are the heralds and advocates of the truth, and with them, God giving his aid, all passes most suitably."

From hospitable Nuremberg Huss travelled to Swabia, on the extreme border of which Constance was situated. Here, too, the courteous kindness and respect with which he was welcomed far surpassed his expectations. At Biberach, some fifty miles from Constance, he disputed with several priests, and other learned men, on the subject of obedience to the pope. The popular satisfaction with the result was such, that he was borne in triumph through the streets. Such a reception, by those who were personally strangers to Huss, shows how ready was the soil of the popular mind for the seeds of reforming truth.

On the third of November the Bohemians arrived at Constance.

From every direction crowds were thronging to the famous council. Multitudes had already arrived, and more were on their way. The buildings of the city were insufficient to accommodate the immense concourse.[1] Booths and wooden buildings were erected outside the walls, and thousands of pilgrims were encamped in the adjoining country. The whole neighborhood presented a curious and novel scene. All classes of society, laity as well as clergy—representatives of every nation, with their peculiarities of costume and manner—the soldier in his armor, the prince followed by his escort, the prelate in his robes, the magistrate with his symbols of authority, servants hastening on errands, thousands providing for the food and entertainment of those who had gathered to the council,—all contributed to make the city of Constance a miniature Christendom. To consult the various tastes of the immense crowd of strangers, there were shows and amusements of all kinds, dramatic entertainments and representations of every description, varied with the solemn or gaudy pomp of religious proceedings. Van der Hardt has preserved, on the large folio pages of his "History of the Council," the pictured insignia of those who were in person, or by deputy, present during its sessions. Amid the infinite multiplicity and diversity of these coats of arms the mind is confused, and constrained to wonder at the scene within the walls of the *Kaufhaus*, where so many of them were blazoned or suspended about the walls. We have kings, popes, patriarchs, archbishops, bishops, princes, dukes, marquises, counts, barons, nobles, knights, ambassadors, cardinals, abbots, masters, each with original or an-

[1] Godeau, xxxvi. 420.

cestral contributions to the heraldry of Europe, with devices that seem to have exhausted the symbolisms of nature and of art. What then must have been the spectacle which the city of Constance presented, when all these dignitaries were gathered within its walls, and each vied with the other in the pomp and magnificence of his attendance and display! Who that walked these crowded streets, or gazed upon the princely robes, the rich and costly attire sparkling with jewels and shining with gold, the waving plumes, the burnished armor, the embroidered standards, the splendid equipage, the lengthened cavalcade, which, as they swept by, seemed to realize some vision of oriental fancy,—who would have imagined that amid such scenes of worldly pomp and pageantry were to be sought decisions and counsels, inspired by the Holy Ghost—sentiments accordant with the doctrines of the Galilean fishermen, or sympathy for the evangelical simplicity of the Bohemian reformer!

But let us not forget that, beneath all this gaudy ostentation of wealth and power, there was present another element, not worldly perhaps, though unconsciously controlled by worldly influences, which deserves a momentary notice. Among those who could claim membership in this most œcumenical of all the councils, were men whom we would have been glad to have found in better company, and whose ability, taste, learning, or devotion, however mistaken, suffices, and more than suffices, for their lack of coronets or heraldric device.

Literature and science were not unworthily represented. By the side of the dignitaries of the church and empire stood several of those whom the after-world honors as the living lights of their age. There in the service, but not in serfdom, to the pope, might be seen Poggio Bracciolini of Florence, one of the most illustrious scholars of his day, his sentiments liberal and manly, and himself possessed with a zeal for literature which was rewarded by the discovery, in the old monasteries, of lost manuscripts of the ancient classics, the writings of Quintilian, Lucretius, Cicero, and others. There, too, was Thierry de Niém, secretary to several popes, and whom Providence seems to have placed near the source of so many iniquities that by his pen they might be consecrated to historic infamy. With these must be recorded also Æneas Sylvius Piccolomini, afterward Pope Pius II., whose fame, as the wearer of the triple-crown, has been long since lost in the greater merit of his pen. There was also, eminent among the members of the council, Francis Zabarella, Cardinal of Florence, a man whose learning, virtues, and moderation secured the respect of all the members of the council, and whose funeral, not long after this, was attended in a most imposing manner by the emperor himself, as well as the highest dignitaries of church and state. The feebleness of the Eastern empire had no need to blush for its representative, when it sent in its behalf to Constance the learned Manuel Chrysoloras, a man whose worth was testified by the gratitude of his scholar Poggio, who erected a handsome monument to his memory. By the side of the epitaph that declares his virtues, were verses composed in his honor by Æneas Sylvius, and inscribed in letters of gold.

But among all who were members of the council of Constance, none occupied a more important position, or exerted greater influence upon the decisions of the body, than John Charlier Gerson, and Peter D'Ailly, Cardinal of Cambray, honored with the appellation of "The Eagle of France." Gerson, for a long time, might be regarded as the master-spirit of the council. As ambassador of Charles VI., king of France, and chancellor of the church and university of Paris, his position was one to give force and effect to his words, and it is not too much to say that he was fully equal to his station. To a character above reproach, and a zeal which rose superior to every obstacle and rejected every seducing influence, he joined a degree of ability for thought, speech, and action which made him *facile princeps*, the foremost man among the foremost men of the council. More than perhaps any other member, he had a well and clearly-devised scheme of his own, a philosophy of ecclesiasticism, which was the product of years of careful and observing thought. Better, perhaps, than any other member, he understood the attitude and relations of the figures on the chessboard of Christendom, and knew the moves to be made to win the game for the church.

For the most part, the Cardinal of Cambray, although raised by John XXIII. to the honors of the purple, occupied an independent position, and was found generally by the side of Gerson. Revered by the latter as his former master, teacher and pupil were now united in common views and common efforts. Both had learned in the university of Paris some lessons in regard to the circumstances and corruption of the church which were not yet lost upon them, and both were men whose fearless integrity rose above the allurements of greatness or the frowns of power.

The universities of Paris, Cologne, Vienna, Heidelberg, Prague, Orleans, Erfurt, Avignon, Bologna, Cracow, and Oxford, were represented at the council. Several independent states and cities sent deputies or ambassadors.

Thus were assembled at Constance, in obedience to the summons of pope and emperor, the component parts of a so-called Christian council, into whose hands were given in trust the suffering interests of Christendom. In the sequel we shall see the results accomplished, such as might be expected of a body of men drawn together by the most diverse and discordant motives, each of them for the most part impelled by an ambition of his own. The thoughtful observer turns his eye away from all the pageantry and pomp that allure the senses, to the humble dwelling of a poor widow, whom Huss compares to her of Sarepta, who received Elijah. In her house the Bohemian reformer found a welcome refuge, if not a secure asylum.

CHAPTER XIII.

ARREST AND IMPRISONMENT OF HUSS.

JOHN XXIII. INFORMED OF THE ARRIVAL OF HUSS. — SENTENCE OF EXCOMMUNICATION SUSPENDED. — HUSS PREPARES TWO DISCOURSES. — THE SUBSTANCE OF THEM. — HE IS NOT ALLOWED TO PREACH. — PROCEEDINGS OF HIS ENEMIES. — MICHAEL DE CAUSIS. — THE OTHER CONSPIRATORS. — THEIR INFLUENCE WITH THE CARDINALS. — ARTS EMPLOYED TO KEEP THE PEOPLE AWAY FROM HUSS. — JOHN XXIII. FAVORED BY THE ABSENCE OF THE EMPEROR. — ANNOUNCEMENT MADE NOV. 1, 1414. — ARRANGEMENTS. — NOV. 3, 1414. — THANKSGIVING FOR THE RECOVERY OF ROME. — INTRIGUES. — DOINGS OF THE CONGREGATION OF NOV. 12, 1414. — SESSION OF NOV. 16. — THE POPE'S SERMON. — BULL READ BY CARDINAL ZABARELLA. — CANON OF THE COUNCIL OF TOLEDO. — OFFICERS APPOINTED. — OPPORTUNE USE OF THE HERESY OF HUSS. — INSIGNIA OF BENEDICT AND GREGORY TORN DOWN. — HUSS CITED TO APPEAR BEFORE THE CARDINALS. — REPLY OF HUSS. — HIS COMPLIANCE. — CARDINAL D'AILLY. — THE CONFERENCE. — INCIDENT OF THE MINORITE FRIAR, DIDACUS. — AFTERNOON CONFERENCE. — ARTCLES OF ACCUSATION. — OTHER CHARGES OF CAUSIS. — HUSS KEPT UNDER ARREST. — INDIGNATION OF CHLUM. — COMPLAINS TO THE POPE. — THE LATTER APPOINTS A JUDICIAL COMMISSION. — HUSS IMPRISONED. — HIS SICKNESS. — CHLUM VISITS THE CARDINALS. — THEIR INDIFFERENCE. — VAIN APPEAL TO THE PEOPLE. — DETERMINATION TO APPLY TO THE EMPEROR. — ARRIVAL OF LATZEMBOCK. — DESPATCH TO BOHEMIA. — THE SAFE-CONDUCT. — CHLUM EXHIBITS IT. — PLACARDS POSTED. — CORRESPONDENCE OF THE EMPEROR AND POPE. — THE MASK TORN OFF. — MANDATE OF SIGISMUND. — HUSS DENIED AN ADVOCATE. — HIS OTHER GRIEVANCES. — THE COMMISSION TO EXAMINE HIS WRITINGS. — THE IMPERIAL MANDATE DISOBEYED. — MOTIVES OF THE POPE.

NOV. 3, 1414 – DEC. 6, 1414.

THE next morning after the arrival of Huss at Constance, the two noblemen who had accompanied him, John of Chlum and Wenzel of Duba, visited the pope to notify him of the fact. They informed him that Huss had come, provided with a safe-conduct from the emperor, and begged to know, without reserve, whether he might remain in Constance free from the risk of violence. The pope's answer seemed frank and cordial. "Had he killed my own brother," said John XXIII., thanking the knights for this mark of deference, "not a hair of his head should be touched while he remained in the city."[1]

No doubt the pope was sincere in his declaration. He did not wish to offend the Bohemian knights. It was his interest rather to secure their favor. It is impossible, from his known character, to suppose that he felt in the least concerned for the fate of Huss, so long as he could be left unmolested himself. The time had not yet come when it was his policy, by an affected zeal for orthodoxy, to avert from his own head the indignation his crimes merited, and concentrate it upon Huss.

During the first few weeks of his residence in Constance, Huss enjoyed a tolerable share of liberty. His sentence of excommunication was suspended, not from any regard for himself personally, but that the city might not be subject to interdict on his account.[2] He was enjoined, however, not to be present at public mass, and to avoid giving any occasion for scandal. At his own lodgings he was left unmolested. Here he conversed with large numbers of persons who came to visit him, vindicating his innonence, and defending his doctrines by word and pen. Each day he celebrated mass in his chamber, in the presence of many who assembled from the neighbor-

[1] Godeau, xxxvi. 44. L'Enfant, 36. (The references to L'Enfant are, after this date, to his "History of the Council of Constance.")

[2] Helfert, 179. Godeau, xxxvi. 420 Huss, however, wrote, soon after his arrival at Constance, (Epis. vi.) "Papa non vult tollere processus."

hood. The bishop of Constance is said to have sent his vicar to prohibit the continuance of the practice, and to represent to him that, as excommunicate, it was not permissible for him to discharge the sacred offices of priest. To this we are told that Huss replied in a somewhat defiant tone, declaring that he paid no heed to the excommunication. But the story rests on doubtful authority, and does not accord with the prudent and conciliatory tone which Huss assumed from his first arrival in the city.

His attention was especially directed towards making preparation for the public audience before the council, in the confidence of which he had set out for Constance. With this object in view he prepared two discourses, which he wished to deliver, and which have been preserved to us in his works.[1] The first of these is substantially a confession of his faith. He declares his assent to the Apostolic creed, protesting that he has never intentionally advanced or defended anything opposed to any article of faith. The Holy Scriptures are, in his judgment, the true rule of doctrinal belief, and sufficient for salvation. He would not exclude recognition of the sentences of the doctors who have faithfully expounded scripture, and he professes his veneration for general and provincial councils, decretals, laws, canons, and constitutions, so far as they are conformed to the word of God. Faith is the foundation of all the virtues which are essential to the service of God. It must precede the confession of the lips and active obedience. Every man is of necessity a disciple of God or of the devil. The

[1] Mon. Hussi, i. 45, 56.

rudiments, the alphabet, of either school is faith or infidelity. He holds, moreover, as he had taught in Bethlehem chapel, that we are not to put faith in the virgin, the saints, the church, or the pope, but in God alone. The highest form of faith is that which is due to Holy Scripture as the primitive standard of truth. A Christian faith necessitates a life of obedience, and hence a person in mortal sin is only a Christian in name, and cannot recite the creed without lying.

On the subject of the church, he presents the same views which he had put forth in his treatise two years previous, but dwells more particularly on the doctrine of the "sleeping church." He admits that souls in purgatory may be benefited by the intercession of the living, and prays Christ to forgive those who had said or insinuated that he denied the intercession of saints. He takes pains to express his regard for the Virgin Mary as our advocate, mediatress, and in some sort the cause of the incarnation, passion, and resurrection of Christ, and consequently of our salvation.

The second sermon of Huss is on the subject of the peace and union of the church. Here he often employs language taken from the writings of Jerome, Bernard, Gregory, and others. The tone of the discourse is less pungent and severe than that of many which were subsequently delivered in the presence of the council. But Huss was not to be allowed to preach. His Bohemian enemies had followed him to Constance, resolved upon his ruin. The principal ones among them were, of course, Stephen Paletz,

Michael de Causis, and Andrew Broda; but besides, there were also Nason, Benesch, Nicholas of Podwein, Nicholas, priest of the Vissehrad, John Stokes the Englishman, and some twelve others.[1] Stanislaus was on his way to join them, when he was struck down by the pestilence and died at Neuhaus.[2]

His enemies had no sooner reached the city, than they nailed placards in all public places, denouncing Huss as a heretic and as excommunicate. Spies were set upon his track, to note his conduct and report his words. His enemies had the largest liberty to vaunt their malignant calumnies, while he was confined almost entirely to his lodgings. They approached the pope and cardinals, and employed all their arts to increase the prejudice against Huss. They bore it ill that the limited measure of freedom which he enjoyed should be extended to him, and they felt that the first step necessary to the success of their designs was to secure his arrest. His course in conversing with those who came to visit him gave them occasion for representing to the cardinals the danger of leaving him any longer at liberty.

The spirit of his persecutors was bitter and unrelenting, as well as unscrupulous. Paletz and Michael de Causis were the most active. As to the latter, he was a fit tool for a conspiracy designed to injure and

[1] Godeau, xxxvi. 427.

[2] Helfert, p. 173, says, "The conservative clergy throughout Bohemia and Moravia imposed upon themselves a tax to meet the expense of sending a deputation to Constance. The deputation consisted of Bishop John the Iron, of Leitomischel, several Bohemian lords, and four doctors of theology." The object of the clergy was to secure the condemnation of Huss.

betray the innocent.[1] He had formerly been curate of the parish church of St. Adelbert, in Prague. He had acquired, moreover, an unenviable character for unscrupulous and greedy avarice. Abandoning his clerical duties, he gave himself up to the pursuits of a fraudful speculation. It was not long before he found his way to court, and became a boon companion of the reckless and drunken king. Abetting, like a true parasite, the schemes of Wenzel, he waited only the fitting moment to abuse and betray the confidence he had gained. Under pretence of advancing a certain royal project for mining, which promised to replenish the coffers of the king, he received for the purpose a large sum of money in advance, with which he absconded in the night. But with money at command, he knew where his crimes would be found venial. He offered his services to the papal court, and John XXIII. could scarcely boast of a more subtle knave or a more serviceable tool. His special business now was one in which his heart, so far as he had any, was enlisted: it was to secure the condemnation of Huss. As a select member of the papal suite, he had the task assigned him of endeavoring to crush a man who had been once his neighbor, and toward whom, beyond question, while at the court of Wenzel, he had professed a warm friendship and respect.

Paletz, Broda, and Stokes, if not more respectable, were at least less infamous. But all of them had been engaged in controversy with Huss, and the bitterness of their zeal was aggravated by unpleasant

[1] L'Enfant, i. 56.

memories. They had felt the blows of the reformer's logic, and had not escaped from the conflict with the prestige of success. Paletz no doubt charged his banishment from Prague to the account of Huss.

Of the other conspirators we have less knowledge. But it throws some light upon their character that they could affiliate with such a villain as Michael de Causis. All, or nearly all of them, had their grievances to avenge. They had pursued Huss at Prague with such means as they could command, and now they had followed him to Constance resolved that he should not escape.[1]

The measures which they adopted proved successful. The cardinals were persuaded to summon Huss before them.[2] Indeed, in the circumstances, it would have been difficult for them to refuse. They were pressed with complaints against Huss, and their attention was drawn to his writings by the studious efforts of his enemies. By the latter they were followed from place to place, visited in their dwellings, and besought to consent to active measures of prosecution. The articles of accusation against him—some of them utterly false—were drawn up with a malicious diligence, and the substance of them repeated wherever it was possible to excite prejudice.

Nor was this all. It was a sore grievance to the enemies of Huss that he should be allowed intercourse with those who thronged to visit him at his lodgings.[3] Attempts were made to induce him to desist from the observance of religious services to

[1] Huss speaks of the violence with which he was assaulted by the Dean of Passau, the pope's agent for the sale of indulgences at Prague.—*Epis.* vi.

[2] Mon. Hussi, i. v. [3] L'Enfant, i. 36.

which citizens were admitted. The limited privilege of access to the minds of others, which he had at first enjoyed, was to be denied him. He had already, at the instance of the bishop of Constance, consented to remain as private as possible, so as not to afford occasion of scandal.[1] But, for still greater security, it was necessary to operate on the minds of the people and induce them to refrain from visiting him. This project the bishop of Lubeck undertook to execute, partly in person and partly by emissaries. The report was studiously disseminated that Huss, as an extraordinary magician, could read the thoughts of all who approached him within a certain distance, and that he was, in particular, an adept in discerning all that might pass in the minds of those who should attend his sermons, not infrequently making his discoveries publicly known.[2] To such arts did his enemies resort to prevent his access to the minds of others. Even this was only preparatory to the more decisive measure of his arrest, upon which his enemies were resolved.

Meanwhile some progress had been made in the affairs of the council. It was doubtless far from disagreeable to the pope to find himself at Constance so much more promptly than the emperor. It afforded

[1] The circumstances of Huss were such as to force him to accept a very humble style of living. He had been but a short time in Constance when his pecuniary means were nearly exhausted. In his fifth letter, Mon. i. 58, he says, "cito deficiam in necessariis." His only companion at this time was the knight Lepka. It would thus appear that John de Chlum must have had other, and probably less humble lodgings. In another letter Huss speaks of the necessitous circumstances of his Bohemian friends in Constance, and the inadequacy of the provision made for them.

[2] This report, according to Huss, was originated by the bishop of Lubeck.

him a favorable opportunity to shape the opening sessions of the council in his own favor. He wished to have it regarded as the continuation, or at least the authorized successor of that of Pisa, to the legitimacy and validity of which he appealed to sustain his own claims as the rightful and sole pontiff. The prolonged absence of the emperor relieved him of one obstacle to the accomplishment of his designs.

The first day of November, 1414, had been fixed for the opening of the council, by the appointment of the emperor and the bull of convocation. By the advice of the cardinals, the pope contented himself with celebrating mass, and adjourning the opening of the council to the third of the month. The announcement made by Zabarella in the pope's name was skilfully worded. "Pope John XXIII. resolved at Lodi to celebrate at Constance a general council in continuation of that of Pisa, and the opening session will take place on the third of November." The inference was plain. The legitimate tenure of his office by John XXIII., to the exclusion of his rivals, was thus coolly assumed.[1]

On the next day six additional cardinals arrived, and were received with great show and pomp. Twelve *Auditores Rotæ*, or judges of the papal court, were appointed, and were conducted by escort to St. Stephen's church, which had been fitted up for the purpose. Monday, Wednesday, and Friday of each week were set apart by them to hear ecclesiastical causes.[2]

The third of November arrived, but the opening

[1] Van der Hardt. [2] L'Enfant, 18.

session was deferred to the fifth. The pope was now ready to proceed. Fifteen cardinals, two patriarchs, twenty-three archbishops, and a large number of prelates were present. At the early hour of seven o'clock in the morning, a congregation was held, to complete all the necessary arrangements. When this was done, all the bells of the city were rung to announce the fact. The procession, swelled by all the clergy in the city, and accompanied by an immense crowd that pressed upon it, moved to the cathedral church. The religious rites usual at the opening of a council were observed, and a sermon was preached by a Benedictine doctor. The next session was appointed for the sixteenth of the month.[1]

Before it arrived, the numbers of the council were largely increased. On the ninth, five cardinals and a large number of bishops and of the nobility arrived, and the pope received the welcome intelligence that his forces had recovered full possession of Rome. The following day was consequently appointed and observed as a day of thanksgiving for the favorable event. In the midst of its solemnities, the patriarch of Constantinople and the grand master of Rhodes entered the city.[2]

Already busy hands were working the wires of ecclesiastical intrigue. Behind the scenes there were plotting and counter-plotting, bargain and sale, log-rolling and bribery, the details of which no history could record. But amid a crowd of competitors, the pontifical schemer was *facile princeps*. If we may believe Thierry de Niem,[3]—and no man had better

[1] L'Enfant, 30. [2] Ib. 31. [3] Van der Hardt gives his testimony in full.

opportunities than himself for observation—the pope wove the net of his intrigue around the council, and, in his palace, the centre of it, watched every thread, and eyed, by means of his partisans, every victim. He surrounded himself with the old associates and "hucksters" of his simony. His court was crowded with them. By their instrumentality, and that of bishops and prominent members of the council bought over to his interest by promised favors, or secured by those arts of which he was a consummate master, he acquired early intelligence of every project, and the means of thwarting it or converting it to his own interest. Every party had its traitors on whom he could rely, and no measure was discussed or agitated so secretly that he did not hear of it before he closed his eyes to slumber. The great majority of the Italians stood blindly committed in his favor.

From day to day congregations were held, at which the policy of the council, and the measures to be taken, were earnestly and sometimes angrily discussed. The great problem of the schism was the one upon the solution of which all minds were intent. At the congregation held November 12th, the pope chanced to be absent. In the exercise of the freedom which his absence permitted, an important paper was read, which, after detailing the steps to be taken for the more full organization of the council, and the proper officers to be appointed, closed with declaring that the union of the church must precede measures for its reformation; that no effort should be spared to unite the church under John XXIII.; that the voluntary cession of the contestants was desirable—but in case of their refusal, they were to be constrained, and treated as enemies and destroyers of the church, in spite of the language of their flatterers, *who claimed that a pope was under no obligation to obey the decrees of a general council.*[1]

The first part of this document contained a recognition of the authority of the council of Pisa, and was doubtless agreeable to John XXIII.; but the latter part was less to his taste, and none ventured to present it to him. In the following congregation, Nov. 15, it was not even noticed. But the pope must soon have had full information in regard to it, and, dissembling his dissatisfaction, must have found it necessary to parry a blow which, aimed ostensibly at others, might yet fall with crushing weight on his own head. He did attempt to parry it, and, as we shall see, the foil he used was the heresy of Huss.

Due provision having been made, the session of the sixteenth of the month was held. John XXIII. presided. The cardinal Jordan de Usurnis celebrated mass, and the pontiff delivered a discourse from Zech. viii .16—"Speak ye every man the truth to his neighbor; execute the judgment of truth and peace in your gates."[2] It is easier to conceive than describe the feelings with which men like Niem must have listened to words in which the pope uttered his own sentence, and heightened, by the contrast of his eulogy on justice, the hue of his own crimes. He exhorted all to carefully consider and heartily communicate whatever could tend to the peace and purity of the church. There were some in the council who were

[1] L'Enfant, i. 32. [2] Ib. 34.

prepared most ungraciously to accept his invitation.

The pope closed his discourse, and Zabarella, taking his stand near the pontiff, read in a loud voice the preamble of the bull of convocation, in which the favorite idea of the pope, claiming the council of Constance as successor to that of Pisa, was again presented. The reading of the bull itself was completed by an apostolic secretary, when the cardinal resumed, addressing the council in behalf of the pope, setting forth, in substance, that having issued his summons for the council, the pope had now, at the time appointed, come with his cardinals to Constance, fully resolved to employ all his means and influence to promote the peace and reformation of the church; and, in order to the prosecution of so holy a work, in which none should presume on his own wisdom, he ordains that, during the continuance of the council, solemn mass should be celebrated every Thursday in all the churches, cathedral and collegiate, secular and regular, of the city; and, to engage all devoutly to assist, he grants forty days' indulgence to all who shall be present—and to priests, with whom he includes all the higher clergy, who are exhorted to celebrate mass, a year's indulgence. All Christians are exhorted to obtain from heaven, by prayer, fasting, alms, and other good works, a happy issue for the council. It was added, that as the principal object in view is the maintenance of the Catholic faith, according to the ancient councils, all who are versed in the writings that concern them, are bound, individually and collectively, to consider well what may contribute to this end, while attention is especially to be directed to errors that for some time past have been reported to have widely spread in certain portions of the world, and *preëminently to those which were originated by Wickliffe.*

To all, the pope assured the largest liberty in setting forth their views. For preserving the order of the council, he cited and commended the canon of the council of Toledo,[1] which enjoined the duty of speaking discreetly and to the point; to abstain from noise or tumult; not to laugh or jeer; not to contend, or conduct with passion or obstinacy, under pain of expulsion and excommunication for the space of three days. This canon, as we shall have occasion to see hereafter, would not have been a bad one to have observed. The reputation of the council would have been better for it.

The names of those nominated as officers of the council were also submitted and approved. Berthold de Ursinis was designated palatine and guard of the council, and to him the protection and security of the body were committed. Notaries, secretaries, and auditors were appointed, and the nominations were unanimously confirmed. The session closed with the announcement that the council would again meet on the seventeenth of the following month.

Up to this time John XXIII. had met with few obstacles in the prosecution of his plans. His time had been carefully improved in strengthening his party, and increasing the number of his adherents. Upon the Italians he could count almost to a man,

[1] L'Enfant, 35.

and the large number of them who were present assured him a powerful minority, if not even a majority in point of numbers. To the Bohemians he had shown himself friendly up to the last moment; but the announcement made in the last session, of the duty of the council to pay special heed to the heresies that had sprung from Wickliffe, foreshadowed the policy which the pope was forced to adopt by the circumstances in which he was placed.

For him, indeed, no subject could have been more welcome than the heresy charged on Huss. In the earnest prosecution of this, he might depend on the support of the large number who identified the views of the Bohemian reformer with those of Wickliffe. So secure did he feel in his own position, that he ventured, on the third day after the session, (Nov. 19th,) to have the insignia of his rivals, Benedict and Gregory, which their ambassadors who had just arrived had set up, torn down from over the doors of their lodgings.[1] The act of violence was perpetrated in the darkness of night,—no one could doubt by whose instigation; but when complained of to the council, the opinions of members were so diverse that no action could be taken. It was for John XXIII. a very opportune measure to divert attention from himself to the heresy of Huss. It gratified the enemies of the latter, and secured for the former that reputation of zeal for the purity of faith which was so necessary as a cloak to his enormities. His recommendations bore speedy fruit. The prosecutors of Huss were encouraged to a more bold and open assault upon him.

[1] Fleury, xxv. 402. Also Van der Hardt at this date.

On the 28th of November a meeting of cardinals was held in the episcopal palace, to take the case of Huss into consideration. He was cited to present himself before them. Two bishops, accompanied by the mayor of the city, and a knight, bore the citation. They found Huss at his lodgings, where he was quietly dividing his time between study and familiar conversation with his friends.[1] They informed him of their errand, stating that they had been sent by the pope and cardinals to request him, in accordance with his expressed desire to give account of his doctrines, to appear before them.[2]

"I did not come here," calmly replied Huss, "with the intention of pleading my cause before the pope and the cardinals, and I never desired any such thing; but I wished to appear before the general council, in the presence of all, and there, openly and plainly, reply, on every point proposed to me, according as God shall inspire me for my defence. Yet I do not refuse to appear previously before the cardinals; and, if they act unfairly toward me, I shall put my trust in the Saviour Jesus Christ, and shall be more happy to die for his glory than live to deny the truth as taught in the Holy Scriptures."

[1] Mon. Hussi, i. 5.

[2] Most absurd stories are related by some of tho historians opposed to Huss. One gives the circumstances of his attempt to escape from Constance. But the basis of such a report could have been nothing more than mere rumor. The story, as related, is quite impossible, nor is there any trace in the letters of Huss, or the statement of his friends, that hints at any such thing; while the statement made by the Bohemians, that, during his stay in Constance up to the time of his arrest, he had not set foot outside of his lodgings, covers the entire period during which he was in circumstances to attempt to escape.

Another story equally baseless is, that he promised a ducat for every hearer that would come to listen to him. A Bohemian narrates the fact, but with the evident suspicion that the report of the promised ducat was originated by the enemies of Huss.

The bearers of the citation conducted themselves toward Huss with gentleness and respect. They had, however, taken the precaution to station bands of soldiers in the neighborhood before presenting the citation, so that resistance, had it been offered, would have been vain. Huss, unsuspicious of the fact, complied readily with the summons. On the lower floor he was met by the mistress of the house, Fida by name, who took leave of him with tears. Struck with a presentiment of death, and deeply moved, he bestowed on her his blessing.[1] He then mounted his horse, and, attended by his noble friend John de Chlum, followed the bishops to the episcopal palace.[2]

The cardinals were already assembled, but it is doubtful whether John XXIII. was present. It was but little more than a week since Cardinal D'Ailly had arrived, and he now, for the first time, met the much defamed Bohemian reformer. So far as severity of language in reprobation of ecclesiastical abuses was concerned, both were equally implicated. The former Bishop of Cambray, now a cardinal, had exhibited as little reverence for papal authority as Huss himself. The two men now stood face to face, and there is reason to believe that the first impression made upon the cardinal by the bearing and language of Huss was far from unfavorable.

Huss saluted the cardinals, and by them was addressed as follows:[3] "Master John Huss, we have heard many things of you, which, if true, cannot be tolerated. Public fame accuses you of having disseminated in Bohemia errors of the gravest kind,

[1] Neander, v. 327. [2] Mon. Hussi, i. 5. [3] Ib.

and such as are manifestly opposed to the Catholic church. We have summoned you here before us, to learn the truth of the case." "Be assured, I beg of you, reverend fathers," replied Huss, "that I would much rather die than be convicted of any heresy, much more of many, and those of the gravest kind, as you express it. And to this end have I cheerfully come to this council, giving my word that if any one can convince me of any error, I will unhesitatingly abjure it."

"It is well spoken," said the cardinals, as they closed their morning session, and withdrew, leaving Huss, with his friend Chlum, in custody. But they had given to his words a meaning which they were never intended to convey. Huss wished to be convinced by reason and scripture. He would not blindly bow to the authority of the pope, cardinals, or council.

During the interval between the morning and afternoon sessions, a monk of the order of Minorite friars approached to converse with Huss.[1] His object was not at first suspected, but when his character and standing were afterwards known, it was suspected that he was a tool of the cardinals, and had been sent by them to entrap Huss while off his guard. In a friendly tone, and with an appearance of ingenuous inquiry, he accosted the prisoner; with insinuating art he assumed the appearance of a simple-minded and ignorant man, anxious to gain instruction. "I have heard," said he, "that many opinions have been attributed to you which are

[1] L'Enfant, i. 57. Mon. Hussi, i. p. 6.

opposed to the Catholic faith, and these things have excited scruples in my mind. In the first place, they accuse you of believing that only bread remains in the sacrament of the altar, after consecration and the pronunciation of the sacramental words." Huss replied, promptly and directly, that the charge was false. "What!" said the monk, "is not that your belief?" "By no means," replied Huss. The monk was disposed to insist yet further, when Chlum, suspecting his purpose, interrupted him, and rebuked him for his impertinence. Excusing himself on the ground of his ignorance and his desire for information, the monk changed the subject. "What do you think," said he, "of the union of the human and divine nature in the person of Jesus Christ?" On this, Huss turned himself to Chlum, and said, in Bohemian, "This fellow, be sure, is not so ignorant as he pretends, for he has proposed to me a most difficult question." Then addressing the monk, he replied, "My brother, you say that you are simple-minded, but by your subtle question I perceive that you are double-minded, and that, under a plain appearance, you conceal a most shrewd and penetrating mind. But whatever you may be, know that this union is personal, inseparable, and entirely supernatural." On this the monk withdrew, thanking Huss for his good instructions. Huss afterward learned from one of the soldiers that this pretended monk was Didacus, one of the most able theologians of Lombardy. He expressed his regret that he had not known it at the time,[1] that he might have improved the oppor-

[1] Mon. Hussi, i. 6.

tunity for a more full and extended conversation. "Would to God," said he, "that all my adversaries resembled him; and fortified by the succor of the scriptures, I should not fear one of them."

Huss and Chlum remained in custody until the re-assembling of the cardinals at four o'clock in the afternoon.[1] They met as before in the pope's chamber. The question now before them was, what should be done with Huss. His enemies, Paletz and Causis, were present, employing all their influence to secure his imprisonment. They urged and insisted that he should not be set at liberty. It is altogether probable that the eight articles of accusation which they had elaborately drawn up, were presented on this occasion. These were to the effect that Huss rejected the doctrine of transubstantiation; that a priest in mortal sin cannot administer the sacraments; that by the church is not to be understood the pope, clergy, or members of the hierarchy, and that its endowment by secular princes is unwise; that all priests are equal, and it is false that bishops alone have the right to consecrate and ordain; that the entire church has no power of the keys, when the whole clergy is in gross sin; and that Huss had contemned his excommunication, having read mass every day on his journey to Constance.[2]

This document had been penned by Causis, and he did not fail, after presenting it, to add other aggravations of the guilt of Huss. He accused him of having been the author of the troubles in the university;[3] of having been the only one there who held

[1] Mon. Hussi, i. 6. [2] Godeau, xxxvi. 435. L'Enfant, i. 40. [3] Ib.

the errors of Wickliffe; of having inflamed the laity against the clergy; and of having gathered to himself a body of adherents who were heretical, and enemies of the Roman church. Hence he inferred that if Huss should escape the severity of the council, he would do more harm than any heretic had done since the days of Constantine; and he therefore supplicated the pope to appoint without delay a commission to examine him, and doctors who should make a careful review of his writings.

It is uncertain whether these accusations and the petition were presented on this occasion, or within a day or two subsequent. However this may be, the cardinals decided that Huss should be kept under arrest. As night approached, the provost of the pontifical palace informed John de Chlum that he was at liberty, but that Huss must remain in custody.[1] The noble knight felt his sense of justice outraged by the announcement of a measure in his view so base and perfidious. Fired to indignation, he complained most bitterly that a worthy and upright man had been lured by false representations into an infamous snare. It was only adding outrage to injustice, when his persecutors, as they passed and repassed Huss, insultingly cried out, "Behold, we have possession of thee; and thou shalt not escape till thou hast paid the uttermost farthing."[2]

Chlum hastened to the pope to inform him of what had taken place, and to remonstrate with him on the violation of his promise. He exhorted him

[1] Mon. Hussi, i. 6.

[2] According to some accounts, these words were uttered as Huss was on his way to prison.

not so unworthily to disregard his plighted faith. John XXIII. declared that he had done nothing against Huss, and, pointing to the cardinals and bishops, exclaimed, "Why do you impute anything to me, when you well know that I am myself here in their power?"[1]

There might have been some weight in this exculpation, if the pope had shown any disposition, then or subsequently, to befriend Huss. But it was too obvious that he was merely the creature of circumstance, and the slave of his own interest. Huss was personally to him an object of supreme indifference, but if he could divert the attention of the council from himself to the business of investigating heresy, he would gain an important object. So far, he saw no reason to interfere with the measures of the cardinals. He in fact acceded to the petition of the prosecutors, and appointed a commission of three,—the Patriarch of Constantinople, the Bishop of Lubeck, and the Bishop of Tiefern,[2]—who were to hear the witnesses against Huss as well as in his defence, and report to the council.

Huss was given over to the charge of the Bishop of Constance, and remained eight days with the Canon of the cathedral. He was taken thence

[1] L'Enfant, 38. Mon. Hussi, i. 6. L'Enfant, 36, says, that on being remonstrated with by the Bohemians, his reply—probably on the first application made—was, "What can I do? your own countrymen have brought it about."

[2] Mon. Hussi, i. 7. The names as here given of the commission are the Patriarch of Constantinople, and the Bishops of Castile and Libus. In the text, I have followed Godeau, xxxvi. 436. To the commission as thus constituted, another was added, probably to examine the writings of Huss. It consisted of four cardinals, Cambray, St. Mark, Brancas, and Florence, with two generals of orders and six doctors. —*L'Enfant*, 41.

(December 6, 1414) to the prison of the Dominican monastery on the banks of the Rhine. His enemies could scarcely have selected a place of confinement more nauseous or unhealthy.[1] The monastery was situated near the spot where the Rhine issues from the lake of Constance. Here he was thrown into an underground apartment, through which every sort of impurity was discharged into the lake. This place at least—more removed from the noise and excitement of the city—might be regarded as sufficiently secure. Huss was left in the custody of the friars.

The noxious stench and effluvia of the place were not long in producing their effect upon the health of the prisoner. In a few hours Huss was thrown into a violent fever, which threatened his life. The aggravated injustice of his arrest and imprisonment undoubtedly contributed to that mental excitement which would exasperate the disease. What must Huss, conscious of his innocence, have thought, in the solitude and suffering of his prison, of the Christianity, the justice, or humanity of men, who illustrated their orthodoxy by such harsh treatment and barbarous treachery as that to which he was now made a victim?

Meanwhile John de Chlum had not relaxed his efforts in the prisoner's behalf. The pope had referred him to the cardinals as the authors of the arrest. He proceeded, therefore, successively to visit the four cardinals who represented respectively the German, English, French, and Italian nations. But they re-

[1] Mon. Hussi, i. 6.

ceived his application with cold indifference. He urged in behalf of Huss the imperial safe-conduct; but the first told him that the safe-conduct derived its authority, in the first instance, from the council itself, who could accept or reject secular documents of a similar nature at their option. The second declared that no faith need be kept with heretics. Shame on the Englishman, whose native good sense told him, even in his bigotry, that he had hit upon the only principle that could afford even a specious justification of the treatment of Huss. The French and Italian cardinals, informed of Chlum's visit, and aware of his errand, closed their doors upon him, and paid him no attention.[1]

Stung to deeper indignation by such unmanly and ungenerous treatment, Chlum rushed out among the people who were gathered about the papal palace, out of sympathy, as he supposed, for the prisoner. How great was his disappointment! The enemies of Huss had subsidized the dregs of the mob in their cause. The priests had dispersed their creatures in all directions to spread the report that Huss had no safe-conduct, but was, in fact, an outlaw. The rumors thus artfully spread, took effect. The rude populace were swayed by the influence, and probably by the gold, of their superiors. With less reserve than they, and with a kindred taste, they took delight in insulting defenceless misery. From one to another the disgraceful falsehoods about Huss were circulated. In vain did Chlum appeal to them for sympathy. Where he was not met by a cold indif-

[1] Van der Hardt relates in full this application to the cardinals.

ference, he was forced to submit to the taunts and threats of the hostile multitude. "A madman and coward, like Huss," they said, "was quite unworthy of such warm sympathy and friendship."[1]

Already it was growing late. The streets were deserted, and the lights extinguished. The faithful and noble knight, overpowered with grief and fatigue, retired to rest. If his eyes closed that night to slumber, it must have been to a slumber disturbed by sad and troubled dreams. But, whatever the meditations of his restless hours, we may at least be sure that they were worthy of an heroic friendship.

Undismayed even by the cold repulses and the abuse to which he had been subjected, Chlum was still resolved to procure the release of Huss. He bethought himself now, as a last resort, to appeal to the emperor himself, whose authority had been trampled on by the violation of his safe-conduct.

In this purpose he may have been encouraged by the timely arrival in Constance of his countryman, Henry de Latzembock, who, with himself and Duba, had been appointed by Wenzel to look after the safety of Huss. Latzembock had been for some time in the suite of the emperor, had accompanied him to Aix-la-Chapelle, and had been present at his coronation at that place on the eighth day of the month. After procuring the safe-conduct of Huss at Spires, and forwarding it to Nuremburg,[2] he continued near the emperor, by whom he was treated with high con-

[1] Some of the facts stated in the paragraph are given by Becker, and others are contained in a small German Life of Huss. I have not been able to verify them by other authórities.

[1] Van der Hardt states that it was here that Huss received it.

sideration. After the ceremony of coronation had taken place, he was dispatched with letters to the pope at Constance announcing the fact. With these in hand, he arrived in the city on the very day of the arrest of Huss. "With what emotions," exclaims a Roman Catholic historian, "must he have seen, if not the chains, at least the imprisonment of Huss!" Undoubtedly he would, in his surprise, share the indignation of his compatriot Chlum; and it is not impossible that the purpose of the latter to apply to the emperor was taken by the advice of Latzembock, or in conference with him.

The very next morning Chlum wrote to the emperor, asking for redress. He detailed the circumstances of the arrest and imprisonment, and entreated him to interfere that justice might be done. To leave no means untried which might contribute to his success, he wrote also a similar dispatch to Bohemia. From day to day, as he traversed the streets of the city, he did not fail to exhibit, as opportunity offered, the large sealed parchment which contained the imperial safe-conduct.

This document read as follows:[1] "Sigismund, by the grace of God, King of the Romans, etc.:—To all princes, ecclesiastical and lay, and all our other subjects, greeting. Of our full affection, we recommend to all in general, and to each individually, the honorable man, Master John Huss, bachelor in theology and master of arts, the bearer of these presents, going from Bohemia to the council of Constance, whom we have taken under our protection and safeguard, and

[1] Van der Hardt, iv. 12.

under that of the empire, requesting, when he arrives among you, that you will receive him kindly and treat him favorably, furnishing him whatever shall be necessary to promote and secure his journey, whether by water or by land, without taking anything from him or his, at his entrance or his departure, on any claim whatever; but let him freely and securely pass, sojourn, stop, and return; providing him, if necessary, with good passports, to the honor and respect of the imperial majesty. Given at Spires, Oct. 18, 1414."

We can imagine something of the patriotic indignation with which Chlum must have exhibited the imperial seal attached to this important document. To blazon abroad more widely the injustice done to Huss, he affixed to the doors of the cathedral and council-house a placard, signed with his own name, in which he stated that an act of unheard-of tyranny had been committed against Professor Huss, that the imperial safe-conduct had been contemned, and that the emperor and the empire would never submit to the insult that had thus been offered to their authority.

The letter of Chlum to the emperor was doubtless despatched by him on the first or second day after the arrest of Huss. Latzembock was the bearer of it, doubtless, and with it he also bore another from the pope to the emperor, scarcely less significant. This last was in reply to one from the emperor to John XXIII., which bore date Nov. 9th, the day after the coronation, and which was full of expressions of affection and filial submission. The pope, in his response, did not fail to reciprocate all these terms of endearment. He congratulated the emperor on his coronation, and besought him to make all diligence to be present at the council, inasmuch as nothing important could be done in his absence.

Such was the character of this curious imperio-pontifical correspondence,[1] which was but the prelude to a conflict of intrigue as embittered as if it had been waged in mortal strife. But the two men knew each other. John XXIII. saw at a glance the respectful and deferential hypocrisy of the emperor, and was not to be outdone in an art in which he was himself an adept. He declared that the emperor's sincere affection for himself and for the holy church afforded him great pleasure, so much so that he thanks the Almighty for it, and receives the glad intelligence of the fortunate commencement of his reign, as an omen of that future success which he will implore of the Lord, to the praise of the divine name, the peace of the church, the strengthening of the Roman empire, and the immortal glory of his imperial majesty. He expresses his zeal to patronize the emperor, "exalting and cherishing so worthy a son, and such an invincible athlete of the Christian faith."

Such was the pope's letter of Dec. 1st, 1414. It was written two days after the arrest of Huss, yet never refers to it in a single line. Who would imagine, from such a correspondence, the clashing and conflicting interests of the two men? Who would imagine that every line was dictated by hypocrisy,

[1] L'Enfant, i. 39.

and that the two correspondents were full of mutual distrust and hatred?

But the mask, so well worn at first, was now to be rudely torn off. The letters of the pope and of John de Chlum, borne probably by the same messenger, Latzembock, reached the emperor at the same moment. He was not slow to comment on the significance of each. If Latzembock was the bearer of both epistles, as he doubtless was, he would not fail to express his own sense of the outrage offered to the imperial authority by the arrest of Huss. Under the impulse of the moment, and moved at least by his own self-respect, if not his own unextinguished sense of justice or the generosity of his nature, Sigismund determined to rebuke the insult offered to his authority. The result, at least, was another letter in this singular correspondence, in a tone altogether different from that which had been hitherto employed. The pontiff and his court had presumed to contemn the imperial authority, and Sigismund was not as yet versed in that peculiar casuistry by which the doctors of the council afterward succeeded in reconciling him to the violation of his plighted faith.[1] In very plain and unequivocal language he now gave vent to his indignation. He sent his ambassadors forward without delay to Constance, sharply insisting on the immediate release of Huss from his unjust imprisonment. Prompt measures were to be taken, and violence employed if necessary, to secure obedience to the imperial mandate.[2]

Meanwhile Huss had been removed from his foul

[1] Helfert, 186, 187.

[2] Van der Hardt, iv. 26.

cell in the Dominican monastery to cleaner and more healthy apartments above-ground. Upon this removal the physicians, with at least professional humanity, had boldly insisted. It is said that the pope, fearful lest Huss should die in prison and the cause of orthodoxy lose the incense of a burning heretic, had directed his own physician to attend the prisoner. However this may be, the health of Huss began immediately to improve.[1]

The commission who had been appointed to hear his accusers and his own defence, did not delay their proceedings on account of the sickness of Huss. They visited him in prison, while yet enfeebled by disease, and presented him with the list of the charges that had been drawn up against him. Huss asked that an advocate might be appointed him to defend his cause, inasmuch as by sickness and imprisonment he was not able to do it himself. The request was denied. He was told that, according to canon law, no one could be allowed to take the part or plead the cause of a man suspected of heresy. One of the later Roman Catholic historians[2] of these events, undertakes to vindicate the justice of this canon.

But this was not the only hardship of which Huss had to complain. The same authority which denied him an advocate, admitted all kinds of evidence against him as a heretic. His enemies—and there were not a few who were glad of such an opportunity to offer their volunteer testimony—were thus invited to become his accusers.[3] In his letters Huss com-

[1] The sickness of Huss must have been severely painful, as well as dangerous. See Epis. li., Mon. Hussi, i. 74.

[2] Godeau.

[3] L'Enfant, i. 41.

plains that every day some new accusation against him was devised, composed of items false and captious, so that he could scarcely find time to answer them.[1] The vexations to which he was subjected by the members of the commission, the insults offered by Paletz and Causis as well as other ecclesiastics, and the artifices and intrigues that were employed to prevent his having a hearing before the council, were enough to drive him to despondency. But in spite of all, his trust in God and the justice of his cause remained unshaken; and the writings which issued from his prison cell attest his incessant activity.[2]

Another commission was appointed by the pope, probably in accordance with the request of his prosecutors, to examine his writings. It consisted of the Cardinals D'Ailly, St. Mark, Brancas, and Florence, two generals of orders, and six doctors of theology. These were busy at their task, while the other commission was gathering up testimony from witnesses whom Huss had no opportunity to confront, and whose names even were studiously concealed.

It was after the commissioners had begun their work, that the mandate of the emperor requiring the immediate release of Huss reached Constance. The instructions of the ambassadors were sufficiently explicit. John XXIII., after his flight from Constance, urges, among other reasons in justification of his course, the peremptory command of the emperor for the release of Huss, directing that in case of resistance

[1] Epis. x., Mon. i. 60. [2] See, besides his Letters, several Treatises. Mon. i. 39–48.

his prison doors should be broken down and he set at liberty. This the pope resented as an interference with his prerogative and the duty of the council. He maintains that Huss had been arrested by his authority, and that the emperor had interfered with the due course of justice in ordering the enlargement of the prisoner.

It is evident, therefore, that the imperial mandate was received, and that its import was understood. But it was not an easy thing to carry it into execution in the absence of the emperor. On this question—however they might differ on other points—the pope and the cardinals, as well as the leading members of the council, were fully agreed. Against their united opposition nothing could be done. Nor does it appear that the imperial ambassadors knew where Huss was confined. This at least is certain, that the command of the emperor was not obeyed. Instead of being released, Huss was more closely confined. His removal to the Dominican monastery preceded but by a few days the arrival of the ambassadors, and may have been effected in anticipation of it. But he was now beyond the reach of the imperial officers, and they were forced to await the coming of the emperor before any decisive steps could be taken.

There were, indeed, some powerful motives which forbade the obedience of the pontiff to the emperor's command. It was his interest to have questions of heresy precede any investigation of the question of the schism. It was something gained, meanwhile, to accustom men to witness the exercise of his own authority, and the bold assumption of his prerogative. In this matter, moreover, he was confident of powerful support. The cardinals and all the enemies of Huss were ranged upon his side.

In such circumstances John XXIII. seemed not unwilling that the papal and imperial authority should come into open conflict. He felt sure of a triumph. It was not a little gained, if, while the sceptre trembled in his hand, and Christendom owned a divided allegiance, he might openly and with impunity venture to trample on the imperial mandate.

CHAPTER XIV.

ANXIETIES OF THE POPE. THE ENGLISH AND FRENCH DEPUTATIONS.

TROUBLESOME QUESTIONS.—MEMBERSHIP OF THE COUNCIL.—VOTING BY NATIONS.—PLAN OF UNION.—THE FRENCH DEPUTATION.—VIEWS OF GERSON.—VIEWS OF D'AILLY.—VIEWS OF CARDINAL ST. MARK.—THEY PREVAIL.—THE ENGLISH DEPUTATION.—PERSECUTION OF THE LOLLARDS.—RICHARD OF LONDON.—THOMAS NETTER.—SPIRIT OF THE ENGLISH NATION.—ROBERT HALLAM.—ULLERSTON.—HIS WRITINGS.—DOCTOR PAUL.—JOHN DORRE.—WALTER DYSSE.—HIS POEM.—THE DEPUTATION ANTI-WICKLIFFE.

DEC. 7, 1414–DEC. 18, 1414.

THERE were several important questions which at this juncture claimed the attention of the council, and, divided with the subject of heresy, the anxiety and attention of the pope. One of these concerned the membership of the council; another was the manner in which the votes should be taken; and still another was the plan to be adopted to promote the union of the church.

Upon the decision of either of these the fate of John XXIII., as pontiff, might depend. As to the first, he had reason for anxiety lest, by the admission of the lower clergy, a majority should be secured adverse to his interests. By means of the large number of obscure Italian bishops who had followed him to Constance, he hoped to be able to carry his measures. Distrustful of the other nations, he could rely upon his faithful Italians, and he did not wish to have their votes lost in those of the multitude of inferior clergy, and of the more secular element furnished from Germany, France, and England.[1]

As to the second question—the manner in which the votes should be taken[2]—the jealousy of the three other nations was excited by the numerical majority of the Italians. If the latter, however, as well as each of the others, was entitled to but a single vote, and the decisions of the council were to be based upon a majority of the votes by nations, each nation being entitled by a majority to determine how its vote should be cast, the Italians, who represented the strength of the papal party, would be able to command in the council but one vote out of four. To prevent such a consummation, urged by the French and Germans, was a favorite project on the part of the pope.

These two questions had been discussed as early as the twelfth of November, and early in December the other was taken up. It was strenuously urged that the wisest course would be to induce the two anti-popes, Benedict and Gregory, by gentle means, if possible, to cede their claims. It was hoped that by the lenity of the council, which was ready to lighten their fall, and secure for them in case of their abdication a favorable reversion, they might be persuaded to adopt this course. Such lenity, it was argued, with a gross inconsistency when the treatment of Huss is considered, was more accordant with the genius of the church, which was bound as a kind

[1] L'Enfant, 70. [2] Ib. 71.

mother to reclaim her erring children by mild and gentle means.

Nothing had been publicly said as yet, in this connection, which bore directly against John XXIII. This was the subject which Niem calls the "noli me tangere."[1] But appended to the schedule for the direction of the council, which had been drawn up in the congregation of November 12th, were certain articles which contemplated the possible necessity of extending the plan so as to include the abdication of John XXIII. But as yet, in the absence of the English and French deputations, the advocates of the measure did not feel themselves strong enough to urge it publicly. Although studiously concealed from the pope, he must soon have learned of it through his spies and the tools of his intrigue, at least if they possessed the skill for which Niem gives them credit; and the apprehension thus excited in the pontiff may be readily conceived.

The arrival of the English and Scotch deputations on the seventh of December, and of the French deputation on the eighteenth of the same month, gave a new face to these important questions, and unquestionably exercised a very considerable influence upon the policy of the council and the measures of the pope. Both these deputations were strongly prejudiced against Huss, and both of them were equally adverse to the favorite projects of the pope. It was not therefore an unwise move on the part of John XXIII. to take the lead in urging on the trial of Huss. He might thus hope to secure the support of

[1] Touch me not. L'Enfant, 31.

the English and French deputations, or at least divert the attention of the council from other matters more threatening to himself.

The views of the French delegation found in John Gerson their ablest representative. Previous to the council of Pisa, he had, on mature investigation, adopted the position which he still maintained. Politically a strenuous upholder of monarchical institutions, he was, strangely enough, an ecclesiastical democrat. In his celebrated treatise "*De Auferibilitate Popæ*," the very title of which was startling, he argues in defence of a republican church polity, and maintains that the church is independent of the pope, and for just reasons may depose him. The membership of a general council should, moreover, represent the church universal. It should embrace not only the higher prelates, but the lower clergy, and even the laity should be admitted, if, as in case of kings, princes, and rulers, they are disposed and able to contribute to the defence and welfare of the church. None, in fact, should be excluded, whose position, advantages, or influence could be of service to the general cause. All such were entitled to be heard, and should be admitted to membership.

Gerson may have been led in part to the adoption of these views by the circumstances of the times. He had no faith in the sincerity of either of the popes, or their respective conclaves. He knew that no reformation of the church was to be hoped for, if left to them and the higher prelates alone. A more popular voice must be heard, and a more popular feeling enlisted, to secure the result.

With these views, in the main, D'Ailly, the Cardinal of Cambray, fully concurred. His treatises that remain show that they were his, and deliberately adopted, long before the assembling of the council of Constance. In some respects, indeed, they nearly approached the positions taken on the subject by the reformers of the succeeding century. Gerson and D'Ailly both held opinions, which they strenuously and openly maintained, which were charged upon Huss as heresy.[1] The latter was far more desponding than his friend in regard to the expected reformation. "If a new pope was to be elected,"—such was his language five years previously to the assembling of the council,—"whence would he come? The cardinals would claim the right of election, and would elevate one of their own number to the purple." What might be expected of such an election he gives us to understand, in comparing the conclave to the priests of Baal, who were all to be thrown to the lions; or to the family of Eli, who were all to be extirpated. "Even if a good pope was elected, the cardinals would not obey him." But at that time he was not a cardinal himself.

In regard to the inherent sanctity or infallibility of the pontiff, the views of D'Ailly were equally bold and original. 'Promotion to the papacy did not make a man holy. Peter was not impeccable.' He charges the alienation of England and Hungary from the Romish church to the avarice of Pope Boniface, so that these kingdoms were still virtually (*acephali*) without a head. He does not spare the simony of

[1] Van der Hardt, tom. i., part iv. See *passim*.

the Roman court. He declares against the multitude, who, by trading in sacred things, had forced their way into the sheepfold. They had not entered in by the door, but by another way, and were truly robbers. He declares, 'that as there is joy in heaven when a sinner repents, so then there is joy in Rome when a prelate dies. His benefices are the carcass around which the eagles exult to gather. An angel from heaven would vainly present his claim to be set over a vacant monastery, unless he paid for it the specified sum; otherwise his petition would not even be listened to.' The question, in regard to one who seeks promotion, is not, 'Are you a fit man, but have you got money?' He then traces the origin of the system of the reservation of benefices to the avarice of the popes, and claims that measures should be taken to restrain this unwarranted usurpation of power.

It seems strange that one holding such views, and openly maintaining and defending them, should have been elevated to the cardinalate by a man against whom they bore so directly as they did against John XXIII. And yet D'Ailly was raised by him to a seat in the conclave (1411). This promotion was, beyond doubt, intended as a bribe to buy him over to the pope's interest. But if such was its intent, it signally failed. The course of the Cardinal of Cambray was independent of papal influence. He carried with him to the council the same opinions which he had previously held. That he knew the pope's character from the first, and that he despaired of any good from that source, is evident.

In the treatise already referred to, he declares 'that the sects which had sprung up in Bohemia and Moravia were directly chargeable to the simoniacal heresy and reprobate acts of the court of Rome. The scandals committed at Prague, and which had spread over the whole kingdom, had been committed out of contempt for John XXIII.' He mentions one of the books of Huss which impugns the papal authority and its plenitude of power, as written on this very account.

In Gerson's works we find at least equal plainness of speech. The university of Paris was an independent republic in the bosom of the church, and though torn by many internal divisions, possessed still a national character, and uttered its decree with magisterial authority. At that period of the papal schism it seemed to have stepped into the vacant chair of papal authority, and to have disputed like a hard master with the popes themselves. Its views in regard to the council were represented by Gerson. On the point now under discussion, as to who should be admitted to a voice in the action of the council, Gerson had said, "let no believer who wished to be heard be denied the privilege, so far at least as he is fitted to teach, or wishes to be taught.'[1] This was the position taken by the Cardinal of Cambray before Gerson's arrival at the council. In a paper carefully drawn up, he maintained that no uniform rule had prevailed in regard to the membership of general councils. This had been dependent in great measure on the object for which they were convoked. In the

[1] Van der Hardt, tom. vi., part iii. 124.

councils of Pisa and of Rome, not only had doctors been allowed to vote, but even secular priests, their ambassadors and proxies. He argued that, if it was intended really to reform the clergy, it would be absurd to exclude the men most interested to secure such a result.

These views of D'Ailly were ably seconded by the Cardinal St. Mark. He demanded where the authority was to be found for excluding the inferior clergy from a voice in the council. He appealed to St. Paul, Jerome, and the Canonists, to substantiate his position that all orders should be equally admitted to co-membership. "According to St. Paul," said he, "the bishop and the priest have the same character, the same dignity, and the pope himself is only the first among priests." The proxies of such as could not themselves be present, as well as royal ambassadors, should be admitted also.

These were the views which finally prevailed,—ecclesiastical republicanism against papal monarchism and infallibility. The success of the opponents of the pope was due, undoubtedly, in great measure, to the fact that in maintaining their position they seemed to recognize the authority of the Pisan council, and thus, by implication, the legitimacy of the pope's election.

In substantial agreement with the views of the French were those of the English deputation. If the university of Paris had condemned the articles of Huss, and had become embittered against the pope and papal iniquity, Oxford was not less outspoken in condemnation alike of whatever savored of Wickliffe, or sanctioned the extravagant corruption of the Roman court. It is not a little instructive to trace the causes which forced the anti-Wickliffe party in England into an attitude of indignant protest against pontifical corruption. Embittered against heresy, they had yet imbibed largely on some points the very spirit of those whom they excommunicated and burned.

It was on the seventh day of December, 1414, that the English deputation reached the city of Constance. Among its members were the Bishops of Salisbury, Bath and Hereford, the Abbot of Westminster, the Prior of Worcester, and the Earl of Warwick, the last attended by a retinue of 600 mounted soldiers.

Cooped up in her island home, England had scarce any European reputation until the fierce forays of her monarchs had established the fame of her prowess on the battle-fields of France. The names of Cressy and Poictiers, for little more than half a century, had, through Europe, become synonymous with English valor. The land of Thomas à Becket was the land of the Edwards also, and in less than twelve months from the opening of the council, the famous battle of Agincourt would give new weight to the vote of the English nation. Henry V., who had just put the crown upon his head, threw aside with his private estate the vices and follies of his youth, and evinced an unwonted regard for the orthodoxy and welfare of the church. There had been in fact a strong reaction going on since the death of Wickliffe, against the measures he had sought to promote.

The ecclesiastical authorities had become alarmed at the progress of reform. The Lollards, as the followers of Wickliffe were called, could no longer be despised. The usurping claims of the papacy to the homage and tribute of the kingdom, the intrusion and impudent assumptions of the mendicant orders, and the general corruption which prevailed in the church, had united the mass of the English laity on the side of reform. The high, proud spirit of the English barons would not brook the arrogance of a foreign priest. Little skilled in the orthodoxy of doctrines, their patriotism recognized only in Wickliffe the champion of the nation's rights. On every side his doctrines spread. The minority of Richard II. left the power and authority of the government in the hands of his uncle, the Duke of Lancaster, a close friend of the reformer. The arm of persecution was not yet strong enough to put any effectual check to the course of the arch-heretic. Arraigned before the ecclesiastical court, a message came from the royal presence commanding them to let Wickliffe alone. Meanwhile throughout many of the counties of England the disciples of Wickliffe were scattered, and they were far from idle. With a primitive zeal they proclaimed everywhere the doctrines of the reformer. The minds of men were not altogether unprepared for their message. "The Complaint of Piers Ploughman," a most severe and scorching exposure of the vices of the clergy and the evils of the times, had been already extensively circulated. No one can peruse it and fail to discover, in almost every line, the plain and sturdy common-sense characteristic of the English people. It is a bold and manly protest against the falsehoods and usurpations that were masked under a sacred name. The English nation also, with singular unanimity, were united in an indignant resistance to the papal claims. In one form or another these came repeatedly before parliament. Even the clergy shrank from a public maintenance of what all were constrained to regard as an insult to the free spirit of the nation. Thus the papal authority was at the lowest ebb. Men spoke freely of the abuses, the impieties, the sensuality, the simony of the papal court. It is true that, from time to time, the Lollards were harassed and imprisoned. But persecution had not yet assumed an organized form, and the active energy of the reformers was busy scattering on every side the seed of evangelical truth. So far had the anti-papal feeling spread, even at Oxford, that it was seriously debated whether the papal bull should even be received. An old historian, Knighton, assures us that two men could not be found together and one not a Lollard. The bishops could not remain a long time blind to the spread of Wickliffe's doctrines. Those who favored the new opinions were cited to appear before the episcopal courts. Some indeed recanted, but others bravely stood the shock, and none were delivered over to the secular arm. Oppression for conscience' sake could not as yet call to its aid the resource of persecuting statutes.

But with the accession of Henry IV. to the throne (1401) a new policy was adopted, less favorable to the spread of the opinions of Wickliffe. Henry IV.

was an usurper, yet the motto of his policy was opposition to tyranny, by which many had suffered. Banished from the realm by Richard II., he had taken refuge in France, and there, with Thomas Arundel, the exiled archbishop who had opposed the arbitrary measures of the court, had laid his plans not only for the recovery of his paternal estates, but for the deposition of King Richard and his own assumption of the crown. In the archbishop he found a useful and efficient ally. Through him he secured the favor of the English clergy and their powerful aid. It has been computed that at this time more than half the landed property of the kingdom was in their hands. Such an alliance as theirs was not, therefore, to be despised. They had need of Henry IV., and he had need of them. The fruits of this alliance were soon seen. Scarcely had the new king mounted the throne, when the writ *de heretico comburendo* made its appearance. Nor was it suffered long to remain a dead letter. The ecclesiastical power could now fall back on the aid of the secular arm. William Sawtré was the first victim of this unhallowed compact. He was a parish priest of St. Omer's, London, and bore the reputation of a good man and a faithful preacher. On the assembling of the first parliament of Henry IV., he demanded to be heard "for the commodity of the whole realm." The sagacity of the bishops quickly detected the danger that might lurk under his free speech. He was arraigned before the episcopal court, tried, convicted, condemned, degraded, and given over to the secular arm. Other victims of priestly hate were not wanting. The fires of martyrdom were repeatedly kindled for those who refused to abjure or recant their imputed errors. The zealous orthodoxy of the English prelates was more and more inflamed against the opinions and the followers of Wickliffe. Commissioners were appointed to examine, and synods held to condemn, his doctrines. The circumstances and policy of the monarch were such that the ecclesiastics could force him to become their tool. They had raised him to the throne, and if he refused to serve their interests they might depose him.

Henry V. pursued the policy of his father, Henry IV., and extended his approval to the measures of the persecuting clergy. Even Sir John Oldcastle, a powerful knight, and a favorite of the young monarch, was given up to their greedy malice, and cast into prison.

It was in such circumstances as these that the English deputation to the council of Constance was selected. It was sure to reflect the persecuting spirit of the church. The name of Wickliffe was odious to the English clergy, and whatever was associated with him or his opinions was already condemned by a partisan prejudice.

No one therefore could be deputed to the council who did not hold every thing connected with Wickliffe in utter abomination. Of the deputation, Richard, Bishop of London,[1] was a conspicuous member. He was one of the council before whom Sir John Oldcastle, Lord Cobham, was summoned, and had taken

[1] I do not find his name on the list of those who first appeared at the council.

an active part upon his trial. Thomas Netter, of Walden in Essex, a Carmelite, and afterward prior of his order, was another member of the deputation. He had been present, and had participated in the sessions of the council of Pisa, and on his return to England had engaged with such zeal in the controversy against the opinions of Wickliffe, as to be designated the fittest representative of the clergy at the council of Constance. By some he was looked upon as the most eminent, and almost the only champion of the faith. Carried away with his partisan fervor, he had not spared the reputation of the king himself, but charged him, not altogether probably without reason, as lukewarm in his purpose to punish heretics. The charge was publicly made, and Henry V. dared not resent it. The author of it was deservedly selected as one who would not be moved by the extreme of compassion towards his victims charged with heresy. The simple fact of his selection for the express purpose of inveighing against the followers of Huss,[1] shows plainly enough the spirit in which the deputation was chosen. The enemies of Wickliffe, and consequently of Huss, were triumphantly in the ascendant. Like a wild beast that has once tasted blood, they were ravenous for new victims. Madly bent on the extermination of whatever bore the taint of heresy, their presence in the council could only give a new impulse to the persecuting spirit to which Huss was already so sorely exposed.

And yet the spirit of the English nation was

[1] Casimir Oudin, iii. 2225.

strongly roused against papal usurpation. To a great extent the deputation to the council sympathized with this spirit. Robert Hallam, Bishop of Sarum, who died at Constance, and whose monument of English brass, sent over by his executors, is still to be seen in the minster of that city, was president of the deputation. Richard Ullerston was his bosom friend, and doubtless reflected his sentiments in a remarkable work published some few years previous to the assembling of the council. Ullerston was a native of Lancashire, and afterward theological professor at Oxford. He pursued his studies under Richard Courtnay,—chaplain as well as blood relative of the Prince of Wales,—a man who boldly dared to vindicate the rights of the university against episcopal usurpation. Such was the general respect for Ullerston's character and ability, that his friend Hallam urgently pressed him to draw up a plan of reform to be submitted to the council. Ullerston acceded to the request. The work, entitled "Ullerston's Petition for Church Reform," is dedicated to Hallam, and was so highly prized by him that "it was scarcely out of his hands during the sessions of the council." The work is divided into several chapters, embracing the various subjects of reform. The first of these is "The Papal Court;" and in describing what a pope should be, every line seems a satire upon the vices of John XXIII. In condemning the simony that prevailed in the church, he does not hesitate to refer to the mystic Babylon of the Apocalypse, "the great mother of fornication and abomination," attributing this title on scriptural grounds to her wealth and pride. In endeavoring to establish the authority of the evangelical standard, he maintains "that Christ did not set Peter over the church to the intent that his gospel should lose its authority, or that Peter should enact laws of greater authority, or that the gospel should be less honored through any act of his successors." Yet so far from this being the case, he declares that "if laws are now spoken of, they are understood to refer to human enactments rather than the gospel. The last is reputed now in the church as of no more binding force than a verse of Cato or a maxim of Seneca." He condemns the practice of elevating unfit men to sacerdotal or prelatical office, arraigns the vices and especially the libertinism of the clergy, while, 'by the abuse of dispensations, wickedness of all kinds is encouraged, and dares to show itself with shameless and unblushing face.' The system of appeals to the court of Rome, so grateful to the papal avarice, but so odious to the English nation, is arraigned and exposed. The avarice of the clergy, their extravagance in dress, their luxury, their mixing themselves up with secular affairs, are indignantly rebuked.

This little treatise of Ullerston,[1] if it had been anonymous, might almost have been mistaken for a sermon of Huss. It is written in the very spirit of Clemengis' famous pamphlet "On the Corrupt State of the Church," every line of which is like a scorpion lash against the iniquities of the times.

Contemporary with Ullerston was another Englishman of kindred spirit, scarcely less bold or able in

[1] Van der Hardt, tom. i., part xxvii.

his exposure of papal usurpation and corruption. Doctor Paul, a priest highly distinguished for his knowledge of the common law, published, about ten years previous to the council of Constance, a work which must have expressed the feelings and convictions of a great portion of the English people.[1] Although, like Ullerston, unsuspected of the least taint of Wickliffe's heresy, he saw with a clear eye the gross abominations and corruptions of the age. His work is entitled "A Golden Mirror held up to the Court of Rome, the Prelates, and the entire Clergy." The plan of it is a dialogue between the apostles St. Peter and St. Paul. It is dedicated to the cardinals, the heads of the clergy, and all the officers of the court of Rome. The writer testifies his grief at the papal schism, and the countless errors which prevailed, heaped up as it were upon his own unhappy age. The law had departed from the priests, and through them had fallen into contempt. The court of Rome was deformed and maimed by errors, from the sole of its foot to the crown of its head. If these assertions seem too bold for him to make, his excuse is, that few dare to utter an open and public rebuke of the prevailing vice and corruption.

The substance and scope of the work are much the same with those of "Ullerston's Petition." "Alas!" says he, "that in these latter times the apostles have left the word of God to serve tables. Each seeks his own and not the things of Jesus Christ." He deplores the fact that "no election to an ecclesi-

[1] Van der Hardt, tom. i., part ix.

astical benefice, even though of the fittest person, and made by divine inspiration, could become effective without money." This abuse he charges upon the court of Rome, "where persons ignorant, scandalous for vice, ambitious, cruel, and every way unfit, are promoted to be bishops. Benefices are bestowed on scullions, pimps, hostlers, and even children. The signature of the pope has its price. Dispensations and indulgences are sold for money, and he is the greatest who is most cunning to deceive, and skilful in sacrilegious traffic. The sum total of devotion is to gain the penny."

From these causes spring the innumerable evils that afflict the church. Those who originate them do not so much guard as crush the church. Instead of feeding the flock, they slay and devour it. The whole work of Doctor Paul is a most energetic protest against papal corruption and usurpation. Huss himself could scarcely have spoken with greater boldness, or have uttered a more indignant rebuke of wickedness in high places.

The same spirit which is manifest in these treatises of Ullerston and Paul, was shown by other eminent Englishmen, who could not be suspected of sympathy with Wickliffe or Huss. Nutter, whose name has already been mentioned as a member of the English deputation, was of this class. One of his associates at the council was John Dorre, whose honest English sense found expression for itself in a figure adapted to the diseased state of the church. His prescription would, doubtless, have had a good temporary effect. His "*recipe* for the stomach of St. Peter, and its complete reformation, given in the council of Constance," is as follows:[1] "Take twenty-four cardinals, a hundred archbishops and prelates, an equal number from each nation, and as many creatures of the court as you can secure; plunge them into the waters of the Rhine, and let them remain submerged for the space of three days. This will be effective for St. Peter's stomach, and will remove its entire corruption." No Protestant doctor surely would have prescribed a harsher remedy.

There was another Englishman whose name should not be passed over in silence. Walter Dysse was an eminent theologian, and a member of the Carmelite order. He was for several years in the service of that master in the art of simony, Boniface IX., and was employed by him in missions to different parts of Europe. At one time we find him in Spain, preaching a crusade against the infidels, and at another engaged in writing against Wickliffe. No man had a better opportunity to observe the general corruption of the church, or the morals of the papal court. Yet, with all the influences that might have sufficed to seal his lips, brought to bear upon him, he dared to speak out in a tone of earnest remonstrance. A poem composed by him on the evils of the age, entitled "The Schism of the Church," is not unworthily appended to the works of Clemengis. This poem consists of only two hundred and sixty lines, but the picture they present shows that it was taken from the same real objects of which his contemporaries have left us the daguerreotype. The author

[1] Van der Hardt, tom. i., part ix., p. 499.

declares himself "at a loss which pope to recognize." "The pastors of the church have become harpies." "The pontiffs and prelates are devoted to their cups and hoards. The church is sold and plundered by those who should cherish her. If you wish to be rich, be wicked; do something that deserves the prison. Ambition and luxury crush the minds of all, and bury them in vice. Sons of the nobility are sent to France to be made doctors. The priest and people are alike. The blind leads the blind. Children learn vile arts sooner than their alphabet."[1]

We have no evidence in regard to the presence of Dysse at the council. He may have been there, however, as a visitor, or even as a member.

We may thus see something of the views and feelings of the English deputation. Animated, many of them, by the fiercest hatred toward Wickliffe and Huss,—in some cases selected for the post on account of the very virulence of their opposition to what they accounted heresy,—they yet condemn without a dissenting voice the prevalent corruption of the church, denouncing it in terms scarcely, if at all, less severe than the reformers themselves. It is a singular spectacle. And yet, unless it is carefully studied, we shall fail to understand the policy which controlled the action of the council.

With the views thus presented and maintained by the English deputation, those of the French coïncided to a great extent, and on whatever policy they might unite, they might be confident of success. The cardinals who had Huss in charge were too shrewd

[1] Clemengis' Opera. Appen. 30–34.

not to observe and take advantage of the circumstances so favorable to their views and interests. They could offset the current of popular opinion in the council against the imperial purpose, nor were they slow to make use of the vantage-ground thus afforded.

CHAPTER XV.

PROCEEDINGS OF THE COUNCIL. HUSS ABANDONED BY THE EMPEROR.

Approach of the Emperor to Constance. — Mass on his Arrival. — The Ceremonial. — Character of the Council. — Sigismund's Influence. — A Field for Intrigue. — The Emperor's Ruling Purpose. — Dark Prospect of Huss. — Chlum Seeks the Emperor. — Cold Reception. — His Letter to John of Lomnitz. — Indignation of the Bohemians. — Their Letters to Sigismund. — The Emperor Ill at Ease. — His Letter. — The Casuistry of the Fathers. — Sigismund Acquiesces in it. — Sermon of Cardinal D'Ailly. — His Remarks on the Duties of the Pope and Emperor. — The Bearing of them on the Case of Huss. — Chlum's Remonstrance. — A General Congregation. — Sermons Preached. — Bold Reproofs. — Sermon of Matthew Roeder. — The New Year. — Emperor Consults with the Cardinals. — Their Demand in Regard to Huss. — Safe-Conducts Given. — The Ambassadors of Gregory. — Opposition of John XXIII. — Prejudice Against Him. — Conciliatory Measures toward Gregory and Benedict. — Cardinal D'Ailly on the Infallibility of Councils. — Legates of Benedict. — Legates of Gregory. — Proposal of John XXIII. — The Way of Cession. — Answer of John XXIII. — Results of his Opposition. — Extreme Measures Proposed. — These Discovered by the Spies of John XXIII. — Canonization of St. Bridget. — Carried without Opposition. — Gerson Writes his Tract on Trying the Spirits. — Bold Suggestions of the Cardinal of St. Mark. — Ability and Character of the Document drawn up. — Rage of John XXIII. — Replies of his Partisans. — Questions Contained in the First. — Refutation of the Cardinal St. Mark in the Third. — Cardinal D'Ailly's Refutation. — Conflict of the Monarchical and Republican Principles in the Church.

Dec. 25, 1414–Feb. 7, 1415.

The English and French deputations had already reached Constance, when the near approach of the emperor was announced. He arrived at Uberlingen, some seven miles from Constance, on Christmas Eve. A message was at once forwarded to the pope, requesting him to celebrate mass in the cathedral church on the arrival of the imperial train. Crossing the lake, the emperor entered Constance at about four o'clock on the following morning. He was accompanied, among others, by his wife Barbara, daughter of the Count Cilley, his daughter Elizabeth, queen of Bosnia, Rodolph, elector of Saxony, and Anne of Wirtemburg.

The Empress Barbara, second wife of Sigismund, was, according to Æneas Sylvius, a woman of infamous morals and abandoned character. While king of Hungary, Sigismund had been seized by some of his powerful subjects and cast into prison. His marriage to Barbara was made one of the conditions of his liberation. This condition, with others less revolting, though scarcely less humiliating, was faithfully observed. The emperor's fidelity to his forced engagements stands in singular contrast with his faithlessness toward Huss.

After a few hours' repose, Sigismund repaired to the cathedral.[1] The pope, prepared to celebrate the pontifical mass, was awaiting his arrival. The emperor assisted in the ceremonial, clothed in the habits of a deacon. The pope is said to have trembled as he listened to the reading of the passage, "There went out a decree from Augustus Cæsar," etc., and saw before him the crowned successor to his imperial power. The throne of Sigismund, magnificently adorned, had been prepared on the pope's right, while, still further on, was the seat provided for the empress. At the side of the emperor, his red cap

[1] The main authority for the statements of this and many of the following chapters, in respect to the council, is to be found in Van der Hardt.

surmounted by the imperial crown, stood, bearing the royal sceptre, the Marquis of Brandenburg, while the Duke of Saxony, as grand marshal of the empire, held aloft a drawn sword. Between the emperor and the pope stood Count Cilley, the father-in-law of Sigismund, holding in his hand the golden apple or globe. When the ceremonies of the mass were completed, the pope presented the emperor a sword, charging him to use it with all his energies in defence of the church. Sigismund received it, with the solemn promise to be faithful to the charge.[1] Little did the pope imagine that in the person of his ally and protector, Frederic, Duke of Austria, he would so soon feel its edge.

By the arrival of the emperor, the splendor and authority of the council seemed complete. Never before had the world witnessed the assemblage of an ecclesiastical body so imposing in its array of power, learning, and talent. The ablest minds of Europe, the highest dignitaries of the church, princes and kings, present in person or by deputy, took part in its proceedings. As to the religious or even moral character of the body, little need be said. It fairly reflected the condition of the Christendom of the day. Gerson left it, disappointed in all his hopes. Neim and De Vrie, as well as others, spectators of its proceedings, paint it in the darkest colors. The opinions of Clemengis in regard to it were not more flattering. It was evident that multitudes, if not the great majority of its members, were drawn to Constance by ambition, curiosity, or the hope of gain.

[1] L'Enfant, 47.

The wishes of the emperor were, to a great extent, the controlling influence of the assembly. With an earnest purpose, clear and definite aims, and a policy as yielding and pliant as the readiest attainment of his ends required, he succeeded to a wonderful degree in shaping its deliberations and decisions. It was one of his maxims, that a prince who knew not how to dissemble was not fit to reign. Thwarted, for the moment, in his plans, he was sufficiently politic to yield to the dominant influence long enough to become its master, and turn it in a direction to suit his designs. Religious, according to the notions of his age, he certainly was—carefully attentive to the ceremonials, however lax in the moralities of a Christian profession. Of his sincere desire to put an end to the papal schism there can be no doubt. From the moment that he saw the imperial crown in prospect, he seemed to feel that he was divinely commissioned to restore peace and unity to the church. His unwearied efforts to this end scarcely allowed him needful repose. But his known and even avowed principles assure us that no rigid or scrupulous conscientiousness would be suffered to obstruct the execution of his purposes. Thrown into a nest of intrigue, he found himself at home among the very masters of the art. To the power and authority of his position, he added the skill, policy, and tact which gave him at last a decided supremacy over every rival.

The glory of restoring peace to the church and reforming it from its corruptions, was Sigismund's idol. It was here that he exposed his weak side to the machinations of those who sought to circumvent him. Whatever purpose, subordinate to his main one, could be shown to interfere with it, was instantly sacrificed. The enemies of Huss were not slow to detect this avenue to the successful prosecution of their plans. Undoubtedly the emperor gave the reformer his safe-conduct in good faith, and was unaffectedly indignant at the slight put upon it. But what was the harm of its temporary violation, if thus a most powerful party in the council could be satisfied, and his own orthodoxy and permanent influence established? The ceremonies of Christmas-day were scarce completed, before both parties, the friends and the enemies of Huss, presented their case to the emperor. A knowledge of the parties, and the circumstances in which they were placed, would allow scarce a doubt as to the result. The friends of Huss were few and feeble. The complaints of John de Chlum were met with derision from the enemies of the reformer. Henry de Latzembock, though undoubtedly friendly to Huss, and enjoying the emperor's favor, was a courtier, and evidently more intent on his own advancement than anxious for the welfare of Huss. It is enough to know that his courage failed him in the hour of trial. After the condemnation of Huss he was suspected of heresy, and chose to abjure the views of the reformer rather than incur the hazard of a suspicion of maintaining them, and thereby sacrificing his hopes of promotion. From him, therefore, no earnest or effectual interposition in favor of the prisoner could be expected. As to the third member of the escort appointed by the king of Bohemia,

Wenzel de Duba, we hear little of him. Huss, indeed, speaks of him in high terms; but he lacked the boldness, if not the devotion of Chlum. The enemies of Huss, on the other hand, were many and powerful. After the steps taken against him by the pope and cardinals, none dared utter a word in his favor. Nor was this all. While he was restrained of his liberty, the malice of his enemies who had followed him from Prague was busy in spreading slanders to his prejudice.

Against such a tide of calumny and envenomed persecution it was vain to expect that the emperor would make a stand. He could not afford thus to risk the alienation of the council and the failure of his most cherished plans. Early on the morning of his arrival, information of it had reached John de Chlum. Without delay he hastened to the imperial residence. On the preceding evening a memorial, drawn up in the name of nearly all the Bohemians in Constance, had been forwarded and presented to Sigismund in favor of Huss. Chlum hoped to receive a favorable answer to the memorial; but, on inquiring for the emperor, he was told that he was attending divine service. Hastening to the cathedral, the noble knight had presented to his view the scene already described. With feelings of dismay, but a smile of pity, he witnessed the celebration of high mass. He saw the emperor, his royal robes laid aside, arrayed in priestly vestments, and, with a taper in his hand, chanting the scripture of the day. It was enough to excite his apprehensions. The imperial and sacerdotal powers were allied together.

Henceforth Chlum found it difficult to obtain a hearing. The subject of his remonstrance was evidently unwelcome. To the emperor the reproachful looks of the indignant knight were more dreadful than the bitterest words. The enemies of Huss were too strong to be withstood even by the imperial power. Sigismund sacrificed his own sense of justice, and respect for his crown and authority, to the dictates of expediency.[1]

Chlum perceived this. Sadly did he write to John of Lomnitz, the lord-chamberlain of Brünn, "Nothing more is to be hoped for from the emperor, who firmly believes that heaven and the pardon of his sins can be obtained through the instrumentality of the priests alone; and the people declare that one who conducts himself so piously in this life will be canonized at his death. Truly, among such saints, our Huss must appear a very devil."

And yet Sigismund was evidently restless under the imputations and censures to which his conduct had given occasion. Remonstrances began to reach him from Bohemia, and he could not remain insensible to the just odium which he had incurred. Intelligence of the arrest and imprisonment of Huss had speedily been borne to Prague, and had excited surprise, grief, and indignation. The outrage offered to the imperial authority, and the injustice done to a man almost idolized by the nation, produced a sudden and violent outbreak of popular feeling. The Bohemian states assembled, and drew up an earnest address to Sigismund, in which they poured out their

[1] L'Enfant, 51, 52.

complaints in a tone of indignant grief. Several letters were successively addressed to him from Bohemia, and even Moravia, urgently supplicating him for redress.[1]

In the first, three of the nobility, speaking in the name of the whole body, informed the emperor that in one of their assemblies they had demanded of Archbishop Conrad if it had ever come to his knowledge that Huss had taught any heresy, and that he had replied that he had never discovered a heretical word in his writings, and that he was not his accuser. This declaration they forwarded in a letter sealed with their own seal, and accompanied with the request that he would restore Huss to liberty, that he might be in a condition to confront his accusers.

A second letter was drawn up still more earnest in its tone. The writers wish respectfully to represent to the emperor, that John Huss had gone to the council of his own free-will, to refute the accusations brought against him and his native Bohemia; that he earnestly desired and urgently demanded to be heard in full council, to present clear evidence of the purity of his doctrine, declaring himself ready to retract any heresy of which he might be convinced; that although he had gone to Constance, provided, as was well known, with a safe-conduct, he had been arrested and confined in a horrible prison; that there is no one, great or small, who does not view with indignation as well as surprise the bold measure of the pope in imprisoning an innocent man, in violation

[1] Mon. Hussi, i. 76, 77.

of the public faith, and without alleging any reason for the act; that so dangerous an example might serve as a precedent for all to disregard the public faith, and expose good men to the designing malice of the wicked. They conclude with the petition that the emperor will promptly set Huss at liberty, that he may justify himself if innocent, or be punished if guilty. "God is our witness," say they, "that it would occasion us the bitterest grief that anything should happen to the dishonor of your majesty; above all, that the stain of so enormous an injustice should tarnish your reputation. It pertains to you, by your discretion and wisdom, to repair the mischief already done, and to hold the whole matter subject to your control." This letter was signed by ten of the nobility, in the name of all.

The feeling of the Bohemian nation generally is expressed, not only in those letters, but in the words addressed to the royal governor, Czenko, of Wartemburg, in the name of the states: "We, Bohemians, demand that he who in the presence of the bishop of the country was fully justified, and in whom not one iota of unsound doctrine was found, should be immediately enlarged from prison, and not surrendered to scorn and contempt through the false witness and calumny of his enemies, and without fair examination."

The subsequent and still more earnest intercessory letters of the Moravian states, openly spoke of the violation of the safe-conduct as being equally disgraceful and prejudicial, prophesied the great mischief that must arise from it, and warned the emperor in conclusion that falsehood does not finally gain the victory over truth.[1]

Sigismund felt himself ill at ease under the imputations of those whom he numbered among the most powerful subjects of the empire, and whose respect he wished to retain. But his attempted vindication only the more clearly exposes the time-serving policy by which he was actuated. In a long letter addressed to the Bohemian states, he attempts to justify himself. He shrank from the reprobation to which public opinion, judging him by his own acts, would doom him. The following extract from his letter illustrates his character, as well as the difficult position in which he found himself placed: "Had Huss accompanied me to Constance, instead of being there in my absence, his affairs would not have taken so ill a turn. God is my witness—and I cannot express myself on this subject with sufficient force—how much the misfortunes of Huss have affected me. All the Bohemians in Constance may have observed my displeasure on account of this act of violence. I should immediately have quitted the city, had I not been withheld from doing so by the threats of the fathers that they would in that case dismiss the council, and therefore I have determined to wash my hands of the whole affair, since, if I adhere to Huss, the assembly will doubtless be broken up."[2] In this passage of the emperor's letter, his policy and shame are at once revealed. He was forced to choose be-

[1] L'Enfant, i. 83. See Helfert also, in his appendix.

[2] This letter, signed by over fifty of the Moravian nobility, is given in full in the Chronicum Abbatis Urspergensis, 404. Also, Mon. Hussi, i. 78.

tween the defeat of his cherished plans and the sacrifice of Huss. He preferred the latter.

The statements of this letter, from which the extract is taken, were substantially repeated in 1417, after the death of Huss. It gives, therefore, the grounds on which Sigismund deliberately chose to rest his defence. In this vindication he says nothing of the casuistry by which the fathers of the council attempted to relieve his conscience.[1] His own good sense told him that it could not but appear contemptible as well as execrable to the whole Bohemian nation. A contemporary historian,[2] and an eye-witness of the proceedings of the council, says, "By long and tedious discourse they persuaded the emperor that by the authority of the decretals he was dispensed from keeping faith with a man suspected of heresy!" Naucherus, who wrote but a short time subsequent to the council, likewise speaks to the same effect: "Sigismund was persuaded that he could not be accused of having violated his promise, inasmuch as the council, which is above the emperor, not having given Huss its safe-conduct, the emperor had no authority to grant it except with the approval of the council, especially where matters of faith were concerned; and the emperor, as a good son of the church, acquiesced in this decision." That this was the case, might be inferred from the emperor's own words. On the subsequent examination of Huss, Sigismund, addressing the reformer, said, "There were those who held that he had no right to give protection to a heretic, or one suspected of her-

[1] L'Enfant, 52. [2] Van der Hardt, tom. i., part ii. Preface speaks of Dacher.

esy." The council itself endorsed this principle by decrees evidently intended to exculpate the emperor, and to counteract the prejudicial reports which were current in regard to the safe-conduct which had been so shamefully violated.

Thus the feebleness or superstition of the emperor coöperated with the malice of the enemies of Huss to ensure his fate.

Whether Sigismund was blinded or not by the casuistry of the fathers, he was constrained to acquiesce in their conclusions. So strong was the prejudice against Huss, and so popular with the members of the council was the course taken in his arrest, that any attempt to rescue him on the part of the emperor would have required a devotion to the cause of truth and justice such as he did not possess. Huss was left unfriended in prison, while his enemies prosecuted their plans against him with all the bitterness of untiring malice.

On the third day after the emperor's arrival at Constance, (Dec. 28, 1414,) Cardinal D'Ailly preached before the assembled members of the council. His subject was, "The Duty of the Emperor, the Pope, and other members, in regard to the union and reformation of the church." In recounting the duties of the pope, who should be the sun of the church, he does not spare John XXIII. "He who lacks the qualifications specified, is only the shadow and image of a pope. If, for instance, a pope forces his way into the church by a criminal ambition; if his morals are disreputable and scandalous; if he governs negligently or tyrannically, he is not to be regarded as the sun of the church! Would to God that the Holy Trinity would dash down these three statues that are set up in the church. Many times have I said it, that as adorable as a trinity of persons is in God, so abominable is a trinity of popes." John XXIII. could not mistake the scope of the cardinal's discourse. To make the matter, if possible, more clear, the latter exposed the pernicious errors of those flatterers of the pope who maintain, to the prejudice of the authority of the council, that the pope is not bound to yield to its decisions, but may set up his own judgment in opposition to it. This opinion, he maintained, was founded merely upon some of the decretals, which were incorrectly understood, and on positive enactments opposed alike to the law of nature and the divine law, and which tended to the prejudice of the church.

As to the part of the emperor in connection with the council, the cardinal held that it was his duty not to preside or to give authoritative decisions in regard to the matters discussed, but to maintain, by the power which he possessed, the resolutions of that body; not entangling himself with questions as to its decrees, or presuming to confirm them, but restraining and subduing all who should resist them in a rebellious spirit.

That such should be the sphere of imperial action, accorded well with the designs of the persecutors of Huss. They sought the protection of the emperor, but had no disposition to allow of his interference with the supremacy of the council. Most evidently the discourse was devised expressly for the occasion, and the public announcement of its positions, which served as a programme of the policy of the council, was intended to bear alike against John XXIII. and against Huss.

The emperor was thus thrown into a hard dilemma. Between his own self-respect and authority, as well as his sense of justice, on the one hand, and the overpowering influence of the council on the other, his position already was most unenviable. As he walked through the streets of Constance, he might perhaps have read, still attached to the doors of the churches, the bold and indignant remonstrance of John de Chlum: "To each and all who shall see or hear these presents:—I, John de Chlum, make known how Master John Huss, bachelor of theology, under the safe-conduct and protection of the most serene prince and lord, Sigismund, king of Hungary, etc., my most gracious sovereign, and under the protection, defence, and guardianship of the most holy Roman empire; and having the letters patent of my said sovereign, the king of the Romans, came to Constance to render to each one demanding it, a reason of his faith in a public audience. This Master John Huss, in this imperial city, under the safe-conduct of my said sovereign, king of the Romans, etc., has been, and is now, detained. And although the pope and his cardinals have been strictly required, in the royal name, by ambassadors of my said sovereign, etc., to release the said John Huss, so that he might be restored to me, they have hitherto refused and still refuse to release him, to the contempt and scandal of the safe-conduct of the king, and the security and protection of the empire and his royal majesty. Wherefore I, the aforesaid John, proclaim that the detention and restraint of the said Master John Huss is executed in utter opposition to the will of my aforesaid sovereign, king of the Romans, since it is in contempt of his safe-conduct and of the imperial protection, and that it was executed on the occasion of the absence of my said sovereign from Constance; for, had he been present, he would never have permitted it. But when he shall arrive, each one should consider that he will be grievously affected at the contempt offered to himself, the imperial protection, and his safe-conduct. Given at Constance, this twenty-fourth of December, 1414."[1] This document was written both in Latin and in German, with the seal of the Bohemian knight affixed. It was made public on the evening previous to the emperor's arrival, and the knowledge of it could not long have escaped him; yet his policy forbade his present interference in behalf of Huss.

On the day following the delivery of the discourse by the cardinal of Cambray, a general congregation was held, to listen to the account from the emperor of the measures he had taken to secure the cession of the anti-popes, or their adhesion to the decisions of the council. The results of these measures belong to the history of the following year. The emperor took occasion to declare his anxiety for the peace and welfare of the church, and that his intended embassy to the king of Spain to induce Benedict XIII. to a cession of his pontificate had been dictated by his anxiety. He demanded that several of

[1] Mon. Hussi, i. 76.

the cardinals should be deputed, with whom he might consult as to the steps which should be taken to expedite the business of the council.

From time to time, during the general congregations, sermons were preached, some of them of a remarkable character. The vices of the popes were not spared. The general and fearful corruptions of the ecclesiastical orders were denounced. In the boldest language the union and reformation of the church were urged. Such was the force of the invective, and such the unsparing nature of the denunciations uttered, that the language of Wickliffe, Huss, and Jerome could scarcely exceed them. Whoever would see a picture to justify the indignant exposures made by these reformers, needs only to review the records of the council. It may seem strange that such freedom of speech should be allowed in that city, where Huss, for the exercise of the same privilege, had been thrust into a loathsome prison. But there was this difference in the two cases, that the members of the council spoke by order of their superiors, and to promote the measures of a strong party with which they were identified, always professing their respect for the church itself, while the reformers relied only on the scriptures for their authority, and were not careful to hide their conviction that the church itself was well-nigh rotten to the core.

On the day following the imperial message to the general congregation, a sermon was preached by Matthew Roeder, theological professor of the college of Navarre, in the university of Paris. It was to this college that Gerson, Clemengis, and D'Ailly had belonged. The discourse of Roeder, who was the friend and colleague of two of them, bore with severity on the simony and ambition of the ecclesiastical order, and forcibly urged the union and reformation of the church. As the schism had already continued nearly forty years, the speaker compared the church to the paralytic in scripture that had been afflicted for thirty-eight years. The rival popes were children contending with one another in the womb of mother church, and by their acts of simony lacerating her with the fangs of vipers. It seems impossible for words to express a more fearful and corrupt state of things than that which he represents as then prevalent. The discourse closed with an eulogy on the emperor, who was now in the interests of the party opposed alike to John XXIII. and to Huss.

The first day of the new year, 1415, was observed by the pope in the cathedral church with religious ceremonial. The large building was crowded by citizens and members of the council. The pontifical benediction was pronounced, and the wine flowed freely to gladden the occasion. John XXIII. was not unmindful of his need of popular support, and while stung by the sermons preached before the council, and the secret measures looking toward his own deposition, did not neglect the effort necessary to counteract their impression.

At the close of the imposing ceremonial, the emperor convoked to a consultation the cardinals who had previously been deputed for this object. There were at this time within the walls of the city, or in its immediate neighborhood, nearly 100,000 persons. To provide for their subsistence, and to maintain peace and order among them, occasioned no small anxiety. After consulting upon measures for this purpose, the cardinals seized upon the occasion to remove the last obstacle that stood in the way of their prosecution of the case of Huss. They demanded of the emperor that he should consult for the freedom of the members of the council, nor suffer their proceedings against Huss to be restricted under the pretext of the safe-conduct which had been granted him. The answer of the emperor was as favorable as could be desired.[1] He declared that the fathers should be free to act, not only in regard to the reformation of the church, but in respect to the case of Huss. He issued a decree to the effect that the council should be free in matters of faith, and might proceed against those who were evidently charged with heresy, in so far that after a public citation they should be judged according to their deserts. And as to threats or alarms, put forth in writing in different localities, that violence would be resorted to in favor of Huss, his royal majesty will see that they are prohibited. By a singular incongruity, the privilege was appended of a safe-conduct to all who, of their own accord, should come to the council. This provision was intended to meet the case of the ambassadors of Gregory and Benedict, who had been condemned as heretical by the previous council of Pisa. The gross inconsistency of the treatment of Huss, with the privilege thus extended

[1] Van der Hardt, tom. iii., part i. p. 32.

to the ambassadors of the anti-popes, plainly shows that the regard paid to a safe-conduct was a mere matter of expediency with the council. To counteract the influence of John XXIII., and to carry out their designs, they wished the ambassadors of the anti-popes to be present at the council, yet were unable to give any assurance, save evident self-interest, about what had already been violated in the case of Huss.

In spite of John XXIII. and his partisans, the cardinal of Ragusa, one of the legates of Gregory, entered Constance, wearing the red cap, the symbol of his official dignity. The event itself foreshadowed the little regard that would be paid to the more grave claims of John XXIII. when they should come in conflict with the policy of the council. It was on this occasion, and in answer to arguments based upon the legitimacy of the Pisan council, that the cardinal of Cambray (D'Ailly) maintained[1] 'that though that council might be properly supposed to represent the church universal, yet it was not necessarily to be inferred that every believer must hold that it could not err, inasmuch as many previous councils, regarded as Œcumenical, are said to have erred. According to some doctors of great authority, a general council may err, not merely in matter of fact, but right, and what is more, in matter of faith. Because the whole church universal alone has this prerogative, that it cannot err in faith.' As to the present council, called by John XXIII., being dependent for its authority on the legitimacy of his elec-

[1] Van der Hardt, tom. ii., part viii., chap. viii.

tion, it was argued that it had been summoned at the instance of the king of the Romans, who must be regarded as the advocate of the church, and bound to act for it in a case of such urgent necessity. This position was sustained by precedents cited from the previous history of the church, while the reception of the ambassadors of Gregory and Benedict was defended by arguments drawn from reason and scripture. These views prevailed, and John XXIII. saw himself subjected to a humiliating defeat.

The legates were received, and their propositions heard. Those of Benedict spoke only of the measures taken or to be taken, for the conference between their master, the king of Arragon, and the emperor. Benedict, master as he was of all the arts of intrigue, hoped thus to be able, with some show of reason, to defer, for a time at least, his cession of the pontificate.

The legates of Gregory seemed more pliant. Their master was ready to adopt "the way of cession" on certain conditions, the substance of which was, that neither of his rivals should be permitted to take undue advantage of his abdication. John XXIII. was not to be permitted to preside in the council, nor have part in its deliberations.

Thus another blow was aimed at the pope. He was continually agitated by new anxieties. The proposal of the conference between Sigismund and Benedict was not at all to his taste. He declared it would be merely lost time to pursue the project, and that it was best that a council should be held at Pisa to confirm the decisions of the previous council. But such a measure, in order to which the pope desired a safe-conduct, mainly however with a view to embroil matters at the conference and prevent any conclusion, was rejected. His pretext for the demand was the promotion of the union of the church by personal conference with Benedict. But the council had not forgotten the game played, to the scandal of Christendom, by Gregory and Benedict some six years previous, and the character of John XXIII. was not such as to inspire renewed confidence of a satisfactory result.

How to dispose of the claims of John XXIII. was now the great question before the council. These claims stood in the way of every measure that had been, or that could be, proposed to promote the union of the church. The cession of Gregory was conditioned only on the abdication or deposition of John XXIII. This indirect attack upon him was not left unanswered. Of the "method of cession" the pope declared his approval so far as it concerned Benedict and Gregory, since to this they were bound by their oath and promise, given previous to the assembling of the council of Pisa. This in fact would be the proper measure for reuniting the church under one head. If by "cession" the authors of the plan meant something different, they should then explain it. As to allowing the partisans of Gregory admittance to the council, it would be an act of injustice to those who, having complied with the decisions of the council of Pisa, have continued in union with the church. As to the proposition that John XXIII. should not preside or participate in the council, it is utterly rejected as unjust and disgraceful, inasmuch as he, as sole legitimate pope, had convoked the council, and was present in person to labor for the reformation of the church. As to freedom of consultation and action in the council, which the legates of Gregory also demanded, no prelate could be released from the engagement into which all enter, of obedience to the pope as their superior; and into any other, none had entered to his knowledge. In conclusion, there was already perfect liberty in the council, and nothing more could be demanded; so that if the partisans of Gregory wished to unite with the council without making any unreasonable conditions, they might do so, and be received with every manifestation of kindness.

The consequence of this opposition of John XXIII. was twofold. The legates of Gregory wrote to him for more full and ample powers, while the attention of the council was more closely directed to measures for setting aside the claims of John XXIII. Secret consultations were held by prominent members. Congregations and conferences were held in his absence. Of their proceedings, however, he was himself well informed. His spies, whom he kept in pay, were everywhere busy. It was in vain that the members present at the consultations took a solemn oath of secrecy. John XXIII. stood ready to absolve them from the guilt of perjury[1] when they revealed to him the measures discussed or adopted. To avoid suspicion, he directed them to visit him at his own palace under cover of darkness. At the hour of midnight,

[1] Niem. Van der Hardt, ii. 390.

or even later, they were summoned to his presence, and from them he learned the proceedings of the previous day. Some of the offenders were detected, and summoned before the council. But however strong the evidence against them, they escaped with impunity. The difficulty of conviction, and the desire to avoid the scandal of their exposure, conspired to shield them, and they were allowed to withdraw from the counsel by its own consent, and thus escape the deserved penalty.[1]

As yet, however, no one dared publicly to advocate the unqualified deposition of John XXIII. This was spoken of rather as possible than probable. Meanwhile he was assuming and exercising all the rights and prerogatives of a legitimate pontiff. He presided in the sessions of the council. He performed the pontifical duties, and celebrated pontifical mass on solemn occasions. At the request of the Swedes, he canonized a countrywoman of that nation known as St. Bridget. Deserting her family, with her husband's consent, she had instituted a religious order, giving out that its rule had been dictated by Jesus Christ himself. The order was called "Of the Holy Saviour," and followed the regulations of St. Augustine. After numerous pilgrimages to places reputed holy, she had died at Rome nearly forty years previously, and had been canonized during the time of schism by Benedict IX. This fact rendered the authority of her canonization doubtful; and the ambassadors of Sweden, Denmark, and Norway, with the deputation of their clergy, presented

[1] L'Enfant, 67.

themselves before a crowded congregation, demanding that the name of Bridget be enrolled on the list of saints. The demand was based on her birth—she was of the royal blood—her piety, her pilgrimages, her revelations, and the miracles which she had performed during her life and after her death. Numerous doctors and licentiates from Sweden came forward to witness to the truth of the claim in her behalf. By solemn oath before the great altar, they confirmed the recital. The canonization was determined on, and Bridget was declared a saint. The ceremony was conducted by a Danish archbishop. After celebrating mass, he placed upon the altar a silver statue to represent the saint. Then raising it in view of the people, he pronounced the benediction, accompanied by an appropriate chant, and the ceremony closed with the *Te Deum*, the ringing of the bells, and strains of music. The prelates, in conclusion, regaled themselves at a sumptuous banquet.

The scene or show was, to some extent, a papal triumph. John XXIII. seized eagerly upon any measures that could promote his interests, or give an imposing appearance to his claims. A slight delay might have robbed him of the privilege of this exercise of his prerogative. The haste with which the measure had been prosecuted had taken all by surprise, and had secured its success. Opposition had no time to take an organized shape. But the alarm was now given, and Gerson seized his pen. He took for the text of his treatise the passage, "Prove the spirits whether they be of God." The claims of canonization are in this work thoroughly sifted; and the evident bearing of Gerson's argument was to throw suspicion on the pretensions of the new saint. He does not forget the passage, "Satan himself is sometimes transformed into an angel of light;" and the reported visions of multitudes are treated with very little respect. But opposition to the canonization was vain. The *advocate of the devil*, as the individual appointed to assail the memory of the candidate is called, as usual, lost his case. The pope enjoyed what Alexander III., in 1170, declared an exclusive privilege of the papal chair. It was an external triumph; but it is questionable whether more was gained than lost by it to the pope.[1]

But while thus in the exercise of the pontifical prerogative, and endeavoring thereby to substantiate his claims before the world, the intelligence reached John XXIII. of the bold measure that had been proposed in the congregations. The letter of Gregory seemed to make the cession or deposition of John XXIII. essential to the success of the only plan for the union of the church which appeared feasible. Respect for the pontiff who had presided at the sessions, and whose authority seemed identified with that of the council, had hitherto hedged him about with a security that shielded his name from public mention in connection with measures for his deposition. But the necessity of the case was breaking down that security. The result was promoted by his own vices, his intrigues, and his spies. One man was at length found to speak the word which, once spoken, would be taken up by a thousand echoes. A variety of

[1] L'Enfant, 67.

measures had been proposed. Speech upon speech had been made in regard to the union of the church. The English and Polish deputations had presented their views. But hitherto everything was of a general character. There was nothing specific, or directly adapted to meet the difficulty of the case. It was at this moment that William Filastre, cardinal of St. Mark, came forward.[1] He saw the fitness of the occasion of which none were willing or bold enough to avail themselves. The letter of Gregory had familiarized the minds of men to the idea of the deposition of John XXIII., and the cardinal resolved to give forth a practical plan for his deposition. He prepared a document, and placed it in the hands of the cardinal of Cambray. It soon came to the knowledge of the emperor. By his means it was transcribed and sent to the several congregations. Thus the very object which the pope had sought to prevent by his presidency in the congregations,—the stifling of discussion in regard to himself by the influence of his presence,—was reached, and by methods most dangerous to the pope himself.

The document was ably drawn up. It showed in every line the hand of a master. The cardinal first lays down the objects of the council. These are two: the first, the peace and union of the church; the second, reformation of the hierarchy. To attain the first, three ways are possible: reduction or forcible subjection of those that refuse to submit; judicial examination and decision of the claims of the contendents; or voluntary cession on the part of all.

[1] Mansi His. of Councils, tom. xxvii. p. 553. L'Enfant, 68, 69.

The two first are rejected for obvious reasons, as tending only to aggravate the difficulty; the last is chosen as the only feasible method to be pursued. The necessities of the church demand that it should be attempted. The obligation of Gregory and Bendict to adopt it is assumed; in fact, permission to abdicate is accounted a favor. The question then arises, whether John XXIII. is bound to adopt this method of settling the difficulty, and in case of his refusal, whether he can lawfully be compelled to do it by the council. As to the obligation of John XXIII., the cardinal holds that the good pastor should be ready to lay down his life for the sheep. The good of the flock should lead him unhesitatingly to adopt such measures as will promote it, even to his own abdication. To refuse to adopt such a course would be to show that he was not the true pastor. Thus John XXIII. was placed in a most unpleasant dilemma. If the true pastor, he should voluntarily resign; if not the true pastor, he should be deposed. Nor should the council hesitate to take action on the pretext of a want of authority. On all those matters which concern the church universal, the council is superior to the pope. Let the case then be laid before John XXIII. Let him be directed to consider the lamentable condition of the church, the monstrosity of a body with so many heads, the danger of the schism becoming permanent; and let him be exhorted to a course which will redound to his immortal honor—to a self-sacrifice that will cover his his own name with glory, while it fills Christendom with rejoicing.

Such in substance was the document drawn up by the Cardinal St. Mark. It was not long before it attained publicity. John XXIII. was filled with surprise and rage. He was by no means inclined to spare the author, a member of the sacred college. But, on the other hand, the cardinal, secure of the emperor's favor, was not disposed to draw back. He went in person to the pope, and avowed the authorship of the document. He declared that his object had been the peace and welfare of the church.[1]

The document of the cardinal had evidently produced a deep impression. Some were almost enraptured with it. Others, however, were enraged. It would not do to leave it unanswered. Some of John's partisans attempted a reply. Their language is anything but complimentary to their opponents. Three papers were drawn up, the two first in the form of questions. By the necessary answers to these, they left the inference to be deduced which should set aside the reasonings of the cardinal:—"Is John XXIII., a pope legitimately elected, to be placed on the same footing with those whom the council of Pisa condemned, and who are therefere to be accounted heretics? May not those who would persuade John XXIII. to such an admission, be regarded as favorers of schism and heresy? Can a true and canonical pope, not charged or suspected of heresy, be forced to abdicate, or be limited in his jurisdiction? Are not those who condemn one not heretical for heresy, and maintain the justice of the condemnation, themselves to be accounted heretics?"

[1] L'Enfant, 68.

The second paper was much to the same purport. The third attempted to refute the arguments of the cardinal by pointing out the contempt which they offered to the council of Pisa, and the injustice they did to John XXIII. If he was not lawful pope, that council was null and illegitimate. It had only increased the schism, while the deposition of John XXIII. would in all probability only give a fourth head to the church. The proposed measure, moreover, would be unjust to the one who was lawful pope; yet, if John were willing to cede, his absent rivals would not submit, and hence the measure would be futile; all justice would be violated by the attempt to enforce it. The true Christ was not to deny his own authority because there were false Christs; and, as to the obligation of the true pastor to lay down his life for the sheep, it was rather a desertion of them to abdicate, and this was only the part of a hireling. In conclusion, the attempt to depose John XXIII. was sacrilegious. It laid violent hands on the Lord's anointed, while it attempted that by force which, if forced, would be invalid and null of itself.

Such were the arguments adduced by the partisans of the pope. Falling back upon the authority of the council of Pisa, their position seemed impregnable. But even here they were not to remain unmolested. The cardinal of Cambray now took up the discussion, and resolved to sustain the positions of the Cardinal St. Mark. His refutation of the papal refutation shows, by the severity of its language and its tone of confidence, the growing strength of the anti-papal party. He commences by uttering his warning against those who come in sheep's clothing, but within are ravening wolves. "These are they in this sacred council who, parasites of power more than lovers of justice, slander the teachers of the truth, whom the apostle calls masters having itching ears." These men he charges with having prepared papers to hinder the action of the council. In reply to them, he takes no issue on the authority of the Pisan council. Granting this to be all that the papal party claim, its example in adopting the method of cession commends itself to approval in the present case. He denies that the attempt to persuade John XXIII. to cede does place him on a level with heretics, and the presumption of favoring heresy or schism must rest rather on the adverse party. But the strength of his argument lies in the authority which he gives to the church universal assembled in general council. It is superior to the pope, and may depose him if the welfare of the church requires it; and if the pope refuses to adopt its decision, he may be condemned as a schismatic, and suspected of favoring heresy; and they who maintain this view are not to be regarded as heretical, but rather the reverse. Moreover, those who condemn the method of cession, calling it unreasonable, unlawful, and unjust, in reality invalidate the foundation of the council of Pisa, and scandalize those who follow its obedience. Finally, those who would make the whole question one to be settled by violence of war, sin greatly against the Holy Spirit, while wisdom directs that of two evils we should choose the least.[1]

[1] All the documents are given in full by Van der Hardt.

Others beside the cardinal of Cambray, though men of less note, joined in the discussion; but their arguments were merely a variation in form of those which he or the Cardinal St. Mark had already adduced.

Such was the spectacle presented by the council at the very commencement of its sessions. John XXIII., with his party, found themselves forced to contend, as it were, for their own existence. The monarchical and the democratic principles of the church had come in conflict. Popular opinion, modified by the gross and growing evils of the schism, gave to the latter a temporary advantage, immensely increased, however, by the odious vices of John XXIII. All the arts of this man only recoiled upon himself. The growing numbers of the council exceeded his power of control. His favors and promotions were too few to satisfy the ambition of the multitude; and men like the cardinals St. Mark and Cambray, strong in reputation and ability, as well as in the favor of the emperor, deprived the lost pontiff of the influence of even a united conclave. It might be foreseen already what must be the necessary result.

CHAPTER XVI.

THE COUNCIL, UP TO THE TIME OF THE FLIGHT OF THE POPE.

Membership in the Council. — Views of the Cardinals St. Mark and Cambray. — Voting by Nations. — Reasons for it. — Interposition of the Emperor in its Favor. — The Order of Business Adopted. — Proposed Charges Against the Private Life of John XXIII. — He Discovers Them. — His Alarm. — Consults with his Cardinals. — The Charges Prudently Reserved. — Method of Cession Adopted by the Nations. — The Form. — The Cession Provisional. — More Definite Form Demanded. — Evasion of John XXIII. — Third Form Demanded. — The Pope Resolves on Flight. — His Difficulty in Attempting it. — Parisian Deputation. — John XXIII. Feigns Assent to the Demands of the Council. — New Form of Cession Presented. — He Accepts it. — The Form. — His Hypocrisy. — Positions Taken by the Germans. — The Second Public Session of the Council. — Ceremonial of Abdication. — Huss Removed to Another Prison. — Congregation at the Franciscan Monastery. — The Policy of the Pope Opposed to that of the Emperor. — The Bull Extorted from the Pope. — Its Evasive Character. — Further Demand on the Pope. — He Resists it. — Gift of the Golden Rose. — Strange Proposal to Elect a New Pope. — John XXIII. Indignant. — Devises Means of Flight. — Cardinal St. Angelo Arrested. — The Pope Complains. — The Emperor Vindicates Himself. — The Pope's Promise. — Dissent of the French Nation. — Indignation Against the Emperor. — Demand Carried to have John XXIII. Appoint Attorneys. — His Measures for Flight. — His Evasive Answer. — Complains of the Air of Constance. — Suggestions of the Bishop of Salisbury. — Flight of the Pope.

Jan. 8, 1415–March 21, 1415.

Meanwhile the question as to the constituency of the council had been decided adversely to John XXIII. The arguments of the cardinals St. Mark and Cambray proved satisfactory to the emporor, and to all who dreaded the numerical ascendency of the Italian, or rather papal party. To have conceded a seat in the council only to the bishops and the higher clergy would have excluded a vast number whose impartiality and opposition to the pope's claims were well understood. It is noticeable that the argument by which the right of membership was demanded, for presbyters as well as bishops, took precisely the same view of the two orders which Huss had presented in his treatise on the church. "An ignorant king or prelate," exclaimed the Cardinal St. Mark, "is nothing but a crowned ass." From the writings of St. Paul, he argued that a bishop and a presbyter must have the same qualifications, inasmuch as the apostle, in describing the bishop, seems to include the presbyter, and passes directly from this to speak of deacons. "By what right, then," he asked, "do you admit one and repel the other, when the last is equally well, if not better, fitted to represent the church?"[1]

Thus the unhappy pontiff was subjected to a new annoyance. A vast number were thus admitted to membership in the council over whom he could exert but a feeble influence, and whose views and policy were adverse to his own. Besides the doctors, of whom the number was very large, the ambassadors of kings and princes, of republics, cities, universities, and other communities, as well as the lower clergy, were admitted under conditions. The pope was chagrined at seeing the votes of his numerous Italian bishops offset by those of multitudes inferior only in ecclesiastical rank.

[1] Van der Hardt gives the arguments of the different parties. See also L'Enfant, 71.

But even yet it was possible for him to command a powerful and influential minority. The hope however which this inspired was now destined to be defeated. At an early stage of the discussion it had been proposed that the votes should be taken by nations. The pope had strenuously resisted the project. He might ply his intrigues among individuals with some chance of success; but if the votes were to be taken by nations, his plans would encounter greater difficulties, while the whole Italian party would command but a single voice out of four.

The pope had on his side the prestige of ancient usage, but the council imagined that they had good and sufficient reason for acting without regard to precedent in a question of such moment. The pope had created as many as fifty new chamberlains, whose devotion to his interests was of course entire. The other nations would not consent to such a fatal preponderance of the Italian party, while the pope on his part was not disposed to yield. From day to day the question became more embarrassing. The whole issue of the council might hinge upon its decision.

In these circumstances the emperor interposed.[1] Clearly perceiving the vital importance of the question, he decided against the pontiff. It was therefore resolved that the votes of the council should be taken by nations, and that as Spain was as yet unrepresented, England, which had hitherto been reckoned with Germany, should be allowed a vote by itself, thus making, with Germany, France, and Italy, the fourth nation in the constituency of the council.

[1] L'Enfant, 72.

The order of proceedings required each nation to have a certain number of deputies, men of learning and ability, composed both of ecclesiastics and seculars, with their procurators, or attorneys and notaries. These deputies had a president, whose term of office was one month. Each nation assembled by itself to discuss the matters that might be brought before it, and when any article had been agreed upon by one nation, it was submitted to the deliberation of the others; and if agreed on in a general congregation of the four nations, it was carried, signed, and sealed before the following session, when it received public and solemn approval. In these preliminary discussions, full liberty was allowed to all to propose, either orally or in writing, whatever they might deem essential to promote the welfare of the church.

Successively defeated in his plans for constituting the council, the pope was still pressed in the most urgent manner to unite with the contestants in adopting the "way of cession." To this he was utterly disinclined. He regarded the demand as insulting and intolerable. But while meeting it in a tone of bold resistance, and even defiance, he was startled from his security by intelligence of a new measure which had been proposed. This was nothing less than a judicial investigation of his life and character. This was his vulnerable point. His private career had been notoriously scandalous. Nothing but the sanctity of his office could have so long shielded him from ignominious exposure. But the steadily increasing hostility which his course provoked, now encouraged an attack upon his reputation and morals.

A series of accusations was drawn up against him, evidently by some one familiar with his career of vice and crime. Niem suspects that the author was an Italian. The charges made were of the most scandalous and horrible kind. The life of the pontiff was described as a tissue of enormity and violence, which outraged all justice, and was the scandal of the church.

The articles were secretly submitted to leading members of the council from Germany and England. It was hoped that an investigation would be demanded, and of its result, if undertaken, no one could doubt. But prudence forbade the measure. It might overshoot its object, and disgrace the papacy as well as its occupant. It might tend to invalidate the promotions which the pontiff had made. Who could say how many of the members of the council would be compromised in the tenure of their titles by an investigation of papal simony? For the present it was deemed best to postpone the matter. Yet the time might come when it could be evoked as a necessary and effective weapon of attack.

Secretly as the whole thing had been managed, it soon reached the ears of the pontiff. His spies were busy, and treachery was sure of its reward. Great was his consternation when he found this new battery opened upon him. Conscious of the weakness of his position, he called together for consultation some of the cardinals and of those whom he had bound to him by favors, and asked their advice.[1] He frankly admitted that some of the charges against

[1] L'Enfant, 73.

him were true, while he maintained his innocence in regard to others. It was his own plan to forestall attack by going before the council, and acknowledging the truth of some of the accusations, falling back, however, on this as an impregnable position, that the pope can be judged and deposed for no fault save for heresy alone. The friends of John XXIII. were at a loss, when consulted, what answer they should return. It was finally agreed that the wisest course would be for the pope himself to take the matter for some days into careful deliberation, and then "adopt such a course as he should deem wisest, in the fear of God." But the enemies of the pontiff were not yet prepared to proceed to extremities. They did not wish to overthrow the See of Rome, but only its occupant. Thus the terror was suspended over his head, and for the present the policy of his foes spared him the crushing blow.

Yet the secret measure had not been without its effect. The knowledge of its having been discussed, the fact that a possibility remained that it might yet be evoked as a weapon of offence in case of necessity, rendered John XXIII. much less disinclined to listen to the exhortations and overtures of the council. On the seventh of February, (1415,) the question of voting by nations had been decided. Meanwhile the charge against the pope had been drawn up. So early as the fourteenth of the previous month, Andrew Lascar, bishop of Posen, and ambassador of the king of Poland, who had just reached the council, addressed the pope in its name, urging him to give peace to the church. Although the method of cession was not mentioned in his discourse in express terms, it was not obscurely hinted at, and the pope was significantly pointed to the example of Christ in laying down his life for the sheep, and urgently exhorted to prefer the glory of its imitation to the power of the keys. John XXIII. must have uneasily listened to an address so guarded in expression but so direct in application. The method of cession was now publicly advocated, and on the fifteenth of February, the German, English, and French nations adopted it, and urged it with such force upon the Italian nation, that they were disposed to yield; and John XXIII. saw himself deserted by those on whom he had most relied. After such a defeat the utter refusal of any form of cession on his part would have been in the highest degree impolitic. It would but exasperate a feeling that could no longer be trifled with. His only hope now was to gain, if possible, some advantage by temporizing.

On the sixteenth of the month the conclusions arrived at in the general congregation of the nations on the preceding day were drawn up and presented to the pontiff.[1] They were as follows: "The sad state of the church, with all the circumstances thereto pertaining, having been duly weighed, three nations, the German, French, and English, composing and representing the majority of this sacred council, have, in order to the restoration of the church, deemed the method of cession on the part of our lord the pope as well as the contendents, the better and more expedient, and that our lord should accept and

[1] Van der Hardt, tom. ii., part viii., chap. xix.

adopt it, to thus carry out the designs of the council; and by his most serene highness our lord the king of the Romans, and this sacred council, he is besought to offer, adopt, and execute this mode of cession." The document was signed by the presidents of the nations, and offered to the pope for his acceptance. Later in the day the council met, at the pope's summons, to receive his answer. It had been carefully drawn up, and was read before the assembly by the cardinal of Florence. It was to the following effect: "Our most holy lord the pope here present, though obligated to it by no vows, oaths, or promises, yet for the peace of Christendom, has proposed, and on deliberation resolved, to give peace to the church even by the way of cession; provided, however, that Peter de Luna and Angelus Corrario, condemned by the Pisan council of schism and heresy, and ejected from the pontificate, shall make a full and sufficient renunciation of the claims which they urge to the pontificate. This renunciation to take place in ways, circumstances, and time to be agreed upon between our lord or his deputies, and deputies from among you."[1]

It was obvious that such a provisional abdication would remain a mere nullity. The conditions would never be fulfilled. The abdication itself, while it necessarily delayed the action of the council till it could take effect, was intended to secure the pope from being molested till such a time as occasion should be given for regaining what had been lost. The several nations, however, took it into considera-

[1] L'Enfant, 73.

tion. They were unanimous in regarding it as too vague, doubtful, obscure, and unreliable, and as utterly insufficient to extirpate the schism, or effect a cession. The pope was therefore requested, inasmuch as he showed a disposition to the way of cession—so it was observed with an artful irony—to express his purpose in plain and simple language that should tend to promote the desired union. In consequence of this request, which the pope did not dare refuse, another form of abdication was drawn up; but this proved even less satisfactory than the first. It gave stronger ground for the suspicion that he had no intention whatever to resign the pontificate. The conditions subjoined to it rendered it altogether unacceptable. In fact, its rejection must have been foreseen by John XXIII. himself, and he could only have presented it in the hope either of gaining time, or dividing his opponents into adverse parties. It was objected to by the council on several grounds: as conditional on the cession of the contendents; as containing expressions in regard to them of an irritative character; as setting a limit of time beyond which it was to have no effect; and as proposing unprecedented measures against the contendents. Another form of abdication was drawn up, modelled after that which had already been presented by Gregory. It was privately presented by the emperor's direction to the pope, but to this he would by no means give his assent.

It was in the interval that followed, that John XXIII. laid his plans for his flight. He saw that the council had him already in their grasp. He resolved therefore to leave Constance, in the hope that by the confusion which his flight, as well as the measures he might take afterwards, would occasion, the council would be broken up. He sent therefore for Frederic, Duke of Austria, with whom he had entered previously into an alliance offensive and defensive in order to his security, and concerted the measures for executing his purpose. But even here he was surrounded by difficulties. A suspicion of his project had already spread abroad. It was even proposed by a portion of the English deputation that the person of the pope should be seized and kept in safe custody,[1] but to this the French deputation would by no means consent. And yet John XXIII. was little more than a prisoner in his own palace. He bitterly complains, in a paper published after his flight from Constance, of the insults offered him before his own doors, and of which the emperor was cognizant. He asserts that he was watched by imperial spies, who intruded upon the privacy of his chamber, and even dared to enter his bedroom to see whether he had escaped.

But the growing unanimity and strength of his adversaries, whom he had vainly hoped to divide—the close watch kept upon his person—the well-known purpose of the emperor, who was resolved that the aims of the council should not be thwarted by papal artifice,—all indicated that before he could hope to escape, he must disarm suspicion by still greater concessions than any he had yet made. With his accustomed duplicity, therefore, he made up his

[1] L'Enfant, 81.

mind to yield a formal acquiescence to the demands of the council, in the hope of thus securing a temporary freedom from molestation, but with the secret resolution, at the earliest possible moment, of denouncing its invalidity as extorted by force.

It was proposed in the council to insert in the form of abdication, "I swear and vow," etc., in order to give it a more solemn and binding character. Upon this point there was a division of opinion, but it was at length carried by the influence of the Parisian ambassadors. On the first of March this new form of cession was presented to the pope in his own palace. The emperor himself and a large number of the different nations were present. In behalf of the council, the patriarch of Antioch presented it, humbly supplicating for it a gracious reception. Objectionable as this new form of abdication, armed with oaths, must have been to the pope, and difficult as he found it altogether to conceal his vexation, there was no alternative but to accept it. Having glanced over the form presented, he replied that it had ever been his intention to restore peace to the church, and that for this purpose he had come to Constance. He added, moreover, that he had already offered to cede his pontificate; that he had done it freely, of his own accord and without restraint, and that he never had been of any other mind. He then read aloud the form of abdication, which had been carefully drawn up by the council in order to cut off any opportunity of evading its conditions:—

"I, Pope John XXIII., for the welfare of all Christendom, profess, engage, and promise, swear and vow to God, the church, and this holy council, voluntarily and freely to give peace to the church itself, by the way of an unqualified cession of my pontificate; and that I will effectually perform and execute it in accordance with the deliberative decisions of the present council, if and when Peter de Luna, Benedict XIII., and Angelus Corrario, Gregory XII.,—so called, each by his obedience,—shall in like manner cede their claims, either by themselves or their lawful attorneys; and that I will do this in case of their cession, decease, or any other circumstances in which my cession will give peace to the church of God, or lead to the extirpation of the present schism."

The demands of the council had now been met by the prompt and well-acted acquiescence of John XXIII. The emperor returned him thanks for the "good and holy oblation" which he had made.[1] The cardinals first, and then other members of the council, followed the example. The pope requested, as if sympathizing with the joy of the occasion, that a session might be held on the following day, in which these proceedings should be publicly ratified.

But the reluctance which John XXIII. had already shown to adopt the course urged upon him by the council had not been without its results. The Germans, who evidently had not looked for the prompt acceptance of the final formula of cession on the part of the pope, had drawn up a series of articles on the subject of the relative authority of the pope and of the council, which admitted of an easy application. They set forth, "that in the matter of

[1] L'Enfant, 77, 78.

schism the council was the supreme judge; that to put an end to the schism there was no way more appropriate, legitimate, and effectual than that of cession; that, without regard to the abdication of Benedict and Gregory, and even in case they should refuse to abdicate, yet if their adherents would unite with the council on condition that John XXIII. should consent to cede, the latter was bound, under pain of mortal sin, to accept and execute the formula of cession presented to him on the part of the nations; that the council may require this of him even with menace, and, in case of his stubborn refusal, the aid of the secular power may be invoked against him in the name of the Catholic church."[1] It is scarcely doubtful that these articles were drawn up with the approval, if not even at the suggestion, of the emperor. A knowledge of them, and a suspicion of the source from which they emanated, could scarcely have failed to satisfy the pontiff, if any doubt had yet remained, that he must surrender at discretion to the supremacy of the council.

John XXIII. occupied his seat before the altar. Turning toward the council, he read the formula of cession presented to him in its name by the patriarch of Antioch, in a loud voice, and word for word. When he came to the expressions "I promise, engage, vow," etc., he knelt toward the altar. Then placing his hand to his heart, he added, "and these I promise to observe." After the reading of the formula, the emperor rose from his seat, thanked the pope in the name of the council, kneeled, and kissed

[1] Mansi, xxvii. 566.

his foot. The patriarch also followed the example, when the choir commenced singing the *Te Deum Laudamus*. The procurator of the council, John de Scribanis, then besought of the proto-notaries of the pope, and the notaries and scribes appointed by the council for the purpose, one or more public documents for a permanent record of the transaction.

It was about this time that the place of Huss' imprisonment was changed. He had been kept hitherto in the Dominican monastery. He was now transferred to that of the Franciscans. The latter was situated in the heart of the city, and was more convenient and accessible, as well as nearer to the papal palace. Of the motives of this transfer we can only judge, from the time and the occasion. The Franciscan monastery was undoubtedly more healthy; but the previous treatment of Huss assures us that this fact could have had but little weight with his enemies. The pope had now taken a new tack to reach the wished-for harbor, and sought undoubtedly to improve the favorable impression made by his acceptance of the demands of the council. It was his purpose to draw off attention from the papal question, and proceed with all expedition in the matter of heresy. It was probably with this object in view that he adopted a measure which contributed to the temporary alleviation of the hardships of Huss' imprisonment, while it brought his case under the daily notice of the council.

It was within the walls of this Franciscan monastery that a general congregation was held on the fourth of March. The emperor, eight cardinals, three hundred prelates, the ambassadors of the kings and princes, including those of Benedict XIII., and the king of Arragon were present. With the latter, at the council's request, a treaty was effected, the object of which was a conference between the emperor and the king of Arragon, who was to be accompanied by Benedict. The cession of the latter seemed now the only obstacle to the peace of the church and the election of a new pope. It was determined that no measures should be taken on the part of the council, pending the proposed negotiation, which should tend to prejudice its success.

The good understanding and mutual regard of the pope and emperor, which had been occasioned by the recent acquiescence of the pope in the demands of the council, were not of long continuance. There was to be no peace for the helpless pontiff while he held any ecclesiastical power. The policy of the council and the conditions of Gregory's abdication required that he should at once sink into a cipher. Nothing could be more repugnant to the purpose or feelings of the pontiff. His conditional abdication had still left him for the present in the exercise of his official authority, and he still claimed his right to continue to preside over the public sessions. But with this concession to his claims, the aims of the emperor as well as of the council interfered. If those claims were allowed, even for the present, the time would come when the difficulty of forcing him to resign them would be even greater than at first. His proposal to continue the sessions and proceed at once to the business of church reform and extirpation of heresy, was therefore rejected. The emperor wished nothing done in his absence for Constance, which should aggravate the difficulty of negotiation with Benedict.

But John XXIII., on the other hand, by no means relished the idea of surrendering his prerogative, or suspending the business of the council. Was the pontifical authority so feeble that it must find shelter under the imperial shadow? Was it not a mere loss of time and to no profit to spend months in such a negotiation as the one proposed? For himself he was willing to undertake any expedition, to visit any city in order to treat with Benedict, or such persons as he should appoint, in order to expedite the proposed arrangement. Some of the views of the pope he boldly avowed.[1] But the council paid them little attention. They had no faith in the honesty of John XXIII. Conjointly with the emperor, they were mainly anxious to take advantage of the conditional cession which he had made. They therefore requested him to expedite, with the accustomed forms, the bull of his abdication. This proposition he treated as an outrageous insult, and abused the prelates who presented it, in such a manner that none were willing again to broach the subject in his presence. The council saw itself forced to have recourse to the imperial authority to vanquish his obstinacy. Sigismund at its request visited him. He found him in a more complaisant mood, and finally induced him to notify his proposed cession to all Christendom, by a bull bearing date the sixth of March, 1415. In

[1] Van der Hardt, tom. ii., part xv., p. 395.

this bull the arts of the pontiff are clearly displayed. He vaunts his love for the church, for whose sake he willingly renounces the possession of the popedom—waives his claims to the pontificate notwithstanding their justice is indisputable—and looks to heaven for the recompense of his self-denial. Nor does he fail to set off the reluctance of Gregory and Benedict to cede, in the most odious light possible.

After the pope had gone so far, it seemed difficult to frame new demands. But the principal object of the emperor and of the council was still unattained. Step by step they had steadily advanced toward their real object, a cession so far conditional only that the emperor, or attorneys appointed for the purpose, could make it absolute at their discretion. Such an instrument might be a powerful weapon to bring Benedict to terms, and it was important that it should be executed before the emperor set out on his journey. The French, English, and Germans were earnest and urgent in their advice to press the pope to execute it. In order to render it more authentic and irrevocable, it was desirable to engage the pope to appoint the emperor himself, with the prelates that should accompany him, or such persons as he should select, his procurators for this purpose. But the proposition was indignantly rejected. The Italians were so displeased with it, that they threatened, if it was urged, to leave the council. For the present, therefore, it was found necessary to defer it.

Closely as the position of John XXIII. was invested, he did not altogether despair. He was still busy in his intrigues. The hope was yet cherished of making the emperor his partisan, or at least securing a larger measure of his favor. Three weeks before Easter he presented him with the golden rose, which he had that day solemnly consecrated according to pontifical usage. Sigismund received it, with large expressions of gratitude and regard. He wore it ostentatiously through the whole city; after which the pope regaled him, together with the secular and ecclesiastical princes, at a sumptuous banquet. But the emperor was not the dupe of papal artifice. He knew the man he had to deal with, and saw the necessity of resorting to measures of intimidation to secure his object. A public congregation was called, on the eleventh of March, in which it was proposed at once to give a pope to the church. The surprise of the papal partisans at this sudden and strange proposition may easily be conceived. It was virtually a declaration that the pontificate was vacant. A discussion arose in which the Archbishop of Mentz took an active part in favor of John XXIII. He declared that if any other were elected, he would refuse to recognize him. For a time the assembly was thrown into confusion; but at length, after the discussion had been continued for some days, it was determined that the nations were at liberty and authorized to take such measures as they should judge most appropriate toward the union of the church and the election of another pope.[1]

The breach between the emperor and John XXIII. now became greater than ever. The last resources of the latter seemed exhausted, and he finally re-

[1] L'Enfant, i. 79, 80.

solved on flight. But his purpose was not one that admitted of easy execution. The report was general that orders had been given for the arrest, or at least the close watch, of all who issued from the gates of the city. Indisposed to run any dangerous risk, and in order to discover the truth or falsehood of the report, the pope directed the cardinal St. Angelo to go to the gates ostensibly to take a walk without the walls. He did so, and was in fact arrested. No sooner was John XXIII. made aware of this, than he summoned a congregation to meet in his palace, in which he addressed a bitter complaint to the princes and the magistrates of the city against this violation of the security and public liberty so solemnly promised to all visitants, and especially to himself. The magistrates threw the blame upon the emperor, and on his part the Archduke Frederic promised that the safe-conducts should be inviolably observed.

The emperor soon learned what had passed in the papal palace. He summoned the next day the three nations, English, French, and German, in order to take measures yet more decisive. The previous demand for the appointment of attorneys on the part of the pope was now renewed. It was resolved that he should be required to engage to grant no permission of absence from the council, nor withdraw himself; that he should not dissolve the council till the union of the church had been attained, nor consent to its transfer to any other place.[1] In respect to the guards stationed in the different places, and of which the pope had complained, Sigismund apologized for

[1] L'Enfant, 80.

it as having been done with the advice of some of the cardinals, who had observed that many secretly withdrew from the council, a course which, if permitted, would draw on its dissolution. The articles, as drawn up under the eye of the emperor, were presented to John XXIII. by the patriarch of Antioch, whose service was rewarded by the pope with the charge of being a false brother, and a secret partisan of Benedict XIII.

On the next day the answer of the pope was given. He promised not to dissolve the council while the schism continued. As to transferring its sessions to another place, he was willing to leave it to the good judgment of the fathers of the council, at the same time giving it to be understood that he was ready to go to Nice, the place of the proposed negotiation between Sigismund and Benedict. As to power of attorney to cede for him, he utterly refused it on various grounds, among others, as implying a dishonorable submission which Benedict would never imitate. In conclusion, he promised to do all that should be judged necessary to promote the union of the church, under pain of being deserted by all his cardinals and prelates if he violated his pledge.

But the point which the pope was so reluctant to yield was not readily abandoned. An assembly of the several nations was held on the following day, in which the subject was again discussed. The French were now undecided, and asked more time for deliberation. The English proposed the pope's arrest in the public assembly, and in presence of the emperor. John XXIII. complains that but for the intervention of the French, they would have proceeded to this extremity. A sort of latent loyalty to the pontiff was aroused by the severity of the measures proposed against him. He was gaining sympathy as a persecuted man. The emperor saw that the moment was critical. He went at once, accompanied by the English, the Germans, and his council, to the monastery where the French were assembled, to confer with the Italian deputation. He presented to the assembly a document, the tenor of which was, to force the pope to appoint attorneys to execute his act of cession, and prevent him from leaving the city. But the French regarded the measure of the emperor as an attempt to overawe them, and insisted on their privilege of deliberating by themselves—a privilege which the other nations had enjoyed. Upon this the English and Germans withdrew while the imperial counsellors remained. The French demanded of the emperor that these also should leave, and that none but himself should be allowed to remain. This demand provoked Sigismund.[1] In a tone indicative of his passion, he exclaimed, as he turned to leave the assembly, "Now is the time to discover who are well disposed toward the union of the church, and at the same time toward the empire." The cardinal of Cambray, who seems to have been satisfied with the conditional cession of the pope, and was indisposed to any further humiliation of the papal authority, regarded the words of the emperor as an implied threat, and withdrew deeply indignant. The four other cardinals, who with him composed the Italian

[1] Godeau, xxxvi. 491. L'Enfant, 81.

deputation, considering their freedom of consultation prejudiced, sent to the emperor, who had not yet left the cloister, to know if they were free to act. He replied, that as for the French they might enjoy perfect liberty of deliberation, and added an apology for the words that had escaped him in a moment of excitement. But as to those who were not of the French nation, they should leave the assembly, under pain of imprisonment. This threat was aimed at the five cardinals who composed the Italian deputation. The French nation was left alone to its own deliberations, and the influence of Gerson and his associates secured a decision agreeable to the emperor. Three nations now united in their demand, that the pope should appoint attorneys to execute his act of cession.

This result was a fatal blow to the last semblance of hope which John XXIII. might have hitherto cherished. Notwithstanding the reluctance of the cardinals of St. Mark and Cambray, who had been the leaders of the anti-papal party, to proceed to this ulterior measure, it had yet been adopted by a majority of the nations. Flight from Constance was the only method which was left to John XXIII. of escaping from the difficulties of his position. Upon this he was fully resolved. His friend Frederic, Duke of Austria, had reached the city but a few days before, and all were suspicious of the object he had in view. The emperor several times gave him warning not to aid the pope in his efforts to escape. On the evening of the twentieth of March, he went in person to confer with the pontiff. He most urgently dissuaded him from the idea of withdrawing from the council. Though guards were stationed at the gates, along the walls, and by the shores of the lake, in order to arrest any that should attempt to leave the city, Sigismund could not yet feel entirely sure of his prisoner. He wished, if possible, to secure his promise not to make the attempt. John XXIII. was too great a master of dissimulation not to be ready to give an answer with which the emperor was fain to be satisfied. He replied that he would by no means leave Constance until the dissolution of the council. The ambiguity of his language left it afterwards to be inferred that he considered the council dissolved by the very fact of his departure.[1]

Scarce had the emperor left, when John XXIII. gave way to his passion. Bitterly did he utter his reproaches and complaints against Sigismund and his adherents. He would now have left him of the golden rose nothing but the thorn. Sigismund heard of the pope's language, but discreetly passed it by. It may have been that there was some truth in the oft-repeated charge of John XXIII. that the emperor had demanded money of him to secure him in his office. The probabilities are indeed against it, but the charge was boldly made out, was not denied, and it was obvious to all that the fate of John XXIII. was in the hands of Sigismund.

John XXIII. had complained, in his last interview with the emperor, that the air of Constance did not agree with him.[2] He found his health giving way under it. Did he ever feel concern for the health of his destined victim, not like himself the inmate of a

[1] L'Enfant, 88. [2] Ib., 82, 83.

palace, but shut up in a prison cell? The emperor, in reply, expatiated to him upon the healthfulness and beauty of many places about the city where he might walk or ride for his refreshment. He even offered to accompany him; but undoubtedly the last companion whom the pope would have selected, would have been the emperor. John XXIII. was not particularly select in the terms by which he characterized his persecutor. He called him drunkard, fool, barbarian, beggar, and names still more opprobrious.

It was on the following day, March 21, that the pope had made his arrangements for flight.[1] Frederic, Duke of Austria, though he stoutly denied all complicity with him, and declared that he cared not a straw for him or his money, had yet given him to understand what measures were to be taken. He had himself, on this day, appointed a tournament without the walls of the city, thus giving occasion for multitudes to pass the gates, among whom John XXIII. might escape unsuspected.

It was towards evening when the pope was prepared to make the hazardous attempt. He was disguised as a groom or postilion. He rode a horse poorly equipped, and was himself wrapped in a large cloak, with a crossbow on the pommel of his saddle. He passed on undiscovered till he reached the banks of the river, where a boat was ready to convey him to Schafhausen, which he reached in safety. Frederic had been at once informed of the pope's flight,

[1] L'Enfant, 84, 85. Fleury, xxv. 450. Godeau, xxxvi. 469. Van der Hardt, *in loco*.

by one of his servants, who had been appointed to observe it, and who came and whispered the intelligence in the duke's ear. No one suspected the nature of the message. The games were continued as if nothing had happened. In due time the duke returned to Constance, and at length rejoined the pope at Schafhausen, a city of his own allegiance.[1]

[1] Cormerim (His. of the Popes) says, (ii. 107,) I know not on what authority, that on the night of his escape the pope made the soldiers who guarded him drunk, and thus, in his disguise as a groom, was able to make good his escape. The story is at least not improbable.

CHAPTER XVII.

SUPREMACY OF THE COUNCIL. THE POPE SUSPENDED. TREATMENT OF HUSS. ARREST OF JEROME.

Consternation at the Pope's Flight. — Steps Taken by the Emperor and Council.— Duke of Austria.— Gerson's Discourse.— The Pope's Letters.— His Apology.— Vain Attempt to Dissolve the Council.— Fourth Session.— Decrees Read. — An Omission. — Dissatisfaction. — Protest of the Pope.— He Goes to Laufenburg. — A New Seal. — Fifth Session. — Decrees of the Former Session Restored. — Wickliffe's Books to be Examined. — Measures for Bringing Back the Pope. — The Duke of Austria Cited. — His Disasters. — John XXIII. at Freiburg. — Letter to the Council. — Wickliffe's Doctrines Condemned. — Controversy Occasioned by the Form of Sentence. — Cardinal of Cambray and Patriarch of Antioch. — Demands Made of John XXIII. — Commission. — Proposal to Exclude the Cardinals. — The Pope at Breisach. — Misfortunes of the Duke of Austria.— Inclined to Submit. — His Advice to the Pope. — Fruitless Conference.— Council Irritated. — Citation of John XXIII. — Of Jerome. — The Duke of Austria Reconciled to the Emperor. — The Archbishop of Metz.— The Pope Deserted.— Commission to Take Testimony. — Force to be Employed.— Evasion. — Tenth Session. — Suspension of the Pope. — Heresy. — Huss Neglected. — Bohemians and Sigismund. — Prison Interview. — Huss at Gottlieben. — Jerome at Constance. — His Flight. — Demands a Safe-Conduct.— Reply.— His Citation.— Leaves for Prague.—Arrest at Hirschau.— Taken to Constance. — Charges Made. — Gerson. — A Doctor of Cologne.— A Doctor of Heidelburg. — The Bishop of Saltzburg. — Confusion. — Peter the Notary Finds Jerome. — Vitus. — Jerome's Cruel Imprisonment.

March 22, 1415–May 24, 1415.

The flight of John XXIII. from Constance produced no little consternation in the city. Many expected the immediate dissolution of the council. The merchants, sensitive to the least popular excitement which threatened riot, closed their shops or packed up their goods, in order to be ready to depart. It was in this emergency that the prudence and decision of the emperor were manifested. Attended by the elector Palatine and most of the court nobility, he marched with the sound of trumpet in procession through the streets of the city, giving his royal word that personal security should be still enjoyed, that the council was not dissolved by the flight of the pope, and that he was ready to defend it to the last drop of his blood. At the same time a writing was nailed to the gates of the palace to which public attention was called. It was an able invective against the conduct of John XXIII. It exposed his bad faith, intrigues, and projects for breaking up the council, and closed with a plea for the continuance of the council and the judgment of the pope according to his deserts.

A congregation was soon held to determine what measures should be adopted in the emergency. It seemed essential to persuade John XXIII. to return to Constance, or at least to appoint his attorneys to execute the act of cession. A deputation of six was appointed to confer with him, of whom three were cardinals, one of the latter, Cardinal St. Mark.

Measures were the same day taken, in an assembly of the princes of the empire, to prosecute the Duke of Austria for his complicity in the flight of the pope. The emperor urged the matter with great energy. The duke was accused of treason and disloyalty to the council, the church, and the empire, and was summoned to appear and answer for his conduct before the emperor and the council. Thus the pope was to be punished in the prostration of the only powerful friend on whom he could rely. Many of the duke's cities at once withdrew their allegiance.

The deputation to the pope had not yet left Constance, when some of the ablest minds of the council, disdaining any longer to demean themselves by controversy or negotiation with him, proposed bolder and more decisive measures. The well-known views and unquestionable ability of Gerson[1] marked him out as their leading advocate. The proposition now advanced was, that a general council was superior in authority to the pope, and might depose him. Gerson made it the subject of a public discourse, which the members of the deputation, although invited, declined to hear. The discourse was able and to the point. It was enforced, moreover, by papers drawn up by the representatives of the university of Paris. One of these, Benedict Gentian, a man of eminent ability, and a doctor of decrees, produced a separate document of similar purport, in which he declared John XXIII. "a stone of stumbling, and a rock of offence." "Who more than he," he indignantly asks, "has scandalized the church of God?" He then concisely argues his "perfect heresy" from the gross and aggravated crimes of which he is undoubtedly guilty.

Meanwhile the pope on his part was not idle. The next day after his arrival at Schafhausen, he wrote to the emperor, his "dearest son," informing him that 'by the favor of Almighty God he was now in the enjoyment of a healthful and salubrious atmosphere.' He exculpated the Duke of Austria from

[1] Fleury, xxv. 453.

all complicity in his flight, and declared that 'now in the enjoyment of health and liberty, he had no purpose to evade his promise.'

The cool impudence of such ostentatious affection could certainly have contributed but little to calm the indignation or change the purpose of Sigismund. Scarcely, however, could he have perused this extraordinary letter, when another missive from Schafhausen reached Constance, and one more clearly indicative of the pope's purpose. He cited all the officials and retainers of the pope's court, under pain of excommunication and deprivation of all their offices, to meet him within six days at Schafhausen. It was plain that his object now was to break up the council. In obedience to his requisition, many left Constance. At the same time he put forth a skilful and specious apology for his flight, which he sent to the king of France and the Duke of Orleans. In this letter he sets forth the difficulties which interested persons had placed in the way of the council's proceedings; complains of the unprecedented measure of dividing the council into nations, each having an equal vote; objects to the obstacles thrown in his way when he was anxious to attend to the trial of Huss; remarks upon the emperor's intrigues, his control over the English and German nations; skilfully appeals to French prejudice in an account of Sigismund's attempt to overawe the deliberations of the French deputation; grows indignant at the restraint imposed upon his own liberty, as well as the insults of the bishop of Sarum, in broaching the proposition which Gerson defended;

and concludes with an account of his necessary flight, in which he contradicts the statements of his previous letter, addressed to the emperor, as to the complicity of the Duke of Austria.[1] John XXIII. could scarcely find fault with Benedict Gentian for calling him a great liar.

But the doctrine which the bishop of Sarum had ventured to state in the pope's presence, and of which Gerson was the public and avowed champion—the superiority of the council to the pope—did not pass unquestioned. Many who had hitherto acted with the majority, began to waver. Was it not evident that such a doctrine would allow the council to annul all that the pope had done, and what security had the cardinals that they should not be deposed as well as their master? The question was already secretly agitated, soon to be brought to a public discussion, whether the cardinals, at least those who were adherents of John XXIII., should be allowed to participate in the deliberations of the council. Already they had taken the alarm. The members of the deputation refused to attend the assembly where Gerson was to discourse. The emperor invited the cardinals to meet and confer with him. Apprehensive of some scheme against the pope in which they could not participate, they declined the invitation. The patriarch of Antioch, whom the pope did not regard with any peculiar confidence, and whom he had called a false friend, drew up an elaborate argument to the effect that the pope is not subject to a general council. It was an answer to

[1] Van der Hardt gives the document in full.

Gerson's discourse. Not without the dissent of some of his colleagues, especially the cardinal D'Ailly, he presented one copy to the emperor, and took good care to send another to the pope.

The deputation to Schafhausen set out on their journey on the afternoon of March 23d. The distance they had to travel was four German or twenty-three English miles. They spent the next day in conference with the pope. One of their number, the archbishop of Rheims, returned on the 25th to Constance. He found the emperor and the principal members of the council assembled to deliberate. His report was far from satisfactory. John XXIII. still professed his readiness to execute the act of cession, but made propositions in regard to the method of it which were quite inadmissible. From day to day the subject was discussed, sometimes giving rise to strange scenes of altercation and confusion. Many of the cardinals, among whom was D'Ailly, were unwilling as yet entirely to break with the pope. They professed their determination to adhere to him until they were satisfied of his purpose to refuse to appoint procurators, in which case they would abandon him and abide by the decision of the council. They insisted that no definite action should be taken previous to the return of the deputation. On one occasion, while they were pleading for delay, and urging the cause of the pope, a copy of the pope's citation, addressed to his officials and requiring them to leave Constance, was brought into the assembly. It had just been nailed upon the gates of the cathedral church. Its announcement took all by surprise.

Even three of the deputation who had just returned from Schafhausen were not prepared for it, though apprehensive that some such a step was intended. The members of the council were indignant at this attempt to dissolve it. It was in vain that the cardinals urged the good intentions of the pope, or the concessions which he had authorized them to make. No faith was reposed in his word. The call was loud and repeated for a public session: "No matter about these; let there be a session," was the cry. It was in vain to resist the demand; the only concession that was granted was, that instead of being held on the twenty-eighth, it was deferred to the thirtieth of the month.

Up to the noon of the last-mentioned day, encroaching upon the time of the session, and in desecration of the sacred hours of the Sabbath on which it was to be held, the altercations continued. Various questions provoked the passions of the disputants. Some, and especially the cardinals, contended that by the pope's flight the council was *ipso facto* dissolved. "What they could not effect by reason," says Niem, "they attempted by their clamor." A question, equally vital, was next raised—the one which Gerson had made the subject of his discourse. Immense results depended on its decision. The cardinals were not blind to the nature of a measure in which they were personally so deeply interested. But public sentiment was against them. The imperial will and Gerson's logic, not unaided by the duplicity of the pope, carried the day. The majority of the nations—the Italians as well as the cardinals dissenting—agreed to report for adoption, at the approaching session of the council, measures necessary to its continuance and the vindication of its authority. These were, the supremacy of the council, in matters vital to the church, over every kind of estate and dignity, even the papal; the guilt and deserved punishment of the pope for attempting to set it aside; and a third article on *the execrable flight* of the pope, of which Gerson secured the insertion, but which was afterwards dropped at the instance of the cardinals. The question of adopting these, renewed all the previous bitterness of feeling. Neither party was inclined to yield. The odium against the cardinals was increased by their obstinacy. Some had refused to attend the deliberations, under pretexts too shallow to conceal their suspected purpose of treating the council as dissolved. Others could not go so far, even in their strong attachment to the council, as to betray the papal prerogative.

Such was the state of things when the fourth session of the council was held on the thirtieth of March. In the absence of the pope, cardinal Jordan de Ursinis was appointed to preside. The decrees were read by Zabarella, cardinal of Florence. The cardinals had taken the liberty to modify the form in which they had been received from the congregation of the nations. As published, they were, in substance, that the council, deriving its power as the representative of the universal church from Christ himself, was superior to all other authority or dignity, even that of the pope; that John XXIII. might not recall his officials, or remove the sessions of the council from

Constance, under penalty of ecclesiastical censure, or measures more severe; that no promotions or deprivations were allowable on his part, to the prejudice of the council, or of those that adhered to it; that no new cardinals should be created, and that those officials of the papal court, who were present in Constance, should enjoy, as before, full and undisturbed liberty of deliberation and action. Besides these, before or after the session, several articles were presented to the cardinals, ostensibly looking to and providing for the execution of the act of cession on the part of John XXIII.[1]

On the following day, when the nations were assembled, complaint was made of the strange omissions and changes in the decrees as read by Zabarella. On their part the cardinals demanded fuller consideration on the omitted points, while the presidents of the nations, after conference with Zabarella, expressed their reprehension of the audacity of the cardinal. It was promptly resolved that the omitted parts should be at once restored, and the decrees be reproduced in their integrity.[2]

Meanwhile the pope, who had obtained information of the proposed measures of the council, through fear or policy, determined to leave Schafhausen. He deemed himself safer at a greater distance from Constance, or at least wished to have it so believed. It gave him opportunity to sting the emperor by the reproach implied in the statement afterward made, that he considered his freedom endangered at Schafhausen. He left the place at about the hour when

[1] Van der Hardt, iv. 86, 91. [2] Ib. 92.

the fourth session of the council was opened. None of his cardinals accompanied him except for a short distance from the city. He made them there witnesses to a written protest against the binding obligation of what he had sworn or promised at Constance, as extorted from him by force and threats.[1] Thus his double game was now fully and finally exposed. In a storm of rain, and on horseback, with few attendants, he hurried on to Laufenberg, thus placing more than double the former distance between himself and the council. Many of the officers of his court returned to Constance. Benedict Gentian says[2] they did not find a good kitchen at Schafhausen, and so came back. Some however remained, undecided what policy to adopt. No sooner were the pope's second flight and his protest known, than several of the cardinals and officers of the papal court, and numbers of the Italian clergy, stole away from the council, most of them, however, soon to retrace their steps, "not without shame."

This second flight of the pope gave the emperor and council the new advantage of showing how John XXIII. had contradicted himself, in the reasons given for his flight, first from Constance and afterward from Schafhausen. It encouraged them to an act which was a virtual declaration of entire independence of the papal authority. A new seal was provided, with which to authenticate the documents of the council. For a device it had on one side the heads of St. Peter and St. Paul, and on the other the

[1] Niem in Van der Hardt, tom. ii., fol. 400. [2] Van der Hardt, tom. ii., fol. 281

words "The seal of the most holy council of the city of Constance." The decision of the emperor, and the persevering energy of the anti-papal party, had now placed them in the ascendant. The cowardly flight of John XXIII., his inconstancy, notorious duplicity, and falsehood, had dispirited his partisans. War was declared against his powerful friend the Duke of Austria, and the emperor was making the necessary preparations for carrying it on.

Such was the condition of things when the fifth session of the council was opened, on Sunday, the sixth of April, 1415. The cardinal Jordan de Ursinis again presided. Eight cardinals were present. As it had been resolved to restore the parts of the decrees which had been omitted in the previous session, Cardinal Zabarella refused to read them. The bishop of Posnania was appointed to fill his place. The decrees, as originally agreed upon, were read, and unanimously adopted. The most important of the previously omitted portions was the one which declared the authority of the council to reform the church in *its head and members.* The supremacy of the council over the papal dignity, which was thus embodied in the decree, was most offensive to the partisans of John XXIII. Four centuries have still left the principle a disputed one. The interest of the popes has ever placed them in the ranks of its bitter opponents.

In this session it was resolved to affirm and approve the sentence of the council of Rome in regard to the books and doctrine of Wickliffe. A commission was appointed to investigate, and report the steps which should be taken. It was, moreover, resolved to write letters in the name of the council to kings and princes, giving a statement of the flight of the pope, and vindicating the body from the charges which he had brought against it.

As it was evident that John XXIII. had no disposition to return to Constance, the council besought the emperor to attempt to bring him back. Sigismund replied that he would do it, intimating at the same time that force might be necessary to take him out of the hands of the Duke of Austria. He then stated the steps which he had taken to reduce the duke to obedience,—well pleased, undoubtedly, to have the approval of the council in an enterprise inspired as much by policy as concern for the church.

Meanwhile John XXIII. had reached Laufenberg. From that place he issued a bull, in which he still kept up his well-feigned anxiety to restore the church to peace and unity. Nor can we be surprised at his expressing his apprehension of danger to his personal freedom when he knew that the troops of the emperor were already on their march to Schafhausen. Sigismund had, in fact, entered upon the execution of his purpose with resolute energy. He was determined to subdue the pride and power of the pope's most powerful champion. On the seventh of April, a citation of the duke, in which he is put under the ban of the empire, and all his subjects are absolved from their oath of allegiance, was nailed upon the doors of all the churches of Constance. Letters were written to different cities of Swabia and the Swiss cantons, urging them to proceed against Frederic as an enemy of the church and empire, and a disturber of the council. It was in vain that the French ambassadors and many powerful nobles interceded in his behalf. Some, who had formerly been under great obligations to the duke, manifested their ingratitude by the readiness with which they abandoned a sinking cause. Forty thousand men, in several bodies, were precipitated upon the cities which owed allegiance to the duke. City after city was taken from him. The Swiss were forced, by terrible threats, to abandon their neutrality and take up arms. John XXIII. did his best to encourage his poor bewildered ally. He looked with confidence yet to the dissolution of the council, imagining that his absence would reduce it to a nullity. In such a case it was probable that the power and influence of the emperor would cease to preponderate, and Frederic might be able to recover what he had lost. But he soon saw himself reduced to the necessity of submission. John XXIII., on his part, deeming himself no longer safe at Laufenberg, fled to Freiburg, a place strongly fortified. On his arrival, he again sent to the council the terms on which he would execute his act of cession. But his demands were too extravagant for the council to allow. They saw themselves made the sport of the pope's duplicity; so that his last letter only served to confirm and strengthen the opposition against him. The cardinals, moreover, were now more inclined than heretofore to abandon the pope. The proceedings of the council were continued in his absence with their former regularity, a commission being appointed to act in his place.

Meanwhile the question of the relative authority of the pope and council was agitated anew. The occasion of it was the proposed condemnation of Wickliffe's writings. As we have already seen, a commission was appointed, (April 7th,) who were clothed with full authority to examine the doctrines of the English heretic, and report the form of process to be adopted for the condemation proposed. This commission, consisting, among others, of Cardinals St. Mark and Cambray, to whom the cause of Huss was also committed, had made their report on or about the eighteenth of the month. By the advice of many eminent doctors who were consulted in the examination of Wickliffe's works, it was agreed that forty-five articles extracted from them should be condemned.[1] These articles, which were read in the session held on the fourth of May, and there pronounced heretical, cannot be regarded as a fair representation of the views of Wickliffe. Some of them are evidently garbled extracts from his writings, while a portion of the others are so distorted as to lose their original meaning. It is obvious, however, in comparing them with the opinions and doctrines of Huss, that the English reformer was by far the most thorough Protestant.

It was proposed also to condemn two hundred and sixty other articles drawn from Wickliffe's writings; but the reading of them for this purpose was interrupted by the French, who complained that they had

[1] Van der Hardt, iv. 150.

not had the opportunity to examine them. It appears, however, that the new list of articles, as well as the principal treatises of Wickliffe, were likewise condemned.[1]

It was indeed a foregone conclusion that Wickliffe should be anathematized as a notorious and scandalous heretic; that his memory should be condemned; and that his body and bones, if they could be distinguished from others, should be disinterred and cast out from ecclesiastical burial. Such was the definitive sentence pronounced by the council in its eighth session, held on the fourth of May.

But in drawing up the form of the sentence, the question was raised whether Wickliffe's condemnation should be pronounced in the name of the pope or the council. Most of the cardinals, and the entire party yet in sympathy with the pope, were united in favor of the former. Thus the controversy in regard to a principle fundamental to the constitution of the whole church was again opened. By order of the council the previous conclusions of the cardinals in regard to the supremacy of the church of Rome, as well as to their own privileges, had been answered and refuted. The patriarch of Antioch, who had gone with the council so far as to be called a false friend by John XXIII., now came forward as the champion of the papal party. "Church power,"[2] he maintained, "was given to the mystic body of the church, so as to pertain especially to St. Peter; from him, as the head, it is diffused through the whole body. But nowhere do we find that Peter ever gave

[1] L'Enfant, 157. [2] Van der Hardt, ii. 295.

a general council power over the pope; consequently the pope is not subject to it. To him belongs *plenitude* of power. Others are therefore subject to him, and not he to them. Councils, moreover, receive their power from the pope. None but God is his judge. A council cannot judge him without his authority." These positions are sustained by a multitude of references to decisions of the popes, opinions of eminent doctors, the canon-law, decretals, etc. Such were the views concurred in by a large majority of the cardinals, and favored by all the partisans of the pope, embracing probably the majority of the Italian nation. The cardinal of Cambray came forward to confute them. Manfully did he undertake the task, well aware, however, that stronger than his logic was the will of the council, resolved to enforce it. "To continue obstinately in schism," said he, "is a heresy, and even an idolatry. In this case it is allowable that a pope should be judged. Besides, is not the pope judged by a human being in the tribunal of his own conscience? The council, moreover, represents the entire church, of which the pope is but a part."

The contention on this matter grew warm and fierce. Only twelve members out of forty,[1] composing the commission of doctors, agreed with the cardinal of Cambray. But, in spite of contradictions even to his face, he was resolved to maintain his ground.

But the policy forced upon the council by the emergency was stronger than arguments drawn from

[1] Several, undoubtedly, were absent. The full number was fifty.

reason or precedent. The question, so earnestly discussed then, has been variously determined since, according to the preponderance of parties. It is still the *touch-me-not* of the Roman Catholic church. But in spite of the overwhelming majority against him in the college of cardinals, D'Ailly was triumphant in the council. Its members were irritated by the frequent subterfuges and delays of the pontiff. They were more than satisfied that he had no intention to cede his office. The only measure that now remained for them was the assertion of the rights and the maintenance of the authority of the council.

On the thirteenth of April the council had deliberated on the terms upon which John XXIII. had wished to negotiate. He demanded of the emperor a safe-conduct, drawn up in such terms as he should dictate; that the council should decree his freedom as well after as before his abdication; that the war against his friend, the Duke of Austria, should cease; and that he himself should remain cardinal and Italian legate, with thirty thousand florins yearly revenue, with authority also over an Italian province. Such terms as these the council was by no means disposed to grant. The emperor was resolved that the Duke of Austria should be humbled, while few imagined that the pope would abide even by the terms he had offered.

In the session held on the seventeenth of April, the council drew up a form by which the pope was to confer a power-of-attorney to execute his cession. The persons to whom this power was to be granted were named in an after decree, and consisted of four from each of the four nations. A committee, consisting, besides the cardinals of St. Mark and Florence, of eminent theologians and bishops from the different nations, was appointed to present to the pope, for his acceptance, the form which had been drawn up. They were instructed, moreover, to demand that he should return from his flight, and select one of the three cities, Ulm, Ravensburg, or Basle, as his place of residence, where the council by its ambassadors might have access to him. Two days were allowed him in which to make his choice. In case of his refusal to comply with the demands of the council, it was resolved that he should be cited to appear and answer to the accusations brought against him. This process, which looked to his deposition, was to be stayed only until answer should be received. In case of his compliance, however, no further steps would be taken.

Meanwhile the council were encouraged in their course by letters from the university of Paris, the only power in Europe the authority and influence of which rivalled that of the papacy. They were addressed, one to the council, one to the emperor, and one to John XXIII., and fully endorsed the policy hitherto pursued. The council on their part drew up letters to kings and princes, giving a statement of the doings of the council and the difficulties with which it had to contend, in which they endeavored to secure their allegiance and support. It was in these circumstances that an event occurred which showed to what a point the influence of the cardinals had declined, in consequence of their extreme reluctance to proceed against John XXIII. In the sixth session, on the seventeenth of April, a prelate,—supposed to have been Benedict Gentian of the university of Paris,—rose and read a paper in which it was proposed that the cardinals should be excluded from the deliberations of the council. It was urged against them, that if their presence were allowed they would be judges in their own cause; that in their election of John XXIII. they had abused their office, and scandalized the whole church; that on the pope's flight from Constance they had followed him, and rendered themselves justly objects of suspicion to the council; that such as had returned, had maintained that the council was dissolved by the flight of the pope, thus virtually arguing their own exclusion; and finally, that while the adherents of John are feed by his gold, their influence will defeat the reform of the church.

No action was taken by the council upon this startling proposition. But the very fact that it could be made with impunity, and without exciting a murmur except among those directly affected by it, is quite significant. On the other hand, the cardinals were indignant at what they considered the insult that had been offered them. They assembled to deliberate in regard to their own rights, and resolved at all hazards to vindicate their own and the papal authority. An "Apology and Vindication" was consequently drawn up, and presented, on the eighteenth of the month, in an assembly of the nations. It was publicly opposed by the cardinal of Cambray. But the answer to it was not given until the second of

May. Previous to this, the cardinals had become more fully sensible of the slight which had been put upon them. Matters had been determined in the assembly of the nations of which they were allowed no knowledge until a short time before the public session, when there was no time to deliberate. They demanded, therefore, that inasmuch as the council was composed of the four nations, of which the English had but there prelates, the college of cardinals should be allowed an equal authority, and be permitted to deliberate and vote as a nation by themselves. Such a demand was little to the taste of the majority of the council. It was consequently refused. The cardinals might deliberate and vote with the nation of their birth, but were not allowed recognition as a distinct body.

Meanwhile the ambassadors to the pope had set out on their journey. It was on the nineteenth of the month that they received their final instructions, and a safe-conduct for John XXIII. in case of his compliance with the demands of the council. But the pope was no longer at Freiburg. Haunted by his fears, and apprehensive of arrest by the imperial army in the neighborhood, he had fled to Breisach. It was his evident purpose to escape from the territories of the empire and seek refuge in France, or put himself under the protection of the Duke of Burgundy. The ambassadors of the council followed him in his flight. They reached Breisach on the twenty-third of April. On the following day they laid the demands of the council before him. They were informed that an answer would be given the next day. In the interval, however, the pope disguised himself and fled, leaving as an excuse to the embassy, that during the night he had received intelligence of danger which threatened him at Breisach. His first stopping-place was at Nienburg, a village two leagues distant. But here again his fears would allow him no rest. Nor was the ground of his apprehensions merely imaginary. The friend on whom he had hitherto relied, the Duke of Austria, was unable any longer to protect, and was in fact about to desert him. One city after another had withdrawn from him its allegiance. The imperial armies were closing around him. If the conflict was to be continued, he could only offer the resistance of despair. He had relied on the fidelity, or at least the neutrality of the Swiss; but the terrors of excommunication and the imperial ban had forced them to take up arms against their ally. Frederic saw the daily defection, and began to despond. John XXIII. alone exhorted him to a manly resistance, and promised him whatever amount of money he might need. He endeavored to persuade him that, at the report of the war, the council, deprived of its head, would be dissolved, and that those who had revolted would return to their allegiance.

But Frederic had another adviser in Louis of the Palatinate, whose sister he had married.[1] Though armed on the side of the emperor, and ostensibly the enemy, Louis was really the friend of Frederic. He represented to the latter the desperate condition of his affairs, the readiness with which the chief cities would throw off their yoke and declare them-

[1] Van der Hardt, iv. 136.

selves free if the occasion was longer allowed; the folly of introducing foreign troops whose presence would only offend and alienate his own party; the fatal policy of allowing the emperor to stir up his subjects to rebellion,—slaying the duke as it were with his own sword; the security to be attained by a reconciliation with the emperor, a thing by no means to be despaired of; and the wise policy of going at once to Constance and throwing himself upon the mercy of the emperor, aided and sustained as he would be by the intercession of powerful friends. These arguments and persuasions of Louis were enforced by the friends and servants of Frederic. He at length yielded to their force, thus leaving John XXIII., unprotected, to manage his own negotiations. He determined to secure his pardon at whatever cost. After having connived at, if not aided, the pope in his flight, and used him as his tool till he discovered that he was but a broken staff, he resolved to deliver him up to the emperor as a mark of his submission; and it was with this view that he returned to Constance. A Swiss historian[1] declares that by Frederic's intervention the pope was prevented from escaping to France. He wished to hold him as a pledge to secure his own pardon. Under the semblance of friendship he wrote to John XXIII. a letter, the results of which, if not so intended, fully accorded with the interests of the council. He told him that he could no longer warrant his security at Nienburg, nor on his proposed route, inasmuch as the troops of the emperor were stationed to intercept him. The

[1] Muller.

duke consequently volunteered the advice, equivalent to a command in the circumstances of the case, that the pope would best consult his safety by returning to Freiburg. No other course was left for John XXIII. than to accept the advice, however unpalatable.

Meanwhile the embassy from the council, deserted at Breisach by the man with whom they had been sent to confer, and indisposed to follow up the fugitive in what they deemed a fruitless chase, had set out on their return to the council. They had already reached Freiburg, and were about to continue their journey, when they were agreeably surprised by information from Louis of Bavaria, who met them at that place, that if they would remain a short time longer, they might have the desired opportunity of meeting the pope, and executing their commission. In a few hours John XXIII. arrived. He was extremely mortified at finding here the men to whom he had shown such antipathy at Breisach, and whom he dreaded almost equally with the imperial troops. They now repeated their demand of a power-of-attorney, and a choice of the proposed cities in which he might reside and treat with the council, declaring that in case of his refusal the council would proceed against him. The mortification of the pope was extreme. There was no longer any possible method of evading the demand. An answer must be given. It was promised by John XXIII., and the ambassadors of the council were to receive it on the following day. The day came, but no answer. The ambassadors at once went to search for the pope. They found him yet in bed, where he received them, as Niem reports, in the most indecent manner. He still refused to grant them a power-of-attorney to execute his act of cession, but promised to send it to the council after them. He merely placed in their hands a list of the demands which he made for himself as the condition of compliance with the wishes of the council. Unable to obtain anything more satisfactory, the ambassadors returned to Constance. At an assembly of the nations, held on the twenty-ninth day of April, their report was made. The irritation against John XXIII. was now extreme. All professed to see in the result of this embassy another illustration of the duplicity and obstinacy of the pope. It was resolved, therefore, that the process against him should be commenced, and that he should be cited before the council to answer to the accusations brought against him. Before the citation was issued, however, the papal grant of a power-of-attorney arrived. But it was loaded with conditions wholly inadmissible. The council voted it unsatisfactory, in spite of the remonstrance of the cardinals.

On the second of May, the seventh public session of the council was held. It was in this session that Jerome, whose arrest was not yet known at Constance, was cited for the second time. The citation of John XXIII. was likewise issued, in which he was charged with the crimes of heresy, simony, corrupt administration of his office, favoring the present schism, and other grave offences, scandalous to the Catholic church. He was accused, moreover, of gross immoralities. His flight, his evasion of the demands of the council, and his opposition to the reformation of the church were not forgotten in the catalogue of his crimes; and he was summoned by a public edict, to be published in the usual manner, to appear within nine days before the council and submit to trial. His refusal to appear should not stay the process.

The second citation of Jerome, to which we have referred as issued at this session, was urged forward by that enemy of the Bohemian reformers, Michael de Causis. He personally attended to the publication of the citation, nailing it, during the hours of public worship, on the doors of St. Stephen's church and the church of the Virgin Mary. His assistants in the work were two fellow-priests of Prague, George de Walschim and Paul de Horowitz. It was not without reason that Jerome complained, on his trial, that he was persecuted by individual envy and malice.

While these things were taking place, Frederic of Austria was industriously looking after his own interests. Abandoning the pope to his fate, he hastened to Constance. It was on the thirtieth of April that he reached the city; but nearly a week passed before he could find access to the emperor.[1] On the fifth of May, Sigismund had assembled the Italian ambassadors and a great number of the prelates of the four nations at a banquet, in the large hall of the Franciscan monastery. He was seated at the further end of the hall when the vanquished prince appeared at the threshold. Frederic advanced, conducted by Duke Louis of Bavaria and the elector of Branden-

[1] L'Enfant, 158.

burg. As he approached the emperor, he bent his knee thrice to the ground. "What do you want?" said Sigismund. "Powerful king," replied Louis of Bavaria, "the Duke Frederic, my cousin, here present, implores your royal clemency. He is ready to bring back the pope; but he requires, for his honor, that no violence be offered the holy father." Frederic confirmed what was thus advanced, and at last moved the emperor, who tendered him his hand. The prince gave up all his domains in Alsace and the Tyrol to Sigismund, and swore fidelity to him as his lord suzerain. The emperor, whose pride was flattered by this scene of Frederic's submission, and who wished to make the most of it, turned to the personages there present, and said, "Gentlemen of the Italian nation, you are acquainted with the name and power of the dukes of Austria, yet observe how I tame them; and learn from this what a king of the Germans can do." Sigismund wished to make an impression that should overawe the partisans of the pope. To this end he sacrificed his true dignity to the bombast of power.

Frederic's submission had been preceded by that of John, archbishop of Mentz, who saw no further hope of success in his attempts to obstruct the proceedings of the council. He had been one of the pope's warmest partisans, but, like Frederic, had no disposition to invite his own ruin by clinging to a sinking cause. Thus John XXIII. saw himself entirely deserted, save by the few partisans and cardinals whose voice was drowned in the loud murmurs of the council. During the nine days allowed for his appearance, the process against Wickliffe and his writings was pressed forward. Their condemnation, referred to already, took place at the eighth session of the council, held on the fourth of May. The citation of John XXIII. had alarmed even the friends who had still followed him in his flight, and had hitherto adhered to his falling fortunes. Day by day some prelate or cardinal might be seen straggling back to Constance. Otho de Colonna, afterward elected pope in the place of John XXIII., was one of the last to desert him. The semblance of a court which had hitherto attended the fugitive pontiff now disappeared. Yet, hopeless as his case was, John XXIII. still obstinately refused to submit to the council. The ninth session was held on the day fixed for his appearance. Prelates, appointed for the purpose, called at the doors of the church for John XXIII. to appear; and, when no person came forward to answer the summons, three-and-twenty commissioners, amongst whom were Cardinals de Ursinis and St. Mark, were designated to hear the witnesses against the pope.

But the council were not disposed to be content with John's absence. His reluctance to appear was foreseen, and the citation was enforced by methods of a more effective kind. Soon after it was issued, the council sent the archbishops of Besancon and of Riga to use their influence with him, to persuade him to return, while the emperor reinforced their persuasions by sending along with them three hundred men, with the Burgrave of Nuremberg at their head. If argument and persuasion could not avail, they were to employ force. On their arrival at Freiburg, their first precaution was to station guards at all the approaches of the city, from fear that the pope might escape their hands. The prelates exhausted their eloquence in urging John XXIII. to return to Constance, but in vain. The pope received them in the most affable and cheerful manner, assuring them of his readiness to comply with their solicitations, meanwhile resolved to play out his last card of negotiation before giving up the game. Again he sent propositions to the council; but these were again refused. His letter, giving notice of his conferring the power-of-attorney on three cardinals, St. Mark, Cambray, and Florence, was read. But the cardinal of Cambray was absent. The cardinal St. Mark declared that he never had performed the office, and would not do it now; while the cardinal of Florence declared his wish to proceed according to the will of the council; but, as there was no reply, at length added that it was hard to be advocate against the whole world. In these circumstances, the whole thing was allowed silently to drop. The power-of-attorney was not read, or even produced.

The tenth session of the council was held on the fourteenth of May. The ceremony of the previous session, calling on the pope to answer to the citation, was repeated. He did not appear, and was declared guilty of contumacy. The commission for examining witnesses against him reported to the council that testimony had been heard sufficient to warrant his suspension. Ten witnesses had been examined. Their words had been reduced to writing, and their depositions were read. The allegations against the pope, as contained in the citation, were considered to be fully sustained, and his suspension from the pontifical office was pronounced. Among the charges against him was that of heresy. To this the cardinal St. Mark excepted, declaring that no witnesses had been heard upon that point. The council, aware of the maxim of the common law that a pope can be deposed only for heresy, and considering John XXIII. guilty of this, at least by implication, were unwilling to allow the force of the cardinal's objection, and the discussion of the matter was deferred to another occasion.

The controversy between the council and John XXIII. had, for the time, absorbed the interest and anxiety of all parties. Meanwhile Huss had been removed from the Dominican monastery to that of the Franciscans only that John XXIII. might more conveniently expedite his processes against him, and thus divert the attention of the council from his own affairs. At the time of the pope's flight, he was under the charge of officers of the papal court. These, when they learned that the pope had fled, deserted their post to follow their master. The keys of Huss' prison consequently fell into the hands of the emperor.[1] The opportunity was one not to be lost. The reformer's faithful friend, De Chlum, accompanied by other Bohemian nobles, immediately waited upon Sigismund in the hope of procuring his release. They pointed out to him the favorable occasion now afforded of delivering an

[1] A German Life of Huss; also, Van der Hardt, tom. iv. 66.

innocent man from indescribable sufferings, while he vindicated his own honor and that of the empire from the contempt to which they had been subjected. Sigismund listened in embarrassed silence. He protested, not without a confusion excited by a sense of his own injustice, that the future destiny of the professor lay not in his hands, but in those of the four presidents of the several nations of the council. All that he himself would consent to was, that the nobles should pay the invalid a short visit in the presence of witnesses. Conducted by the emperor's attendants, the Bohemians proceeded to the Franciscan convent. There they found Huss, to outward view, a pitiable object. He lay stretched on a miserable couch, emaciated, and wasted almost to a skeleton. On the ground before him lay a small strip of paper. They picked it up, and though the writing upon it was scarce legible, it told the story of the neglect which would soon have saved the stake a victim. "If you still love me, entreat the emperor to allow his people to provide for me, or else enable me to find sustenance for myself." Such were the words they read.

Huss had formerly been scantily supplied from the pope's kitchen, but since his flight had been entirely overlooked. For three days the weak, enfeebled prisoner had been without food. Meekly and uncomplainingly did he endure what God had seen fit to suffer wicked men to inflict upon him. At the melancholy sight, the bearded warriors were melted into tears, but their resentment was roused. "With uplifted hands and eloquent eyes, they besought

Heaven to give them, at some future period, an opportunity of avenging with their swords" such inhuman cruelty and injustice. Undoubtedly Sigismund might thank his own policy, in allowing such treatment of Huss, for the bitter wars that afterward ravaged his Bohemian dominions. The meeting of Huss and his friends, says the chronicle, was very melancholy, and the parting was still more sad; for all those brave men loved Huss as their father, and their hearts were full of gloomy forebodings. When the sufferer had received the last embrace of his countrymen, he sank back fainting on his chains. The next day he was given over by the emperor and the council to the rigid custody of the bishop of Constance. By the order of the latter he was conveyed by water to the castle of Gottlieben. Armed men accompanied the prisoner till they reached the spot on the banks of the Rhine, three miles distant from Constance. He was thrown into the tower, and treated with a severity which would have been harshness even to the greatest criminal. Irons were fastened to his feet, and during the day he might move the length of his chain, but at night he was chained by his arms to the wall. With such inhuman cruelty,—enough to crush the boldest spirit,—Huss was to be prepared to stand up alone against a host of enemies that thirsted for his blood. Undoubtedly there were men among them who would deliberately prefer to browbeat an invalid, or argue with one too weak to defend his own cause, than contend with the living, vigorous energy of thought and action that had electrified a whole kingdom.

It was but a few days after the removal of Huss to Gottlieben,—on the fourth of April,—that his friend and associate, Jerome of Prague, arrived at Constance. The misfortunes and sufferings of Huss had become known in Bohemia. An intense sympathy was felt in his behalf. His cruel treatment, and the danger to which he was exposed, became the subjects of daily conversation. Men began to blame Jerome that he should have left his companion and brother in faith to contend alone and unsupported against a host of enemies. But their complaint was ill-founded, as the event showed. On his departure from Prague, and more especially after his imprisonment, Huss had exhorted his friend to preserve himself for better times.[1] He was ready and willing himself to become a sacrifice, if one was demanded, but he could not consent to have the cause of truth deprived of so able and faithful a champion as Jerome. In the generous mind of the latter, however, the blame imputed to him, and to which he was so sensitive, outweighed every other anxiety. He immediately quitted Bohemia and hastened to Constance. His countrymen, to whom he presented himself, were terrified by his arrival. They knew too well the spirit that had been shown in the treatment of Huss to dare to trust it further. They at once pronounced his journey useless, since all hopes of his friend's release from prison were at an end. But Jerome was resolved to see Huss if possible, and exert himself on his behalf. By some means he seems to have secured admittance to him;[2] but when he saw his gloomy prison, the

[1] Mon. Hussi, i. 75, Epis. liv.

[2] Van der Hardt, tom. iv. 103.

chains upon his limbs, and the harsh treatment to which he was subjected, his apprehensions of the vanity of any effort in his behalf enforced the persuasions of the Bohemian nobility, and he withdrew from Constance, where his own liberty was endangered, and where spies were on his track.

Yet he had already learned from other sources, facts that excited all his fears. Since his arrival in the city, he had mingled, without being known, with the crowds of people about the streets, and had overheard disastrous intelligence. It was said that John Huss would not be admitted into the presence of the council; that he would be judged and condemned in secret; that he would leave his prison only to die. Jerome was struck with alarm, and thought that all was lost.[1] A violent terror seized on him, and he took to flight as suddenly as he had come. It is even stated, so precipitate was his departure, that he left his sword at the inn where he had alighted.[2] The news of his arrival had already spread abroad, and he was searched for in every direction. But it was soon ascertained that he had left the city.

By the aid and counsel of his friends, the Bohemian magnates, he withdrew to the neighboring free city of Uberlingen. Here deeming himself more secure, his calmer reflection led him to take those steps which his generous and impulsive nature had caused him to overlook on his departure from Prague. The precaution was indeed tardy, and one from which he could not expect any great result; yet the sanguine hope of contributing to aid Huss, the bitter fear

[1] Bonnechose, 72. [2] Mon. Hussi, ii. 349, 354.

that without such aid as he might render his doom would be sealed, and the shame of fleeing for his life only to bear back the sad message of hopeless effort to his friends at Prague, impelled him to do what he could in his friend's behalf. He wrote to the emperor and the council, asking each to grant him an open and unequivocal safe-conduct, provided with which he might appear at Constance and justify himself and Huss from all calumnious accusations brought against them. He grounded his claim on the fact of his having come to Constance of his own accord, without being summoned there like Huss. The answer he received was too ambiguous to allow him to repose any confidence in it. The emperor made the only reply that could reasonably have been expected from him after what had occurred. He refused a safe-conduct. Most probably it was his wish that Jerome would remain as far away from Constance as possible. The affair of Huss had already given him too much trouble, and Sigismund was anxious for the attainment of an object with which the trial of Jerome, or the confusion incident to his presence at Constance, might be expected to interfere.[1]

The council replied to Jerome's request in strange terms. They granted him what they chose to call a "safe-conduct," but what was, in reality, a document of quite another character, and which illustrates only too well the real object in view—the arrest and condemnation of Jerome himself. It was a very different document from that which Huss had received:—

[1] L'Enfant, iii. Mon. Hussi, ii. 355.

"The sacred synod, forming a general council at Constance, assembled by the Holy Spirit, and representing the universal church militant, recommends Jerome of Prague, calling himself master of arts in several universities, to be well-conducted, even unto sobriety, and to do nothing beyond what is necessary for being well-conducted. . . . *As we have nothing more at heart than to catch the foxes which ravage the vineyard of the Lord of hosts*, we summon you, by these presents, to appear before us as a suspected person, and violently accused of having rashly advanced several errors; and we order you to appear here within a fortnight from the date of this summons, to answer, as you have offered to do, in the first session that shall be held after your arrival. It is for this purpose that, in order to prevent any violence being offered you, we, by these presents, give you a full safe-conduct, as much as in us lies, *excepting always the claims of the law, and that the orthodox faith does not in any way prevent it;* certifying to you, besides, that whether you appear within the specified time or not, the council, by itself or its commissioners, will proceed against you as soon as the term shall have elapsed. Given at Constance, in public session, the 17th of April, 1415, under the seals of the presidents of the four nations."[1] Another account informs us that the cardinals wrote under Jerome's petition, "We grant you our protection to this place, but not back again." This was at least candid.

Dissatisfied with the answer which had been re-

[1] Van der Hardt, iv. 106–119. Also L'Enfant, i. 127.

turned to his petition, Jerome determined to make one more effort. Our historian[1] assures us that he returned to the council, and affixed his appeal for a safe-conduct in all the public places,—on the city gates, the doors of the churches, the monasteries, and palaces of the cardinals. If he did, indeed, for a few hours return to Constance, it must have been by stealth; and his appeal, we may presume, was made public by means of the Bohemian nobility. It was unquestionably the same in substance with that which he had previously presented.

The answer of the cardinals to the application of Jerome was somewhat delayed. As no answer arrived for several days, the Bohemian knights represented to him the uselessness of his attempt, and earnestly pressed his return home. Sad at heart, he commenced his journey back to Prague. He saw the uselessness of all his efforts in behalf of Huss, and was uneasy at the manner in which he apprehended his return would be interpreted. He was, however, bearer of a document in which seventy Bohemian nobles, present at Constance, gave testimony to his having come there; that he had done all in his power to render reasons for his faith; and that he had departed from Constance only because he could not remain there in safety.[2]

Such disappointment and provocation as he had experienced at Constance had not increased his pru-

[1] Van der Hardt. L'Enfant, i. 3. I cannot but express my doubt on this point. Jerome's return is very improbable, and the placards were affixed as early as May 7. Besides, from his own statements, given on his first examination, it seems evident that he never received the council's safe-conduct, although it is not improbable that he may have learned the tenor of it from his countrymen.

[2] L'Enfant, i. 136. mmimmgm

dence. He proceeded on his way, declaiming everywhere openly, and without precaution or moderation, against the council. He was still the same man as ever, full of generous and noble impulses, but often impetuous and violent. Conscious of his integrity, and listening only to his own strong convictions, his words and acts were rarely regulated by a calculating or cautious prudence.

On the 24th of April, Jerome had reached Hirschau, a small village of the Black Forest, situated on the Rhine. It was here that the curé persuaded him to stay and dine in his house, where he had invited several others of the clergy.[1] Common prudence would have led Jerome to decline the invitation. He accepted it, however, and took his seat at the table with men whose suspicions were soon excited by what they deemed the heretical language of the stranger. The course of conversation led, as might have been expected, to a discussion of the merits of the council then assembled at Constance. The mind of Jerome was at once carried back to the prison and the wrongs of Huss. His indignation mastered his discretion. He so far forgot himself as to call the council "a school of the devil, a synagogue of iniquity." Such terms could not fail to give deep offence. Some of the priests went at once and laid them before the officer in command of the town, by whose orders Jerome was arrested.

Hirschau was a city of the upper Palatinate, and it was not long before intelligence of what had occurred reached the palgrave then residing at Saltz-

[1] L'Enfant, i. 136.

bach. By his orders Jerome was cast into prison and bound with chains, while information of his arrest was sent to the council. The latter immediately besought the palgrave to send him bound to Constance. He promptly complied. Jerome was chained to a cart, his heavy irons clanking upon his limbs, and conveyed to the city—which he reached on the 24th of May. Here Louis, Duke of Bavaria, brother of the count Palatine, waited the arrival of the victim. Surrounded by a multitude equally brutal with himself, he began to pull and drag Jerome by his chains.[1] He led him about in this cruel and savage manner through the whole city. At length he stopped at the convent of the Minor Friars, where the priests were assembled to receive him. Jerome was led in like a wild beast by his chain fastened to a manacle, in order to be examined. The letter of the palgrave informing the council of Jerome's arrest, and[2] his citation published after his withdrawal from Constance, were read to him. One of the bishops then addressed the prisoner, demanding of him why he had fled and not obeyed the citation to appear before the council. "I withdrew," replied Jerome, "because I had not obtained a safe-conduct either from you or the emperor, and besides, I was aware that I had here a great number of mortal enemies. I never received the summons of the council. Had I known of it, I swear to you that I should at once have returned, aye, if I had already reached

[1] Op. Hussi, ii. 350, 355. L'Enfant, i. 182.

[2] Jerome was cited three times to appear before the council. The first citation was on April 18; the second, on May 2; and the third, on May 4. On May 23 he was brought back to Constance.

my own country."[1] In evidence of the refusal of a safe-conduct and of the danger of his appearing before the council, Jerome referred to the document presented to him by the Bohemian nobles, which had been taken from him at the time of his arrest, and which was now in the hands of the council.

The reply of Jerome produced much sensation. Great noise and confusion ensued. A multitude of persons accused Jerome, and volunteered to give evidence against him. He had visited all the universities of Europe, and the fame of his eloquence, if not the vanquishing force of his arguments, had excited the jealousy and envy of many who were here present. He had the rancor of the doctors and the petty passions of former antagonists arrayed against him. The illustrious Gerson did not neglect the occasion which his present position afforded him, to exult over a man whose pride of intellect was fully equal to his own.

After the tumult had somewhat subsided, the Parisian doctor addressed the prisoner. Gerson was not unaware of Jerome's argumentative skill, for they had known each other at Paris. He therefore recurred at once to the old subject of dispute on Universals and Ideas. Gerson was a Nominalist, Jerome a Realist. "Jerome," said the former,[2] "when you came to Paris, you fancied yourself with your eloquence to be an angel from heaven. You troubled the university, broaching in our schools many erroneous propositions with their corollaries, and especially in the matter of Universals and Ideas, beside many other

[1] L'Enfant, i. 183. [2] Mon. Hussi, ii. 350, 365. Van der Hardt, iv. 215, 216.

things of a scandalous nature." "Master Gerson," replied Jerome, "I answer you, that what I proposed in the schools of Paris, and what I answered to the arguments of the masters, I proposed philosophically, and as a philosophical thinker and a master of that university. And if I proposed anything which I ought not to propose, let me be instructed in what respect it is erroneous, and I will be corrected and set right with all humility." At this point Jerome was interrupted by a doctor of the university of Cologne, who rose and said, "When you were at Cologne, you brought forward several erroneous arguments." "Will you mention, first of all, one error that I maintained?" asked Jerome. "None occurs to me at present, but they shall be objected to you hereafter," was the reply of the doctor, disconcerted by the unexpected question. A doctor from Heidelberg now became Jerome's accuser. "When you were at Heidelberg," said he, "you maintained grave errors with regard to the Trinity. You represented it there under the figure of a kind of shield, comparing the Trinity of persons in the divine nature to water, snow, ice, etc." "What I wrote and represented at Heidelberg" said Jerome, "I am ready to assert, write, and represent again. Let me know in what respect I have erred, and I will humbly recant the error." A murmur now arose in the assembly, several calling out, "Let him be burned, let him be burned." "If it be your pleasure that I should die," resumed Jerome, "in the name of God, be it so." The bishop of Saltzburg, the only one of the council who showed the least feeling of compassion, here interposed between the judges and the prisoner. "Not so," said he, "not so; for it is written 'I will not the death of a sinner, but rather that he should turn and live.'" This single tone of mercy was drowned, however, in the redoubled noise and vociferations of the assembly. The clamor and tumult of the accusations brought against him were such that all orderly proceedings were at an end. Jerome was committed, bound, to the charge of officers of the city, and the assembly broke up.[1] Towards evening, Peter Maldoniewitz, better known by the name of Peter the Notary, an attendant on John de Chlum, and a faithful friend of Huss and Jerome, roamed about in the neighborhood of the house where the latter had for the time been lodged.[2] Drawing close to one of the windows, Peter called out to Jerome, who heard and recognized his voice. "Welcome, brother," was Jerome's instant exclamation. Welcome, indeed, must one have been who came to cheer and encourage him in the gloomy prospect now before him. "Strengthen thy soul," continued Peter; "be mindful of that truth which thou hadst so often in thy mouth when thou wert at liberty, and thy limbs were free from shackles. My friend, my master, do not fear even to face death for it." "Yes," said Jerome, "you know that I do not fear death. We have often spoken of it, but now must we see what it can do to us."[3]

The soldiers interrupted this moving conversation

[1] The account of this scene may be found in Van der Hardt and L'Enfant. Also Mon. Hussi, ii. 354, 355.

[2] In the narrative contained in Mon. Hussi, ii. 351, he is called *unus de familia M. Huss.* His name is afterwards spoken of as Peter.

[3] Mon. Hussi, ii. 351, 356.

between the friends, by repulsing Peter with violence and threats. He mournfully bade farewell to Jerome, and withdrew. His heart was filled with grief.

Scarcely had he gone, when another person came up,—a servant of John de Chlum, named Vitus. Scarcely had be begun to speak with Jerome, when he was seized by the soldiers, and found no small difficulty in recovering his liberty.

The charge of Jerome was committed to John Wallendrod, archbishop of Riga. The selection of such a man for the office, although it fell to him probably as president of the German nation, was in keeping with the harsh treatment which Jerome had already received from the council. The archbishop removed him the same night from his temporary prison to the dungeon of a tower in the cemetery of St. Paul, where he ordered him to be heavily ironed. His chains were riveted to a lofty beam in such a way as to prevent his sitting down, whilst his arms were forced by fetters to cross on his neck behind, compelling him to incline his head forward and downward. Such is the description given by old authors and by those who were spectators of his imprisonment, in their accounts of his life. For two days he was kept in this posture. His only food was bread and water. No one of his Bohemian friends knew or could ascertain where he was. At last Peter Maldoniewitz discovered his circumstances through one of the keepers of the prison. By his means Jerome was allowed the indulgence of better food.[1]

[1] Van der Hardt, iv. 218.

Had the council resolved to establish against themselves the truth of the charge made by Jerome? Had they determined, by their treatment of their prisoner, to make it manifest that they were indeed "a school of the devil, a synagogue of iniquity?" They were murdering their prisoner by inches. Nature could not long endure such aggravated and cruel inflictions. Jerome's health soon gave way. His life was at length in imminent danger. He now demanded that a confessor should be allowed him, and his request was granted. Some of his irons were taken off. His health at length was restored, and for a whole year he was the tenant of a prison.

CHAPTER XVIII.

THE COMMUNION OF THE CUP. THE BOHEMIANS AT CONSTANCE.

COMMUNION OF THE CUP. — MATTHIAS OF JANOW. — ORIGIN OF THE RESTORATION OF THE CUP. — JACOBEL AND PETER OF DRESDEN. — THESES DISCUSSED BEFORE THE UNIVERSITY. — PREVAILING OPINION IN FAVOR OF THE CUP. — JACOBEL DEFENDS IT. — REPLY TO HIM. — BRODA'S TREATISE. — JACOBEL'S REFUTATION. — HIS CONSTANT REFERENCE TO SCRIPTURE AUTHORITY. — HIS REPREHENSION OF APPEAL TO THE SECULAR ARM. — HIS ELOQUENT CONCLUSION. — HUSS CONSULTED. — HE SUSTAINS JACOBEL. — THE UNIVERSITY VINDICATED BY JACOBEL. — ALARM AT CONSTANCE. — JOHN THE IRON, OF LEITOMISCHEL. — HIS ELECTION AS BISHOP. — AN ENEMY OF HUSS. — THE BOHEMIANS INDIGNANT. — THE BISHOP'S WRITTEN REPLY. — ANSWER TO THIS AND "THE APOLOGY FOR THE COUNCIL," BY THE BOHEMIANS. — THE SAFE-CONDUCT OF THE EMPEROR. — EVIDENCE OF JOHN DE CHLUM. — CASE OF HUSS. — FALSEHOODS CIRCULATED IN RESPECT TO HIS COURSE IN REGARD TO THE CITATION FROM ROME. — CLAIM THAT HIS SAFE-CONDUCT SHOULD BE REGARDED AND HE BE FREELY HEARD.

MAY 14, 1415–MAY 18, 1415.

IT was in this tenth session of the council, (May 14th,) that a new subject was presented for discussion. This was the use of the cup in the eucharist, a practice long discontinued by the church, but now revived at Prague. This practice, or communion in both kinds, as it was called, had prevailed in the Greek church from the earliest times; and the intimate relations which had subsisted between that church and the churches of Bohemia had not been without their influence in introducing it anew in the city of Prague. The Bohemians, moreover, had not all forgotten their traditions of a Sclavonic Bible, and religious services celebrated in their national language. Even when the Latin practice had become prevalent under Charles IV., in the fourteenth century, and the communion in both kinds was no longer publicly allowed, there were still those who sought the enjoyment of their Christian liberty in the secrecy of private dwellings, and in the depths of forests.[1]

As the Bible became more known and read, the minds of men were led to ponder over the original institution of the sacrament. The difference between the ancient original, and the modern corrupted practice, could not escape their notice. Discussion necessarily arose, and a doctrine so palpably appealing to the senses as the use of the cup could not fail to make a deep impression upon the minds of the multitude. The result was, that wherever the Bohemian reformation triumphed, there was a disposition favorable to arguments for the restoration of the cup.

We have already seen that the practice did not originate with Huss. We find no reference made to it in connection with his name, previous to his arrival at Constance. He may have considered it a matter of minor importance, or, without having made a careful examination of it, may have silently acquiesced in the prevalent opinions. Doubtless it would not have been wise to have made the claims of a mere outward rite the basis of an appeal which could be enforced only by a living apprehension of the spiritual truths of the gospel. Huss was already a prisoner at Constance, when the doctrine of the cup began to be discussed at Prague. Two of his friends, both of

[1] Gieseler expresses doubt on these points, maintained by Schröckh.

them doctors, and numbered among his adherents, were the leaders of the new movement. As to Jacobel, the most noted of these, we scarcely need the testimony of one who was afterward a pope,[1] that he was a man of the highest eminence for learning and integrity. He was a zealous defender of evangelical views, and an uncompromising enemy of ecclesiastical corruption. He sought the purity of the church, and carefully studied its original constitution. His views and feelings led him strongly to sympathize with Huss, and his study of the Bible opened his eyes more and more clearly to the prevalent errors of the times. After the departure of Huss for Constance, he seems to have succeeded, in great measure, to his position in the esteem and regard of the people. He was curate of the parish of St. Michael, in the city of Prague, and was also connected with the university. Scarcely had Huss left the city, when Jacobel, undeterred by fear of consequences, began to propose and defend the use of the cup. The subject, if we are to believe Æneas Sylvius, was first brought to his notice by Peter of Dresden. This man seems to have cultivated the acquaintance of Jacobel, as one of spirit kindred to his own. He seized a fitting occasion to speak to him on the subject of the use of the cup, and expressed his surprise that a man of his learning and devotion had not detected the error that had so long prevailed in the church. He pointed out the inconsistency between the present practice of the church and the original institution of the sacrament, quoting

[1] Æneas Sylvius. His. Bohem.

the language of Christ, "Except ye eat the flesh of the Son of man, and *drink his blood*, ye have no life in you." The attention of Jacobel was at once arrested. He determined, therefore, to investigate the subject. He found the early traditions of the church and the authority of the fathers altogether on the side of the original form of the ordinance. His resolution was quickly formed, and he immediately took measures to secure the restoration of the cup in the eucharist. His influence was great among his own congregation, and his popularity might have secured the adoption by them of his own views without tedious discussion. He chose, however, to bring the subject in the first place before the university, and according to the customs of the day proposed *theses* upon the subject, which he was prepared to maintain and defend (March 25.) Meanwhile one of his colleagues[1] came over to his views, which he no longer hesitated to present to the people from the pulpit (March 29.) It was not long before he ventured on the introduction of the cup, a measure which the mass of the people readily approved, and which was applauded highly by a great majority of the members of the university. It was from the clergy that the opposition with which he had to contend sprang. Jacobel was driven out from his own church, but the doors of the St. Martin's church were opened to him, and he was here received with a hearty welcome. He continued, therefore, to publish and defend his views, in spite of all the obstacles thrown in his way. The next step, therefore, against him was to attempt

[1] Sigismund Rsepansky, of the church of St. Mary. Becker, 94.

to write him down. The doctors were urged to attack him with the pen; but Jacobel did not fail to answer them in a triumphant manner. The controversy soon attracted the attention of the nation. All Bohemia was interested in it. Conrad, the archbishop of Prague, attempted to smother the flame by excommunicating its author. But Jacobel was not thus to be silenced. He only preached with renewed energy in contempt of the sentence launched against him. Supported by the people, he continued his labors under the very eye of the archbishop. The clergy, driven to desperation, had but one resource left. They determined to apply at once to the authority of the council. It was a countryman of Huss, and one of his bitterest adversaries, John, bishop of Leitomischel, who was charged with the commission of denouncing the heresy of Jacobel.

The controversy that now arose was one that the council could not compose.[1] First the pen, and then the sword, were called into requisition; but pen and sword both proved powerless to suppress the popular conviction in favor of a rite so clearly established by scriptural authority and ancient precedent as the use of the cup. In this controversy Jacobel proved himself a man of fearless spirit and superior ability. He maintained his theses, not only from scripture, but by copious references to the fathers, the scholastics, some of the popes, and the canon law. From all

[1] In order to give a clearer and more connected view of the proceedings connected with the introduction of the use of the cup in Bohemia, I have here presented the early history of the controversy which it occasioned, anticipating somewhat the order of events. Jacobel's reply to Broda could scarcely have seen the light before the death of Huss, although it must have been produced at about that time.

these he drew the conclusion that the administration of the sacrament to all Christians, under the form of bread and wine, is the word, the law, the truth, the ordinance, and the gospel of our Lord Jesus Christ, his apostles, and the primitive church,—a practice never to be annulled or changed by any custom, however ancient, of the Roman church, nor by the constitution or decree of any pope or council.

The first reply to Jacobel was anonymous, and seems to have been written at Constance. Its tone indicates that matters had not yet proceeded to an open rupture. It is addressed to Jacobel personally, and in it he is styled brother, and eloquent preacher of the word of God. Jacobel is reproved for his disregard of ecclesiastical authority, and his innovation upon the sacred rites of the church. The applause which he met is incidentally referred to, and in a manner to show that the immense majority were ranged upon his side. His contempt for the archbishop's excommunication is then noticed, and an attempt is made to refute his argument in his own defence—the argument drawn from that commission of Christ, "Go ye into all the world," etc.

Other subjects, besides the one of the cup, are drawn into controversy. Jacobel is reproached for having taught that tithes are merely alms, that may be withdrawn by the secular power from an unworthy clergy. His conduct in preaching beyond his own limits, going from church to church throughout Bohemia, and thus spreading his views, is charged as highly reprehensible. He seems to have strongly insisted on reducing the clergy to the simplicity, if not poverty, of their early state, that, avoiding pomp, avarice, and luxury, they may more freely preach the word of God. His antagonist paradoxically maintains the present condition of the church to be superior to that of its primitive state, moulded to a more ornate, devout, and honorable form, and that the wealth and power of the clergy were necessary and useful to the restraint of popular vice and error. His argument against the communion of the laity, under the form of the cup, shows ingenuity, if not sophistry. The multitudes in the desert were fed with bread alone. Christ at Emmaus broke the bread, but nothing is said of the wine. Had he wished that all should commune under both forms, he would have invited his own mother, as well as the seventy disciples, to be present at the institution of the ordinance. The only argument that even seemed to bear directly upon the subject, was the practice under the Old Testament, enjoined by the law, that the priests should drink the wine and the honey presented in offerings; and to none but the Levites was this allowed.

It was not by such shallow reasonings and incongruous citations as these that Jacobel was to be driven from a position so impregnably fortified as his own, by the plain language of scripture. His antagonist can meet him here only by the unsustained assertion, that the passage on which he relied was addressed solely to the apostles and their successors; and his interpretation of this passage, in reference to spiritual eating and drinking, places him in a position where consistency would require him to go yet further. A Quaker's argument would have left him entirely indefensible in observing any outward form of the ordinance whatever. But, abandoning the ground of scripture, and almost altogether neglecting the argument from the writings of the fathers, he enlarges on the inconvenience that would result from allowing the cup to the laity. He maintains, that caution requires to avoid the incongruity and the great guilt that are in danger of being incurred, from spilling the blood of Christ upon the robes of the women, or suffering it to wet the beards of the men, or fall to the ground. He cites the decree of Pope Pius, that if a drop of the consecrated wine should by negligence be spilt upon the earth, or upon a cloak, the sin should be expiated by forty days of prayer and fasting, with abstinence from the mass for the same space of time. If the drop has fallen upon a stone, the stone is to be rasped, and the fragments deposited with the sacred relics. If it fell upon a cloak, the cloak was to be burned. If upon the sod, it was to be licked up with the tongue, and the sod laid away in the sacred repository. From all this Jacobel's antagonist infers, that if a layman should spill a drop of the consecrated wine upon his beard or garment, he ought with his beard and garment to be burned up and thrust to the bottom of hell, unless he should repent. The reason given against the administration of the cup to the sick at a distance is, the danger of the fall of man or beast. If, then, the sick may commune under one form only, why not all, he asks. The danger of the wine turning to vinegar; the difficulty of many persons in drinking or even enduring the smell of wine; the great size of the vessels that would be necessary if all were to commune; the difficulty of raising the vessel in time of war, when thousands were to partake,—are subjects successively noticed; and, to conclude all, it is maintained that the flesh of Christ necessarily includes the blood, so that the laity and clergy do in reality receive the same, that is, Christ, and one no less or more than the other.

The writer then proceeds to sustain his positions by the authority of the Roman church—an authority necessarily binding upon the consciences of all. He cites the language of St. Augustine, "I would not believe the gospel if the authority of the Catholic church did not induce me thereto," and then maintains that as the Catholic and Roman church has established the form of communion, the question is thereby finally settled.

In this reply to Jacobel, we find by incidental allusions that he had allowed or authorized other changes at Prague which were regarded in the light of innovations, and as revolutionary if not heretical in their nature. He had taught that the parishioner is not bound to confess to his parish priest, or receive the communion at his hands only; but in case he is unworthy or vicious, another may be applied to. He refused to recognize the authority of the pope as superior to that of the parish priest in the matter of absolution, or even in some other respects. Popular songs had been introduced, which were sung in the streets, the markets, and the churches,—some of them, we are given to understand, far from complimentary to the character of the prelates, and these Jacobel refused his influence to suppress. On these accounts also, his antagonist reproves him, closing his treatise however, in language which shows a high esteem for Jacobel as his *brother*, asking pardon for anything improper, wrong, or displeasing which he may have uttered, and expressing his willingness to be corrected in whatever fault he may have fallen.

This anonymous letter to Jacobel was soon followed by a treatise quite similar in character from the pen of his townsman, Andrew Broda, residing at the time at Constance.[1] The similarity is indeed so striking that we can have no hesitation in ascribing both to the same source, though the latter treatise is more harsh and severe.

Jacobel does not suffer Broda's treatise to pass in silence.[2] He commences his reply by protesting, as he declares he had formerly done in the university when the subject was brought before it, that in this most important matter, as in every other, he had no intention to say, write, or maintain anything presumptuously in opposition to the holy Catholic church of Jesus Christ, or against the true Christian faith and the perfect law of God; and if anything of this sort should escape him, through ignorance, inadvertence, or the imperfection to which he confesses himself subject, he revokes and retracts it, subjecting himself to the correction of those to whom it belongs to restore the erring. He refers to the numerous treatises in which he had already defended the use of the cup, and in which he had sustained himself by

[1] Van der Hardt, iii., part xv. [2] Ib. part xvi.

the authority of scripture and of holy men, and then proceeds to refute the arguments of Broda, *seriatim.* This he does in a manner most complete and triumphant. He adverts to Broda's false glosses on the authorities which he had cited, whether from scripture or the fathers, exposing his gross perversions of their original meaning, and detecting not only the weakness of his opponent's arguments, but the dishonest reasoning and sophistry by which the author himself could scarcely have been deceived. Broda had objected to Jacobel that he refused to receive the authority of eminent doctors, but the latter has manifestly the advantage when he exposes his opponent as rejecting the authority of those whose words he could not pervert. Broda, relying upon pontifical decrees and decisions, had held that the pope, with cardinals, prelates, and bishops, could not err. Jacobel boldly avowed an opposite belief. He triumphantly appealed to their avarice and simony, as well as other vices, which plainly showed that they entered not by the door into the sheepfold. Such a church as the one called the Roman, made up of such materials, Jacobel boldly asserted, might err in life and doctrine, calling evil good, and light darkness. He even cites papal authority from the decretals to sustain him in his position. Broda had demanded of Jacobel that he should with him give faith to the legends of the church, but Jacobel, without absolutely rejecting them as false, everywhere manifests his decided preference for the authority of scripture. His opponent asks him when the church first began to depart from the purity of its early practice, and for how long a time the use of the cup had prevailed in the primitive church. "Why," answers Jacobel, "does the doctor put such a question to me, when by reason of the malice with which he pursues me he would not receive or believe the truth if I should utter it?" He then refers Broda to the scriptures for an answer. "When the abomination of desolation was first to be seen in the holy place; when iniquity began to abound, and the love of many to wax cold throughout the whole church; when impious men, true to their nature, began to pollute the sanctuary; when fraud and forgery found their way into the church, then this sacrifice was taken away from the people, and the cup was withheld."

Broda had called him a disciple of Antichrist, because he would not obey the commands of those *who occupied Moses' seat.* Jacobel replies that he had never refused to receive their commands when accordant with the gospel, but "to our scribes and Pharisees, commanding what is opposed to God's law," he had never allowed that obedience was due. In such a case their excommunication was frivolous and vain. The seeming curse, humbly endured by the innocent, would be changed to a blessing. Here he cites the example of Chrysostom, who, though excommunicated and banished, was afterwards recalled, against the will of his superiors, and who, while thus pretendedly excommunicated, did not cease to preach to the people. "Why then," he asks, "should not I imitate these holy men in preaching and ministering to the people, notwithstanding my pretended excommunication?"

Broda had charged Jacobel with disturbing the peace of the church. To this Jacobel replies, that to observe the law of the gospel to the saving of souls and the glory of God, is not to sin against charity; while Christ himself, in saying "I came not to bring peace, but a sword," showed that the peace of wicked men ought to be disturbed. It was better, he maintained, that offences should arise than that the truth should be betrayed.

The silence of Broda on the corruptions of the church, or the gentleness with which he treats them, is not passed over by Jacobel in silence. He maintains that his opponent is, on these grounds, in danger of being himself suspected of simony. As to confessing in cases by law reserved, Jacobel maintains that this had rarely been done; but, in cases of necessity, he could not refuse those who, like some of the priests themselves, had been pursued by hatred, because they had zealously congregated to hear the preaching of the word of God.

Throughout the whole argument of Jacobel we are struck by the reverence with which he bows to the simple authority of the scriptures. He indeed refers to the eminent names in the history of the church, whose views upon the matter in dispute manifestly coincided with his own. But he does not forget that even Peter and Paul were once at variance; and the name of Thomas Aquinas is no authority with one who openly points out his gross departure on other subjects from the plain doctrines of the gospel. Laudable practices there well might be, instituted for the church, to promote or facilitate the observance of evangelical truth; but never could these be suffered to preponderate over the authority of Christ's express commandments. Here was, in reality, the turning point of the whole controversy. Jacobel had assumed the true Protestant ground. Broda's position was utterly indefensible, unless the authority of the pope and of the Romish church was allowed to supersede the express commands of the author of Christianity himself.

Nor did the evident aim of Broda to bring in to the aid of his arguments the power of the secular arm escape the notice of Jacobel. He showed that the *restraint* which Broda spoke of, quoting from Augustine, was but another name for the adoption of violent measures on the part of the civil power to suppress hated opinions. Jacobel commits his cause to the Supreme Judge, who alone could not err, while he vindicates the language of St. Augustine from the sense in which it was employed.

The conclusion of Jacobel's defence displays a deep consciousness of the rectitude of his purpose, the danger which he incurred, and the unspeakable importance of that cause in which the individual was but a humble instrument of the divine glory.

"I am fully aware," he says, "that by what I have done I have laid myself open to the malicious assaults of many, who, stung by envy, will taunt where they cannot argue.

"I know that I am thrusting my hand into the fires of hatreds; but I here attest that, according to my ability in this matter of faith, I preach and defend the ministrations of the cup to the laity, and I exhort others to do the same to the end, that the kingdom of lust and of Antichrist may to some extent be purged, and the spirit of fervor and devotion, so long extinct among Christian nations, may be revived; and that some may be moved to that holy zeal of God for the edification and restoration of the house of God, that will cry out, 'Do good in thy good pleasure, O Lord, to Zion, that the walls of Jerusalem may be built!' I beseech each reader, therefore, to prove these or whatsoever other of my words, and hold them each even to the end; and I desire to be corrected by any such, if I have said anything at variance with the truth, or anything not accordant with the rule of charity.

"I therefore request all to whom this present writing shall come, piously and charitably to interpret and accept it for God's sake. And whether I have lapsed in word, assertion, opinion, or superfluity of words, or possibly in too excessive and severe reprehension of the doctor, or in any words of a satirical turn employed for rebuke, so as to excite passion, or in my zeal, if perchance not according to knowledge, or by unfit expression of truths,—for all these, I say, I ask pardon.

"And I subject myself to the correction of him who is Lord of all, and of his creature whom he would have deputed for this purpose.

"But if in these writings there be that which is fit and useful, for this be praise and glory to God forever and ever. Amen."

The discussion upon the subject was kept up between the advocates and the opponents of the *utraque.*

The adherents of Huss were divided in opinion. The subject was one which the practical nature of his mind had never led him closely to investigate. The more palpable and gross corruptions of the church, which had a more direct and obvious bearing upon morals and religion, had absorbed his attention. But circumstances had now arisen in which it was no longer permitted him to remain silent. His opinion was requested. What it would be, could scarce have been to his friends a matter of doubt. The respect of Huss for the scriptures, as the sole and supreme authority for the truth of doctrine, was not inferior to that of Jacobel. He, too, would decide each question by the law of Christ as laid down in the written word. Throughout his trial, his appeal was constantly made to its divine authority; and all he asked was to be convicted of his error from the sacred page, or be absolved on the ground of conformity to its doctrines. The answer of Huss to the question proposed was an approval of Jacobel's doctrine. He was not blind to the danger which he incurred by expressing this approval. Yet he shrunk not from that fidelity to his convictions which was so eminently characteristic of him. From his prison at Gottlieben his voice was heard; and those of his adherents who had withheld their approval from what they regarded as an innovation of Jacobel, no longer withstood it. The doctrine of the use of the cup prevailed by an overwhelming majority. The voice of the university was almost unanimously in its favor. The absence at Constance of the most virulent opponents of Huss allowed it greater harmony and unanimity in its decisions. What support and sympathy Jacobel received from this quarter may be judged from the manner in which he speaks of it in his defence. "The members of our university," said he, "do not strut about in a remarkable and sumptuous costume, in order to set off their dignity the more. They are not of the class of whom our Lord speaks, as loving the first places at feasts and synagogues, in order to be saluted at public places and to hear themselves called, Master! Is it not a disgrace to the church, as St. Jerome says, to preach Jesus Christ, poor, crucified, in want of everything, with bodies loaded with fat, with well-fed faces and vermilion lips? If we are in the apostles' places, it is not merely in order to preach their doctrines, but to imitate their mode of life."

Intelligence of the state of things at Prague had reached Constance, and begun to excite alarm. Broda's interposition had proved of no avail. It had only given occasion for a triumphant refutation, which made the adherents of the old doctrine feel how untenable was their position. The teachings of Jacobel, already possessed of a stronghold in the university, were spreading more widely every day throughout Bohemia. It was at this period, when the approval of the new doctrine on the part of Huss was strongly suspected but could not be proved, that Broda found a powerful ally in a fellow-countryman and a former antagonist of Huss. John the Iron, as he was not inappropriately called, bishop of Leitomischel, denounced the innovation of Jacobel before the council. Personal hostility undoubtedly embittered him against Huss and Jacobel. His election as bishop was opposed by Wenzel and a large body of the reformers, as well as by Conrad, archbishop of Prague. The council of Constance, however, decided in his favor; and the energies of the soldier, the general, and the bishop, all which characters he had sustained, broke out in virulence against the Bohemian reformers. Although without any authority as yet for the assertion, he sought to implicate Huss in the recent transactions at Prague by ascribing to him the origin of the innovations. To aggravate the odium against the reformers, he represented the wine for the communion,—the blood of Christ, as he called it,—as carried about in flasks all over the kingdom, and exposed to innumerable hazards.

The denunciations of the bishop could not be passed over in silence. They excited a deep feeling of indignation on the part of the Bohemians in Constance, who regarded the charge as utterly unwarranted, and slanderous to their nation. It did not escape their notice that its natural effect would be to aggravate the difficulties of Huss' position, and excite a stronger prejudice against him in the minds of his judges. They were aware of the severity and hardships to which he was subjected in his prison at Gottlieben. They knew that the process against him was already commenced, and was urged forward by the bitterest malice. It was therefore with affectionate solicitude for his welfare, as well as indignation at his unjust treatment and apprehension excited by the denunciation of the bishop, that, in the afterpart of the day, (May 14, 1415,) on which the latter had made his charges, they insisted that Huss should at once be set free, or at least that his imprisonment should be lightened, and a public audience be allowed him. They also manifested their dissatisfaction at the defamatory reports to which the bishop had given utterance to such a degree that he felt called upon to make some reply.

On the sixteenth of the month, two days later, the opportunity was given. The bishop presented a written answer. The substance of it is the expression of his zeal against the followers of Wickliffe and Huss. This, he declares, and no wish to defame the Bohemian nation, is the motive by which he is impelled. Of the abuses which he declares had prevailed in connection with the communion of the cup, all is narrowed down to one or two specifications, and these narrated to him on the authority of others, in all probability with gross exaggerations. At the worst, they could fairly be regarded only as exceptional cases, noticeable for their very singularity. But besides the reply of the bishop, an apology for the council, drawn up by its order, was also read. To its false statements, as well as the misrepresentations of the bishop, the Bohemians felt constrained to reply. The apology denied that Huss had received his safe-conduct until fifteen days after reaching Constance, and expressed astonishment that the Bohemians should speak of Huss as innocent when he had already been condemned and excommunicated by the pope on the ground of contumacy, because, his life endangered, Huss chose to appear at Rome only by his procurators! For this cause, and for venturing to 'harangue' after his arrival at Constance, he was to be considered an arch-heretic, in utter violation of the principle that a man is to be accounted innocent until tried and found guilty. The Bohemians asked a delay of two days to prepare their answer. The request was granted, although the council refused to set Huss at liberty. This confirmed their apprehensions in his behalf, and the question in regard to the cup at once subsided, in their view, into one of secondary importance. They were wise enough, moreover, not to wish to entangle the main subject in new difficulties, and their reply turns, therefore, chiefly upon this alone. They declare first, in regard to the assertion that they had been ill-informed as to several matters which had been made grounds of complaint, that they wish to make a more full and clear statement of the case; not to retort the charge upon the members of the council, but to enable them to discern and judge the real state of things.[1] The Bohemians first propose to correct the error of the council in saying that they had been ill-informed in regard to the safe-conduct, and that it had been secured for Huss by his friends and partisans fifteen days after his arrival in Constance. To this the Bohemian nobles answer—especially John de Chlum, whom this point principally concerned—that on the very day of Huss' arrest, the pope had asked, in the presence of a great number of his cardinals, whether Huss was provided with a safe-conduct from the emperor. To this Chlum had replied, "Most holy

[1] Van der Hardt, iv. 208. *Et seq.*

father, know that he has one." And when the question was repeated, the same answer was given. No one, however, asked to have the safe-conduct exhibited. On each of the two following days, Chlum had complained to the pope that Huss was detained in violation of the safe-conduct, at the same time exhibiting it to the view of many persons. And, in confirmation of his statement, he refers to the testimony of many lords, bishops, soldiers, officials, and eminent persons of the city of Constance, who themselves, on that occasion, saw the document and heard it read. John de Chlum, therefore, was prepared, under any penalty whatsoever, and against all denial from any source, to prove and manifest, in the clearest manner, the truth of his assertions. The Bohemian nobles, moreover, refer, in confirmation of their statement, to the many princes and nobles attendant upon Sigismund's court, who were present when and where the safe-conduct was given by the royal mandate. Hence the fathers of the council might perceive that not the Bohemian nobles had been ill-informed, but rather those persons who had carried to the fathers such false reports, and who really do injustice to Sigismund and his chancellors as well as the Bohemian nobility, as if the safe-conduct had been surreptitiously obtained. They therefore urge that the fathers of the council would no more give ear to such unfounded reports, undeserving of credit, but hear both sides, and let the truth be manifest.

They then proceed to consider the assertion that Huss was already condemned. The mockery of all the forms of justice, by which the court appointed for his trial had proceeded to sentence him unheard, is exposed to a just reprehension. The facts of the case are simply and clearly stated. As to the citation, the Bohemian nobles profess to know nothing except by common fame. But as to his non-appearance personally, they declare that it was solely owing to the danger which he thereby incurred. His procurators, who had appeared for him at Rome, had been shamefully treated. As to his excommunication, they knew from his own lips that he did not meet it in a spirit of contumacy, but endured it under appeal. The evidence in regard to this, which they are prepared to exhibit, is perfectly conclusive. As to Huss having preached in Constance after his arrival in the city, as his enemies had reported of him, the Bohemians answer—and especially John de Chlum, here present with Huss, and who resided with him from the time of his first arrival in Constance[1]—that he never had preached, or, from the time of his arrival up to the day of his imprisonment, had even set foot beyond his own lodgings.[2]

The fathers of the council had professed not to understand what the Bohemians meant by the toleration and courtesy shown to heretics condemned by

[1] I cannot reconcile this with the statement in one of Huss' letters, unless Lepka and Chlum are the same. See page 335.

[2] Van der Hardt. Huss says, (Epis. v.,) in his letter to Prague, written shortly after reaching Constance—"Venimus sine salvo conductu." This letter, we have strong reason to believe, fell into the hands of Causis, and was by him exhibited to the council. The natural inference would be that Huss did not receive a safe-conduct till after he reached Constance. But, in a subsequent letter, evidently referring to the perverted use which had been made of this, he says, that the expression was designed merely with reference to a safe-conduct of the pope. This probably affords the correct explanation of the matter.

the Pisan council. They were in doubt whether reference was had to the contending or schismatic popes, or to others, but asserted that even heretics, coming to the council on the business of union, were to be tolerated and respected. The Bohemians reply, that whichever was meant, all they ask is that Master John Huss may enjoy the same freedom which they enjoyed. Coming to the council as he did, of his own accord, and no way compelled, only to declare his faith, and in whatsoever respect he might be shown to have strayed from the word of God and the unity of the church, to be reconciled and restored; and that this was not only his motive, but that of his favorers and adherents, who composed, in fact, a majority of the Bohemian nation. He had desired also to purge the realm from the infamy attached to it by false reports.

The Bohemians close their reply by thanks to the council for their favorable answer to their principal request, that the matters concerning Huss should be expedited—a request in which the whole kingdom of Bohemia is united with them.

But the papal question was one which seemed to the council most important at the present juncture, and it was to this that their attention was now directed.

CHAPTER XIX.

THE POPE DEPOSED.

The Deposition of John XXIII. a Necessity.—The Emperor's Resolve.—The Contumacy of the Pope Declared.—Exception of Cardinal St. Mark.—Sitting of the Commission for Procuring Testimony.—The Witnesses.—List of Accusations.—Suppressed Articles.—The Fifty-four Others.—The Eleventh Session.—Report Approved.—The Result Communicated to the Pope.—His Reception of it.—His Reply.—Information Sent to Him of his Proposed Deposition.—His Affected Submission.—His Letter to the Emperor.—Inconsistency of the Pope.—Frederic Gives the Pope up.—He is Left Guarded at Ratolfcell.—Abjectness of John XXIII. in Prison.—Eleventh Session.—Report from the Pope to the Council.—The Sentence of Deposition Read.—Unanimously Assented to.—The Cardinal of Florence Put Down.—The Sentence Carried into Execution.—Precautions in Regard to a New Election.—The Pope Informed of his Deposition by the Council.

May 19, 1415–May 31, 1415.

The judicial deposition of a pope by the assembled representatives of Christendom stands upon the page of history as a recorded fact. Yet a large number of those assembled at Constance had regarded the proposal to sit in judgment upon John XXIII. as something sacrilegious. To them he was the Lord's anointed, and the theory of papal infallibility was exalted by them into a doctrine of faith. But the force of circumstances was too strong for any theory which would absolutely block the progress of the council. The interests of Christendom, or at least of the bishops and prelates, absolutely required that the scandal of schism should no longer be endured. It was a nuisance to be abated. It was a standing text for heresy. It was a grievance to the nations; and, what was more perhaps in the eyes of the emperor, so long as it continued, Europe had reason to tremble for fear of Moslem invasion.

It was on the sixteenth of May, at two o'clock in the afternoon, that the commission for procuring testimony against the pontiff, in order to his deposition, held their first session. They met in the episcopal palace, attended by the proper officers of their court. Nearly forty witnesses were summoned before them, and sworn to give true evidence.[1] John XXIII. was, moreover, cited to see and hear the testimony which should convict him of the crimes with which he stood charged. These crimes were recited in language shockingly plain. His profligate course in the alienation and plunder of ecclesiastical property, and his scandalous life and morals, stained with simony and almost every vice, were to be the subject of investigation. And yet even this statement of his crimes was too lenient. Truth, however, would not consent to anything less, and decency could tolerate no more.

But John XXIII. had no disposition to hear or see the testimony to be produced against him. The commission for examining witnesses therefore proceeded in his absence. The testimony of thirty-seven persons was taken, some of them holding distinguished places in the church, and all of them men of note. Ten of the number were bishops. One

[1] Only ten made their appearance at first.

was the grand master of Rhodes, and several were officers of the apostolic chamber, and even secretaries of John XXIII.

The list of accusations was composed of sixty-six[1] articles, all attested and proved. The conclusion of all was, that John XXIII. was stiffnecked, stubborn, a hardened and incorrigible sinner, and a favorer of schism, and as such, as well as on other accounts, was entirely unworthy to hold the office of the pontificate. The Vienna manuscript list of the articles closes with the just reflection, "What judgment must be formed of the cardinals who elected John XXIII., acquainted as they were with his simony and his infamy in other respects! After having sworn to elect the best man among them, what must they themselves have been, if they have judged that among them all there was none better than he who has been proved by so many witnesses to have been simoniacal, a traitor, a homicide, guilty of rape, arson, and incest, the debaucher of members of religious orders, and a man guilty of a sin more grievous still than these!" Who can deny the justness of the inference? What invectives of Huss could be so severe as a simple statement of the facts attested before the commission?

In fact, several of the articles in the list of impeachment were suppressed by the council. At least fourteen of the most odious and scandalous charges which had been reported as proved, in the assembly held on the twenty-fourth of May, were not produced in the public session subsequent. These suppressed

[1] Van der Hardt gives seventy. Some are mere repetitions.

articles were mostly specifications of fact, in regard to which witnesses could not be mistaken. They recited the reckless, undutiful, lying, and licentious conduct of this pontiff's youth, precocious in almost every kind of depravity; his course as the principal minister and agent of simony for Boniface IX., by means of which he amassed the immense wealth that secured him a cardinalate; his proceedings as legate of Bologna, in subjecting that city and church to tyrannical extortions and violence, as well as unheard-of cruelties, massacring, torturing, and driving into exile many of its citizens; his actual sale of several parochial churches and many ecclesiastical benefices to lay persons, who took possession of them, and placed priests over them according to their own caprice; his conferring an important office upon a bastard son of the king of Cyprus, aged only five years, revoking the grant only on condition that the king should be reimbursed the amount of the purchase-money he had paid, that he should himself receive six thousand florins, and the son of the king an annual pension of two thousand, besides an office that brought in a revenue of ten thousand more; his poisoning his predecessor, Alexander V., as well as his physician, in order to open the way to his own election as pontiff; his acts of fornication, adultery, incest, and sins of the most abominable impurity, that cried to heaven for vengeance; his sale of unlawful dispensations for enormous sums; his bargaining away, alienating, and spending the revenues and tribute due to the Roman church; his sale of the sacred relics of John the Baptist, in the convent of St. Sylvester, for fifteen thousand ducats, and which he would have given up if he had not been miraculously detected, while those who complained of the proceeding had been banished or imprisoned; and his maintaining stubbornly, before reputable persons, that there was no future life or resurrection, and that the souls of men perish with their bodies, like brutes.

Such were, in substance—as decently expressed as possible—some of the suppressed articles. Of those not suppressed, and which were made the ground of his deposition, there were, in all, fifty-four; but of these it must suffice to give a few as specimens. In these his course is recited mainly from his elevation to the pontificate. It was maintained[1] that "he is universally regarded as an oppressor of the poor, a perverter of justice, the supporter of iniquity, the defender of simonists, the bond of vice, the enemy of all virtue, the mirror of infamy as well as a slave of lasciviousness; that he pays no heed to the public consistories, is always plunged in sleep or in his pleasures, and that all who know him speak of him as a 'devil incarnate;' that from the date of his pontificate he has been guilty of the most scandalous and reckless simony,[2] disposing at his caprice of the property of the church, selling the same benefice to several persons at once, and forbidding the courts to hear parties complaining, or to render them justice; that

[1] Van der Hardt, iv. 197.

[2] Sir Robert Walpole might have taken lessons of bribery from John XXIII. Venal himself, he thought every man had his price. Niem says of him, (Cormenin His. of the Popes, ii. 100,) "The holy father was an intruder, who broke in the pontifical gate with a golden axe, and closed the jaws of the Cerberuses who guarded the threshold, by casting to them the remains of his festivals, to prevent their barking at him."

he had spurned the fraternal exhortations of the cardinals, and the remonstrances of others, urging him to desist from his course; that he had sent a layman, a merchant of Florence, into the dioceses of Cambray, Tournay, Liege, and Utrecht, empowered to collect tithes, and excommunicate such as refused to obey him, thus amassing prodigious sums of money; that after having exhausted the revenue of the patrimony of St. Peter, he had invented new imposts, or increased those already established, in a most oppressive manner, and had finally given up the capital, in spite of his own promise, to plunder and pillage, filling city and country with robbery, murder, and sacrilege, leaving the women exposed to a brutal soldiery, and many persons of the court to assassination, plunder, the gallies, or perpetual imprisonment; that his criminal and hateful life had provoked universal complaint, yet when the emperor Sigismund had remonstrated with him and secured the promise of reform, he had violated that promise, falling back into all his former excesses. The list of charges then recites the duplicity and falsehood of which he had been guilty after his arrival at Constance, and the utter disregard which he had shown to his own engagements. On such grounds as these, evidently sufficient without including the suppressed articles, the council resolved to proceed with the steps necessary to the final sentence—the solemn deposition of John XXIII.

The eleventh session was opened in solemn form on the twenty-fifth of May. The Cardinal de Vivieres presided; and the emperor, with all the cardinals then in the city, the princes, envoys, and ambassadors, was present. The commission for hearing witnesses on the subjects of accusation against the pontiff were called upon for their report. It was read *seriatim*, each charge accompanied by a mention of the number and quality of the witnesses by whom it was proved. The report was approved by the council, and five cardinals were named to notify the pope of what had been done by the council in its present session.

The cardinals departed at once for Ratolfcell, where the pope was residing. As he had already been suspended, and had laid aside the insignia of his dignity, their greeting was not as usual with the kissing of his feet, but only of his mouth and hands. Some authorities intimate that, but for the presence of other members of the council, the cardinals would have rendered him the usual homage. He received the proceedings of the council with every mark of profound submission. He saw himself in their hands, and knew all further resistance was hopeless and could but aggravate the conditions of his treatment. Undoubtedly he hoped, by an assumed contrition and acquiescence, to soften the resentments which his conduct had excited. To the communication of the cardinals he did not trust himself—whether from fear or prudence or exhaustion—to reply orally. He sent in to them a document drawn up by his own hand, and which the cardinals bore back with them to the council. In this reply he assumes the most penitent and submissive airs, showing himself still, in this most desperate condition of his affairs, the consummate actor that he was. He declares 'his purpose to submit himself absolutely to the orders and decisions of the council;' expresses his readiness to cede his office, whether at Constance or any other place which the fathers shall be pleased to appoint; far from opposing the sentence which the council should pronounce against him, promises that he will ratify it by all means in his power, and in whatever form should be prescribed; but yet prays the council, 'by the bowels of divine mercy, to spare his honor, his person and estates, as far as may be, without prejudice to the union of the church.'

It was on the twenty-sixth of May that the cardinals, who had returned from Ratolfcell, reported to the council the success of their mission, and the favorable answer of the pontiff. A new commission was then appointed, consisting of two bishops and two abbots accompanied by notaries, to lay before him the articles and grounds of his deposition, in order that he might reply to them if he saw fit. They were also to inform him that the sentence of his deposition would be read on the day following, which he might be privileged to hear if he chose. But John XXIII. had heard enough already. Manifesting toward the commission the same spirit of resignation as upon a former occasion, he declined even the reading of the articles of accusation which had been presented for reply, declaring that he did not need to see them, inasmuch as he held the council to be infallible, and would not recede from the act of submission which he had put into the hands of the cardinals. He only begged them to spare his honor and his fortune, and present the emperor with a letter which he had written him containing the same request.

This letter is valuable as another illustration of thè character of its author. He wears the mask to the last, with the same easy and well assumed impudence. He calls the emperor, in his address, his *dear son*, assuming still the authority of pope. After passing an eulogy upon his prudence and other virtues, especially the clemency and generosity with which he had pardoned the most grievous offences, he reminds him of their former friendship, and urges the claims upon the emperor which his devoted service and fidelity had imposed.

But Sigismund was not the dupe of this artful and tardy humiliation. It was the result of the extreme measures which had overtaken its author, and had been preceded by a course of conduct on his part which exposed it only to contempt. He had spread his accusations of the bad faith of the emperor all over Europe. He had employed all his resources to defeat the cherished purpose of Sigismund in giving peace to the church. Yet, with a kind of scrupulous honesty, the council resolved to pay him back a fair price for his submission. He was informed that, in consideration of it, the sentence of his deposition, which was to have taken place on the twenty-seventh of May, would be deferred until the twenty-ninth, and that its severity would be somewhat relaxed. John XXIII. received the announcement with the best possible grace, but his condition now was anything but enviable. He was a prisoner at Ratolfcell, under the charge of four guards appointed by the council, each of these a member of it and representing one of the four nations. Frederic, the duke of Austria, had been forced, as the price of his restoration to favor, to take the pontiff into custody and deliver him over to the council. Accompanied by members whose fidelity could be relied upon, and who were to see that the task was faithfully executed, he had arrested the pontiff, and brought him as far as Ratolfcell. Unwilling himself probably to appear in Constance with his prisoner, he sent word to the council that John XXIII. refused to proceed further, and would only submit to the necessity of force. The council, therefore, averse to harsh measures which might possibly react against themselves, permitted him to remain at Ratolfcell. It was here that the deputations of the council had met him, and it was from this place, under the custody of his guards, that his letters of submission were dated. Their true value was probably accurately apprèciated by the council, when, in consideration of them, they deferred for two days the sentence of his deposition.

In his imprisonment, John XXIII. seems to have sunk into almost abject despair. Those were gloomy days to him in which he awaited the pronouncing of his sentence. He was carefully guarded by day and by night.[1] His old servants, with the exception of his cook, were all removed, and new ones appointed. Eight members of the council, two from each nation, were appointed, by their presence and society, to relieve the tedium and solitude of his im-

[1] Niem, Lib. ii., c. xx. See Van der Hardt.

prisonment, a humane regard which was not shown in the case of Huss; yet the trembling pontiff could have scarcely appreciated such consideration, as he gave up into their hands "the ring of the fisherman" and the insignia of his office.

On the twenty-ninth of May the twelfth session of the council was held. The emperor, with all the cardinals, princes, and ambassadors, was present. The passage of scripture read was one appropriately significant: "Now is the judgment of this world, and the prince of this world is cast out." After the usual preparatory ceremonies, the late deputies to the pope made their report. They stated that the articles of his indictment had been presented to him, and he had been informed that if he had any opposition to offer he might be at liberty to do so; to which he made reply, that he had done much for the union and welfare of the church, even offering to cede his office. He readily acknowledged that he had basely abandoned the council, and now he would rather—saving the welfare of his soul—have died on the very day of his flight, than have done a thing so reprehensible. Against the sentence of the council he had nothing to offer in his own defence; but, according to the tenor of a writing which he had drawn up, and now placed in the hands of the cardinals deputed to visit him, desired and promised, standing in their presence, to conform himself to every ordinance, deliberation, and decision of the said holy council, ratifying every process issued by it against himself, and asserting that to the articles against him he had no other answer to make. The council he declared to be most holy, infallible, and a continuation of the Pisan, promising that neither at Bologna, nor at any other place where he might be present in person, would he speak a word against it. Let the sentence, he said, when pronounced, be presented to him, and he would receive it with head bared, and with all respect, and would, as far as lay in his power, ratify, confirm, approve, and acknowledge it. In fact, all that had been done by the council against him he did at once and from that moment ratify, approve, and confirm, promising never at any period to oppose it.

After this report was given in, Martin Porrée, bishop of Arras, arose and read the sentence of deposition. Three bishops and the patriarch of Antioch ascended the platform with him, and took their places by his side. The sentence of a deposed pope deserves to be given entire. It was as follows:[1] "In the name of the holy and indivisible Trinity, the Father, the Son, and the Holy Ghost. Amen.—The most holy general council of Constance, in the Holy Spirit lawfully convened, invoking the name of Christ, and having the fear of God only before their eyes, having examined the articles drawn up and presented in this case against the lord pope, John XXIII., together with the evidence sustaining them, his voluntary submission, with the entire process of this cause, doth, after mature deliberation upon the same, pronounce, decree, and declare, by this definitive sentence, produced in writing, that the clandestine withdrawal of the aforesaid lord pope, John XXIII., from

[1] Van der Hardt, iv. 281.

Constance, and from this sacred council,—his departing by night, at a suspicious hour, in an unbecoming and disguised garb,—was unlawful, and to the church of God and to the said council notoriously scandalous, tending to disturb and obstruct the peace and union of the church itself, an encouragement to its protracted schism, inconsistent with the vow, promise, and oath given by Pope John to God, the church, and this holy council; that Pope John himself is a notorious simonist, squandering the goods and disregarding the rights, not only of the Roman, but of other churches—a perverse administrator of the spiritualities as well as temporalities of the church—by his shameful life and detestable conduct, grossly scandalizing Christian people, both before and since his accession to the papacy, even down to the present time; that, after proper and kindly admonitions again and frequently repeated, he has pertinaciously persevered in his aforesaid wickedness, thereby rendering himself notoriously incorrigible; and that he, on account of the aforesaid and other crimes set forth in the process of the said cause against him, ought, as unworthy, useless, injurious, to be deprived and deposed from the papacy, and its entire administration, both spiritual and temporal;—and the said holy council doth remove, deprive, and depose him, declaring all Christians, of what state, condition, or dignity soever, absolved from all obedience, fidelity, or oath of allegiance; forbidding all the faithful from receiving, naming, adhering to, or obeying him, thus deposed, any longer as pope. The said holy council also makes good, from certain knowledge and plenitude of power, each and every defect in this preceding sentence; and condemns him by this same sentence to stay and remain in some good and fitting place, under the safe custody of the emperor Sigismund, the most devoted champion and defender of the Catholic church, as long as in the view of the said holy general council the welfare and the union of the church of God shall require. Other fitting penalties to be inflicted for the said crimes and enormities, according to canonical sanction, the said council reserves, to be declared and inflicted at its own good pleasure, as the rigor of justice or the measure of mercy shall require."

Such was the sentence that invaded the sanctuary of infallibility, and dragged down "the Lord's anointed" from his throne. It was the deliberate and well-weighed act of representative Christendom, urged on by the most catholic emperor Sigismund, and sanctioned by the ablest, wisest, and best men whom the council could boast among its members. When the sentence had been read, the president of the council, Cardinal John, bishop of Ostia, arose and asked if any one then present, great or small, rich or poor, had anything to say against the aforesaid definitive sentence, or against its being pronounced. If any such were present, he invited them to arise and declare their views in the name of the council, allowing them full liberty of expression: and in case no one arose, each was to be considered as consenting to the sentence. Not a voice was heard. If any still felt an attachment to the unfortunate pontiff, they were unwilling to testify it before the council in this hour of his desperate fortunes. John XXIII. had not a John de Chlum to stand by him to the last, and, at the risk of all things earthly, vindicate his innocence. He, at least, fell unpitied and unwept. No prayers like those which commended the imprisoned Huss to the care of Heaven, were breathed forth with sighs and tears in his behalf. He fell as a criminal; Huss as a martyr.

After the momentary silence—more eloquent than words—which ratified the judgment of the council by a tacit but unanimous consent, the several presidents of the nations arose, and in their behalf responded their *placet* to the sentence that had been read. The presiding cardinal answered in behalf of the college of cardinals. The vote was taken thus by the whole council. At this moment the cardinal of Florence arose. He was the youngest member of the college of cardinals, a man of great ability and daring. He had ventured on a previous occasion to set himself as the organ of the will of the college, against the whole council, omitting the reading of a portion of one of the decrees of that body—a portion exceedingly important as bearing upon the pope and cardinals—on his own authority. The council had resented the proceeding; and now, when Zabarella arose with a written document in his hand, and asked permission to read it, their former jealousies and suspicions were reawakened. He was greeted from every side by an almost unanimous shout "*Non placeret.*" He was thus forced to resume his seat, and silently acquiesce in what had been done. Doubtless his purpose was to present in some form a protest, but such was the state of feeling in the council that he was not allowed to proceed. Whatever it might have been, it could scarcely, from such a source, have had any influence to change the result.

It now only remained to carry the sentence into execution. So far as the council itself was concerned, there was no delay. The archbishop of Riga, the keeper of the seal and arms of John XXIII., presented them to the council. It was then demanded by Henry de Piro, the procurator of the council, that the seal should be broken and the armorial bearings effaced. This was done on the instant, with unanimous consent, by the hands of Arnold, the goldsmith of the pope. Five cardinals were at the same time appointed to notify John of his deposition. They were instructed to urge him to acquiesce in his sentence with a good grace, and to threaten him with more severe treatment if he offered any resistance. The council knew how to manage their prisoner. They could take the measure of his hopes and fears, but Huss, they were soon to find, was not a man of the same stamp.

Nothing more was done at this session except to take some precautionary measures in regard to the election of a new pope. The council resolved and decreed that no steps should be taken towards such an election without their advice and consent, or, in case they should be, they were to be accounted null and void. It was forbidden to recognize as pope any person who might be elected in such a case, under the severest penalties. All customs, statutes, or privileges interfering with this decision, were pronounced invalid. Thus the democratic principle in the council, under the lead of men like Gentian and Gerson, triumphed. The monarch of the church was deposed, and the oligarchy of the cardinals at the same time suspended from the exercise of their authority as electors of the ecclesiastical sovereign.

A decree also was passed forbidding the reëlection of either of the three contendents for the papacy, and a commission appointed to summon and secure the attendance of the absent prelates. The last was a wise and necessary measure. The council was in danger of dissolution, and coercion was necessary to keep it together after the deposition of the pope, and in the expected absence of the emperor on his journey to Spain, where he was to take steps for reducing Benedict, the most refractory of the popes.

John XXIII. awaited in his prison at Ratolfcell the announcement of his sentence. On the thirty-first of May, the cardinals deputed to make it discharged their commission. They presented his sentence to him in writing, and asked whether it met with his approval, or whether he had anything to say against it. He took the, to him, dismal document from their hands, and read it in silence. He promised them a reply within the space of a few hours. Early in the afternoon he sent for them to receive his answer. It was the answer of one reduced to submit to the most humiliating terms, yet true to his habitual hypocrisy, striving to gloss his answer with the fairest show of repentance and sincerity. "The tyrant of Bologna," "the poisoner of Alexander V.," "the incarnate devil," gave his full confirmation to the sentence; acknowledged himself deposed from the papacy, and ratified his expressed purpose to submit to the council's decisions, by a long and tedious document subscribed by his own hand. The most overbearing of tyrants had become the most abject of slaves.[1]

[1] For an elaborate vindication of the supremacy of the council over the papal authority and dignity, see Richerius (vol. ii.) on the council of Constance. He enumerates the practical decisions of the body by which this principle is endorsed, and the sanction which Martin V. extended to its proceedings. It is difficult to evade the force of his conclusions. Either the proceedings of the council were the merest farce, and more than savored of heresy, or papal supremacy and infallibility must split on this rock.

CHAPTER XX.

HUSS AT GOTTLIEBEN. PRISON EXAMINATION.

Condition of Huss at Gottlieben. — His Remarks on the Deposition of John XXIII. — On the Profligacy of the Council. — Views of Clemengis. — Of Niem. — Huss Cites the Proceedings of his Enemies in his own Justification. — His Cheerful Courage. — Strength of his Faith. — His Love of Truth. — His Humility. — New List of Accusations. — Charged with the Heresy of the Cup. — Petition of Huss' Friends. — His Protestation. — Falsehood of the Charges. — Demand that Huss should be Set Free or Heard. — Sigismund Engages to Secure for Huss a Public Audience. — The Answer of the Council. — Advice of Chlum. — Confidence of Huss. — His Main Anxiety. — His Visions. — Anxiety of Chlum. — Bitter Malice of Paletz and Causis. — John XXIII. Removed to Gottlieben. — False Honor Done Him. — Strange Juxtaposition by the Side of Huss. — Contrast of the two Men. — Lament of the Pope. — Just Retribution. — Removal of the Pope. — Huss on the Cup. — The Friends of Huss Present their Document to the Council. — False Report. — Prison Examination. — Anxiety of Huss' Friends. — His Constancy and Answer. — Account of the Examination. — What was Meant by Submission. — Explained by his Protestation. — Gerson and D'Ailly. — Their Agreement with Huss on Many Points. — Their Nomination. — Scholastic Antagonisms. — Huss Less Trammelled by such Prejudices.

May 31, 1415–June 1, 1415.

The case of John XXIII. was now disposed of, and the council was ready to proceed with the trial of Huss. In his prison at Gottlieben the Bohemian reformer, conscious of his innocence, had somewhat impatiently awaited the hour when he might declare and vindicate his faith before the assembled council. For more than two months he had been removed from nearly all communication with his friends at

Constance. He was closely confined, and his treatment was such as might have been expected from the harsh, stern character of the man to whom he was given in custody. During the day he was only allowed to move the length of the chain attached to his feet. By night, his arms were made fast to the wall. Well might his Bohemian friends earnestly remonstrate, and seek to have his trial expedited.

But even in his prison, Huss was a watchful observer of the remarkable events that were transpiring around him. He investigated and approved the doctrine of Jacobel in regard to the cup, and exhorted his friends to acquiesce in the seeming innovation, which only restored to its simple completeness a sacrament which had been mutilated during the corrupt ages of the church. He did not neglect, moreover, to make use of the sentence against John XXIII. to confirm, in this hour of trial, the faith and devotion of his disciples at Prague. The unveiled crimes of that wretch whose excommunications had been launched against him, were a more than sufficient justification for his own course and language. "Courage," says he; "you can now give an answer to those preachers who declare that the pope is God on earth; that he can sell the sacraments, as the Canonists assert; that he is the head and heart of the church by vivifying it spiritually; that he is the fountain from which all virtue and excellence issue; that he is the sun of the Holy Ghost, and sure asylum where all Christians ought to find refuge! Behold! already is this head severed as it were with the sword; already is this terrestrial God bound in chains; already are his sins unveiled—the gushing fountain is dried up—the heavenly sun is dimmed—the heart is torn out, that no one may again seek an asylum there."[1]

Huss then adverts to the cruelty of his persecutors, as well as to the corruption of his judges. In a tone of indignant invective, he exclaims, "The council has condemned its chief—its proper head—for having sold indulgences, bishopricks, in fact, everything; and yet among those who have condemned him are many bishops who are themselves guilty of the shameful trafic! . . . O profligate men! why did you not first pull out the beam from your own eye. . . . They have declared the seller to be accursed, and have condemned him, and yet themselves are the purchasers. They are the other party in the compact, and yet they remain unpunished."

This language of Huss is fully sustained, nay, is far exceeded in keenness and sting of invective, by men who were members of the council, or who carefully and anxiously observed it from a distance. Gerson himself, in his treatise written at a later period, handles the council if possible more severely. Clemengis[2] describes those assembled,—but "not truly in Christ's name,"—to seek the peace and unity of the church, as "carnal, for the most part bent on their pleasures, not to say their lusts." "These carnal sons of the church do not only have no care or apprehension of spiritual things, but they even persecute those who walk after the Spirit, as has been the case from the days of just Abel, and will be to the end of

[1] Epis. xiii. [2] Clem. Op. p. 69.

time. These are the men who fly together to the church merely to seize upon temporalities, who lead in the church a secular life, conspire, covet, plunder, rejoice in preëminence, not in profiting others, oppress and rob their subjects, glory in the honor of promotion, riot in pomp, pride, and luxury, who count gain godliness, sneer at such as wish to live holily, chastely, innocently, spiritually, calling them hypocrites. . . . Of such men the church is full this day, and scarcely, in whole chapters or universities, can you find any others. . . . Are men like these, the ones to exert themselves for a reformation of the church—men who would account such a reformation the greatest calamity to themselves?" Such was the language of one of the ablest and best men of his day. And yet even this scarcely equals in severity that of Niem, former secretary of John XXIII., and present as a personal attendant upon the sessions of the council. He speaks of the prelates as pastors that feed themselves and scatter the flock. He lays bare the rottenness of the church, from the sole of the foot to the crown of the head, from the plain tonsure of the priest to the tiara of the pope. Well might Huss, supported by such testimony, and with a keener sense of spiritual purity and corruption than even these men possessed, declare, "Such are those spiritual princes, who declare themselves, forsooth, to be the true vicars and apostles of Christ—who give themselves the appellation of 'holy church, and the most sacred and infallible council;' which, however, proved itself fallible enough when they adored John XXIII., and bent the knee before him, kissing his feet and calling him the 'Most Holy,' whereas, all the time they knew him to be a homicide, a man of most flagitious life, stained with simony, and a heretic, as their judgment declares. . . . May God forgive them; for with such knowledge of the man, they named him pope! . . . And now Christendom is without a head on earth—possesses Jesus Christ alone as chief to direct it; as the heart to give it life; as the fountain to water it with the seven gifts of the Holy Spirit; as the always sufficient refuge, to which I have recourse in my misfortunes, firmly believing that there I shall always find direction, assistance, and plenteous vivification; and that God will fill me with an ineffable joy in delivering me from my sins and from a wretched existence. Happy then are they who, in observing his law, perceive and detest the vain pomp, avarice, and hypocrisy of the Saviour's enemies, and patiently wait for the coming of the Sovereign Judge and his angels."[1]

It is difficult for us to withhold our sympathies from this prisoner at Gottlieben, calm in conscious innocence, and firm in an integrity of purpose which all his misfortunes were insufficient to crush. There he is, within those cold, damp walls, a helpless victim in the hands of his foes, and his doom predetermined. Sharing now, as he had not at first, the well-grounded fears of his friends, his mind is fully made up to meet the worst. Not a word, implying doubt or fear, escapes his lips. Not a sentence of bravado drops from his pen. He is at peace with himself and God. Not even the harshness of his treatment provokes a

[1] Epis. xix.

single utterance inconsistent with his habitual gentleness and charity. He cherishes no resentments. Without a single trace of obstinacy—willing ever to listen to argument—inviting correction if he has erred—he is yet true to his convictions, resolved sooner to perish himself than sacrifice one iota of the truth. All his letters from this Patmos of his exile breathe a noble Christian spirit. Christ is his "sufficient refuge," to which he has recourse in his misfortunes. He cannot expose the iniquity of his persecutors, but, like his Master, he at the same time exclaims, "May God forgive them." If, in some of his previous acts and writings, violent or bitter expressions had been provoked by the zeal of his indignation, no trace of them is any longer to be found. Rarely has even a martyr faith won more signal triumph than when, in the castle of Gottlieben, a patient endurance was crowned with grateful hope and even joy. "This declaration of our Saviour," says he, "is to me a great source of consolation; 'Blessed are ye when men shall hate you, and shall reproach you, and cast out your name as evil for the Son of man's sake. Rejoice ye in that day, for behold, your reward is great in heaven.'"

It would be difficult to find anywhere more clear and decisive evidences of a simple love of truth for its own sake than were exhibited by Huss. His was not the self-importance of a leader, or the pride of a champion. He possessed, indeed, a clear and strong intellect, a fearless spirit, a fervid and powerful eloquence, but his estimate of himself was always humble. His own life, in his esteem, was nothing by the side of that cause to which he was willing to devote it.

Such was the man who, the moment John XXIII. was deposed, claimed the attention of the council. Scarcely was the sentence pronounced, when his case was brought before them. His bitter enemy, Michael De Causis, had not been idle. While Huss was in prison, new grounds of accusation against him were sought out. The former list, however it may have been modified, was now prefaced with the charge of heresy in the use of the cup. It was inferred that, inasmuch as the adherents of Huss at Prague had adopted this innovation, he was therefore its author. Many of the council may have supposed the inference just, and perfectly conclusive. Causis himself, however, must have known its falsehood. But the design of the measure was manifest. It was intended to prejudice the council, and poison the minds of his judges against the prisoner. Undoubtedly it did have this effect, although its falseness was subsequently detected. The other articles, the character of which will soon be noticed, were drawn up with great care and skill, and betray the malice in which they originated.

The friends of Huss were aware of what was going on. They saw the skilful web of accusation which the cunning art of his enemies was weaving to entrap him. Nor on their part were they idle. Again and again they had remonstrated against the injustice of Huss' imprisonment. On this day (May 31) they again appeared, still more solicitous in their petitions that Huss might be enlarged, and a hearing be granted him. The emperor was absent at the opening of the congregation, when their petition was read, and consequently did not hear it. The Bohemians, therefore, as the assembly broke up, gave a copy of it into his hands for his private inspection. It was the production of the Bohemian nobility present in Constance, and was signed by them in behalf of their countrymen. It was a candid and manly plea for the reformer. It sets forth, first, the fact that their former communications had been treated with neglect; that in vain they had requested the fathers of the council to consider the lame and impotent charges against Huss the productions of malice and envy on the part of his jealous rivals; that the reformer himself, in all his acts, scholastic and ecclesiastical, and especially in his preaching, had made, and was wont to make, protestations of his readiness to yield to the truth whenever convinced of it. It was hence fair to be inferred, in regard to his intentions, that he neither would nor did wish, in his books, treatises, instructions, and public preaching, to write, speak, or maintain anything which he clearly knew to be erroneous, scandalous, seditious, offensive to pious ears, or heretical, as the malice of his enemies had charged; but that his grand aim and purpose had been, in all respects, to conform himself to the teaching of gospel truth, and the holy doctors who had commented on the Sacred Scriptures. And if, in any respect, he should be found in fault, or by others ill-understood, he wished from these sources to be corrected, directed, informed, and enlightened, and by no means to defend or sustain any article contrary to the most holy Roman church and to Catholic faith.

"Wherefore," the Bohemian nobles proceed, "since, Right Reverend Fathers, notwithstanding all this, his bitter foes, impelled by great hatred, extract isolated and disconnected passages from his books, rejecting the qualifications or the intent of them, or at least overlooking them, not adverting to the distinctions proper to be observed, and thus put together against him articles which are false and framed artfully to this end, that, despite all charity, they may depose him from his office and put him to death, in violation of the safe-conduct openly granted him by the emperor to secure him against all these intrusions of his enemies which produce in Bohemia these disquietudes and contentions which the emperor so greatly desires to see composed;—therefore the said nobles and barons do petition that—the preceding matters, and the dishonor from them resulting to the said kingdom and its people being considered—you would on your part interfere, and appoint method and process by which the said Master John Huss may, by men enlightened and masters of Holy Scripture, who are here present and shall be deputed for this purpose, be carefully heard upon all the articles charged against him, so that his own meaning and that of the doctors may be declared along with the distinctions proper to be made, in which matters his accusers are inconsistent with themselves. Thus, also, let the deposition of witnesses be heard, many of whom are, and long have been, his most bitter enemies, whose wanton instigation would lead to his condemnation, though held a captive and unheard; since from such methods your majesty may be more clearly informed in regard to the truth, while he is ever ready to submit himself to the decision of the most holy council. For you have been informed, through the plausible lies and tricks of his slanderers, that Master John Huss has obstinately persisted for a long time in articles of a most dangerous character, which representation you will then be able to understand clearly the falsehood of."

In proof of this the Bohemians adduce the public testimonial of the bishop of Nazareth, inquisitor at Prague, which we have already seen. They then petition the fathers of the council, that inasmuch as Huss had not been condemned or even convicted, he might be released from the chains and fetters by which he was grievously deprived of his freedom, and placed in the hands of bishops or commissioners of the council specially deputed for the purpose, that he might have opportunity to recover strength, and might more carefully be examined by the said commissioners. And, for greater security, the barons and nobles pledged themselves that Huss should not be allowed to escape from the hands of the commissioners until the final issue of the affair.

The paper of the Bohemians was read and discussed by the fathers of the council. Yet, moderate and even humble as the request was, there was no disposition to grant it. But in Sigismund's bosom there was found the policy of a ruler, if not the justice. Such a request from such a source was entitled to respect, and doubtless the emperor felt more than suspicious of the interested motives of the enemies of Huss. It was not without a strenuous effort on his part that the portion of the request which asked for a public audience of the reformer was granted. John de Chlum at once hastened to announce the welcome intelligence to the prisoner. "To-day," he writes, "the king, assembled with the deputies of all the nations, spoke of your case, and contended for a public audience. It was finally and definitely resolved that it should be allowed you. Your friends are also insisting on your removal to some more airy place, that you may be refreshed and restored to strength."

The answer of the council, as read by the patriarch of Antioch, deserves to be given. It was, that as to the first point, the protestation of Huss, the future would show whether it was true and reliable. As to the assertion that the adversaries of Huss had improperly and wickedly cited isolated passages from his books, this was to be shown in the issue of the cause. If it was found that Huss had been unjustly accused, then his enemies would be overwhelmed with lasting disgrace. But in regard to sureties, the deputies of the council could not, with a safe conscience, receive them, even though a thousand were given in behalf of a man in whom, on no condition, faith was to be reposed; but to this they would attend, that on the fifth of the next month (June) Huss should be brought to Constance, that he should have full and free opportunity of speaking before the council itself, and that they would hear him affectionately and kindly. How well their promise was kept will be manifest in the sequel.

Meanwhile Huss patiently endured the martyrdom

of his cruel imprisonment. Oppressed with chains, and his health giving way under the severity of his prison life, his purpose was still unshaken to witness, if occasion should demand it, a good confession. In the weakness of the flesh, the spirit triumphed. His noble friend Chlum did not forget to exhort him, "In God's name, and for the sake of the truth, take good care not to desert the holy cause through any fear of losing this wretched life; for it is for your great benefit that God visits you by this trial." But a mightier than man was his counsellor. The greatness of the cause in which he was engaged filled his thoughts. He ardently anticipated his trial, in the hope of an opportunity to vindicate the claims of truth. Though at times disheartened by the malice of his enemies that threatened to crush him unheard, he seems yet to have cherished the hope that some, at least, would be found in the council to respond in approval of his views. In default of this, he could not believe that the assembled representatives of Christendom would unite in opposing the testimony of scripture, or rejecting it as the test and standard of doctrine. How sadly he was to be disappointed in all this, we shall soon have occasion to observe.

All the anxieties of Huss for his own person were lost in his deeper anxiety for the interests of a pure and scriptural Christianity. His musings by day and even his dreams by night constantly presented to his view that Saviour whose example, unworthy as he was, he gloried to imitate. It is not surprising that in his prison he should have been visited by visions and dreams which one might easily be led to regard as prophetic. One of these—that which concerned the vain attempts of the priests to efface the paintings and inscriptions on the walls of Bethlehem chapel—has been already referred to. There were others of which he makes mention in his letters, but to which he declares, himself, that he attached slight importance.[1]

"Occupy your thoughts with your defence, rather than with visions," said John de Chlum, in a gentle reproof, which attested his own good sense and his anxiety for his friend. He deeply and sadly felt the danger which impended over Huss, and could not bear the thought that such a life should be risked by any neglect of preparation, or any over confidence of the final result. Jerome was already in prison, and of his deliverance there was little prospect. It was too much that Huss also should be lost to future service, in the cause of which he and Jerome were the ablest champions.

Huss did not altogether neglect preparation for his own defence; but how oppressively discouraging were the circumstances in which it was to be made! His imprisonment, his harsh treatment, his failing health, his severe pain in his teeth,[2] as well as other bodily ailments, which cost him so many sleepless nights, his exclusion from the society of his friends, his ignorance of the various methods of his enemies to prejudice his cause, his inability to divine what new changes would be made in the articles of his accusation, or what new articles might be framed, and the depressing conviction that his prosecutors, who had free

[1] Epis. xxxiii. [2] Epis. xxxvii.

access to the minds of the members of the council, would spare no effort to secure his condemnation; all conspired to dishearten him, and overwhelm him with foreboding. From time to time his trial had been deferred, and even in his prison Paletz and Causis, who accompanied the judicial committee appointed to visit him, had insulted even his helplessness and misfortunes. They were bent, moreover, on depriving him of the privilege of a public audience. They knew the power of his eloquence, and they did not wish to have the experiment of it tried upon the council. He had been denied an advocate. They would also have him condemned unheard. But here they were defeated by the more just, if not manly and honorable, policy of Sigismund.

By one of those strange series of events which characterize the processes of this world even, as providential retributions, Huss was not to leave his prison at Gottlieben until his great antagonist, John XXIII., now deposed from the papacy, was immured in the same walls. The ex-pontiff had received, with every mark of contrite submission, the announcement of his deposition. For this well-played farce the Jesuit Maimbourg does not hesitate to enroll him among the noblest martyrs of the church, and for his self-sacrificing spirit place him in merit by the side of St. Peter himself. How much he deserves such eulogy, the hypocrisy, simony, and corruptions of his life might enable any one unversed in Jesuit casuistry to judge. He merely cried "quarter" when the knife was at his throat. The threat of the council, that further obstinacy should be met with severer penalties, was hung *in terrorem* over his head. The report of his submission reached the council on the first day of June, and, in considerate appreciation of his ostentatious humility, the holy fathers determined on placing him in closer and safer custody. On the third day of June, therefore, he was removed by their order from Ratolfcell to Gottlieben, occupying a cell in the same prison where Huss was confined. It is doubtful whether the two men met. It is enough that they now found themselves in this strange juxtaposition. The last time that they had stood face to face, the proud, tyrannical, and hypocritical pontiff had seemed to occupy a position superior to any earthly tribunal. Soon his selfish policy marked Huss as a scapegoat for his own sin. Denied the luxury of exulting over his victim, he spread his complaint of the emperor over Europe, and howled forth his rage that the policy rather than the justice of Sigismund had snatched the victim from his tiger claws. Now the tiger himself was caged, and Huss might, if he had chosen, have enjoyed the disgrace of his foe. His own turn for exultation had come. But he chose rather to see in this event the demonstration of the futility of his own excommunication,—a demonstration which was not to lose its effect upon the Bohemian nation.

Moralists might discover an important lesson in the contrast presented by these two men confined in the same fortress. One was the coward tyrant of Christendom, taking counsel of his fears, and adopting in regard to himself language, if true, as degrading as it was submissive. The other, weak and exposed as he was to the inveterate malice of his foes, had no terms to offer but those of submission to the supremacy of truth alone,—a supremacy which his foes also must finally acknowledge. One had alienated all the friends he ever had. The other had not only bound his former friends closer to him by his steadfast integrity, but had won the hearts of his jailers to sympathy, compassion, and admiration. There, in one cell, might be seen the ex-pontiff, on whose head rested a weight of crime that could scarce have found its parallel in the lives of the Herods and the Neros—crushed by infamy as well as by chains—a whining supplicant, cringing to lick the hand that inflicted his blows—stripped of all his honors, and his name made the by-word of reproach. Here, in another, was the victim of bigoted and jealous malice, and yet, with an integrity and purity of character on which his bitterest enemies could not fix a stain, awaiting in the calm consciousness of his innocence the assaults of calumny—sustained by strength and grace imparted from above—turning his prison-cell into a Bethel, and with faith in God exultant in every prospect, whether of acquittal or of death. One of these prisoners humbles himself before men; the other before God only. One represents Barabbas; the other, in his patient endurance of injustice, calumny, and scorn, reminds us of the example of his divine Master.

The ex-pontiff had few if any to commiserate his fate. The name of Huss will be respected and honored while truth has honors for her martyrs.

The spectacle of the dethroned tyrant of Christendom excited wonder, but not pity. A chronicle of the time[1] introduces him uttering the lament:

> "I who but late was seated on a throne,
> Must now in bitterness lament my fall;
> In my high place of power I ruled alone,
> My feet the kiss of homage had from all.
> Now to the lowest deep of shame I'm hurled,
> A victim to the penalty of crime,
> The laughing-stock and scandal of the world,
> Gazed at in scorn—the wonder of my time.
> Once every land its gold laid at my feet,
> Now wealth delights not, not a friend remains;
> From me, cast down so low from my high seat,
> Let those be warned whom glory false sustains."[2]

Neither of the prisoners was to remain at Gottlieben. Even within stone walls and carefully guarded, the ex-pontiff was in too immediate proximity to the council. He was soon detected in his old business of intrigue. There was some danger lest the party in his favor might be revived. At least it was not to be doubted that, inspirited by his countenance, his partisans might be ready at the first opportunity to obstruct its further proceedings. He was accordingly committed by the emperor to the charge of the elector, and by him conveyed first to Heidelberg,

[1] Engelhusen Chron. quoted by Van der Hardt, iv. 299.

[2] The following is the language of the original Latin version:

> "Qui modo summus eram, guadens de nomine Præsul,
> Tristis et abjectus nunc mea fata gemo.
> Excelsus solio nuper versabar in alto
> Cunctaque gens pedibus oscula prona dabat.
> Nunc ego pænarum fundo devolver in imo,
> Et me deformem quemque videre piget,
> Omnibus ex terris aurum mihi sponte ferebat,
> Sed nec gaza juvat, nec quis amicus adest.
> Cedat in exemplum cunctis quos gloria tollit,
> Vertice de summo quando ego Papa cado."

and afterward to Manheim, to be kept in closer custody.

Before the removal of Huss to Constance, his friends sought the opportunity of obtaining his views in regard to the doctrine of the communion of the cup.[1] On the very day, (May 31,) therefore, on which it was determined that a public trial should be granted him, the Bohemians requested him, through their common friend John de Chlum, to give a clear and full statement of his views on this disputed question, together with the reasons by which they were supported.[2] "We have to ask," writes the Bohemian nobleman, "of you, most beloved, that you will give us in writing your deliberate and argumentative opinion on the subject of the communion of the cup, if such shall seem good to you, that it may be shown at the proper time to our friends. For on this subject the minds of the brethren have been somewhat divided, and many have been disturbed."

Huss at once complied with this request of the Bohemians. In his reply to Chlum, he says, "As to the sacrament of the cup, you have in writing what I wrote when in Constance, with the reasons that led me to adopt the views there presented. And I know not that I can say anything more in regard to this sacrament, except that it is sustained by the gospel and by Paul's epistles, and was observed in the primitive church. If it may be, seek at least permission to have it administered to those who ask for it in a devotional spirit."

[1] Van der Hardt, iv. 291. [2] Epis. xlvii.

The friends and the enemies of Huss now felt alike that the critical moment was at hand. On the first day of June, the former presented to the council a document which they had drawn up, showing that Huss had come to Constance, provided with a safe-conduct, in order to render reasons of his faith on every point upon which he should be called in question, and by no means with the intent obstinately to defend everything; but, if he should be better informed, resolved, in such case, to recant and change his views.

It was on this same day that the commission of the council visited Huss in his prison at Gottlieben. Notwithstanding the engagement of the council and the emperor that Huss should be heard, there were those who persisted in opposing the audience that had been promised him,[1] and to further their plans, the calumnious report was spread abroad that a sedition was to burst forth upon his arrival. Nothing could be more improbable, although the idea may possibly have entered the heads of some of the more hot-headed partisans of the reformer. Paletz and Causis accompanied the commission. In the secret interrogatories that took place, all means were tried, even to insult and threats, to shake the constancy of Huss. His friends, who knew of what materials the deputation was composed, were not without disquietude in their apprehension of the result. But Huss, debilitated and weakened as he was by sickness and severe imprisonment, was not to be awed

[1] Huss says (Epis. xliii.) that he was told by his enemies that he could not be allowed a hearing unless he paid 2,000 ducats for expenses.

by terror any more than seduced by promises. It was the wish of his friends that he should refuse to answer any question put to him thus in private. They saw no security for him but in a prudent reserve, or even absolute silence. They knew the violence of his adversaries, and were fearful of its effect upon a frame already so enfeebled by a long and harsh imprisonment. But, worn and enfeebled as Huss was, the spirit within him that was to brave the fires of martyrdom, was still unsubdued. True to the calm constancy of his life, he did not suffer himself to be intimidated, nor to use, as he justly might have done, any severe language. In one of his letters he depicts the troublesome and annoying nature of the inquisition to which he was subjected, a harshness of proceeding which might well have provoked angry retort. "Let my friends," said he, "be under no alarm on the score of my answers. I firmly hope that what I have said under the roof will yet be preached upon the house-tops. Every one of the articles has been presented to me separately, and the question has been asked whether I persisted in desiring to defend it. My answer was, that I would not do so, but would await the decision of the council. God is my witness that no reply has seemed to me more suitable, since I had already given it under my own hand that I did not wish to maintain anything obstinately, but was willing to receive instruction of any one. Michael de Causis stood by, with a paper in his hand, urging the patriarch to use force to make me reply to his questions.[1]

[1] Epis. xlviii.

The bishops then came in and interrogated in their turn. . . . God has permitted Causis and Paletz to rise up against me for my sins. The one examined and remarked upon all my letters, and the other brought up conversations that had taken place between us many years back. . . . The patriarch would insist upon it that I was exceedingly rich, and an archbishop even named the very sum I possess,—namely, 70,000 florins. . . . Oh! certainly my sufferings to-day were great! One of the bishops said to me 'You have established a new law;' and another, 'You have preached up all these articles.' My answer simply was, 'Why do you overwhelm me with outrage?'"

Berthold Wildungen,[1] one of the deputation who visited Huss, has himself given an account of this interview, which, in the main, agrees with that of Huss, omitting, however, its most odious features. The number of articles submitted to Huss was thirty. His declining to defend them, and offering to submit to the correction of the council, was afterward used against him in the public audience. It is evident that he saw the futility of any private defence which he might offer, and preferred that the council, instead of the deputation, should be the judge of his views. Certainly no intention to submit his convictions, without argument or instruction of his error, could ever have entered his mind. He was not disposed to allow the council, any more than the pope, to usurp to themselves the authority of the word of God. He merely referred himself, as he felt in duty bound,

[1] See Van der Hardt.

to the decisions of the council, based, as he had the right to demand that they should be, upon the plain doctrine of the Sacred Scriptures. His friends were disquieted at the report perversely spread abroad by his enemies, in regard to his submission. They feared that he had already offered some sort of retraction. But this was not the case. "I never promised," he says, in a letter written a few days later, "to submit myself to the council except conditionally; and at several different audiences—as already previously in public—I have protested that, as to the demand that I should retract, I desired to submit myself to the instruction, direction, and justice of the council, whenever I could be made to see that I had written, taught, or maintained anything opposed to truth." This protestation was repeatedly made by Huss, from the time when he left Prague for Constance up to the conclusion of his trial. As the articles were now read to him, he gave the sense in which they were held, sometimes denying the one presented to be the expression of his views, or pointing out the perversion to which another had been subjected. To prevent any misstatements or alterations, Huss reduced his replies to writing.

Among the most influential opponents of Huss were those members of the council who represented in its sessions the university of Paris and the royal court of France. Of these men, Gerson was the acknowledged leader. Cardinal D'Ailly, his former instructor, sympathized with him on most of the controverted questions of the day, and from their position, as well as the remark which the former of these men afterward made—namely, that had Huss been properly defended he would have escaped—it is to be presumed that their influence against the reformer was decisive of his fate. And yet, to the observer of passing events, not initiated into a full knowledge of the secret currents of influence combining with, or counterworking one another beneath the surface, such violent hostility as those men manifested toward Huss is quite inexplicable. In many points they agreed with the Bohemian reformer. They had no more respect for the papal power, and would have paid no more regard to its excommunication, than Huss himself. Their exposures of the iniquity and corruption of the Roman court are as horrid and startling as any that were ever heard within the walls of Bethlehem chapel at Prague. It might have been supposed that these men, alike able, learned, and indignant at the gross corruptions of the church, sanctioned and exemplified in the lives of her own dignitaries, would have welcomed in Huss a brother reformer. But calumny had already poisoned their minds against him. Rivals and enemies had represented him to them as a heretic. His partial endorsement of the views of Wickliffe had in their eyes identified him with that hated Englishman. A strong party, resolved to glut their vengeance upon the latter, even at the price of robbing his grave and insulting his bones, thirsted for some living victim, and swept strong minds around them along in the tide of their own sympathies. To all this, however, must be added the fact, the weight of which at this day we are scarcely able to appreciate, that scholastic differences aggravated the animosity of the Paris deputation against Huss. The latter belonged to the school of the Realists, while the former were the avowed and leading champions of the school of the Nominalists. For full two centuries from the days of Roscelin and Abelard, France had been a battle-field for these contending parties. At times the result of the conflict seemed doubtful. Abelard, who was a Nominalist, with all his noted ability, fell before the unrelenting assaults of his powerful adversary, Bernard, and was branded as a heretic. But his views survived, and continued to spread until they had made the university of Paris their strongest fortress. In vain had popes and councils attempted to stay the tide of opinion. Abelard's bones rested quietly in their grave, but over his helpless dust the battle was fought which more than avenged him. The Nominalists gained at last the supremacy, but the hard-fought battle had left behind it deep scars, and bleeding wounds that refused to be healed. Alienation and bitter hostility still were cherished in the minds of the opposing parties. They who triumphed—and Gerson among them—doubtless remembered the humiliation of past defeats, and it was no unimportant object in their esteem that a general council for the reformation of the church should lend its sanction to the views which they maintained. Several of them, therefore, reproved in Huss the Realist as much at least as the heterodox preacher. Scholastic feuds were carried into the theological arena, and even men whose general integrity we are bound to respect were blinded, in the heat and strife of party feelings, to the nature of their acts. In the person of Huss, Realism was virtually triumphant at Prague; and when he stood before his judges, their prejudices were already aroused, and his case was really prejudged.

In regard to Huss, we have no evidence that he reciprocated the strong antipathies or party feelings of his antagonists. His philosophy was never made prominent, while his course was shaped simply by his sense of duty and his theological convictions. The cause of a pure Christianity excited in him a deeper interest than the dialecties or disputations of the schools. His philosophy did not obstruct—it may perhaps have promoted—the practical bearing of his words. His soul was too full of the great truths of scripture to have room left there for the play of passions which are roused by scholastic partisanship.

It was in such circumstances as these that Huss appeared before the council—a combination of opposing influences arrayed against him, from the conspiring antagonism of which little was left him to hope. Prejudice had built up, as it were, between him and the conscience of the council, an impenetrable wall of granite, from which argument, appeal, and remonstrance alike recoiled. This was manifest in the first steps of the process taken by the council against the reformer.

CHAPTER XXI.

FIRST AUDIENCE OF HUSS BEFORE THE COUNCIL. SECOND AUDIENCE.

Removal of Huss to Constance. — Council Assembled to Consider his Case in his Absence. — Peter, the Notary. — The Emperor Informed. — Forbids any Hasty Decision by the Council. — Their Reluctance to Obey. — Books of Huss Sent to the Emperor. — First Appearance of Huss Before the Council. — Charges Read. — Confusion in the Council. — Huss Cannot be Heard. — Luther's Description. — Calmness of Huss. — Cardinal of Ostia. — Complaint of Huss. — He is Required to Recant. — Confusion such that the Council Adjourns. — Assembly of June 7. — Eclipse. — Sigismund Present. — His Weakness. — Articles Read. — The Cup. — Transubstantiation. — The Cardinal D'Ailly. — Philosophical Subtleties. — Nominalists and Realists. — Reply of Huss. — The English Doctors. — Huss Dissents from Wickliffe. — John Stokes. — Remarks of the Cardinal of Florence. — Noble Reply. — Zabarella Rejoins. — New Article on Approval of Wickliffe. — Whether Tithes are Alms. — Statements of Huss as to his Course. — Sbynco. — The Burning of the Books. — The Appeal of Huss. — He Justifies it. — Article on Appeal to Arms. — On the Discord Produced by his Doctrines. — Statements of Huss. — Nason. — D'Ailly. — The University. — Nason's Remarks. — Paletz Confirms Them. — Council Adjourns. — Huss Called Back. — D'Ailly Seeks to Prejudice the Emperor. — Huss Replies. — Chlum's Answer. — D'Ailly Urges Submission. — Sigismund on his Safe-Conduct. — Bids Huss Submit. — His Reply. — Clemency of the Council. — Letters of Huss. — Anxiety About his Debts. — Few Friends of Huss in the Council.

June 1, 1415–June 7, 1415.

It was on the fifth of June, 1415, that Huss was removed from the prison at Gottlieben, where he had remained for more than two months, and brought to Constance. But even here he was not permitted to meet his friend, Jerome. The latter was confined in the tower of St. Paul's Cemetery, while the former was placed in the monastery of the Franciscans, where he was to remain, for the greater part of the time loaded with irons, till the hour of his martyrdom. Well does the annalist[1] add, as he notes the period of this the last imprisonment of Huss, that 'he was to take leave of his cell, not of his constancy; of his life, but not of his faith.'[2]

The council, however, contemning even the forms of justice, did not wait for his appearance before they proceeded to take measures that were meant to be decisive of his fate. Several hours before his arrival at Constance, and not only in his absence but in that of the emperor, the fathers of the council, with the cardinals and bishops, assembled in public congregation. The place selected for the assembly was the monastery of the Franciscans, in which Huss was to be confined. Articles were produced and read, accompanied with the alleged proofs, which were said to have been selected from his books and treatises. The object of such a proceeding, so strangely at variance with the course which they were virtually pledged to pursue, was sufficiently obvious. If the council's condemnation of Huss' doctrines could not thus be secured, a full opportunity at least was allowed his enemies to ply their arts of slanderous invective and false crimination. But among those present at the council, there was one indignant spectator of this grossly unjust proceeding. The good notary, Peter Maldoniewitz, the one who, two weeks before, on the arrest of Jerome, had discovered the

[1] Van der Hardt, iv. 306. [2] Carcerem non constantiam, vitam non fidem linqueret.

secret prison in which he was confined, and offered him consolation, sympathy, and kindness, was present in his official character, and gathered, from what he heard,[1] that the doctrines of Huss would speedily be condemned, perhaps before his arrival. He therefore hastened to inform his friends and countrymen, Chlum and Duba, of what the council proposed to do. On receiving this intelligence, these men promptly communicated it to the emperor. Sigismund shared to some extent the indignation of the Bohemian nobles. He dispatched, on the instant, the elector Louis of Bavaria and Frederic burgrave of Nuremberg to the assembled members, seriously enjoining upon them not to determine anything in the cause of Huss until they had heard him, and heard him, moreover, with calmness and impartiality. He directed them also to send him whatever erroneous articles they might detect, giving them to understand that he on his part would submit them to the judgment of good and learned men.

Such a message was far from acceptable to the council. They bore it ill, that having deposed a pope, their own supremacy should not be fully acknowledged by the emperor. With the first part of his command they were forced to acquiesce, and gave orders to have Huss brought before them; but on the second point they met the emperor's demand by an absolute refusal. They declined to send him the erroneous articles. To this they were impelled as well probably by their fear of the result if the matter was to be left in his hands, as by their res-

[1] Van der Hardt, iv. 307. Mon. Hussi, i. 12.

tiveness under his assumed control. Meanwhile Duba and Chlum, taught by experience to distrust the fair dealing of the council, handed to the princes whom the emperor had sent, the several volumes of the writings of Huss, from which the articles objected against him had been extracted. By a reference to these, the bad faith of his adversaries might the more readily be detected, or, if the extracts were correct, they might be verified.

Huss, now removed from Gottlieben, was brought in the course of the day for the first time before the council.[1] The elector and the burgrave, having handed in the volumes of his writings, withdrew, and left Huss alone in the midst of his enemies. Exasperated as they were by the obstacles thrown in their way by the emperor, they were not in the best mood for hearing a man whose case they had already prejudged. The books of Huss were presented to him. He was asked if he acknowledged them as his. He replied that he did, promising at the same time to correct whatever error could be pointed out in them. "I will rectify," said he, "any mistaken proposition which any man among you can point out, with the most hearty good-will."

The reading of the articles charged as erroneous was then commenced. After one had been read, and Huss had shown a disposition to reply to it, the true spirit of the assembly broke forth. He had scarcely uttered the first word, when there arose

[1] The main authorities for the facts pertaining to the trial of Huss are Van der Hardt, who is most full and complete, and the accounts given in the works of Huss, i. 12–29. L'Enfant has given a fair and full digest from these authorities.—Pp. 200–235.

throughout the whole assembly such clamor and disturbance that the hearing of him was altogether out of the question. The scene was renewed as the council proceeded from article to article. If the notary Maldoniewitz is to be believed—and he was present at the scene, gazing upon it with anxious interest—the proceedings of the assembly were characterized rather by the ferocity of wild beasts than the grave deportment and thoughtful attention of Christian doctors, assembled to discuss and decide the gravest questions. At length, as the storm lulled somewhat, the voice of Huss was heard appealing to the Sacred Scriptures. This was too much for the patience of the council. "That is not the question," was the outcry which burst forth from every side. Some uttered accusations against the prisoner, while others laughed him to scorn. Any attempt which he could make to secure a hearing was perfectly futile. He ceased for a moment, and his enemies began to enjoy their triumph. "He is dumb," cried they; "it is evident that he has taught the heretical proposition contained in the article." "All," said Luther, in describing the scene in his own energetic language, "all worked themselves into rage like wild boars; the bristles of their back stood on end; they bent their brows and gnashed their teeth against John Huss."[1]

But, in the midst of all the taunts and insults that were heaped upon him, Huss was not depressed or dismayed. "There were given to me," he says, "boldness and presence of mind."[2] Two of the articles

[1] Luther's Latin letter appended to the letters of Huss.

[2] Van der Hardt. "Magno se animo fuisse præditum."

charged against him were stricken out. There was not evidence to sustain them. "The same fate," writes Huss, at the close of the day, "is augured for many of the others." One of those probably which were dropped was the one that concerned the doctrine of the cup. The council readily perceived that, whatever might be the views of Huss upon the subject, he was not the originator of the innovation at Prague; and if he was condemned for them, the sentence might strike further than they desired. Huss justly complained of the confusion and clamor of the occasion. Causis insisted that his books should be burned. Yet there were men more favorably inclined. Huss speaks well of the cardinal, Bishop of Ostia, who usually presided over the deliberations of the council. He was the son of a poor peasant of Brogni. A swineherd in his youth, he was never ashamed of his origin. By his merit he had risen to high station, and in his elevation preserved a sympathy for the poor and unfortunate. Huss speaks of him as father, and commends the kindness which he experienced at his hands. One of the Polish doctors also showed himself friendly. Even the Bishop of Leitomischel, who had denounced Jacobel, seemed somewhat softened in feeling toward Huss.

But his friends were few in number, and their voices were drowned in the clamors of this judicial mob. No order was preserved. The members of the council cried out against Huss, while they interrupted one another at the top of their voice. "I supposed," cried the prisoner, "that there had been more fairness, kindness, and order in the council."

Upon this the Cardinal of Ostia addressed Huss: "When we saw you in the tower, you spoke in a more modest manner." "With good reason," replied Huss, "for there no one vociferated against me, and now all do." "They tried," says Huss, in speaking of the scene at a later period, "to frighten me from my constancy in the truth of Christ; but they could not vanquish the strength of God in me. They would not deal with me on the ground of the authority of the Sacred Scriptures, as those noble lords, Duba and Chlum, prepared as they were to incur infamy for the truth of God while they stood firmly by my side, can testify." These men had been authorized by the emperor to be present with Huss on his trial. With what indignation must they have heard the reply to Huss when he asked to be instructed in what respects he had erred. "As you ask to be informed," said the presiding cardinal, "you must first recant your doctrine, according to the prescript of the fifty masters in Sacred Scripture."

As the clamor continued and increased, and the eyes of Huss, gazing over the assembly, met only enemies where he had hoped to find impartial judges, he was forced to express his surprise. "I anticipated," said he, "a different reception, and had imagined that I should obtain a hearing. I am unable to make myself audible over so great a noise; and I am silent because I am forced to it. I would willingly speak were I listened to." The more moderate members of the council were disgusted. The agitation and confusion were too great for calm deliberation. A fair audience of Huss was utterly impossible in the circumstances. Those who were anxious for the reputation of the council urged an adjournment, insisting that the case should be deferred to another occasion. Their views prevailed, and the council stood adjourned to the seventh of June.

The next day upon which the council met (June 7) was ushered in by a solar eclipse. The sun's disc was almost wholly obscured, and the superstition of the age regarded it as a strange omen.[1] It was not till the eclipse had wholly passed away, and at about one o'clock in the afternoon, that the council reassembled in the hall of the Franciscan monastery, where they had met before.[2] Sigismund took good care to be present. The Bohemian noblemen had given him an account of what had taken place at the first audience, and conjured him to be present at the second sitting, to preserve order.

Huss was led into the assembly loaded with chains, and attended by a numerous body of soldiers. He was placed directly in front of the emperor, whose imperial word had been pledged for his security. The feelings of Sigismund on such an occasion were scarcely to be envied. He came now, undoubtedly, in the hope of saving the prisoner from condemnation, and restraining the excessive zeal of his prosecutors. He persuaded himself, in all probability, that his influence with the council, and with the prisoner also, would be decisive. But he had failed rightly to estimate the strength of religious conviction on the part of one, or of prejudice and venomous hostility on the part of the other. Little did he realize,

[1] L'Enfant, 200. [2] Mon. Hussi, 12, 13,

while he exulted over the deposition of a pope, that in the hands of the council he was himself to become the blind instrument of his own infamy.

The two bitter enemies of Huss, Paletz and Causis, had neglected nothing which could contribute to secure his condemnation. The presence of the emperor only incited them to redouble their efforts. Apprehension of the shame of defeat, if their victim was suffered to escape them, aggravated the bitterness of their zeal. The audience opened with the reading of the articles of accusation. They were fitly presented, as they had been mainly drawn up by Causis. In the first of these he sought to identify the cause of Huss with that of Wickliffe, and thus overwhelm it in the same obloquy. "John Huss," said he,[1] "has taught in the Bethlehem chapel, and in other places in the city of Prague, many errors among the people, some of them drawn from the books of Wickliffe, some of his own getting up, and he has diligently defended them, with extreme obstinacy. In the first place, he has taught that after the consecration and the pronunciation of the words in the Lord's supper, the material bread still remains, and this is proved by the testimony of several witnesses." The names of four of them, Protiva, Pecklo, Benesius, and Broda, were specified.[2]

To this charge Huss replied, with a solemn adjuration, that he had never taught such a doctrine. "Only this," he would confess, "that when the archbishop of Prague had wholly prohibited the use of that expression, *bread*, he could not approve this

[1] Van der Hardt, iv. 308. [2] Mon. Hussi, i. 13.

mandate of the archbishop, inasmuch as Christ in the sixth chapter of John had spoken of himself eleven times as the bread of angels that came down from heaven to give life to the world, but that he never had spoken of material bread."

Upon this Huss was addressed by the Cardinal of Cambray, who belonged to the school of the French theologians, and who like them was embittered against the Realism of Huss on philosophical grounds. Holding a paper in his hand, which he said he had received the day before, he addressed the prisoner: "John Huss, do you hold that universals are derived from particulars?"[1] This was a test question of philosophy. Huss replied to it in the affirmative, strengthening himself with the remark, that thus St. Anselm and others had believed. "It follows, then," replied the cardinal, "that after the consecration, the material substance of the bread remains. And this point I thus prove: because after the consecration, while the bread is changed and substantiated into the body of Christ, as you now say, either the wonted substance of the material bread remains there, or it does not. If it remains, the charge is true; if not, then it follows that at the cessation of the particular the universal itself ceases."

By such reasoning this "hammer of heretics," as he was proud in his day to be called, attempted to smite down Huss, and force him either to renounce his philosophy, or admit that the material bread remained after consecration. His passions as a parti-

[1] Ponisne universalia a parte rei?

san had thrown him into the strange attitude of a champion of orthodoxy, contending as a philosophical polemic. The fate of Huss was made to hinge upon the syllogisms and the technicalities of the schools. It is scarcely possible to conceive the more than *odium theologicum* which, at that period, characterized the feelings mutually of the Nominalists and Realists. This bitterness had continued through centuries, the heirloom of successive generations. These contending sects carried their fury so far as to charge each other with the "sin against the Holy Ghost." It is worthy of note that the Nominalists, in their subsequent letter to Louis, king of France, do not pretend to deny[1] that Huss fell a victim to the resentment of their sect. Undoubtedly this article of accusation which Causis had drawn up, and of the falsehood of which he could scarcely have failed to be aware, had been introduced by a malignant ingenuity, and with the purpose to array against Huss the philosophical prejudices of the whole French deputation. It gave an opportunity to bring to bear upon him all the arts of their scholasticism, and the rigor of an inflexible and pitiless logic. It placed him directly in conflict with the ablest and most disciplined intellects of Europe, and left him at the mercy of all the sophistical snares with which they might endeavor to entrap him.

But Huss, believing as he did in the doctrine of transubstantiation, was prepared by his own belief with an unanswerable reply. In this case, he admitted that the *universal* ceases, inasmuch as transub-

[1] Dugald Stewart, i. 94.

stantiation is a miracle—the substance disappearing in this case, though remaining in every other.

Upon this an English doctor interposed. He wished to present a new edition of the cardinal's argument, and prove, from what Huss admitted, that material bread remains after consecration, thus condemning him by inference—a course of all others most unmanly and odious. But Huss treated it as a puerility with which even the boys in school were familiar, and at once answered it. Another English doctor now proposed to prove that material bread remains after consecration, inasmuch as it is not annihilated. To this Huss replied that, although not annihilated, it yet ceased to be bread in particular, by its transubstantiation into the body of Christ.

Here another Englishman interrupted him, by saying, "In my view, Huss seems to speak in the same subtle way that Wickliffe did.[1] For the latter granted all that the former does, but held also that material bread remains after consecration, in the sacrament of the altar. Moreover, that whole chapter,[2] *Firmater credimus*, he perverted so as to confirm his erroneous opinion." To this Huss replied, denying that he had spoken anything but with sincerity and from conviction. "Was then," asked the Englishman, "was that body of Christ, which was born of the Virgin Mary, suffered, died, rose again, and is seated at the right hand of God the Father, wholly and truly present in the sacrament of the altar?" This was the vital question, at least in the view of

[1] Mon. Hussi, i. 13. [2] From the decree establishing the doctrine of transubstantiation.

every Englishman. Wickliffe's denial of the doctrine of transubstantiation was the head and front, theoretically at least, of his offending. But Huss candidly and manfully disavowed the views which the English reformer held upon this point. Upon this the minds of some of the English members of the council became somewhat softened toward him. They had, with their characteristic common sense, little sympathy with the subtle and scholastic distinctions of the French doctors. If Huss was to be proved guilty of rejecting the doctrine in question, they wished the proof to be such that a plain man could understand it. Probably few of them could fairly comprehend the technicalities of the Nominalist philosophy, or, if they did, some at least must have regarded it with aversion. "What use," exclaimed one, "of all this disputation about *universals*, which has nothing to do with faith? This man, as far as I can see, has correct views in regard to the sacrament of the altar."

All the English doctors did not share this opinion. The present charge was a vital one in their view, and the smoke of Huss' funeral-pile would be far more grateful incense to their nostrils if he could be burned as a disciple of their old enemy, Wickliffe. Unwilling even yet to give up the point, Doctor John Stokes returned to the charge. "I saw," said he, "at Prague a certain treatise ascribed to this John Huss, in which it was distinctly stated that after consecration the material bread remains in the sacrament." "With all due respect," replied Huss, calmly conscious of his innocence of the charge brought against him, "With all due respect, this is not the case."

Unable by these methods to substantiate anything against the prisoner, on this charge at least, they returned to the various testimony which had been sworn against him. John Protiva,[1] parish priest of St. Clement, at Prague, added to his testimony, that Huss had, when the authority of St. Gregory was adduced against him, spoken of that holy man as a jester or a wag. To this Huss replied, that in this matter injustice was done him. He had ever accounted Gregory a most holy doctor of the church.

Upon this the ardor of the prosecution somewhat abated. The course of his enemies was perhaps producing something of a recoil of feeling in favor of the prisoner. The false charge, and Cardinal D'Ailly's absurd attempt to prove it upon Huss by inference, were enough upon reflection to excite sympathy among the more moderate members of the council.

At this moment, when the heat of the dispute had somewhat subsided, the cardinal of Florence came adroitly to the rescue of a bad cause. "You know," said he to Huss, "that in the mouth of two or three witnesses every word must be established. But now, as you perceive, there are almost twenty men, of great credit and authority, some of whom heard you themselves, while others testify from common fame and the reports of persons who did hear you, whose testimony bears against you. All give such decisive

[1] Protiva had occupied the pulpit of Bethlehem chapel before Huss, and it is not improbable that envy had something to do with his present course.

evidence of the truth of what they testify, that we can not disbelieve them. How you can defend your cause against so many, and such eminent and reliable men, I can not see." The aim of the cardinal in this assumed tone of moderation was obvious. He wished to persuade Huss to an unconditional recantation, at once, probably, to dispose of the whole matter, and, out of regard for the emperor and the Bohemians, to save the prisoner's life. But Huss was not to be thus entrapped into a violation of his convictions. "I call," replied he, "I call God and my own conscience to witness, that I never have taught, or even thought of teaching, as these men have dared to testify in regard to what they never heard. And even though there were many more arrayed against me, I make more account of the witness of the Lord my God, and of my own conscience, than I do of the judgments of all my adversaries, which I regard as nothing."

It was a noble reply, worthy of the man and of the occasion. But the fathers of the council could not appreciate the spirit in which it was uttered. Undoubtedly the cardinal of Florence spoke the feelings of the more moderate portion of the council, when he rejoined, "We cannot decide according to your conscience, but we must of necessity be satisfied with the most clear and reliable testimony of these witnesses. Nor do they assert these things against you as you say, impelled by some grudge or malice, but fortify their testimony with the reasons alleged for it, savoring in no respect of malice, and in regard to which there is no room left for doubt. As to your saying that Master Stephen Paletz is suspected of sinister designs by you, and that he has craftily selected those articles from your books, which will hereafter be brought forward, you seem to me in this matter to do him injustice. In my opinion, he has proceeded in this matter in such good faith, that he has presented the objectionable matter in milder language than you employed in your books. I hear, moreover, that other excellent men are likewise suspected by you, and you have asserted as much in regard to the chancellor of Paris, (Gerson,) than whom there is not another person in Christendom more eminent in merit."

The reply of Huss is not given, but the language of the cardinal was obviously as much addressed to the assembly as it was to the prisoner. "Should I live," says Huss, in one of his letters, "I will reply to the chancellor of Paris;[1] if I die, God will answer for me at the day of judgment.[2]

The result as to the first article seems to have been, that it was, however reluctantly, abandoned.

The article was next read in which Huss was charged with obstinately teaching and defending the erroneous articles of Wickliffe, in Bohemia.[3] The malice in the drawing up of this charge is manifest at a

[1] Cormenin relates (ii. 199) that on his trial, Huss was addressed by Gerson, who told him that he "must either break or bend." To this Huss replied, "I would rather that they should put a mill-stone about my neck, and cast me from heaven into the sea, than deny the truth. . . . . Let your infernal proceedings take their course. Give John Huss to the flames. But ere a century passes, there will spring from those ashes an avenger who will proclaim anew the truths I have taught, and for which you would condemn Christ himself, should he return to earth." I find, however, no such account given by reliable historians.

[2] Epis. I. 21.

[3] Mon. Hussi, i. 13.

glance. "I never have taught," said Huss, "the errors of Wickliffe or of any other man. If Wickliffe scattered abroad the seeds of error in England, let Englishmen themselves look after it."

In proof of this charge, however, it was adduced in evidence, that he had resisted the execution of the sentence against Wickliffe's doctrines, which was first passed in the council at Rome, and afterward published at Prague by Archbishop Sbynco, upon the advice of several of the most learned doctors. "Because," replied Huss, "they were condemned in such terms as these, viz: that not one of them was accordant with Catholic faith or doctrine, but was either heretical, or erroneous, or scandalous;" and besides, for conscience' sake he could not consent to such a sweeping assertion, and especially in view of Wickliffe's doctrine that Pope Sylvester and Constantine erred in endowing the church; and again, that a pope or priest, in mortal sin, could not consecrate or baptize. "This article," said Huss, "I have qualified, so as to say that such a one, because he is then in mortal sin, and is an unworthy minister of the sacraments of God, consecrates and baptizes unworthily."

Hereupon the accusers of Huss, with their witnesses, insisted that this article of Wickliffe was adopted and expressed by Huss in so many words, in his book against Paletz. "Verily," replied Huss, "I refuse not to die, if you will not find it there, qualified just as I have said."

The book was brought. Upon opening to the passage, they found it written precisely as Huss had stated. Again he added, that he had not dared to agree with those who condemned the doctrines of Wickliffe in a lump, on account of that article of his that tithes are purely alms.

Upon this point the cardinal of Florence chose to make a stand.[1] The voluntary bestowal of tithes was a sore doctrine to the prelates. Huss was met by the following syllogism:

"Alms must be voluntarily given, without debt or obligation; tithes are not given voluntarily, but from debt and obligation; therefore they are not alms." Huss replied by denying the major proposition, sustaining himself by a reference to Christ's words, in the twenty-fifth of Matthew, where the rich are obliged to give under pain of everlasting condemnation. Yet these gifts were alms, so that alms are given with debt and obligation. Here he was interrupted by an English bishop. "If," said he, "all of us are under obligation to the performance of the six works of mercy there recited, it follows that the poor who have nothing to give must be condemned." To this Huss replied, that he had spoken specifically of the rich, and of those who possessed the means of charity, and had said that they were under obligation to bestow alms under penalty of condemnation. Proceeding then to speak of the minor proposition of the cardinal's syllogism, by showing that tithes were at first freely given, and afterward were required by authority, he was cut short by the refusal of the council to hear more upon the point.

[1] L'Enfant, 204.

He then proceeded to state other reasons why he could not with a clear conscience give his consent to the wholesale condemnation of Wickliffe's articles, asserting, moreover, that none should be condemned until the reasons of such condemnation, drawn from Holy Scripture, were first adduced. "And of this same opinion," said Huss, "were many others, both doctors and masters of the university of Prague. For when Sbynco, the archbishop, had commanded that all the books of Wickliffe, gathered up throughout the whole city of Prague, should be brought to him, I myself, on handing to him some of Wickliffe's books, asked him to detect and note down any error that they might contain, that I might publicly acknowledge it. But the archbishop, without designating so much as one, cast all the books that were brought him, together with mine, into the fire. And yet he had received no command to this effect. By artful means[1] he had unfairly obtained, through the bishop of Sarepta, a bull from Alexander V., requiring that the books of Wickliffe, on the ground of their many errors, not one of which was mentioned, should be withdrawn from general circulation. Relying upon the authority of this bull, the archbishop imagined that he could easily bring the king and nobles of Bohemia to give their assent to the con-

[1] Cormenin (His. of the Popes, ii. 99) says that Alexander V. was drunk when he granted Sbynco's request. "At the conclusion of one of these dinners, the holy father, who had drunk extravagantly, granted to the deputies of Sbynco the bull which they asked for, and designated four masters in theology, and two in the canon law, to second the archbishop in his pursuit after those who taught the doctrines of Wickliffe, whether in public or private; he gave them full power and authority to hand them over to the secular arm if it were necessary, to repress their disturbances."

demnation of Wickliffe. But in this matter he was mistaken. Nevertheless he did not fail to call together certain theologians, to whom he committed the business of examining the books of Wickliffe, and judging them according to the canons. These theologians with one consent condemned them to be burned. Upon the report of this proceeding, the doctors, masters, and scholars of the university unanimously (those theologians excepted who pronounced the condemnation) petitioned the king for a stay of proceedings. The king granted the request, and sent a deputation to the archbishop to inquire into the matter. To this deputation the archbishop promised that he would not proceed further without the king's decree. Upon this, notwithstanding his fixed purpose to burn the books of Wickliffe on the following day, the matter was passed over, and for the time deferred.

"Meanwhile Alexander V. died. The archbishop, fearing lest the bull which he had received of him would prove no longer serviceable, called his adherents together, shut fast the gates of his court, and committed Wickliffe's books to the flames. To this act of injustice he added, moreover, one still more outrageous. On the authority of Alexander's bull, he published an edict forbidding any man longer, under pain of excommunication, to preach in the chapels. Upon this I appealed to the pope, and upon his death to John XXIII. who succeeded him; and after my case had been pending for nearly two years, and my advocates were not admitted to a hearing in my defence, I appealed to Christ the Sovereign Judge."

Here Huss paused. The question was put to him whether he had received absolution from the Roman pontiff. He replied that he had not. He was then asked whether it was lawful for him to appeal to Christ. "Truly," answered Huss, "I do here affirm, in the presence of you all, that there is no appeal more just or final than that which is made to Christ; for appeal in the legal sense is nothing more than to implore the aid of a higher judge for relief from the decision of an inferior. But what judge is there above Christ? Who can discern more in accordance with the rules of justice and equity than he whom no deceit can draw into error? and who can more promptly aid the wretched and the wronged?"

With a devout and serious spirit Huss had uttered these words—the spirit in which his whole defence was conducted; but their utterance brought down upon him at once the jeers and mockery of the whole council.[1]

Another article against Huss was then read. It was to the effect that, in order to confirm the allegiance of the simple and unlettered crowd among whom he preached, to the doctrines of Wickliffe, he had ventured to relate what occurred in England, when many monks and learned men had assembled in a certain church to dispute against Wickliffe. "They were unable," Huss was charged with saying, "to convict him of error, when suddenly the doors of the church were burst open by lightning, and the enemies of Wickliffe scarce escaped without harm." It was added, moreover, that he had said "that he wished his soul might be where Wickliffe's was." To

[1] Van der Hardt, iv. 311.

this Huss answered, "that some twelve years before the theological works of Wickliffe had been introduced into Bohemia, and after the perusal of some of his philosophical writings, he had said that they afforded him great satisfaction, and that when he was convinced of the stainless life of Wickliffe, he had said that he hoped that Wickliffe was saved; yet, though he doubted that he might be condemned, he would that his soul might be where John Wickliffe was."[1] The utterance of these words was another signal for the outburst of jeers and derision from the grave fathers of the council.

Another article was then read.[2] Huss was charged in this with advising the people to resist, if necessary, the assaults of their enemies by force of arms, after the example of Moses; and that on the day following this advice, public handbills were widely circulated, to the purport that each should be armed effectually with the sword, and that brother should not spare brother or nearest kindred.

To this Huss replied, 'that the whole of it was a false accusation of his enemies. But he had admonished the people, while preaching from the words of the apostle in regard to the helmet of salvation and the sword of the Spirit, that they should all arm themselves with these in the defence of gospel truth, and, to avoid all chance of calumny, he had carefully added, not with the material sword, but with that which is the word of God. But as to the public intimations, or the sword of Moses, there was no truth in it.'

[1] Mon. Hussi, i. 108. [2] L'Enfant, 205. Van der Hardt, iv. 311.

The next article charged—as supported by testimony—that many scandals had sprung up from the doctrine of Huss. At first he had sown discord between the ecclesiastical and political authorities, which resulted in the persecution and spoliation of the bishops and the clergy; and, moreover, he had, by the discord introduced into the university of Prague, effected its ruin.

The reply of Huss was a brief statement of facts: "None of these things," said he, "has taken place by any fault of mine. The dissension between the ecclesiastical and political authorities was a prior occurrence. Pope Gregory XII. promised, upon his election, that he would lay down the pontificate when the voice of the cardinals should demand it. He was elected on this condition. In opposition to Wenzel, king of Bohemia, also king of the Romans, he bestowed the imperial title upon Robert, duke of Bavaria. A few years after this, when Gregory refused at the instance of the cardinals to lay down his office, they sent letters to the king of Bohemia, urging him, in common with them, to refuse obedience to Gregory. They encouraged him, moreover, to expect that by the authority of a new pontiff he might be able to recover the imperial dignity. Swayed by these motives, the king yielded to the urgency of the cardinals, and refused obedience to both Gregory and Benedict. In this matter the Archbishop Sbynco, along with the clergy, was opposed to the king; and many of the priesthood, on this account relinquishing the duties of their office, left the city. Among these was the archbishop himself, who first tore open the sepulchre of St. Wenceslaus, and, in opposition to the will of the king, burned the books of Wickliffe. As a consequence, the king readily allowed some of the goods of these persons, who had thus fled of their own accord, to be plundered."

This simple statement of unquestionable facts was a sufficient exculpation of Huss. But to defeat the favorable impression, an individual named Nason, a member of the council, rose and declared that 'the clergy refused the performance of the divine offices, not because they were unwilling to swear obedience to the king, but because they were stripped of their property and their privileges.'

The cardinal of Cambray volunteered his confirmation of what Nason had said. "It is proper that I should here state," he remarked, " what has just been recalled to my mind. In the same year in which these things took place, I was at a certain time just setting out upon my journey from Rome, when several Bohemian prelates met me. I asked them what news they brought from Bohemia. "A most disgraceful transaction has happened there," said they. " The entire clergy have been stripped of their privileges, and shamefully treated."

Huss still affirmed that the case was as he had stated it. To the other portion of the article, accusing him of the ruin of the university of Prague, he replied by maintaining that the German nation had not left from any fault of his. "The founder of the university, Charles IV., had granted to the Bohemians three votes, and to the German nation one; and when his son, the present king, restored this principle of its founder, the Germans were aggrieved, and of their own accord left the city, binding themselves by oaths and the severest penalties never to return. I admit, I confess, that I approved, from patriotic motives, this proceeding of the king, to obey which I was in duty bound. And that you need not imagine I misrepresent the facts of the case, here is Albert Warentrapp present, who was at that time dean of the faculty of arts, and who upon his departure from the city, took the same oath that was taken by the other Germans. He, if he is willing to state the truth, will easily clear me of this suspicion."

Warentrapp was about to speak, but the council was indisposed to hear him. Nason, however, was more readily listened to. "I am," said he, "sufficiently acquainted with this matter. At the time when these things took place, I was in the court of the king, where I saw the masters of the three nations, Germans, Bavarians, Saxons, and Silesians, with whom the Polish was reckoned, come as supplicants to petition that the right of suffrage which they had exercised might not be taken from them. The king promised that he would see to it that their request should be granted. But John Huss, with Jerome and others, persuaded the king otherwise, and this too, although at first he was much provoked against them; had charged them with the disturbances that had taken place, and had even threatened to let the flames solve the matter for them. Be assured therefore, most reverend fathers, that the king of Bohemia never really favored these men, whose audacity is such that they would not hesitate to meet me with a base reception, though lately, to a high degree, enjoying the royal confidence."

Paletz did not fail to seize upon an occasion so favorable to add the weight of his testimony. "Yes," said he, "most reverend fathers, not only learned men of other nations, but of Bohemia itself, have been driven out by John Huss and his counsels, some of whom are yet in exile in Moravia." "How," asked Huss, "can this be true, when I was not at Prague at the time when those men you speak of left?" Their banishment had in fact occurred after he had withdrawn from Prague.

But the council had now grown weary, and it was time to adjourn. Huss was left to the charge of the archbishop of Riga, to whom Jerome also had been committed. As they were leading him away, the cardinal of Cambray called him back. "John Huss," said he, in the hearing of Sigismund, "when you were first brought before us, I heard you say that unless you had chosen to come to Constance of your own accord, neither the king nor the emperor could have forced you to do so." The object of this remark was obvious. To prejudice the emperor against Huss was to rob the prisoner of his last hope of justice. The plan of the cardinal was as unmanly as it was unjust. Huss did not deny the statement. "With all respect, most reverend father," said he, "I confess that I used such language. For unless I had chosen to come, there are princes enough in Bohemia, who regard me with the most kindly feelings, who could with the greatest ease have kept me in some secret and safe place, to prevent my being forced to come here, even against the will of the king and of the emperor."

At these words the countenance of the cardinal changed. "Observe," said he, indignantly, "Observe, I pray you, the presumption of this man." The remark was not lost upon those to whom it was addressed. A murmur of passionate comments arose. But the brave Chlum was not the man to leave Huss undefended. "John Huss," said he, "has spoken the truth. I agree with what he has said; for even I, humble as my power and position are in Bohemia, could easily have defended him for a whole year, against the power of both these kings. How much more could more powerful lords with their more strongly fortified castles have done it!"

The cardinal was not prepared for this. "Let us pass these things over," said he. "I urge and advise you to do what you promised when you were in the castle,—submit yourself to the sentence of the council. If you do this, you will best consult your safety and standing."

The course which the cardinal advised was such, doubtless, as would tend to propitiate the council. It was easy to perceive that such a solution of the matter would afford great relief, even to men who thirsted for the blood of Huss, but felt some hesitation to commit a deed the consequences of which might be disastrous. Sigismund snatched at this solution. If the prisoner would but admit the virtual supremacy of the council in all matters of faith; if he would conciliate their offended dignity by submission, Sigismund would feel strong enough to rescue him from the hands of his foes. With this view he sought himself to enforce upon Huss the advice of the cardinal. To give it more force, or to satisfy his own conscience, he volunteered a refutation of some of the false reports that had been circulated in regard to the safe-conduct. "Although," said he, "there are those who say that you received letters of public faith from us, through your friends and patrons, only after you had been fifteen days under arrest,[1] yet we can prove, by the testimony of many princes and persons of distinction, that you received these letters from us before you left Prague,[2] by the hands of those lords, Wenceslaus de Duba and John De Chlum, to whose loyal care we committed you, that you might suffer no injustice, but that the privilege of speaking and answering before the council, in regard to your faith and doctrine, might be fully secured to you. And this, as you see, the most reverend lord cardinals and bishops have so allowed that we are much obliged to them; although there are some who say that we have no right to afford protection or countenance to one who

[1] From this language of the emperor it is obvious that the assertion made by the enemies of Huss was not merely that he had been fifteen days in Constance before receiving his safe-conduct, (as stated on pp. 499, 500,) but that he did not receive it till the order for his liberation from the emperor reached Constance, some two weeks after his arrest. It is not improbable that various accounts of the matter was given by different individuals, some of them admitting that the safe-conduct was received by Huss fifteen days after reaching Constance, while others, aware that this would still leave the council under the stigma of having contemned the imperial authority, modified falsehood to serve a purpose, and gave it the form which the emperor was honest enough to expose.

[2] In this the emperor was mistaken. L'Enfant, 208.

is a heretic, or is even suspected of being such. Now, therefore, we give you the same advice as the lord cardinal, that you defend nothing with obstinacy; but in all those things adduced against you, on credible testimony, that you submit yourself to the authority of this most holy council, with a becoming obedience. If you pursue this course, we will see to it that for our own sake, and that of our brother and the whole kingdom of Bohemia, you be discharged by the council itself, with good grace, and fitting penance and satisfaction. Otherwise, the leaders of the council shall have what they determine in regard to you; for we surely will never countenance your errors and stubbornness. Yea, with our own hands we will make ready the fire for you, sooner than suffer you to persist in that stubbornness which you have hitherto shown. It is our advice that you choose to abide by the judgment of the council."

Huss replied briefly to this address of the emperor, by expressing his deep gratitude for the clemency which he had shown in regard to the safe-conduct.

Here he was reminded that he had said nothing in regard to the charge of obstinacy. At the instance of Chlum, he then added, "I call God to witness, most indulgent emperor, that I never conceived the purpose of defending anything with extreme stubbornness, and that I came here of my own accord with this intent, that if any one could give me better instruction, I would unhesitatingly change my views." Upon this the soldiers led Huss forth to take him to his prison, and the assembly dispersed.

The language in which Sigismund addressed Huss

decisively refutes the false allegations made in the council in regard to the safe-conduct. It was, however, a mistake of the emperor to suppose that Huss received the safe-conduct previously to his leaving Prague. It was expedited on the eighteenth of October, and on the third of November Huss reached Constance. The document, as we have seen, met him on his way, at Nuremberg. The emperor supposed it had been received by him at Prague; and to all intents and purposes it was as valid as it would have been if he had received it there. The false pretence of the council was thus refuted.

In regard to the clemency which Sigismund asserted had been shown to Huss by the council, we readily perceive that here also he labored under a misapprehension. He had probably taken but little pains to inform himself of the treatment of the prisoner, and his views in regard to what an innocent man might claim of the council were evidently of the crudest kind. If calumny, hard usage, derision, and insult were clemency, then, as the "tender mercies of the wicked," they were "cruel" indeed.

The letters of Huss enable us to follow him from the public scene of audience to the solitude of his cell. Nothing that had hitherto been said or done had in the least shaken the strength of his convictions. He could but wonder at the ignorance, the incapacity, and prejudice that had been manifested on the part of the council. "Oh! if a hearing were granted me," so he wrote, "in which I could reply to such arguments as they might bring against the articles contained in my treatises, then do I believe that many of those who cry out would be compelled to be dumb. As God in heaven wills, so let it be."[1] Such was the firm and yet submissive spirit of the man, confident of the justice of his cause, but humbled in the dust before God. Again he writes, "Let all the Bohemian knights apply to the emperor and the council, and demand that, as the emperor and council had promised, he might in the next audience be briefly allowed to state what he had to retract, and at the same time give his explanations. Thus, if held to their own words, the emperor and the council would be forced to yield this privilege. "I will then," says Huss, "speak out the truth without reserve; for rather would I be consumed by the fagots, than kept so miserably concealed by them; for then all Christendom would learn what I finally said." Over confident, perhaps, of the result of such an appeal, and anxious above all for a fair opportunity to state his own case, Huss was willing to lay down his life as a sacrifice to the cause of truth. To Chlum, whom he called his most trusty patron, he wrote, "May God be your rewarder. I desire that you should not leave this council till you have seen the end." "Oh!" says he, "much would I prefer that you should see me led to the stake, than that I should be kept so treacherously in the dark. I still have hopes that Almighty God, through the merits of the saints, may deliver me out of their hands." Here we see his evident anticipations of a fatal result of the trial, enlivened, however, with some faint hopes of escape, and the truly martyr faith which lifted him far above

[1] Epis. xxxiv.

all human terrors. He felt that he was deeply wronged by the course which the council pursued, restraining him of the liberty of a full and free defence, and prejudging his case on the testimony of his bitter and relentless foes.

He begged his friends to let him know the hour at which, on the next morning, he should be led forth to trial. We can readily imagine the prayerful and meditative preparation to which previous hours would be devoted, while he sought from heaven a spirit of devotion to the cause of truth, and strength to sustain him in the hour of trial. He desired his friends, moreover, to pray for him, that if he must await death in the prison, he might endure with patience. He lamented that he had not been able to repay many of them for their services, and sent to request that they would be content, and excuse him on the ground of his want of ability. He knew not who was to repay those that had lent him money in Bohemia, unless it were the Master, Christ, on whose account they had lent it to him. Still he expresses the wish that some of the more wealthy would settle up his affairs and pay his poorer creditors. What a comment was this on that calumnious insult which had been offered him at Gottlieben, when an archbishop had named the value of his property as 70,000 florins, and the patriarch insisted that he was exceedingly rich! Base minds could not account for, or comprehend, the conduct of Huss without ascribing it to base motives.

What but the power of faith—what but the presence of his divine Master with him in his cell, could have sustained the spirit of the suffering Bohemian? He had no earthly resource upon which he might rely, or from which he could draw comfort and encouragement. The embittered malice of his adversaries had enlisted nearly the whole strength of the council upon their side. Skilfully had they appealed to old prejudices, and strongly had they bound together the conspiring elements of bigoted and partisan feeling. If there had been any whose secret sympathies were on the side of Huss, they were forced to conceal them. But if any, they were few in number. "They cry out, nearly all of them," said Huss, "like the Jews against our Master, Christ." Among the whole multitude of the clergy, he knew of but one friend, a Polish member, beside the one father who subsequently endeavored to effect a compromise between him and the council.

CHAPTER XXII.

THIRD AUDIENCE OF HUSS BEFORE THE COUNCIL. ARTICLES OF ACCUSATION.

Third Audience of Huss. — Thirty-Nine Articles. — How Drawn Up. — Language in Regard to his Recanting. — Charged with Writing Falsehoods to Bohemia. — The Book "On the Church." — Predestination. — No Outward Badge or Office Makes a Man a Member of the Church. — The Reprobate Never a Member of the Church of Christ. — Judas Never a True Disciple. — The Church Composed of the Predestinate Alone. — Peter Never the Head of the Church Catholic. — The Pope, Christ's or Antichrist's Vicar, According to his Life. — Simonists and Wicked Priests Err as to the Sacraments. — Papal Dignity an Imperial Gift. — No one Without Revelation can say he is Head of any Particular Church. — No Pope, unless Predestinated, the Head of any Church. — The Pope's Power Null if his Life is Vile. — His Holiness and his Revenues. — The Cardinals no Successors of the Apostles except by Holiness. — Heretics not to be Given Up to the Secular Arm. — The Civil Authority Should Constrain the Priesthood to Do their Duty. — Ecclesiastical not Scriptural Obedience. — Appeal to Christ Against Excommunication. — Cardinal D'Ailly. — Evil Men do Evil Deeds. — Questions and Replies. — The Priests Bound to Preach. — Cardinal of Florence. — Excommunication no Excuse for Silence. — Ecclesiastical Censures are of Antichrist. — Interdict not to be Imposed.

June 8, 1415.

The third audience of Huss was held in the Franciscan monastery on June 8th. The emperor was present, and along with Huss appeared his constant friends, Duba, Chlum, and Peter the Notary.

Upon the appearance of the prisoner, thirty-nine articles were read, which were ostensibly selected from his writings. To these were appended the answers which he had given them at his private examination in prison. Most of these articles—twenty-six out of the whole number—were said to have been extracted from his book *De Ecclesia.* Those passages which had been fairly selected, Huss acknowledged. The others had been drawn up by Paletz in such a manner that he disclaimed all responsibility for them.

In his prison[1] Huss was charged with having said that in case he should, while at Constance, be obliged with his mouth to retract any of his doctrines, it would be no retraction of the heart, inasmuch as what he had preached was the pure doctrine of Jesus Christ. The reply of Huss was, that this article was a tissue of falsehood, but that he had indeed written to his friends at Prague, exhorting them to pray to God in his behalf, and to remain steadfast in the doctrines of Jesus Christ, inasmuch as they could not but know that he had never taught the errors charged upon him by his enemies, nor must they be troubled if it should so happen that he should be crushed under the false testimony of his enemies.

They reproached him again for having written to Bohemia that the pope and emperor had granted him an honorable reception, and had sent two bishops to engage him in their interests. "It is a manifest falsehood," said Huss, "for how could I have written to Bohemia that I had been well received of the pope and the emperor, when on my arrival at Constance I wrote back that it was not known where the emperor was, and when I had been three weeks

[1] L'Enfant, 209. Mon. Hussi, i. 15. Van der Hardt, iv. 314.

in prison before he arrived? What great reason had I for writing back from my prison to Bohemia that I had been highly honored at Constance? It is plainly a sarcasm spread by my enemies, who think that I have been too highly honored by being imprisoned."

The following articles[1] are those which had been first presented to Huss in his prison, and which were now exhibited against him in the council. The order and arrangement of them had been somewhat changed, some things having been added and some struck out. Huss had drawn up a copy of them, with his answers to each, previous to his appearance before the council.

"I, John Huss, unworthy minister of Jesus Christ, master of arts, and bachelor of divinity, do confess that I have written a certain small treatise bearing the title, "*Of the Church*," a copy of which was shown me, in the presence of notaries, by the three commissioners of the council, the patriarch of Constantinople, the bishop of Castile, and the bishop of Lebus, the which commissioners, in reproof of the said treatise, delivered unto me certain articles, saying that they were drawn out of the said treatise, and were written in the same. Of which articles, the first is:

"1. 'There is but one holy Catholic church, which embraces all the predestinate.' This proposition I confess to be mine, and it is confirmed by the comment of St. Augustine upon the Gospel of John.

"2. 'St. Paul was never any member of the devil,

[1] Given in almost the same language by Van der Hardt, L'Enfant, Fox's Martyrs, and in the works of Huss, i. 15–26.

although he did many things like those committed by the enemies of the church. And St. Peter in like manner fell into the horrible sin of perjury and denial of his Master, by the permission of God, that he might the more firmly and steadfastly rise again, and be confirmed!' My answer is, this proposition is sufficiently proved in the book itself. For it is expedient that the predestinate should fall into such sins. Here it is plain that there are two ways of separating from the church. The first is not to perdition, as is the case with the elect. The other is to perdition, by which certain heretics are, by deadly sin, divided from the church. And yet, by the grace of God, they may return to the fold of our Lord Jesus Christ, as he says in John x., 'Other sheep I have which are not of this fold.' The same thing is also proved by Augustine on John, and in his ninth dist. on penitence.

"3. 'No part or member of the church is ever entirely separated from the body, because the grace of predestination which binds it thereto does not fail.' My answer is, this proposition is found in the book in these words: 'As the reprobate of the church go forth out of the same, yet were they never members thereof, since no part of it may finally fall away, inasmuch as the grace of predestination which binds it thereto fails not.' This is proved by the thirteenth chapter of First Corinthians, and the eighth chapter to the Romans. 'All things work together for good to them that love God.' And 'nothing shall separate us from the love of Christ.' All which is more fully treated of in the book itself.

"4. 'The predestinate, although not now in a state of grace, according to strict justice, is yet ever a member of the holy Catholic church.' I answer, this is an error, if it is to be understood of every one that is predestinate. For in the book at the beginning of the fifth chapter, speaking of the ways of belonging to the church, it stands written, 'there are some in the church only by an inadequate faith, and others according to predestination, as Christians predestinate, now in sin, but who shall return into a state of grace.'

"5. 'There is no place of dignity, nor any human election, nor any outward sign, that makes one a member of the holy Catholic church.' Answer. This proposition is thus expressed in the book. 'These sophistries will be detected by considering what it is to be in the church, and what it is to be a member or part of the church; and this membership is produced by predestination, which secures grace in the present and glory in the future world; and not by any place of dignity, any human election or outward sign. For the traitor Iscariot, notwithstanding his election by Christ, and the temporal gifts which were granted him for the office of an apostle, and notwithstanding his being reputed a true apostle of Christ by the people, yet never was a true disciple, but only a wolf in sheep's clothing, as Augustine asserts.'

"6. 'A reprobate man is never a member of holy mother church.' Answer. This passage is contained in the book of the church, and it is there sustained at length by the thirty-sixth Psalm, the fifth chapter of the Epistle to the Ephesians, and by St. Bernard, who says, that the church of Jesus Christ is his own body, more plainly than that which he delivered up to death. Moreover, in the fifth chapter of my book I have said, 'All will grant that the holy church is the Lord's threshing floor, in which, according to faith, the good and bad, the predestinate and the reprobate, the chaff and the wheat, are found, according to the exposition of St. Augustine.'

"7. 'Judas was never a true disciple of Jesus Christ.' Answer. I do confess it. It is proved by the fifth article above laid down, and by Augustine on penitence, dist. fourth, where he treats of that passage in the second chapter of John's first Epistle, 'they went out from us, for they were not of us.' 'He knew,' says he, 'from the beginning who they were that believed on him, and who should betray him, and said: therefore I said to you before, no one cometh unto me, except it be given him of my Father; and after this many of his disciples left him.' These are called disciples in the language of the gospel, and yet they were not truly such, for they did not abide in his word, as he said, 'If ye shall abide in my word, then are ye my disciples.' Inasmuch as they did not persevere as true disciples of Jesus Christ, they are not, however they seem, truly sons of God. They are not such with him, who knows what they shall be, and discerns the evil from the good. Such is the language of St. Augustine. It is equally plain that Judas could not be a true disciple of Christ while he continued in his avarice. For the Saviour himself had said, when Judas was present, as I suppose,

'Unless a man shall renounce all that he hath, he cannot be my disciple.' Inasmuch, therefore, as Judas did not renounce all, according to the intent of Christ, and so follow him, because he was a thief and a traitor, (John vi. 12,) it is plain from the words of Christ that Judas was not a true but a false disciple. For which reason, Augustine, (upon John,) showing how the sheep hear Christ, says, 'But what hearers, suppose we, are sheep? Judas heard, but he was a wolf; he followed the shepherd, but, disguised in sheep's clothing, sought to betray the shepherd.'

"8. 'The body of the predestinate, whether in a state of grace or not, compose the holy church, which has neither spot nor wrinkle, but is pure and immaculate, and is called by Jesus Christ, his own.' This article Huss acknowledged, and cited the words of his book in which they were contained. 'The church, in the third place, is understood and taken for the whole body of the faithful, whether they be in a state of grace according to present righteousness or not. And this thus becomes an article of faith, concerning which Paul speaks in Eph. v., "Christ loved the church, and gave himself for it," etc.. What believer can doubt, let us ask, but that *the church* here signifies all the predestinate, of whom we must believe the Catholic church is composed—the spouse of Christ, finally to be presented holy and without spot. Whence that holy Catholic church is objectively an article of faith, in which we are bound firmly to believe, according to the symbol, "I believe the holy Catholic church;" and of this church do Saints Augustine, Gregory, Jerome, and others speak.'

"9. 'Peter never was, nor is he, the head of the holy Catholic church.' Answer. This proposition is deduced from the words of my book as follows: 'It is granted, indeed, that Peter, from the corner-stone of the church (*a petra ecclesiæ*) which is Christ, had humility, poverty, firmness of faith, and consequent blessedness, not that by those words of scripture, "Upon this rock (*Petram*) I will build my church," Christ means to build his whole church militant upon the person of Peter; for on the Rock, which is Christ, from which Peter received his strength of faith, Christ would build his own church, since Christ is the head and foundation of the whole church,—not Peter.'

"10. 'If he who is called Christ's vicar, follows Christ in his life, then is he his vicar; but if he walks in an opposite course, then is he Antichrist's agent, contrary to Peter and to the Lord Jesus Christ, and the vicar of Judas Iscariot.' Answer. The words of my book are, 'If now he that is called Peter's vicar walks in these aforesaid paths of purity and virtue, we believe that he is truly his vicar, and chief pontiff of the church which he rules. But if he pursues opposite courses, then is he the agent of Antichrist, contrary to Peter and the Lord Jesus Christ.' Hence Bernard, in his letter to Pope Eugenius, writes, 'Thou delightest and walkest in great pride and arrogance, and art surrounded by all various splendor. What benefit do the sheep receive? If I durst say it, these are rather the pastures of devils than of sheep. This was not the practice of Peter, neither did Paul grow thus wanton. In these matters you have succeeded not Peter, but Constantine.' So speaks Bernard. Then follows in my book, 'If in his morals he lives the reverse of Peter, and gloats on mammon, then is he the vicar of Judas Iscariot, who loved the wages of iniquity, selling his Lord and Master, Christ.'"

At the reading of this last clause, the bishops and doctors tossed their heads in proud derision, and exchanged looks with one another that expressed their feelings better than words.

"11. 'All simonists, and priests of a dissolute life, do hold false opinions in regard to the seven sacraments, in regard to the keys and offices of the church, the censures, the rites and ceremonies, the worshipping of relics, indulgences, and the orders of the church.' Answer. The words of my book are, 'This abuse of power do they practice, who sell and buy and acquire, by simoniacal methods, the sacred orders of the church, making importunate exactions for the sacraments, living in avarice, lust, luxury, or whatsoever is shameful, and thus polluting the priesthood. For although in words they profess that they know God, yet in deeds they deny him, and consequently do not truly believe in God, and, as disobedient children, hold a false opinion of the sacraments of the church. And this is most evident, inasmuch as all such despise the name of God, according to that saying of Malachi, "Unto you, O priests, be it spoken, which do despise my name."'

"12. 'The papal dignity was derived from the

Roman emperors.' Answer. My words are, 'the pre-eminence and endowment of the pope emanated from the imperial power. And this is proved by the ninety-sixth "distinction;" for Constantine granted this privilege to the Roman pontiff, which was confirmed by other emperors, so that as Augustus was above other kings, so the Roman pontiff before other bishops should be called specially the father of the church, and this in regard to outward adornment and splendor and benefactions of the church. Notwithstanding which, the papal dignity has its source immediately in Christ in respect to the spiritual administration and rule of the church.'"

Here the reading was interrupted by the cardinal of Cambray. Turning to Huss, he said, "Yet in the time of Constantine the general council of Nice was held, in which the highest place was given to the bishop of Rome, although, for honor's sake, ascribed to the emperor. Why, then, do not you, John Huss, say that the papal dignity was derived from the council instead of the emperor?" Huss replied, that he attributed the elevation of the popes to Constantine only so far as the donation of this emperor was concerned.

"13. 'No one may reasonably affirm without revelation, either of himself or of any other, that he is the head of a particular church.' Answer. I confess this to be in any book, where it immediately follows, 'Although in a holy life he may hope and trust that he is a member of the holy Catholic church, the spouse of Christ; yet, according to the saying of the preacher, "No man knoweth whether he be worthy, and have deserved grace and favor, or hatred." And Luke xvii., "When ye have done all ye can, say that ye are unprofitable servants."'

"14. 'It ought not to be believed that the pope, whatsoever he be, may be the head of any particular church, unless he be predestinated and ordained of God.' Answer. I admit it. And thus it is proved: otherwise, a Christian must needs believe and confess a falsehood when saying that such or such a one is the chief of such a church, while the church may be deceived, as was the case in Agnes. The same thing also appears from St. Augustine.[1]

"15. 'The pope's power is null and void, unless in life and morals he be conformed to Christ or to Peter.' Answer. My words are, 'that one who is thus a vicar is bound to discharge the part and fill the place of his superior, from whom he has received vicarious power; he should, therefore, be conformed in life and morals to him whose place he occupies. For, otherwise, the authority he claims is null and void, unless there be this conformity, and thus with it the authority of him who appoints.'"

And John Huss here added before the council in explanation, that he regarded the power of such a pope as did not reflect the life of Christ, frustrate and void, with regard to the merit and reward that

[1] Both this article and the answer are somewhat obscure. The reply, as given by Fox, has no application whatever. Huss undoubtedly wished to maintain, from this case of the female pope Agnes—a case which the council seems not even to have disputed or questioned in the least—that one might bear the outward office and dignity of the pontificate, who was not really to be regarded or obeyed. The case he cited silenced all cavil; the story of Agnes was not then rejected, and the grave fathers of the council were constrained to let the article pass in silence.

should attend it, but not as respects the office itself. "But where," asked several, "is this gloss in your book?" "In my treatise against Stephen Paletz you will find it," replied Huss. Upon this the members of the council exchanged smiles of derision.

"16. 'The pope is accounted most holy, not because he is the vicar of St. Peter, but because he has great revenues.' Answer. In this my words have been perverted and mistaken; for thus I wrote, 'He is not most holy because he is the vicar of Christ, or because he has large revenues, but if he be the follower of Jesus Christ in humility, gentleness, patience, labor, and above all, charity.'

"17. 'The cardinals are not the manifest and true successors of the apostles of Jesus Christ, unless they live after the apostolic pattern, observing the commandments and counsels of Jesus Christ.' Answer. It is so stated in my book, and the proof of it is this: 'If they climb up any other way than by that first door, Jesus Christ, then are they thieves and robbers.''

Here the cardinal of Cambray interrupted the reading. "Behold," said he, "in respect to this and other articles already read, he has written things in his book more detestable than anything which the articles contain. Truly, John Huss, you have not observed discretion in your preaching and in your writings. Should you not have adapted your sermons to your audience? For what need or use was there of preaching to the people against the cardinals when none of them were present? It had been better to have told them their faults to their face than scandalously proclaim them to the laity." The cardinal did not presume to deny the truth of the article. His own writings as well as speeches had been as unsparing in regard to the whole Roman court as those of Huss. The whole charge was thus reduced by him virtually to one of imprudence. To this Huss replied, "Most reverend father, there were then present at my sermons priests and other learned men, and for their sake, and to bid them beware, my words were spoken." "You do an evil thing," said the cardinal, "for by this sort of sermons you tend to spread disturbance in the church."

"18. 'No heretic after ecclesiastical censure should be given up to the secular arm, to be subjected to capital punishment.' Answer. My words are, 'There should be shame for their cruel proceedings, specially as Jesus Christ, Bishop of both the Old and New Testaments, would not judge the disobedient by civil judgment, or put them to death.' This is plain from the twelfth chapter of Luke, from the second and eighth of John in regard to the woman taken in adultery, and from Matthew xviii., 'If thy brother shall sin against thee,' etc. So, therefore, I say that he who is a heretic ought first to be instructed kindly, justly, and humbly, from the Sacred Scriptures, and reasons drawn therefrom—the course pursued by Augustine and others who disputed with heretics. But if there are those who utterly refuse to desist from their errors after all suitable instruction has been given, then I say that they should be subjected to corporeal punishment."

Even this degree of toleration, short of what is now universally demanded, was too far in advance of the age to be allowed. The good sense of Huss, and the kindly and humane spirit in him which had been cherished by the study of Christian truth, would not allow him to approve any harsh methods of dealing with men charged with error. But this noble advance beyond the bigotry of his age was the occasion of a new charge of heresy. While Huss was stating his views, one of his books was taken up by his judges, who turned to a certain paragraph in which he inveighed against those who deliver over a heretic not yet convicted to the secular arm, saying, that "they are like the chief priests, scribes, and Pharisees, who said, as they delivered over Christ to Pilate, 'It is not lawful for us to put any one to death;' and yet, according to Christ himself, who said, 'therefore he who betrayed me to thee hath the greater sin,' they were greater murderers than Pilate himself." The reading of this passage produced much commotion in the council. Indisputably true and just as the sentiment was, it seemed to be placing a bar between the bigots of the council and their destined victim. It was a picture of the very course which they intended to pursue, presented in an odious but true light. Turning to Huss, some asked, "Who are they that are like the Pharisees?" a question equivalent, doubtless, to that of the traitor asking at the last supper, *Is it I?* But Huss was at no loss for a reply; "All those," said he, "who give up to the civil sword any innocent man, as the scribes and Pharisees did Christ." "No, no!" cried they; "but you here speak of the doctors themselves." Upon this the bishop of Cambray repeated his stale attempt to work upon the prejudices of the council. "Surely," said he, "they who drew up the articles have proceeded with great gentleness, for his writings contain things more atrocious still." Such was the expressive comment of one of the most enlightened and able cardinals of the church, on a doctrine which at the present day no man, unless steeped in inquisitorial bigotry, ventures to dispute.

"19. 'The nobles of the world should constrain the priests to the observance of the law of Christ.' Answer. My words are, 'Those of our party, in the fourth place, do insist and preach that the church militant is composed of parts, according as Christ has ordained, viz., of the priests of Christ who truly keep his law, and of the nobles of the world, who should constrain to the observance of Christ's ordinances, and of the common people also, ministering to each of these parts according to the law of Christ.'

"20. 'Ecclesiastical obedience is an obedience invented by the priests of the church, without any express authority of the Sacred Scriptures.' Answer. I confess to these words as written in my book. 'It is to be remarked that obedience is threefold—spiritual, civil, and ecclesiastical. The spiritual is that which is due simply on the ground of the law of God, according to which the apostles lived, and all Christians are bound to live. The civil is that which is due to the laws of the state. The ecclesiastical is that which has been devised by the priests of the church without the express authority of scripture. The first kind of obedience wholly excludes from itself all evil, both on the part of him who commands and him who obeys; according to Deut. xxiv., "Thou shalt do whatsoever the priests of the house of Levi shall teach you, according as I have commanded them."'

"21. 'He that is excommunicated by the pope, yet who, declining the judgment of the pope and general council, appeals to Christ, is preserved safe from the harm of all excommunication.' Answer. This proposition I do not acknowledge, but I did complain in my book of the many aggravated charges brought against me and mine, and that I had been refused an audience in the papal court. For when I had appealed from one pope to his successor, it was of no advantage to me, and to appeal from the pope to the council would be too tedious an affair, and attempting an uncertain security against the charge. For this reason I finally appealed to Jesus Christ, the Head of the church. For he is so much the more to be preferred to the pope in deciding causes, inasmuch as he cannot err, nor deny justice to him who asks it righteously, nor, in accordance with his own established law, can he condemn an innocent man."

Here the cardinal of Cambray addressed Huss: "Would you be above Paul, who appealed to the emperor and not to Christ?" "And am I," replied Huss, "though I were the first to do this thing, to be accounted a heretic? And yet Paul did not appeal to the emperor of his own motion, but through the revealed will of Christ who appeared to him and said, 'Be thou firm and constant, for thou must needs go to Rome!'" Huss went on to repeat the substance of his views in regard to appealing to Christ, but his statements were met by the open derision of the council.

"22. 'The deeds of an evil man are evil, of a virtuous man, virtuous.' Answer. My words are, 'It is further to be remarked, that human actions are directly divided into two classes, virtuous and vicious. This is evident inasmuch as, if a man is virtuous and performs any act, the act is virtuous; and if he is vicious, whatever he does is vicious. Because as vice, which is called crime, that is, mortal sin, infects universally the acts of its subject, that is, man,—so virtue vivifies all the acts of the virtuous man, insomuch that, being in a state of grace, he is said to be prayerful and deserving, even while he sleeps, as in some way still working, as says Augustine, as well as Gregory and others. And this is evident from Luke vi., "If thine eye," that is, thine intention, "is single," undepraved by the blinding power of sin, "thy whole body," that is, the sum of thy actions, "shall be full of light," or pleasing to God. "But if thine eye be evil, thy whole body shall be full of darkness." And 2 Cor. x., "Do all things to the glory of God." And 1 Corinthians, in the last chapter: "Let all your deeds be done in charity." Whence the whole course of life, through charity, becomes virtuous, and, without charity, becomes vicious. And this may be proved from Deut. xxiii., where God says to his people, that if they will keep his commandments, they shall be blessed in the house and in the field, going out and coming in, lying down and rising up. But if they will not keep them, they shall be cursed in all these things. The same thing is evident from Augustine upon the Psalm, where he infers that the good man glorifies God in whatever he does. And when Gregory says that the sleep of the saints is not without merit, how much more that action while proceeds from the purpose of the will, and which consequently is virtuous? On the other hand, in regard to him who is in a state of criminality, that holds good which took place under the law,—whatever he shall touch shall be unclean. On this, moreover, that passage bears which was above cited from Malachi. Gregory the First, *in ques.*, says, "We therefore pollute the bread when we unworthily approach the altar, and we drink the pure blood while ourselves steeped in impurity." Augustine, upon Psalm cxlvi., says, "If by the excess of voracity beyond the due bound of nature, you neglect to restrain yourself and choke yourself with drunkenness, however loudly your tongue may sound the praise of God's grace, you life blasphemes against him."' "

When this article had been read, the cardinal of Cambray rejoined, "But scripture says that 'we all sin;' and again, 'if we shall say we have no sin, we deceive ourselves, and the truth is not in us.'" "But," said Huss, "scripture there speaks of venial sins, which do not exclude necessarily virtuous habits, but are tolerated along with them." Here a certain master, an Englishman named William, interposed: "But these sins are not tolerated along with those habits by any principle morally good." Huss cited again the passage from Augustine on the cxlvi. Psalm. "But what," cried they all at once, "has that to do with it?"

"23. 'A priest of Christ living according to his law, having a knowledge of scripture and a gift for edifying the people, ought to preach, notwithstanding any pretended excommunication. And again, if a pope or other prelate commands a priest in such circumstances not to preach, he ought not to obey the command.' Answer. My words are these: 'Notwithstanding any pretended excommunication, whether threatened or inflicted, a Christian should keep the commandments of Christ.' This is plain from the language of Peter and other apostles when they say, 'We ought to obey God rather than men.' From this it follows, that a priest of Christ who lives according to his law, having fitness by knowledge of scripture, etc., ought to preach notwithstanding any pretended excommunication. This is evident, inasmuch as (Acts v.) priests are commanded to preach the word of God. We, I say, have been commanded of God to preach and testify to the people. This is evident also from many other passages from the Sacred Scriptures, and from the holy fathers which were cited in my book. The second part of the article follows in my book in these words: 'From this it is plain, that for a priest to preach, and for the rich to give alms, are not matters of choice, but command. It is plain, moreover, that if a pope or other prelate should forbid a priest in such circumstances to preach, or a rich man to give alms, the subject of command should not obey.'"

Huss added, moreover, "In order that you may rightly understand me, a pretended excommunication, as I call it, is one that I regard as unjust and discordant to the rules to be observed, as well as opposed to the commands of God. A priest fitted to preach successfully, should not on account of it cease to preach, or be in fear of damnation."

The members of the council then objected to him that he had called such an excommunication a benediction. "And in truth," replied Huss, "I say the same thing now, that excommunication, by which any one is unjustly excommunicate, is a benediction to him in the sight of God, according to that language of the prophet, 'I will curse your blessings;' and again, 'they shall curse, but thou shalt bless.'"

Upon this the cardinal of Florence, who kept a notary at his side to minute down whatever he should direct, said to Huss, "Yet there are canons which show that even an unjust excommunication is to be dreaded." "It is true," said Huss, "for I remember that there are laid down eight causes why excommunication should be dreaded." "No more than that?" asked the cardinal. "It may well be that there are more," answered Huss; and here the discussion on this point rested.

"24. 'Every one who receives by special commandment the office of preacher, and thus enters upon the priesthood, should keep the charge committed to him, notwithstanding a pretended excommunication.' Answer. My words are these: 'From what has been said, therefore, it is plain that whoever, by special command, shall take the office of preacher, and enter upon the priesthood, should obey the charge given him, notwithstanding a pretended excommunication.' And again, 'With no Catholic should it be suffered to be brought into question, that a man sufficiently instructed is bound to advise the ignorant, to teach those that are in doubt, to correct the lawless, to avenge the injured, as well as discharge other works of mercy. Since, moreover, he who is sufficiently provided to minister alms for the body is bound to do it, much more does this hold true (Matt. xxv.) with respect to spiritual alms.'

"25. 'Ecclesiastical censures are such as are of Antichrist, which the clergy has devised to exalt itself and enslave the people; if the laity will not obey the clergy in their every wish, they multiply their avarice, protect malice, and prepare the way for Antichrist. But it is plain proof that these censures proceed from Antichrist, which in their processes are called fulminations, in which the clergy proceed especially against those who make bare the iniquity of Antichrist, usurping to themselves, to the highest degree, the ecclesiastical powers. These things are found in the last chapter of the book on the church.' Answer. I deny the form of statement. Yet this subject is fully laid down in chap. xxiii."

During the examination, members of the council—some of them at least—were busy in searching out not only the passages referred to, but others of a confirmatory character. Some bearing upon the last article were discovered, undoubtedly pointed out by the more bitter enemies of Huss, which were regarded as still more paradoxical and offensive than what had been cited. These also were read, thus bringing out against Huss passages which he had no opportunity to verify or examine. "Surely," exclaimed the cardinal of Cambray, as the passages were read, "these things are much more aggravated and scandalous than those recited in the articles."

"26. 'Interdict ought not to be imposed upon a people, inasmuch as Christ, the highest priest, neither on account of John the Baptist, nor for any injuries that were offered to himself, imposed an interdict.' Answer. These are my words: 'For I complain that for one priest's sake an interdict is imposed, and thus all the good cease from praising God. But Christ, the highest priest, when that prophet, than whom a greater has not been born of women, was detained in prison, did not impose an interdict. Nor when Herod had beheaded him, nay when he himself was stripped, beaten, blasphemed by the soldiers, scribes, Pharisees, etc., not even then did he inflict his curse, but he prayed for them, just as he had taught his disciples to do in Matt. v.; and following out this doctrine, the first vicar of Christ said, 1 Pet. ii., "In this are ye called, because Christ suffered for us, leaving us an example that we should follow in his steps, who, when he was cursed, cursed not again." And Paul, (Rom. xii.,) pursuing the same thought, says, "Bless them that hate you."'"

Numerous were the passages which had been selected from the writings of Huss, which were arraigned as objectionable. But the attention of the council was now directed to the articles extracted from the treatise against Paletz.

CHAPTER XXIII.

THIRD AUDIENCE CONTINUED.

Seven Articles from the Treatise of Huss Against Paletz. — A Pope or Prelate in Deadly Sin is, *ipso facto*, no Pope or Prelate. — Embarrassing Subject for the Council. — The Grace of Predestination Unites the Church and each of its Members to its Head. — A Wicked Pope a Son of Perdition. — A Wicked Pope or Prelate is no Pastor, but a Thief and a Robber. — Objections. — The Pope not "Most Holy." — A Pope Legitimately Elected, if of Evil Life, Enters not by the Door. — Paletz's Remarks. — Reply of Huss. — The Condemnation of the Forty-five Articles of Wickliffe Unjust. — Six Articles from the Treatise Against Stanislaus. — A Majority of Electoral Votes Cannot Make a Man Christ's Vicar. — A Reprobate Pope is not the Head of the Church. — Christ Sufficient to Rule His Church. — Remarks of Huss upon it. — Peter was not Universal Pastor. — The Apostles Ruled the Chuch without a Pope. — Remark of an Englishman. — How to Deal with Huss. — Conclusions. — Cardinal D'Ailly Addresses Huss. — Some Reluctant to Doom Huss to the Flames. — He is Urged to Submit. — The English Deputation. — Gerson. — Huss States his Purpose and Desire. — Cardinal D'Ailly Perverts its Meaning and Demands Submission. — Reply of Huss. — Pleads Conscience. — The Emperor's Advice. — Terms of Submission. — Reply of Huss. — Demand Repeated. — The Priest in Silk Cassock. — Reply of Huss. — Paletz. — The other Works of Huss. — His Conscientiousness. — Insists on a Further Hearing. — Slanderous Interpretation of a Sentence of the Pope. — Exhaustion of Huss. — False Charge in Regard to the Three Men Beheaded at Prague. — Paletz. — Paletz and Nason on the Inflammatory Sermons of Huss. — The Oxford Letter. — Pause in the Proceedings. — Protestation of Paletz. — Of Causis. — Of Huss. — Remark of Cardinal D'Ailly. — Disposition of Paletz. — The Council Adjourns. — Chlum Cheers Huss. — Conclusions and Policy of the Emperor.

June 8, 1415.

From the treatise of Huss against Paletz seven articles were extracted, which were now exhibited, (June 8,) along with the others, against the prisoner.

1. "If pope, bishop, or prelate be in mortal sin, then is he no longer pope, bishop, or prelate." Answer. "This article I acknowledge, and refer you to Saints Augustine, Jerome, Chrysostom, Gregory, Cyprian, and Bernard, who further say that he who is in a state of mortal sin is not a true Christian, much less pope or bishop. Of whom it is said, Amos viii., 'They have reigned, yet not by me; they became princes, and I knew them not.' But yet we grant that a wicked pope, bishop, or priest is an unworthy minister of the sacrament, through whom God baptizes, consecrates, or otherwise works to the benefit of the church. And this point is more largely handled in the book, with reference to the authority of the holy doctors. Yea, he who is in mortal sin is not worthily king before God, as is plain from 1 Kings xv., where God, by Samuel, declares to Saul, 'Because thou hast rejected my word, I will reject thee from being king.'"

While this article was undergoing discussion, the emperor was standing in the recess of a window of the building, in conference with the Elector Palatine and the Burgrave of Nuremberg. Their conversation was in regard to Huss. The prejudices of the emperor had been already excited to an unusual degree, and he at length let fall the expression that there never was a more dangerous heretic. It was at this moment that Huss was speaking in regard to the unworthy king of Israel, and the occasion it afforded for confirming the prejudices of the emperor was one which the council was not willing to lose. He was therefore called, and Huss was bid to repeat what he had just said. He at once complied, making a slight correction. The emperor, to the disappointment of the enemies of Huss, quietly replied, "There is no man who lives without sin." The Cardinal of Cambray, however, showed more excitement and passion. In an angry tone he cried out, "Was it not enough that, contemning the ecclesiastical state, you have tried to spread confusion through it by your writings and teachings? Now, it seems, you are attempting to cast down kings from their dignities." Paletz, moreover, felt himself called upon to maintain his own ground. He began to cite authorities by which he would prove that Saul was still king even when he had heard the words of Samuel, and that on this ground David had forbidden any one to slay him—not on account of his personal holiness, for he had none, but on account of his anointing as king. Huss commenced his reply by quoting Cyprian as saying that *he* could by no means claim the Christian name who did not resemble Christ in his conduct. "But," exclaimed Paletz, "see how he stultifies himself in saying what is nothing to the purpose. For even though any one be not a true Christian, is he not therefore a true pope, bishop, or king, inasmuch as these are but the titles of offices, while Christian is a name implying moral worth? And so any one may be a true pope, bishop, or king, even though he be not a true Christian." But here again Paletz found himself going too far. The old doctrine of the church, which warranted the crusades, and added one of its most precious jewels to the crown of papal prerogative, was that an infidel king had no authority from God to reign, and that he might justly be deposed. How then could one not a Christian retain his office? But Huss was as ready to meet Paletz with the tongue as with the pen. An illustration of the matter occurred to him which he promptly used. "If, then," said he, with admirable tact, and with a logic pertinent to the matter in hand—"If, then, John XXIII. was true pope, why did you depose him from his office?" The question was one to embarrass the council, and the emperor came to its relief. "But the masters of the council," said he, "did of late agree on this very point, that he was true pope, but on account of his notorious wickedness, by which he scandalized the holy church of God and wasted its energies, he was deposed from his office." It would have been impolitic for Huss to argue with an emperor. And yet it would have been easy for him to have exposed the double edge of his argument, worthy of commendation in after days by Jesuit murderers of kings, as well as Puritan judges that passed sentence on an English monarch. John Gerson, at least, charged to secure from the council the condemnation of the regicide principles of John Petit, might well have listened uneasily to the imperial logic. But the authority of the speaker forbade all comment.

2. "The grace of predestination is the bond by which the body of the church and each of its members is indissolubly united to its head." Answer. "I confess to this, that it is my doctrine, and it is proved by the text from Rom. viii., 'Who shall sep-

arate us from the love of Christ?' And John x., 'My sheep hear my voice, and I know them, and I give unto them eternal life, and they shall never perish, neither shall any one pluck them out of my Father's hand.' This connection of the body of the church with Christ its Head is spiritual, not carnal. I understand by the church the body of the predestinate."

No reply seems to have been offered to this article. The doctrine which it contained is one on which the church of Rome, and in all probability the council, were divided. Any attempt at discussing it might have seriously affected the unanimity of the proceedings.

3. "If a pope is wicked, or, more, a reprobate, then, like the apostle Judas, he is a devil, a thief, and a son of perdition, not the head of the holy church militant; since he is not, in fact, a *member* of the militant church." Answer. "My words are as follows: 'If a pope is wicked, and especially if he be a reprobate, then is he as Judas was, a devil, a thief, and a son of perdition. How, then, is he the *head* of the holy church militant, when he is not even *a member* of the holy church militant? For if he be a member of the holy church, then would he be a member of Christ; and if a member of Christ, then would he cleave to Christ through the grace of predestination and present righteousness, and he would be of one spirit with God, as the apostle reasons, (1 Cor. vi.,) where he says, 'Know ye not your bodies are the members of Christ?'"

4. "A pope or prelate who is wicked or reprobate

is not truly a pastor, but a thief and robber." Answer. "The text of my book is as follows: 'If he be wicked, then is he a hireling, of whom Christ says, "He is not the shepherd, neither are the sheep his; therefore, when he seeth the wolf coming, he fleeth, and leaveth the sheep." And so indeed every wicked and reprobate one does; such a wicked and reprobate pope or prelate, therefore, is not a shepherd, but is truly a thief and robber,' as is more fully shown in the book."

Huss perceived the ease with which his enemies might pervert the meaning of his words, and thus renew against him the charge which had excited the anger of the Cardinal of Cambray. He therefore added the remark—"I limit all that I have said in regard to such persons to the question of their worthiness, and it is in this sense that they are not truly or properly popes or shepherds in the sight of God. But as it respects the mere office or standing among men, they are popes, pastors, priests." Upon this, a monk who sat behind where Huss was standing, and who, clothed throughout in silk, could have little fancied the simplicity of the primitive pastors, arose to speak. "My masters," said he, "see to it that Huss do not deceive himself and you by such glosses as these. For perhaps they are not in his book. For I lately had a dispute with him on those articles, in which I said myself that a wicked pope is not true pope as respects worthiness, but as respects office he is. He is now therefore making use of those glosses which he has heard from me. He does not draw them out of his own book." "But," said Huss, turning round to address the monk in person, "did you not hear that so it was read out of my book? And this very matter is clearly illustrated in the case of John XXIII., who may be seen as he was, whether true pope or true thief and robber." But the point was a sore one to the council. They were forced into a position which the friends of the Duke of Burgundy could accept more readily than Gerson might like. The cardinals and bishops, turning one to another, as if to give mutual assurance, said that John XXIII. was true pope, and treated Huss with derision.

5. "The pope is not, nor ought to be called *Most Holy*, even as respects office, for on this ground a king also might be called most holy. Even torturers, lictors, and devils might, for the same reason, be called most holy." Answer. "My words are different. I spoke thus: 'The objector must needs say that if any one is most holy father, then he most holily observes *that* paternity; and if he is most wicked father, then he keeps *that* paternity. Likewise, if he is most holy bishop, he is best bishop; and when he says that pope is the name of office, then it follows that that man, a pope wicked and reprobate, is a most holy man, and consequently, as respects that office, is best. And since any one cannot be best, as it respects office, unless he discharge that office in the best manner, it follows that a wicked and reprobate pope does not discharge the duties of his office in the best manner. For he cannot discharge them so, unless he is morally good. Matt. xii. "How can ye speak good, when ye yourselves are

evil?"' And then it is added afterward, 'And if by reason of his office the pope is called most holy, why, by reason of his office, should not the king be called most holy, since, according to Augustine, the king represents the Deity of Christ, as the priest does his humanity. And why should not judges, yea, executioners, etc., not be called holy, when they hold the office of ministering to the church of Jesus Christ?' These, with many things beside to the same purpose, are to be found in the book. And I do not know," added Huss, "the ground on which I should call the pope most holy, when of Christ only it is said, 'Thou alone art holy; thou art Lord alone, etc.;' with great reason would I call Him Most Holy."

To the remarks of Huss on this point, no reply appears to have been made by any member of the council.

6. "If a pope lives in a manner opposed to Christ, even though lawfully and canonically elected as it respects human choice, yet has he climbed up some other way than by Christ." Answer. "The language I used is this: 'If the pope lives in a manner opposed to Christ, in pride, avarice, etc., how is it that he does not climb up into the sheepfold by some other way than the humble door, the Lord Jesus Christ? And granting, as you say, that he might ascend by lawful election, which I call election made first of all by God, he would not stand in his office by the authority of the common human ordinance, so as to climb up some other way. Now, Judas Iscariot was orderly and lawfully elected to the office of bishop, as Christ says in John vi., and yet he climbed up some

other way into the sheepfold, and was a thief, a devil, and a son of perdition. Did he not ascend up some other way when the Saviour said of him, "He who eateth my bread shall lift up his heel against me?" The same thing is proved by the letter of Bernard to pope Eugenius.'"

Paletz hitherto seems for the most part to have listened quietly. But his equanimity was now disturbed. The old spirit of controversy was awakened anew, and the disputant and the persecutor were one. "See," cried he, "see this madness and folly! For what can be more mad than to say Judas was elected by Christ, and yet climbed up some other way than by Christ?" "But yet," replied Huss, "both are true. He was elected by Christ, and yet climbed up some other way, for he was a thief, a devil, and a son of perdition." "But," asked Paletz, "cannot one be orderly and lawfully elected to the papacy or the episcopate, and afterward lead an unchristian life? In such a case he would not climb up some other way." "I say," answered Huss, "that whoever enters upon the episcopate, or like offices, through simony, not with the purpose of laboring in the church of God, but of living in delicacy, pleasure, luxury, and pride, such a one climbs up some other way, and, according to the gospel, is a thief and a robber."

7. "The condemnation of the forty-five articles of Wickliffe is unreasonable and unjust, and the ground alleged for it is fictitious, viz., that none of them is catholic, but each of them is heretical, erroneous, or scandalous." Answer. "In my book I wrote

thus: 'The forty-five articles of Wickliffe were condemned on the ground that no one of them was catholic, but each of them either heretical, or erroneous, or scandalous. O doctor! where is your proof? You feign a cause for the condemnation which you do not prove,' and more in the treatise to the same effect."

Then said the Cardinal of Cambray, "John Huss, you said that you would not defend any of Wickliffe's errors; and now it is plain, from your books, that you have publicly advocated his articles." "Most reverend father," replied Huss, "I say the same thing now that I said before—that I will not defend the errors of John Wickliffe, or of any other man. But inasmuch as it seemed to me to be against conscience to consent to their unqualified condemnation without proof against them from scripture, on this account I was not willing to consent to their condemnation; and because, moreover, the ground of it, which is of a complex nature, cannot be verified of each of them in its several parts."

Six other articles charged against Huss were now adduced. They contained selections from his treatise against Stanislaus. They were as follows:

1. "The fact that the electors, or a majority of them, give their consent *viva voce*, according to the practised usage, to the choice of any person, does not legitimately elect him, or prove that he is on this account the plain and true successor of Christ, or Peter's vicar in the apostolic office, but only his more abundant labors to the proper good of the church, while he has from God a grace more eminent for this

end." Answer. "In my book it is as follows: 'It stands in the power of unworthy electors to choose a woman to an ecclesiastical office, as is plain from the case of Agnes, called pope Joan, who occupied the papacy for two years and more. Yea, it is in their power to elect a robber, thief, or devil, and consequently they may elect Antichrist! And it is in their power to elect, through motives of love, avarice, or hatred, a person to whom God cannot grant approval. And thus it is plain that, not from the simple fact that the electors, or a majority of them, *viva voce*, give their assent to any person, according to human usage, is this person, on such grounds, legitimately elected, nor is he therefore the evident successor or vicar of the apostle Peter, or of any one else in ecclesiastical office. Therefore they who in a manner most accordant with scripture, yet without the direction of revelation, proceed to the matter of election, pronounce in favor of him that is elected only on probable grounds. Whence, whether the choice of the electors be good or ill, it is the works of the elected which we must credit, for according as any one in a worthy manner promotes the welfare of the church, he has the grace from God, the more abundantly bestowed to this very end.'"

2. "A reprobate pope is not the head of the holy church of God." Answer. "As I wrote in my book, 'I should be glad to receive a satisfactory reason from the doctor, why that question is of an infidel nature, viz., if the pope is reprobate, how is he the head of the holy church? The truth cannot suffer by argument. Was it reasoning against the faith

when Christ asked of the scribes and Pharisees, Matt. xii., "Ye generation of vipers, how can ye, being evil, speak that which is good?" And now, behold, I ask the scribes, if the pope is reprobate and of viper brood, how is he the head of the holy church? Let the scribes and Pharisees answer,—those, namely, who exercised a controlling influence in the council at Prague. For it is more possible that a reprobate should speak that which is good, since he may be at present in a state favoring it, than be the head of the holy church of God. Moreover, the Saviour, John v., in arguing with the Jews, asked, "How can ye believe, who receive glory one of another, and seek not the glory which cometh from God only?" And I, in like manner, ask, How can a pope, if he be reprobate, be the head of the church of God, while he receives glory from the world, and seeks not the glory that comes from God only? For it is more possible that a reprobate pope should believe, than that he should be the head of the church of God when he receives glory from the world.'"

3. "There is not a particle of evidence to make it appear that there should be but one head in spiritual matters, ruling over the church, yet ever conversant with the church militant." Answer. "I confess it. For what a consequence is this! The king of Bohemia is the head of the Bohemian realm, *therefore* the pope is the head of the whole church militant. For Christ in spiritual matters is the head, ruling the church militant, much more necessarily than the emperor must needs rule in temporal matters. Inasmuch as Christ, who sits at the right hand of the

Father, must necessarily rule over the church militant as its supreme head, and there is no sign of evidence that there must be one head in spiritual matters ruling the church, who is ever to be conversant with the church militant, unless some infidel would heretically assert that the church militant should have here a permanently abiding city, nor seek one to come. And further, it is made plain in the book how illogical is the proof from analogy of a reprobate pope being the head of the church, to a reprobate king being the head of the Bohemian realm."

4. "Christ would rule his church better by means of his true disciples scattered through the world, without such monstrous heads." Answer. "In the book it is as follows: 'And though the doctor say that the body of the church is sometimes headless (acephalous), we nevertheless truly believe Jesus Christ to be head over all his church, unfailingly ruling it, infusing into it energy and sensibility even to the day of judgment. Nor can the doctor give a reason why the church in the time of Agnes, for two years and five months, was without a head, living, in respect to many of the members of Christ in a state of grace; but for the same reason it might also be without a head for a long course of years, since Christ, without these monstrous heads, might better rule his church by means of his true disciples scattered throughout the world.'"

Upon this there was a shout,—"Now, behold, he is turning prophet!" Members of the council took occasion to sneer at the prisoner, and ridicule his words.

Undisturbed by the interruption, Huss proceeded.

"But I say that the church in the times of the apostles was infinitely better ruled than it is now. And where is the inconsistency, or indignity to Christ, in saying that he would rule the church better—without those monstrous heads that there were, but just now—through his own true disciples? And at present we have no such head at all, and yet Christ does not fail to rule his church."

The argument of Huss was irrefutable by those to whom it was addressed. It was, therefore, treated with—not argument, but—derision.

5. "Peter was not universal pastor or shepherd of the sheep of Christ; much less is the pope of Rome." Answer. "Such was not the language which I employed. In my book it is as follows: 'It is plain, in the second place, from the words of Christ, that he did not define the whole world to Peter for his jurisdiction, nor so much as a single province, and in like manner neither to the other apostles. Some of them, nevertheless, preached the gospel through many regions, others in more limited districts, passing from place to place. This was the case with Paul, who labored more than they all, and who visited in person, and converted many provinces. Whence to each of the apostles, or his vicar, as much people or territory was committed as they converted or confirmed in the Christian faith. So much might suffice, and there was no restriction of jurisdiction save from their own insufficiency.'"

6. "The apostles and faithful priests of the Lord have ably ruled the church in all things necessary to salvation, before the office of the pope was introduced."

"And so too might they possibly do still, even if there were no pope to the day of judgment," said Huss.

Here again the cry was, on the part of the council, "Lo, he is turning prophet!"

But Huss calmly proceeded. "Yes, it is true," said he, "that the apostles ably ruled the church before the introduction of the papacy, and assuredly to better purpose than it is ruled now. And their faithful followers might do the same. And, behold, now we have no pope, and perhaps this state of things may yet continue a year, or even more."

This article disposed of, a certain Englishman, turning to Huss, addressed him thus: "John Huss," said he, mixing a personal taunt with a skilfully devised accusation, "you pride yourself upon these writings, claiming to be their author, but these views are those of John Wickliffe, rather than yours."

Thus closed the reading of the articles of accusation laid to the charge of Huss. A discussion now arose in the council in regard to the steps to be taken with the prisoner. At last the method of procedure to be pursued was resolved upon. Three positions were taken in regard to Huss. In the first place, he was to confess that he had erred; secondly, he was required to promise that he would never teach again the same doctrines; and thirdly, he should be required to recant the articles charged against him.

The Cardinal of Cambray now addressed Huss. "You have heard," said he, "of how many atrocious crimes you are accused. It is your duty now to consider what course you will take. Two proposals are submitted to you by the council, one or the other of which you must accept. The first is, that you suppliantly give in your submission to the judgment and sentence of the council, and endure, without remonstrance, whatever shall be determined in regard to you by the common voice. If you shall take this course, we shall, out of regard to the honor of his most merciful majesty, the emperor here present, and his brother, the king of Bohemia, as well as for your own sake and your salvation, proceed toward you with all due kindness and humanity. But if you still purpose to defend some of these articles which have been laid before us, and demand a further audience, we will not deny you the privilege. But you should reflect that here are so many men, and of such learning, and have such strong and efficient arguments to urge against your articles, that I fear lest any further wish to defend them could be carried out only at your great inconvenience and danger. I say this to you by way of admonition, and not as a judge."

Undoubtedly the cardinal spoke the policy of the council when he advised Huss to submit. There were some things in the prospect of burning such a man not altogether agreeable. It might not tend to quiet the troubles of Bohemia. It would be undoubtedly somewhat distasteful to the emperor. It would be more for the glory of the council to have a man like Huss acknowledge, to his own confusion, its orthodox supremacy and judicial infallibility. The show of moderation in the cardinal's advice to Huss must, however, have appeared in the prisoner's eyes as the bitterest irony. He could see, as well as the cardinal, that his enemies in the council were in the immense majority, and that it was useless to discuss further with men, "enlightened" as they were by the common interest they had in suppressing a dangerous assailant. His own apprehensions by this time must have taught him to prepare for submission to the council, or for martyrdom.

When the cardinal had given his advice, others seized the occasion to urge Huss to submission. Some of them, doubtless, were led to do this by a genuine sympathy for the prisoner, and a conviction that, with all his errors, as they viewed them, he was a man of honest intention and real ability. Many of the English deputation undoubtedly thirsted for his blood, and the taste already acquired by them in the execution of the writ *de heretico comburendo*, would have been gratified by another sacrifice that should testify their abhorrence of Wickliffe. But there were others who, in listening to Huss, must have been disarmed of their prejudices. Gerson had been one of the bitterest in his invectives against him, but his voice was not heard again on his trial; he listened and reflected on what he heard: and it is a just comment on the change that must have been wrought in his feelings, that he afterward publicly declared that if Huss had been properly defended he would not have been condemned.

To these exhortations addressed to him, Huss was not indifferent. He had not the false pride that would lead him to a stubborn persistence in any doctrine or position which he could be convinced was false. In a submissive tone, and a manner corresponding to his words, he said, "Most reverend fathers, I have already said, repeatedly, that I came here freely, of my own choice, not to defend anything with stubbornness, but if in any point whatsoever my views were incorrect, to submit to be instructed with a cheerful readiness. I ask, therefore, that I may have further opportunity to declare my views, in behalf of which, unless I bring plain and sufficient proof, I will readily submit to your direction in all respects, as you require." Upon this, some member of the council shouted, at the top of his voice, "Notice the sophistry of his words. *Direction*, he says, not *correction* or *decision*." "Yes," replied Huss, "as you wish it,—direction, correction, or decision; I protest before God that I spoke in all sincerity of mind."

"Well, then," said the Cardinal of Cambray, mistranslating—perhaps intentionally—the language of Huss, "since you subject yourself to the instruction and favor of the council, this is the decree approved, first, by sixty doctors, of whom some have left, though their place has been supplied by others, and then by the whole council, without an opposing voice: first, that you confess that you have erred in those articles which have been alleged against you; then that you promise, on oath, not to think or teach any of those errors for the future; and finally, that you publicly recant all those articles."

Many members of the council beside the cardinal, urged Huss to pursue this course. It remained to be seen what effect these various persuasions would have upon his mind. "Again, I say," he replied, to the exhortations addressed him, "that I am ready to be instructed and set right by the council. But in the name of him who is the God of us all, I ask and beseech of you this one thing, that I may not be forced to that which, my conscience repugnant to it, I cannot do under peril of the loss of my soul—recant, by oath, all the articles charged against me. For I remember reading, in a book of Catholic authority, that to abjure is to renounce an error previously held. Since, then, many articles have been charged against me which it never entered my mind to hold or teach, how can I on oath renounce them? But in respect to those articles which are indeed mine, if any one will instruct me to different conclusions, I will readily yield to your demand."

What unprejudiced judge could fail to see and approve the justice of the prisoner's request? With no show of stubbornness, with the humility of one who only sought to know the truth, he asks the least with which his conscience will allow him to be content.

But the emperor's conscience was more elastic. Confident that, to save his life, a man might strain some points, he attempted to reason Huss out of his position; and the reasons of an emperor are equivalent to a command. A lion's paw may at first rest upon its victim with a velvet pressure, but it only hides his bloody claws.

"How is it," asked Sigismund, "that you cannot renounce these articles that are falsely charged against you, as you say? I should have no objection to renouncing all errors whatsoever. Neither does it thence directly follow that I have held any error." The reply of Huss indicated good sense and conscientiousness, as well as respect for the emperor. "Most merciful emperor," said he, "the word has a very different signification from that in which your majesty has used it."

"In that case," said the Cardinal Zabarella, of Florence, "a written form of abjuration shall be presented you, sufficiently mild and proper. You will then easily be able to consider whether you will adopt it or not."

Without allowing Huss opportunity to reply, the emperor repeated the terms which had been laid down by the Cardinal of Cambray. "You have heard," he said, "the two ways that have been presented to you for settling this matter: First, that you publicly renounce those errors of yours that have now been plainly condemned, and subscribe to the decision of the council; in which case you shall experience marks of favor. But if you persist in defending your opinions, the council will probably determine to proceed in your case according to the laws of heresy."

"Most merciful emperor," said Huss, "I refuse not my consent to anything whatsoever that the council shall decree concerning me. I only except this much, that I may not sin against God and my conscience, and say that I have professed and taught those errors which it never entered my mind to teach or profess But I beseech of you, if it may be, that you will grant me the further privilege of declaring my views, that I may answer, so far as is proper, in respect to those points that have been objected against me, especially on the subject of ecclesiastical offices."

Upon this, several of the council began anew to urge upon him to submit. It was the same story over and over again. They wished no further discussion. "You are of age," said the emperor, somewhat provoked at the persistence of Huss in demanding to be heard further; "you can easily comprehend what I told you yesterday, and here again to-day. We are forced to believe testimony most worthy of our faith. For if scripture says, in the mouth of one or two witnesses every word shall be established, how much more by the testimony of so many men, and persons of such standing as those who have testified against you! If you are wise, therefore, you will accept the penance which the council shall impose, with a contrite heart, and renounce your evident errors, promising on oath that you will hereafter hold and teach the contrary. But if you will not, there are laws by which you will be judged by the council." To enforce the intimation of severity contained in the last clause of the emperor's words, an aged Polish bishop added, "The laws in regard to heretics are plain enough in defining the penalty which must be inflicted."

Still Huss persisted in his former purpose. He could not recant conscientiously all the articles charged against him; for some he had never held. He wished to be heard further. This just request, which they were reluctant altogether to deny, irritated them, and they cried out that he was obstinate.

This exasperation of the feelings of the council permitted those who were implacable in their hostility, a further opportunity to exaggerate the dangerous character of Huss. A priest, in his silk cassock, and otherwise splendidly dressed, called out, "He should on no condition be allowed the privilege of recanting; for he wrote to his friends, that though his tongue might swear, he would still retain his mind unsworn. No credit is therefore to be allowed him."

To this calumny Huss calmly replied, in language such as he had used before, that he was not conscious to himself of holding any error. "But," said Paletz, "of what use is this your protest, asserting that you will defend no error, and especially Wickliffe, and yet you do defend him?" And with these words Paletz adduced nine articles of Wickliffe in testimony, and publicly read them. "When I and Master Stanislaus," said he, "in the presence of Ernest, Duke of Austria, preached against these articles at Prague, Huss defended them, not only in his sermons, but in his published works, which, if you (turning to Huss) will not exhibit, we will." To this the emperor assented.

"I have no objection," said Huss, "to your presenting not these only, but also my other books."

To one who had regarded merely his own safety, the course which Huss chose to pursue would doubtless seem unwise. It was evident that the council had heard enough for their own satisfaction. They had now sat for several hours, and had grown weary of the discussion. But the devotion of Huss to his own conscientious views of truth forbade his acquiescence in the proposal of submission. His life was a matter of inferior importance, in his esteem, to the establishment and spread of correct views of the doctrines which he taught. He moreover felt, undoubtedly, that he might justly claim of the council, and of the emperor in virtue of his promise, a full and patient hearing. His trial for heresy was, in fact, a trial for his life, and he should at least have the privilege of a full defence.

But his request to be further heard, instead of being granted with a lenient and judicious kindness, was met by the effort to bring up against him, and overwhelm him with, new charges. Not content with what had been drawn up—with at least some show of system—by the commission of the council, individuals came forward, each presenting some separate charge.

Among these new articles was one in which Huss was charged with having slanderously interpreted some sentence of the pope. Huss denied having made, or even seen it, till it had been shown him in prison by the commission. "Who was the author of it, then?" he was asked. Huss answered that he did not know, although he had heard that Master Jessenitz was the author. "But what," they asked again, "are your views of the interpretation?" "How can I say," replied Huss, "when, as I told you, I never saw it except so far as I have heard of it from you?"

With such a cross-fire of questions they persevered for some time in their efforts to embarrass Huss. It was persecution of the most cruel and severe kind. He had now been subjected for several hours to the ordeal of examination. He had passed the previous night with scarcely a moment's rest from pain in his teeth. His health had suffered from his long imprisonment; and here he was, surrounded by a whole assembly embittered against him, in which he could scarce discern a single friendly face. It is surprising that he should have so far been able to command his faculties as to reply at all to the ensnaring questions addressed to him. Still his enemies persevered in trying to overwhelm him with accusations.

Another article was read, in which it was stated, in regard to the three men that had been beheaded at Prague, that they had been led by the doctrines of Huss to treat the pontifical letters with contempt; and that by Huss, with studied pomps and honors, they had been exalted and preferred in one of his public harangues to the rank of saints. Nason, a former courtier of Wenzel, of whom mention has been already made, arose and affirmed that the article was true, adding that he himself was present at the time when the king of Bohemia had given orders that those blasphemers should be punished.

"The statements," said Huss, "are false, both that the king gave the command, and that I had them pompously borne to their burial, since, in fact, I was not present on the occasion. You are therefore at the same time doing injustice to the king and to myself." Paletz arose to refute this statement of Huss, although careful not to give it a direct denial. "It was forbidden," said he, "that any one should speak against the pontifical bull. This was enjoined by the edict of the king. Those three men did speak against the pontifical bull. For this reason, by virtue of the royal edict, they were beheaded."

The views which Huss really held upon the subject, he did not—nor, had he wished, was he able to—disguise. They are found fully stated in his book, "*De Ecclesia:*"—"I suppose they had read the Prophet Daniel, where it is said, 'They that understand among the people shall instruct many, yet they shall fall by the sword and by flame, by captivity and by spoil, many days, . . . and many shall cleave unto them with flatteries.'" And afterward, "How is this fulfilled in the case of these three laymen, who, not consenting to, but contradicting the falsehoods of Antichrist, exposed their lives, and many did cleave to them by flatteries, who, frightened by the threats of Antichrist, turned and fled, and went away backward."

This passage could leave no doubt of the real views of Huss as to the papal bull, or the injustice of the execution of the three men. After its reading, there was silence for a short time, the members of the council exchanging looks of surprise. Paletz and Nason were among the first to speak, and prosecute the advantage they seemed to have gained. They stated that Huss, in his public address, had so inflamed the people against the magistracy, that a great multitude of the citizens openly opposed them, and went so far as to say that they, like the three that had been executed, were prepared to die for the truth, and this tumult had with difficulty been quieted by the gentleness of the king.

Several Englishmen now presented a copy of a letter which they said had been forged at Prague, purporting to have come from the University of Oxford, and stated that this had been read to the people at the suggestion of Huss, in order to commend John Wickliffe to the citizens. The letter was read in the council by the Englishman, who then turned to Huss and asked him whether he had publicly rehearsed it to the people.

Huss confessed that he had done it, inasmuch as it had been brought to Prague by two scholastics, under the seal of the university.

"Who were these scholastics?" they asked.

"That friend of mine," said Huss, pointing to Paletz, who, unfortunately for himself, had in the matter been intimately associated with Huss—"That friend of mine knows one of them as well as I do. With the other I have no acquaintance whatever."

"But where is he?" they asked again. "I have heard," said Huss, "that he died on his return to England." Paletz felt that silence on his part in regard to the other scholastic would be impolitic. "He was not an Englishman, but a Bohemian, and he brought with him a bit of Wickliffe's tombstone, which these persons, who follow his doctrines, worship as though it were some sacred relic. It is plain, therefore, with what design this whole thing was executed, and that the entire responsibility rests upon Huss."

Upon this this Englishmen produced another letter, under the seal of the university, of a tenor directly opposite to that of the former; but this mode of proceeding, which brought forward no specific doctrine which Huss could explain, or in regard to which he could ask to be set right, could afford him little satisfaction. He was altogether too much exhausted, even had he been disposed, to defend himself. In regard to the contradictory letters of the University of Oxford, there can be but slight grounds for questioning them. Both probably were genuine, inconsistent as their contents were. There seems to be no doubt that, long after the death of Wickliffe, his views had a stronghold in the university. Archbishop Arundel affirms that Oxford was a vine that brought forth wild and sour grapes. Of these the fathers had eaten, and the children's teeth had been set on edge. In consequence of this, the whole province of Canterbury was represented as tainted with novel and damnable Lollardism, to the intolerable and notorious scandal of the university. We can see nothing, therefore, improbable in supposing that, in some period when the views of Wickliffe were more than usually popular, his friends may have seized the occasion to employ the seal of the university to attest their public acceptance. There is other collateral evidence to support this conclusion. But however this may be, Huss at least did not design to make any reply to the accusation, whether it was that he felt too exhausted, and wished to reserve what little strength still remained for a more important object, or that he scorned to notice an imputation so inconsistent with his principles, or so injurious to his character, or possibly so weak and unimportant in itself.

After the Englishmen had finished, there was a general pause. Huss would have been more than mortal if he had been still ready to proceed after all the fatigue and assaults to which he had been subjected; and even his accusers, numerous as they were, seemed to have exhausted all their ammunition of accusation. The council were evidently at a loss what to do. They were not quite ready to take the final step. They paused, hesitating, on the brink of a decision the results of which might be such as their forecast would not choose to fathom.

At this fitting moment Paletz arose, and solemnly protested, in the presence of God and his imperial majesty, and the most reverend fathers, cardinals, bishops, etc., that "in this accusation against John Huss he had not been moved by any hatred or malice toward him, but only to be faithful to the oath which he took with his doctoral degree, that he would be the unrelenting antagonist of every error to the prejudice of the holy Catholic church." As if to crown the suspicious solemnity of the act by the ludicrously horrid, his associate, the wretched villain Michael de Causis, arose, and went through the same form of solemn protest.

"But I," said Huss, conscious of his integrity, and undoubtedly indignant at the sacrilegious villainy of Michael de Causis—"But I commend all this matter to the Judge in heaven, who will judge the cause of both parties with impartial justice." Who does not feel that the prisoner occupied a far more enviable position than one at least of his accusers, whom we cannot, by any stretch of faith, acquit of perjury?

The Cardinal of Cambray, in a tone of affected moderation, addressed the council. "I cannot enough admire," said he, "the gentleness and humanity of

Master Paletz, which he has shown in laying down the articles against John Huss; for, certainly, there are things in his books more atrocious, as we have heard." The cardinal might have understood what he called "gentleness" better, if he had but fully been acquainted with the facts of the former intimacy between Huss and Paletz. The last, undoubtedly, had sought merely to lay down such points as he could prove, and not be worsted in argument before the council by a former rival, with whose ability, in their past controversies, he had become fully acquainted. Paletz, probably, with all his animosity, merely sought the humiliation and not the life of Huss; and his general course and character were respectable by the side of his villain-associate. We can readily believe that his own partisan spirit had carried him away so far that he really believed himself sincere in his efforts.

The day was now drawing to a close. The council as well as the prisoner must by this time have been thoroughly exhausted. Further proceedings were deferred to the next day. The council adjourned, and Huss was given in charge of his keeper, the bishop of Riga, to be placed in prison and kept under guard.

One at least of his friends followed him. It was the faithful John de Chlum, who knew well how severely he had been tried, and how much he needed the sympathy and strength of friendly counsel. Few were the words that he could seize the opportunity of addressing to the poor, exhausted prisoner; but they were words of cheer, and Huss welcomed the consolation they afforded, so genial after the tempests that had assailed him, so needed in this the hour of his loneliness and desertion.

As the assembly broke up, the emperor gathered the more prominent officers and members of the council around him, and addressed them on the subject of the trial. "You have heard the many and aggravated charges against John Huss, sustained not only by strong testimony, but, moreover, also by his own confession, each of which, in my judgment, is deserving of death by fire. In case, however, he shall comply with what is required of him, let him be forbidden to teach, or preach, or reside in Bohemia. For it is by no means clear that if he should be again allowed to preach, and especially in Bohemia, but that, trusting in the graciousness and favor of his followers there, he may return to his former views. And, moreover, he may also scatter new errors abroad among the common people, in which case the last error would be worse than the first. I think, moreover, that his condemned articles should be sent to my brother the king of Bohemia, to Poland, and to other regions where the minds of men have become imbued with his doctrines, together with the edict that whoever shall continue to hold those views shall be punished by the combined power of the secular and spiritual arm. Thus this mischief may possibly be met, if the branches along with the root be torn up thoroughly. But let the bishops and other prelates who have labored in these regions to extirpate this heresy, be commended, by the unanimous suffrage of the council, to the kings and princes in whose allegiance they are. Finally, if any intimate friends of John Huss are found here at Constance, let them also be held in severe restraint, and especially his disciple Jerome." "But," said several, "it is our hope that when the master is punished, the disciple will show himself more pliable."

The emperor could no longer be regarded by Huss with hope or confidence. He had taken the side of his enemies. There was much brought out on the trial to alienate his feelings from the prisoner. Undoubtedly, moreover, the emperor saw that the demonstrations of public feeling in the council were such as warned him against placing himself in its way. Instead, therefore, of struggling against the current—a vain effort that would only prejudice the success of his own favorite schemes—he determined to put himself at its head, and at once lead and control it. From his words it is obvious that he did not contemplate, notwithstanding the violence of some members of the council, the fatal issue of these proceedings. He did not expect that Huss would be put to death, but only silenced. Undoubtedly he hoped that by leading the current of feeling it would be in his power to interpose at the right moment, and adjust the whole matter according to the dictates of his imperial wisdom. He was but feebly aware, even yet, how strong and resistless—slave of his policy as he was—were the chains of influence in which he was himself bound. He had allowed the council to be hounded on after their victim, and it passed his power to call them back.

END OF VOL. I.

www.ingramcontent.com/pod-product-compliance
Lightning Source LLC
LaVergne TN
LVHW021056110826
845150LV00001B/84